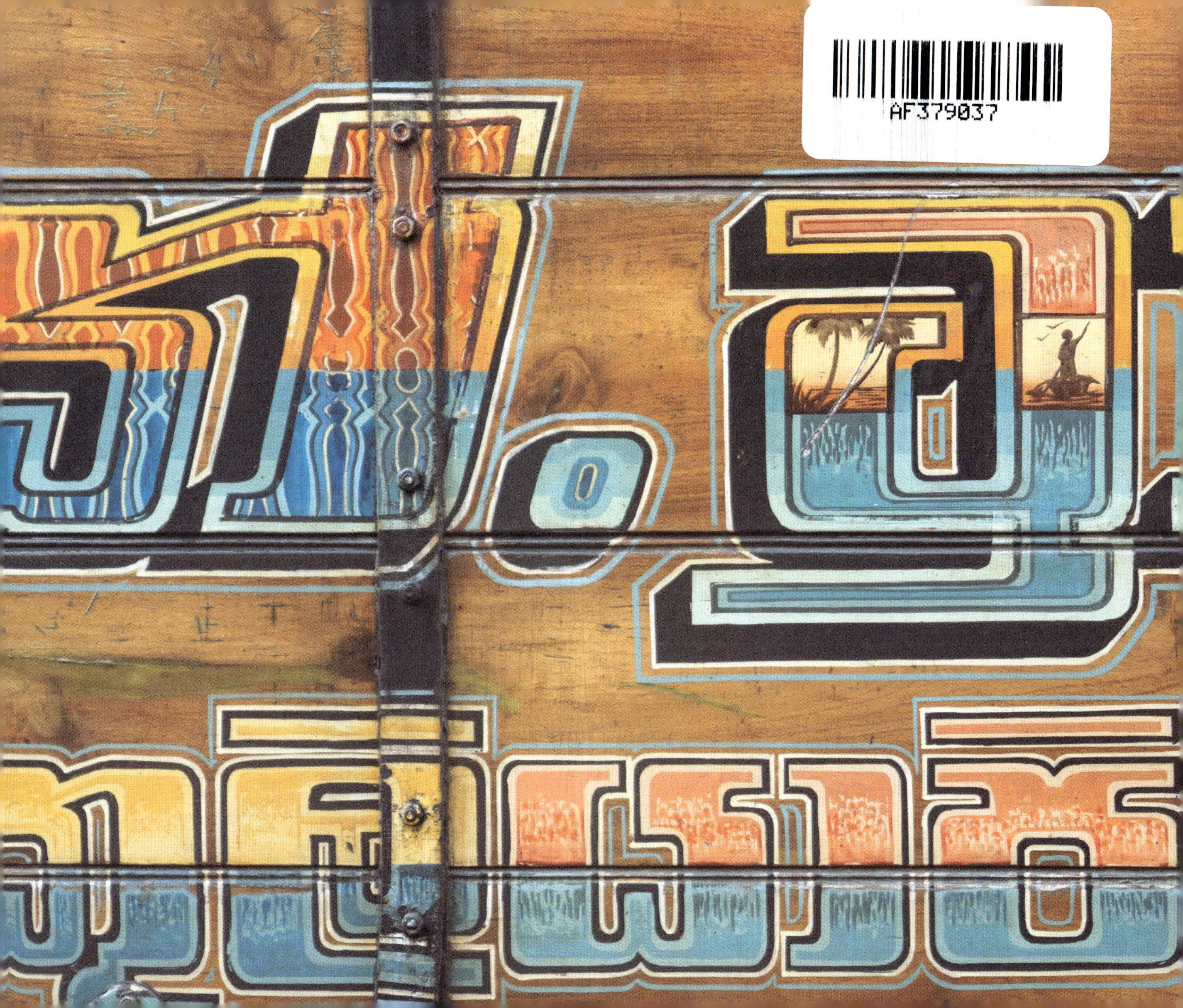
AF379037

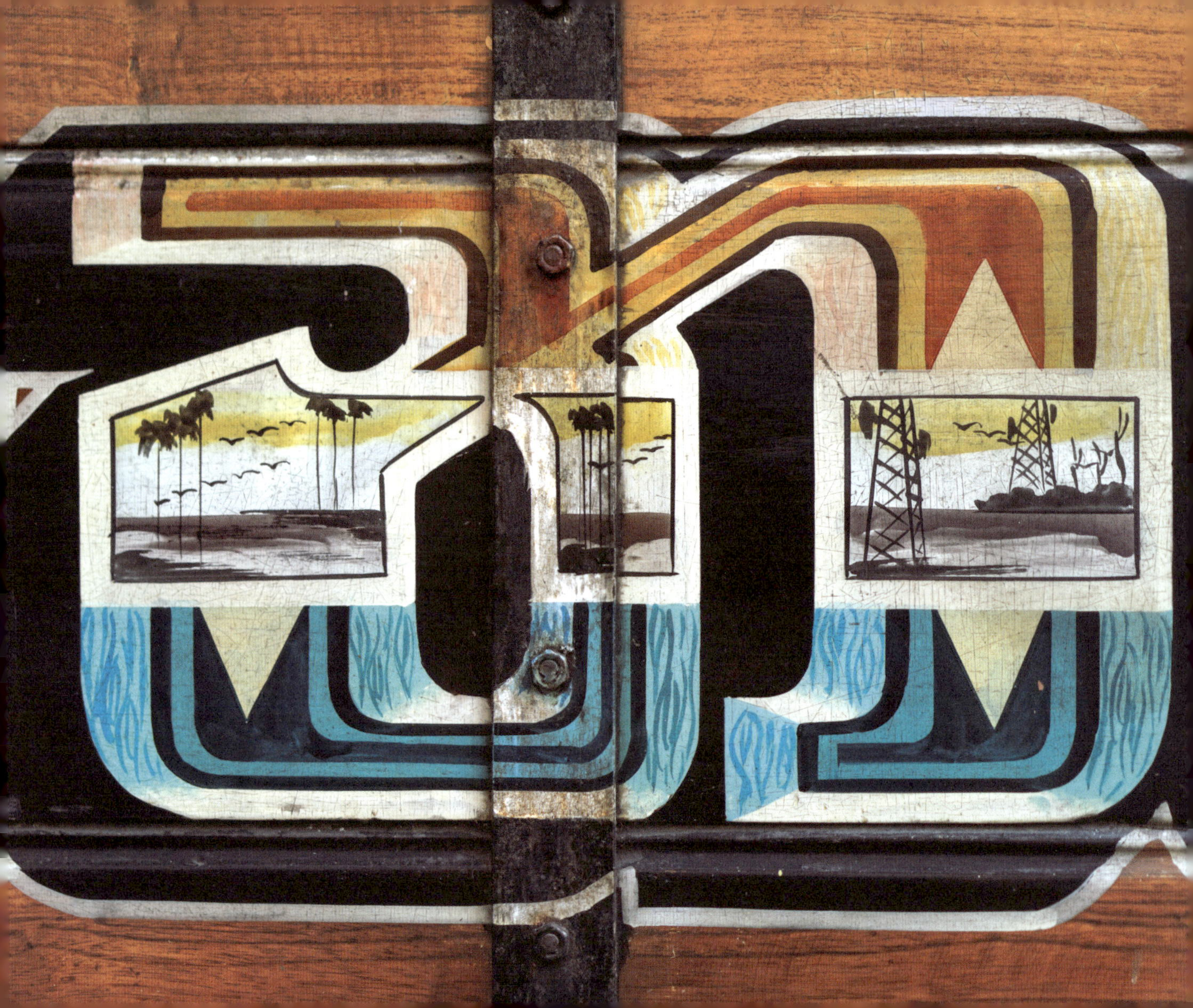

DECORATED VEHICLES OF SOUTH ASIA

TRUCKS and TUKS

CHRISTOPHER HERWIG

FUEL

Introduction

Riya Raagini

A pair of *kajal* (kohl) laden eyes, a colourful *parandi* (tassel), a soaring bird or even revered gods and goddesses – such symbols are painted by self-taught artists onto the trucks and tuks of the Indian subcontinent. All carry with them a story, personal to the individual driver, yet shared within a collective consciousness of myths, fables, faiths and traditions. At any given moment a vibrant collection of colours, poetry and totems can be found travelling the roads and highways. These living, breathing, moving metaphors traverse the narrowest of mountain turns and muddiest of tracks – the arteries that keep the Indian subcontinent alive.

Sajavat (ornamentation and decoration) has long been an essential part of everyday life across South Asia. It can be found not only on vehicles, but also adorning well-decorated homes, as in the flowering motifs of *alpana* (traditional folk) designs, or the heavily embroidered traditional *kantha* (quilts). Even before modern vehicles appeared in the region, people were decorating every conceivable mode of transport, from bullock carts to boats. Naturally, when trucks, tuk-tuks and rickshaws began to arrive in the early 20th century, they were embellished in a similar fashion.

Accounts of the origins of truck art (and by extension tuk-tuk and rickshaw art) differ slightly in each of the South Asian countries. Having been developed by individuals independently and unsystematically, a definitive source is difficult to establish, appearing instead to be the result of a combination of several disparate factors: in Pakistan, the importation of a large number of British Bedford 'Rocket' trucks following World War II; in India, the growth of truck manufacturing with companies such as Tata and Ashok Leyland; in Nepal, the opening of the Rajpath from India to trucks in 1955 (the first drivable road to reach Kathmandu from the outside world); in Sri Lanka, the introduction of trucks to serve areas inaccessible by rail; in Bangladesh, the transformation of Dhaka (the 'Rickshaw Capital of the World') after the country gained independence in 1971.

Between the 1950s and the 1980s truck art developed considerably, encompassing popular South Asian aesthetics alongside evolving traditional motifs. This was particularly reflected in the practice of filling every inch of a 'canvas', inspired by the way Indian and Pakistani cinema billboards had become louder and more kaleidoscopic in appearance. These in turn, had been influenced by the Pop Art and psychedelic movements which had arrived from the West in the 1960s. The first vehicles to be painted in this fashion were the mini-buses of Karachi. The approach quickly transferred to local trucks, the range of decoration continually expanding. Some truck cabs have interiors so heavily decorated with metal strips and fluorescent reflector tapes that they are known as *disco gaari* (disco cars).

That vehicle art continues to evolve in unexpected directions, incorporating and juxtaposing influences from numerous, sometimes seemingly contrasting worlds, is perhaps mainly due to the small *karkhanas* (workshops) and the skill of their artists. With no formal artistic education (in most instances) they are taught on the job, training under an *ustad* (master artist). Simultaneously they learn to develop their individual imagination using ephemera from their immediate surroundings (posters, picture books, calendars etc.) as inspiration. With this inexhaustible supply of material, they are able to produce new hybrids, while adding unique variations to established motifs. In this way, the work they

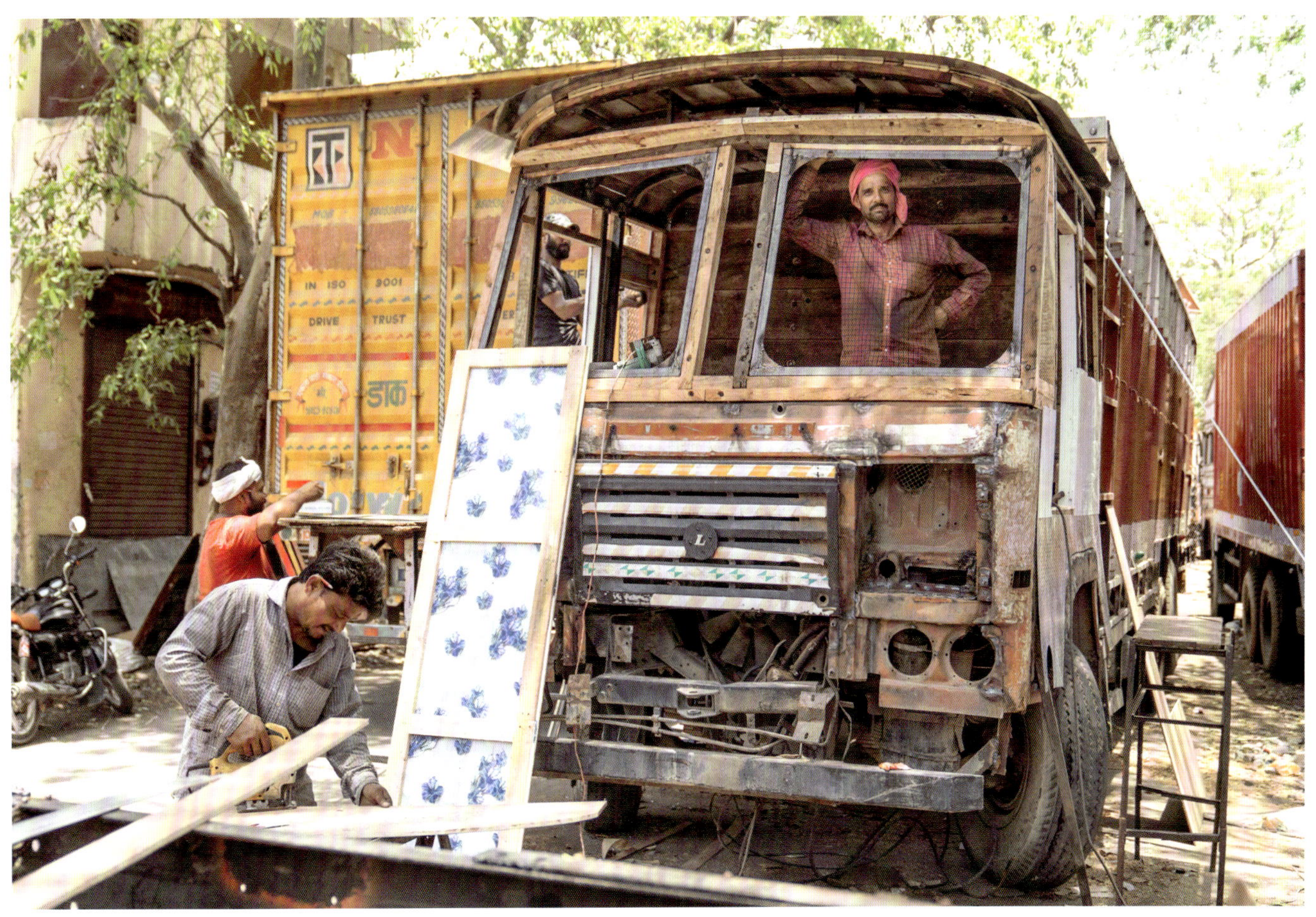

TATA
IN ISO 9001
DRIVE TRUST

produce continuously reflects changing social realities and interests in a unique, unrestricted manner.

The average Indian goods truck covers around 300 kilometres a day, with drivers spending most of the year away from their family and friends. It is a tough life, contending with corrupt officials and local mafias, driving in challenging terrains and weather conditions, with only their *rani* (queen) – in the form of their truck – to console them. Provided government regulations don't intervene, the extent to which a truck or vehicle might be decorated is boundless and hardly ever restricted by the utilitarian purpose of the vehicle. For a driver, the truck isn't simply a carrier of goods, but their very own *dulhan* (bride) with whom they spend the majority of their time, finding solace in moments of monotony and loneliness. Consequently, trucks are embellished with bridal symbols and cab interiors mimic bridal rooms – stuffed full of colourful fabrics, *parandis* (silk hair ornaments), mirrors, pom-poms and tassels, to such an extent that practically every inch is covered. This treatment of a truck – not simply as a dull and distant workplace, but as an integral, even romantic, part of a trucker's everyday life – explains why most drivers who are also owners of their vehicles are prepared to bear the considerable cost of decorating them, often around 30 percent of their value. While much of the imagery appears random – mythical worlds of pure white stallions, famous football players and pastoral scenes – the form and choice of symbols, style and typography are largely reflective of a contemporary, globalised South Asia, complete with its own set of heroes, myths and nostalgias.

The unrelenting pressures of long-haul driving, combined with basic living conditions and the danger of accidents, explain the ubiquity of talismanic objects, symbols and religious motifs. A pair of women's eyes are painted on the front or back of the truck acts as a charm to ward off *nazar* (the evil eye). In Pakistan, a large wooden peak is built on the front of the trucks in the shape of a tiara. Known as a *taj* (crown), this elaborately decorated area is often adorned with Islamic quotations and iconography, or with auspicious symbols like the swastika or the leaf of a bodhi tree. Similarly, in both India and Nepal, Hindu gods and goddesses like Shiva, Parvati and Ganesha can be found on truck panels, ensuring that, through faith, both truck and driver will remain accident free.

Across areas of Pakistan, Nepal and India, a shoe or slipper dangling from the back of a brightly painted truck, or painted shoe in the style of a Punjabi *jooti*, is more than a warning symbol not to cross the driver of the truck, it also hints at one of the origins of the artform itself. The motif of the shoe probably originated from the *Sardar* (Sikh) drivers of the Punjab region, who were among the first truck drivers and owners of the subcontinent. The motif was subsequently adopted by followers of different faiths and belief systems, at the same time as an independent language of vehicular art – with shared symbols, warning signs and assemblages – developed in parallel. This use of a shared visual language is also visible in the appropriation of symbols and portraits such as those of the Sikh Gurus and saints, adopted by the Muslim drivers in Pakistan, to portray their own prominent *Sufi* saints and *Ulma* (scholars of Islamic law and theology).

The fusion of folk and popular traditions, both accidental and intentional, is significant. In rickshaw art, the ancient folk traditions of Bangladesh (which are derived from the intermingling of the Ajanta and Tibetan traditions) are combined with local designs to develop new forms of urban vernacular folk art. With trucks, from the moment of purchase, rituals and *poojas* (acts of homage and worship) are performed that often bind the religious beliefs of the owner to the truck. These connections can also take the form of Islamic quotations and iconography demonstrating a devotion to Allah, or painted *deeps* (butter lamps) and swastikas for Buddhists and Hindus, or crosses and likenesses of the Virgin Mary and truck names like 'Infant Jesus' (p40) for Christians.

A common underlying visual theme is masculinity, with the emblem of a handlebar moustache indicating a type of stereotypical male fearlessness associated with the occupation of being a driver. Symbols of gearboxes or hubcaps are painted alongside (in the form of kill markings), as if keeping a score of the number of cars the trucker has hit. Other images display visions of macho culture that do not necessarily represent the personality of the driver, but are rooted in more widely held perceptions of heroes and aspirations. Typically, the backs of trucks are adorned with portraits of favourite political figures, national heroes, celebrities, or ideals that the truckers or truck artists connect with on some level. Bruce Lee deserves a special mention in this regard, as he occupies an important place in South Asian truck art. After becoming popular in Pakistan, he was the first non-native celebrity to appear on Pakistani trucks – albeit in a style rooted in the aesthetics of the genre, usually surrounded by *phulkari* (floral and geometric) inspired designs.

Other common subjects include national heroes like Pakistan's founder Muhammad Ali Jinnah (1876–1948) who is often referred to as *Quaid-e-Azam* ('Great Leader'), and the country's national poet, Muhammad Iqbal (1877–1938). Over time the inclusion of heroes and figures has changed to reflect more recent events. Since the first Battle of Swat (2007) where the Pakistani Army defeated the Taliban, images of army general Raheel Sharif (1956–) have also become commonplace. Portraits of Imran Khan (1952–), the former cricketer and ex-prime minister, who has become a controversial figure in Pakistani politics, can also be found.

The selection of figures for portrayal on the backs of trucks demonstrates the sensitive balance of tradition and experimentation that countries like India, Bangladesh and Pakistan practice in their everyday politics and culture. The presence of revolutionary, anti-colonial heroes such as Chandra Shekhar Azad (1906–1931) and Bhagat Singh (1907–1931) on trucks throughout India is a good example. Both

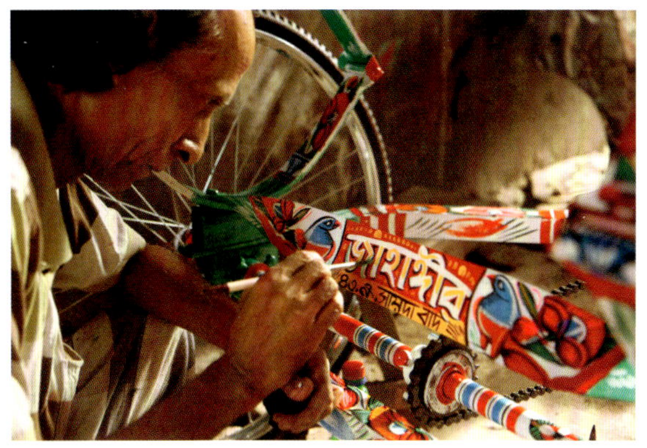

personify a youthful, high-spirited interpretation of *aazaadi* (freedom), *shaheedi* (martyrdom) and *inquilab* (revolution). Despite the disconnect between their modern manifestation and the socialist ideology of their historical context, a common recognition and respect for their courageous actions remain.

Alluring portraits of modern, cleavage-revealing, Bollywood -influenced women adorn the rickshaws of Bangladesh. Where the art of the region (particularly in Islamic countries) normally adheres to more restrictive symbolic motifs, here representations of women follow their own rules. These depictions can be interpreted as a form of resistance against the broader control of art by the upper classes in the country, as well as indicating the more moderate nature of Bangladesh, heavily influenced as it is by Indian politics and culture. Principally, these vernacular portrayals of female beauty assert a specific Bangladeshi identity, in opposition to the strict religious practices imposed by Pakistan between 1955 and 1971, when Bangladesh was East Pakistan.

In Nepal it is believed that at certain hours, female ghosts called *kichkanya* are attracted to truckers and will attempt to seduce them. In such instances, the interior and exterior fabrics and decorations of the vehicle serve to indicate the presence of another woman, signs that ward off the *kichkanya*, who continue their search for a victim elsewhere.

In Dhaka, the capital of Bangladesh, rickshaws frequently carry an image of a Royal Bengal tiger, sometimes depicted as a mother figure, nursing her cubs. The tiger is integral to the mythical world of *Bonbibi*, the lady of the forest, who protects mangrove workers from *Dakkhin Rai* (a deity in the form of a tiger, who rules over beasts and demons).

Birds and animals are also common: loyal parrots, vibrant peacocks, graceful eagles and brave lions are all part of an ever-expanding menagerie, conveying significant folkloric meaning, alongside character traits that correspond to the owner or driver's cultural ideals. The coterie also extends to mythical creatures such as *Buraq* (Lightning), the supernatural winged horse-like creature, with the head of a human, believed to have flown the Prophet Muhammad from Mecca to Jerusalem; and the legendary *Zuljanah*, the white horse of Husayn ibn Ali, famed for his strength, endurance and devotion – all indispensable qualities for a good driver.

Some motifs and practices which initially appear unconnected to traditional forms of worship have, through repetition and custom, become part of trucking folklore and could be conceived as acquiring a parallel religious status in their own right. In Nepal for instance, truckers place mirrors by the side of the road at sharp bends, partly to act as a reminder to other motorists of the difficulties they face, but also as a form of faith and communication between the drivers themselves. This practice may have originated at the Mulkot Mirror Wall on the BP Koirala Highway, which connects the Kathmandu Valley with the Eastern Terai region. Known as one of Asia's most dangerous roads, here mirrors are offered to the goddess Seti Mata Devi (renowned for her self-sacrifice to uphold her husband's honour) to ward off potential accidents.

Paintings of architectural structures such as the Taj Mahal, or even more distant landmarks, unlikely to have been visited by the artists in person, such as London's Tower Bridge or Australia's Sydney Opera House, can be found on all kinds of vehicles. The scale, extravagance and intention of these scenes vary depending on the origins of the truck, as well as the driver's nationality and cultural background. In Bangladesh, this category of image is a place where flamboyant fantasy meets rural reality. It is common to see depictions of (for example) a luxury car in front of a hut, or a helicopter about to land in a humble backyard. By contrast, in parts of India, Pakistan and Sri Lanka, miniature portrayals of idyllic landscapes, such as peasants harvesting crops, or riverside vistas complete with coconut palms, are usually painted on the sides of a truck, or on small niches at the rear. These romanticised naturalistic scenes are supposed to convey strength to the truckers, giving them a sense of respite from their harsh existence on the road. In Pakistan they are also interpreted as the trucker's imagined Islamic *Jannah* (paradise), a place of eternal bliss for those who have lived a righteous life. In reality, these images are mostly inspired by western calendars depicting scenes of Switzerland.

In Sri Lanka, such landscapes are framed within three-dimensional letters painted onto the trucks, often stating the origin and destination of the truck itself. Similarly, small pictures of boats or aircraft painted onto the sides of the lorries will signify that their cargo is destined to be delivered to a port or airport. Boats are a particularly popular motif in Bangladesh, as they form an important element of rural transport, as well as being an election symbol of the Awami League, one of the country's major political parties.

These examples of a common trucker's language can be found across South Asia; a number are still prevalent, despite losing their original meaning over time. The universal phrase 'HORN O.K. Please' or 'Horn Please' is generally accepted to date from the period when Indian trucks were manufactured

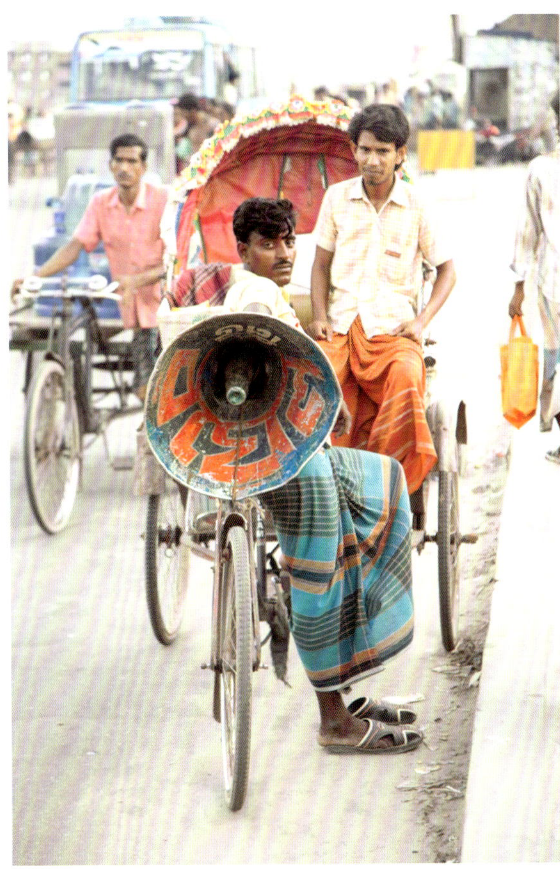

Dhaka, BANGLADESH

without wing mirrors, the sounding of the horn serving as a signal to the driver that someone was overtaking them. Although all trucks now have mirrors, the tradition of painting this request onto the backs of trucks endures.

Assertions of nationalist narratives and cultural identities such as, 'Together we are [Tamil; Buddhist; Sinhalese; Hindu; Muslim; Christian] Sri Lanka', have become common themes in truck art. In the majority of cases there is no official government directive as to how these proclamations are phrased or reproduced, these decisions are made directly by the trucker or left to the artist. Patriotism is also expressed in imaginary scenes of war involving tanks, jeeps, F-16s and jet fighters – motifs especially prevalent in Pakistan on trucks dating from the 1970s, usually referencing the Indo-Pakistani wars of 1965 and 1971. Furthermore, anti-aircraft guns and missiles are also popular as a means of demonstrating the country's readiness for battle and its ability to defend itself against any incursion.

Social and political messages engaging directly with the public form an important part of the painting tradition. Famously, rickshaws were used to depict realistic scenes of torture inflicted by the Pakistani army during the Bangladesh Liberation War (26 March–16 December, 1971). The plight of rural women at the hands of the army was so vividly pictured that the Dhaka Municipality imposed a ban on these paintings 'for the sake of decency'.

The phrase 'Use dipper at night' (pp70, 79) is often found rendered in colourful typography on the back of trucks, reminding drivers to lower their headlights to avoid blinding oncoming traffic. In 2016 the phrase was co-opted by the National AIDS Control Organization and Tata Motors (one of India's largest truck manufacturers) in an innovative campaign to promote safe sex among truck drivers in India – they produced the 'Dipper' condom, aimed specifically at truck drivers. Research had found that approximately two million long-distance truckers were regular clients of sex-

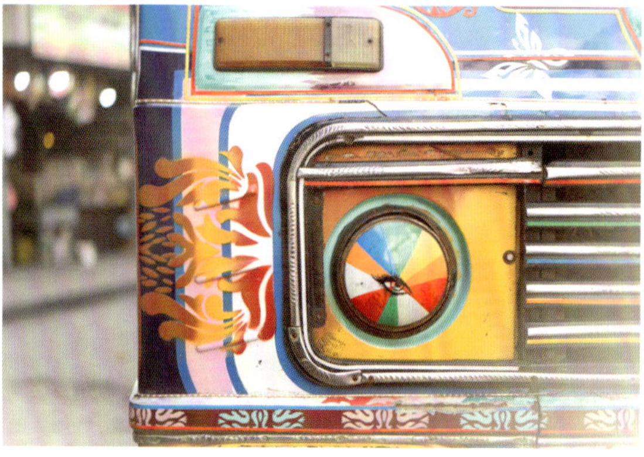

workers and that their awareness of STDs and HIV/AIDS was very low. Available at petrol stations and tyre shops, the Dipper condom appealed to the drivers' sensibilities and became a great success, with 45,000 sold in the first month.

While the Dipper campaign utilised an existing phrase from the transport lexicon, the reverse also occurs, with truckers incorporating government slogans into their truck's decoration (with or without incentives). Drivers and painters from Delhi's Sanjay Gandhi Transport Nagar area consistently use official phrases, a practice that can also help with the complicated process of legally registering a vehicle.

A classic of this genre is the popular slogan 'Jai Jawan Jai Kisan' (Hail the Soldier, Hail the Farmer), used by India's second prime minister Lal Bahadur Shastri (1904–1966) to galvanise the military and increase food production during the 1965 war against Pakistan; a more recent example is the phrase 'Beti Bachao Beti Padhao' (Save Daughter, Educate Daughter), the rallying cry of a campaign launched by the Government of India in 2015, in an attempt to encourage women's education and help balance the country's male to female ratio. Whether the use of such slogans on trucks is the result of governmental pressure or not, their subject matter reflects the stark essence of standards of living in the subcontinent, a reality which is often at odds with the false sense of progress and modernity that the region's governments attempt to portray to the wider world.

Of course, words painted onto trucks are not only confined to the political, they also comprise truck *sahitya* (literature) – texts that express poetry, humour, notions of romance and the individual personality of the driver, owner or artist. In Nepal the late poet Narayan Bhakta, celebrated for his protest songs against the Panchayat system (1961–1990), is considered to be the grandfather of truck *sahitya*, becoming famous for his compositions which resonated with trucker society. In Bangladesh, *Dhakai kutti Bengali* (the Dhakaite dialect) is used to express the local quirky, sharp, quick-witted sense of humour. In Sri Lanka, this literature takes the form of tuk-tuk 'wisdom', with popular aphorisms such as 'He who flies not high, falls not low' and 'You have to understand first and to be understood second'. In India and Pakistan, trucks are decorated with various poetic verses, humorous and romantic phrases, quotes, simplistic sayings and *mukhras* (literally meaning 'face', referring to the first two lines of a song, that set the mood and theme of the tune).

Sayings like 'This neem tree is no less than the *chandan* [sandalwood], this city of Delhi, no less than London', signify that although the driver might be poor and his life difficult, he treasures what he has. Many phrases convey messages of safety, both for the trucker and other road users, sometimes with a hint of irony: 'Drink less my dear, for Iraqi water [meaning alcohol] is very expensive!' As truck driving remains largely a male-dominated domain, countless texts are concerned with the longing for (and appreciation of) a lover or a muse. In particular, lines from romantic *shayari* (a type of Urdu poetry) are very popular: 'Do not be restless in someone's love, do not wait for me, for I do not belong to this place.' These phrases intend to offer a small glimpse into the difficult lives of truckers.

Today the whole industry of truck art is facing increasing challenges, confronting a range of new obstacles, affecting the entire production line from artists and tape-wallahs to shopkeepers and mechanics. In January 2020 the Government of Nepal imposed new restrictions for truck decoration. The display of truck literature, scenes and poems was prohibited, the authorities declaring not only that they are offensive, but also that they constitute a dangerous distraction to other drivers. The enforcement of this law initiated the erasure of the tradition of truck literature and is viewed by critics as an attempt to curb criticism and free speech.

In Bangladesh, the two-stroke 'baby-taxi' has now been completely banned, resulting in the loss of a unique artist's canvas. In Dhaka authorities have begun the eradication of slow-moving traffic (such as rickshaws) from major streets. During the 'Clean Sri Lanka' campaign of 2025, police launched a controversial crackdown on tuk-tuk operators, requiring the mandatory removal of ornamental accessories, claiming that they violate the Motor Traffic Act.

In Pakistan, Islamic fundamentalists belonging to the FATA (Federally Administered Tribal Areas), Swat and Dir Districts constantly pressure drivers to remove human and animal imagery from the trucks, driving truck artists out of these areas and shutting down their workshops. The fear of persecution or having their cargos looted or damaged has forced drivers with painted and embellished trucks out of these regions, while new trucks, decorated in abstract, minimal designs, have replaced them.

In India, truck literature has been subjected to stricter legislation following the Motor Vehicles (Amendment) Act of 2019, which recommends harsher penalties for violation of traffic rules, including any vehicle modifications that vary from the manufacturer's standard specification.

As well as legal obstacles, truck art is also facing economic and technological issues. A significant number of artworks are being replaced with stickers and customised, reflective, radium tapes, the majority of which are imported from China. Not only are they cheaper by virtue of being mass-produced, but they also save time, negating the need to employ a skilled artist to hand paint or spray vehicles. Rarely offering regional variations, they are steadily and surely steering the artform towards homogeneity.

However, the chaos of the subcontinent, with its elastic notions of time, prolonged chai-breaks and unorganised, non-institutionalised structures, continually finds ways to circumnavigate regulations. Despite repeated efforts by the Bangladeshi government to reduce the number of rickshaws, the figure has grown significantly. This is in part due to the increase in unregistered rickshaw-wallahs (the poorest citizens in Asian countries) who are indifferent to such edicts. Meanwhile Nepalese truckers are evading the ban on truck art by rendering large-scale images of gods and goddesses like Buddha, Ganesha and Parvati on their trucks. These religious depictions trap local authorities in their own moral dilemma, as the removal of sacred images is largely frowned upon.

The birth of 'truck art' (and by extension vehicular art) in South Asia is a result of an unofficial and unregulated means of expression finding its own space within the public realm. It is a constantly adapting language that continues to defy those that attempt to control it. Truck art articulates the dialogue between happiness and pain experienced by the drivers, acknowledging the difficulties inherent in their lives – their beliefs, loves, religion, romance, heroes and principles: all coexist on these ever-moving canvases.

SRI LANKA

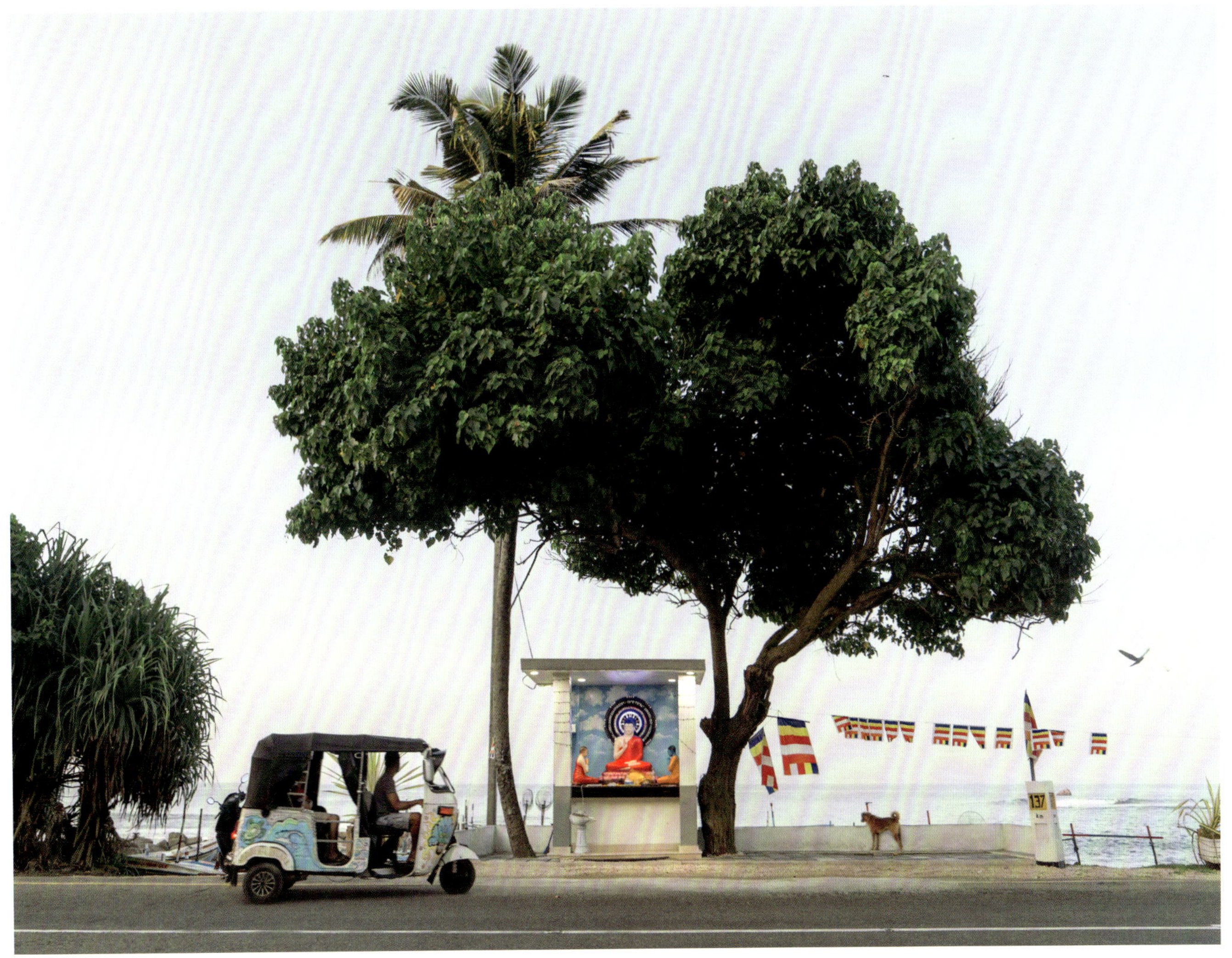

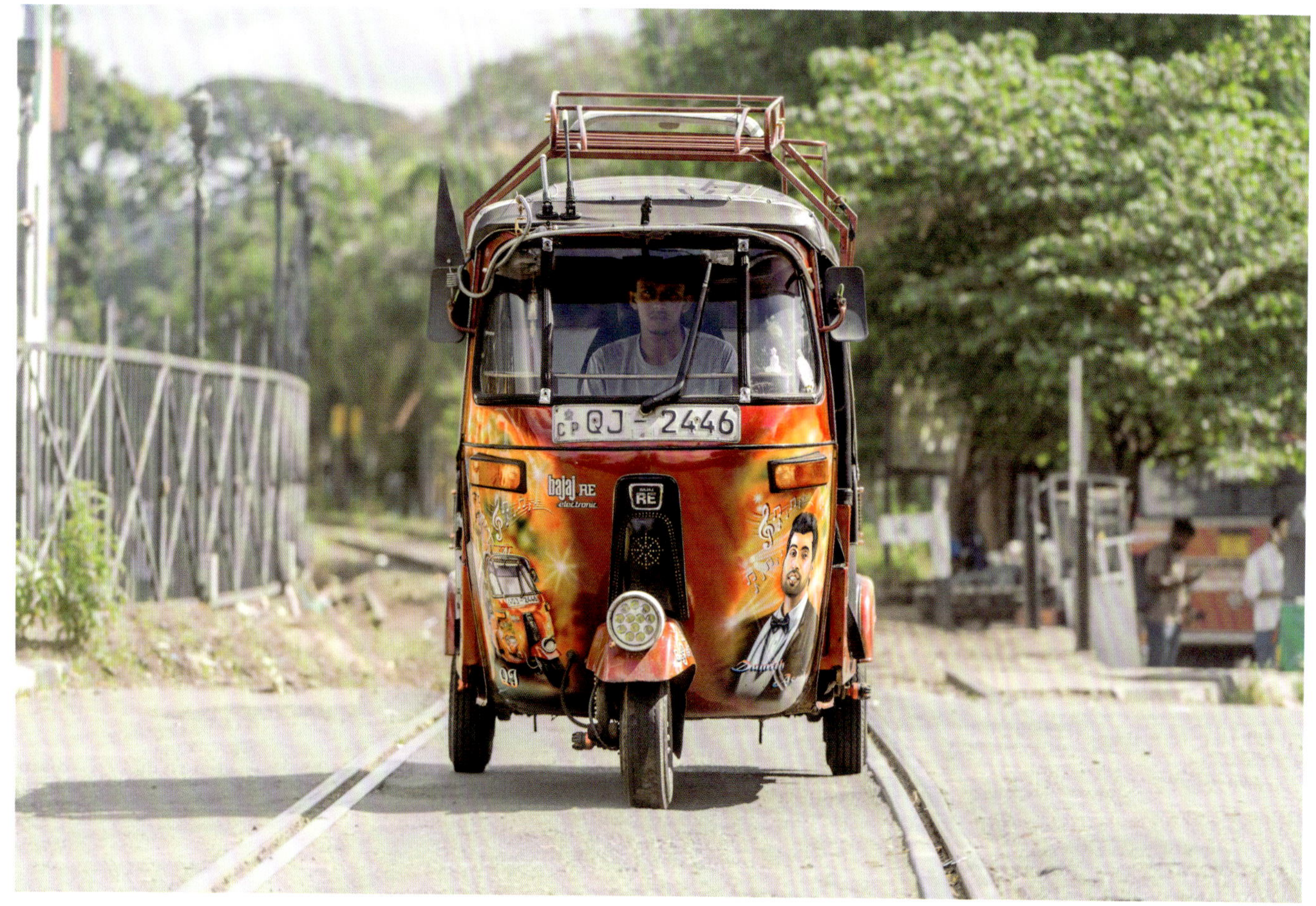

14   Kandy, SRI LANKA

Ahangama, SRI LANKA

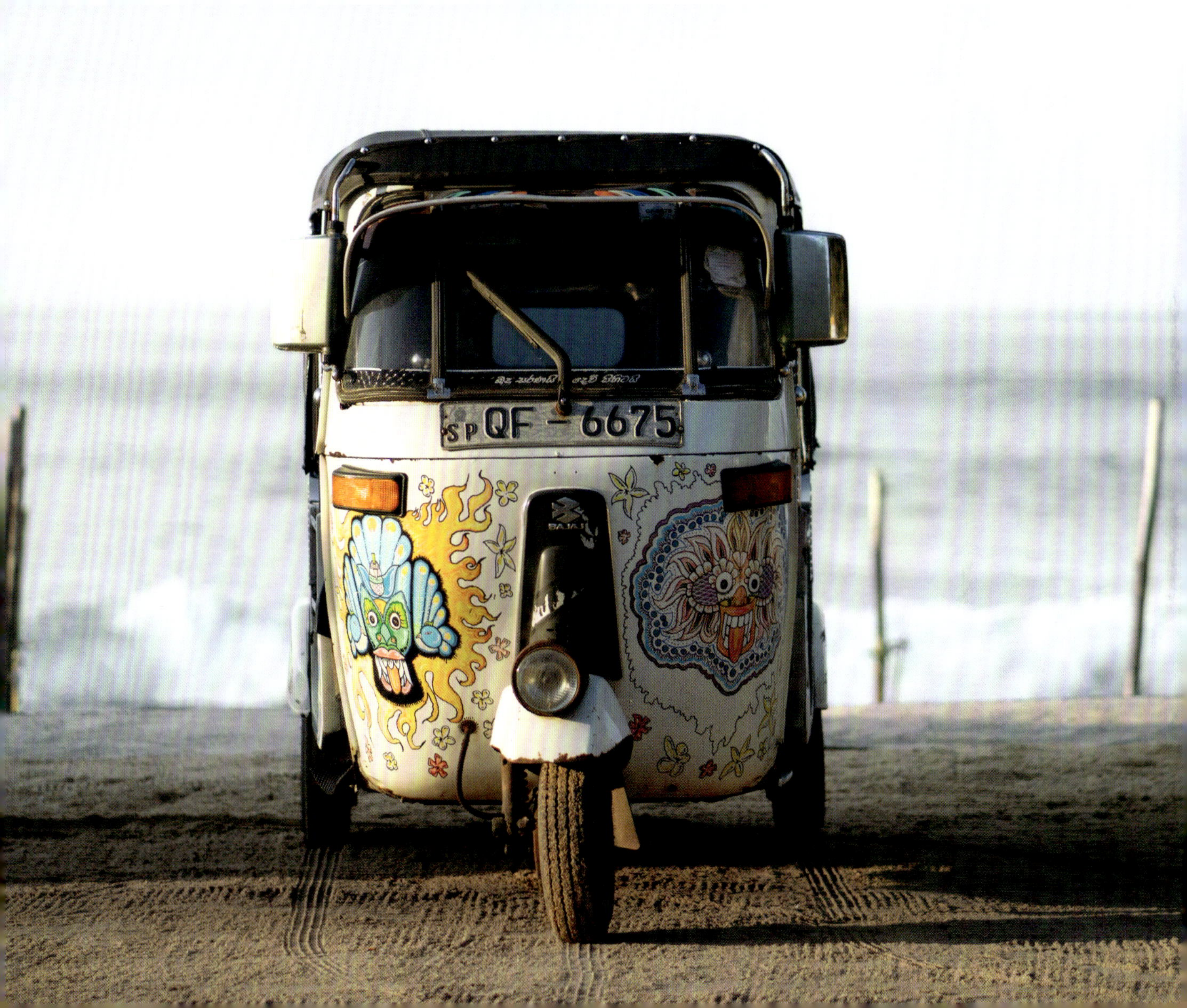

SP QF - 6675
BAJAJ

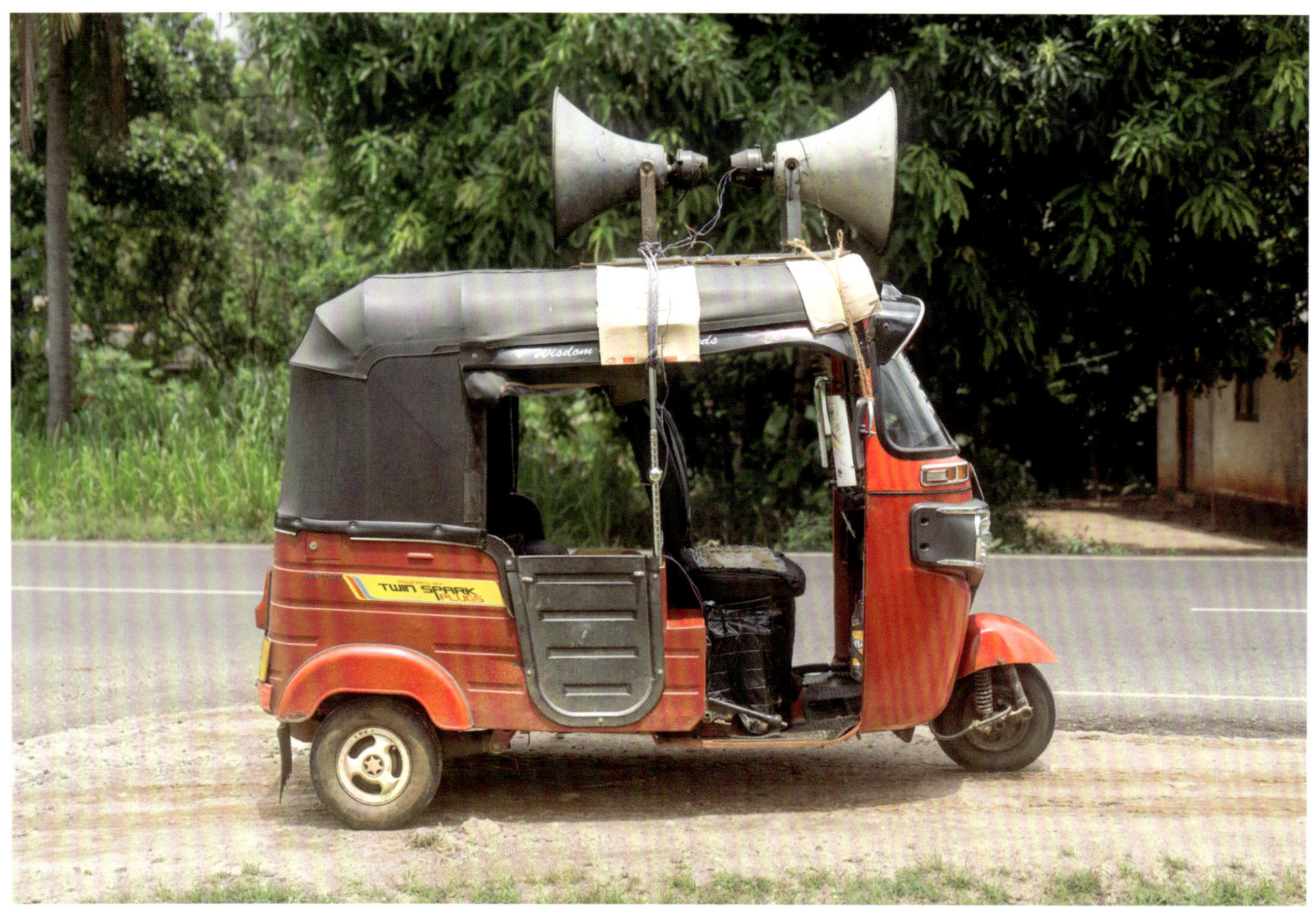

16   Dambulla, SRI LANKA

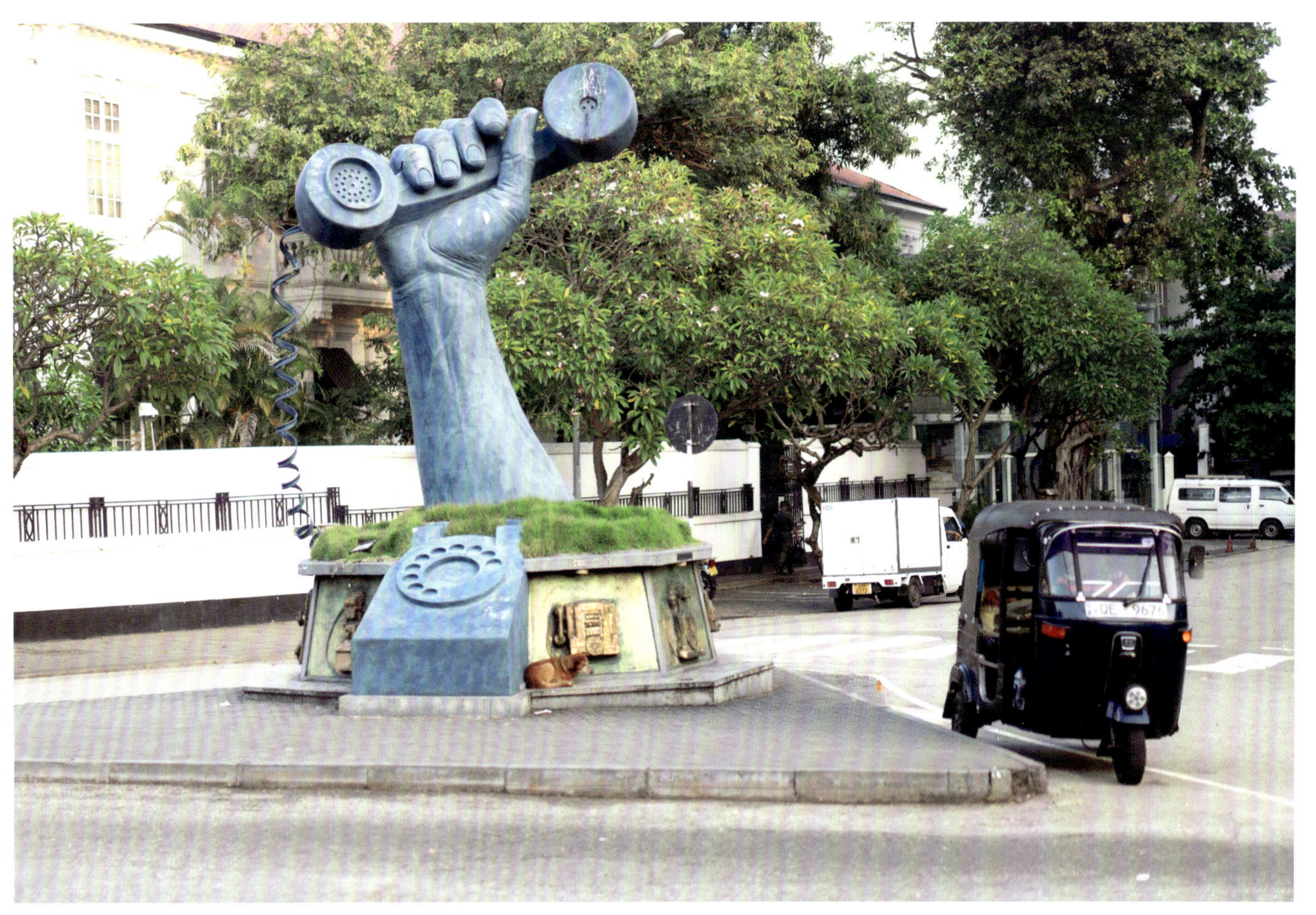

Colombo, SRI LANKA   17

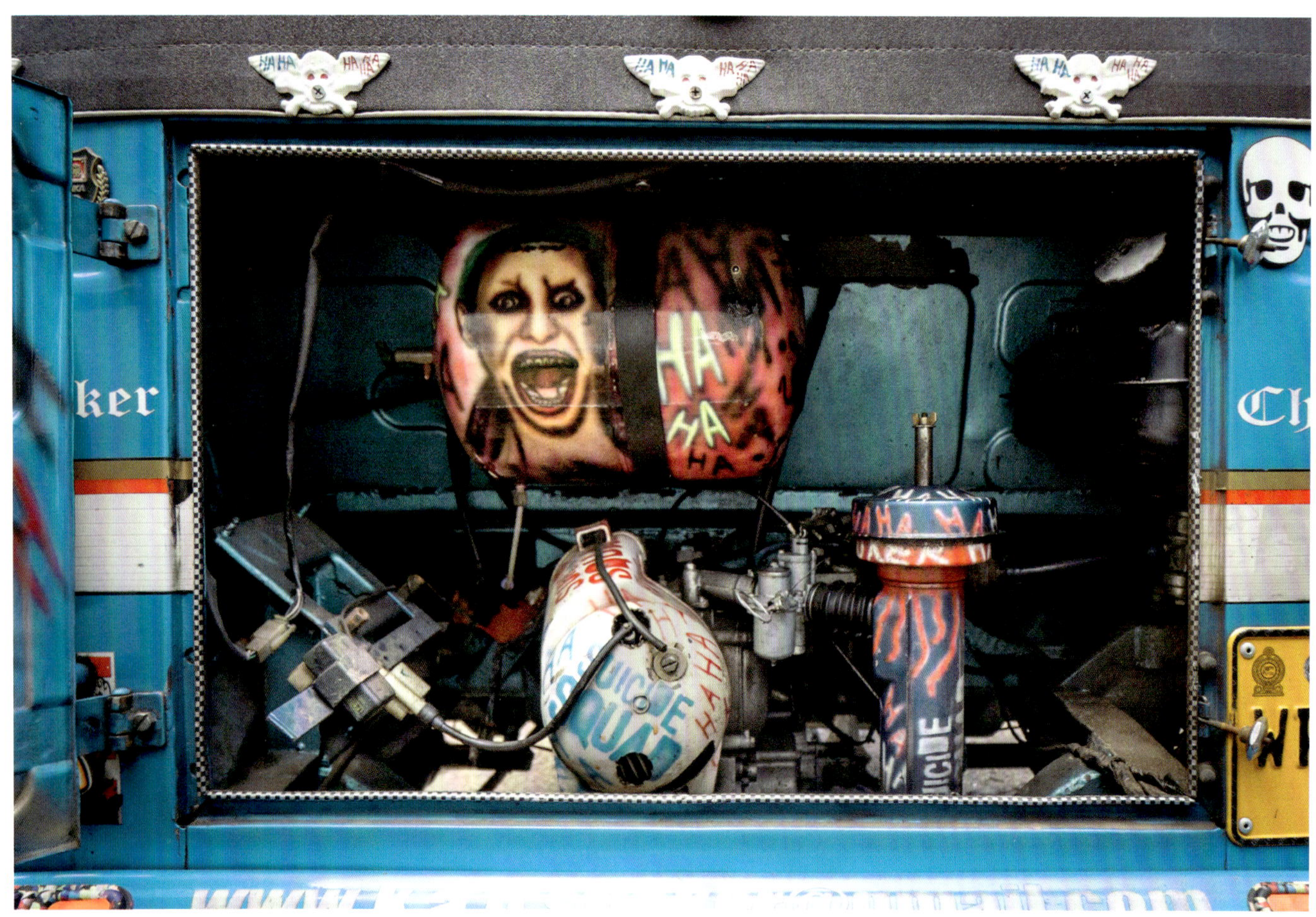

 Kiribathgoda, SRI LANKA

overleaf: Ratnapura, SRI LANKA

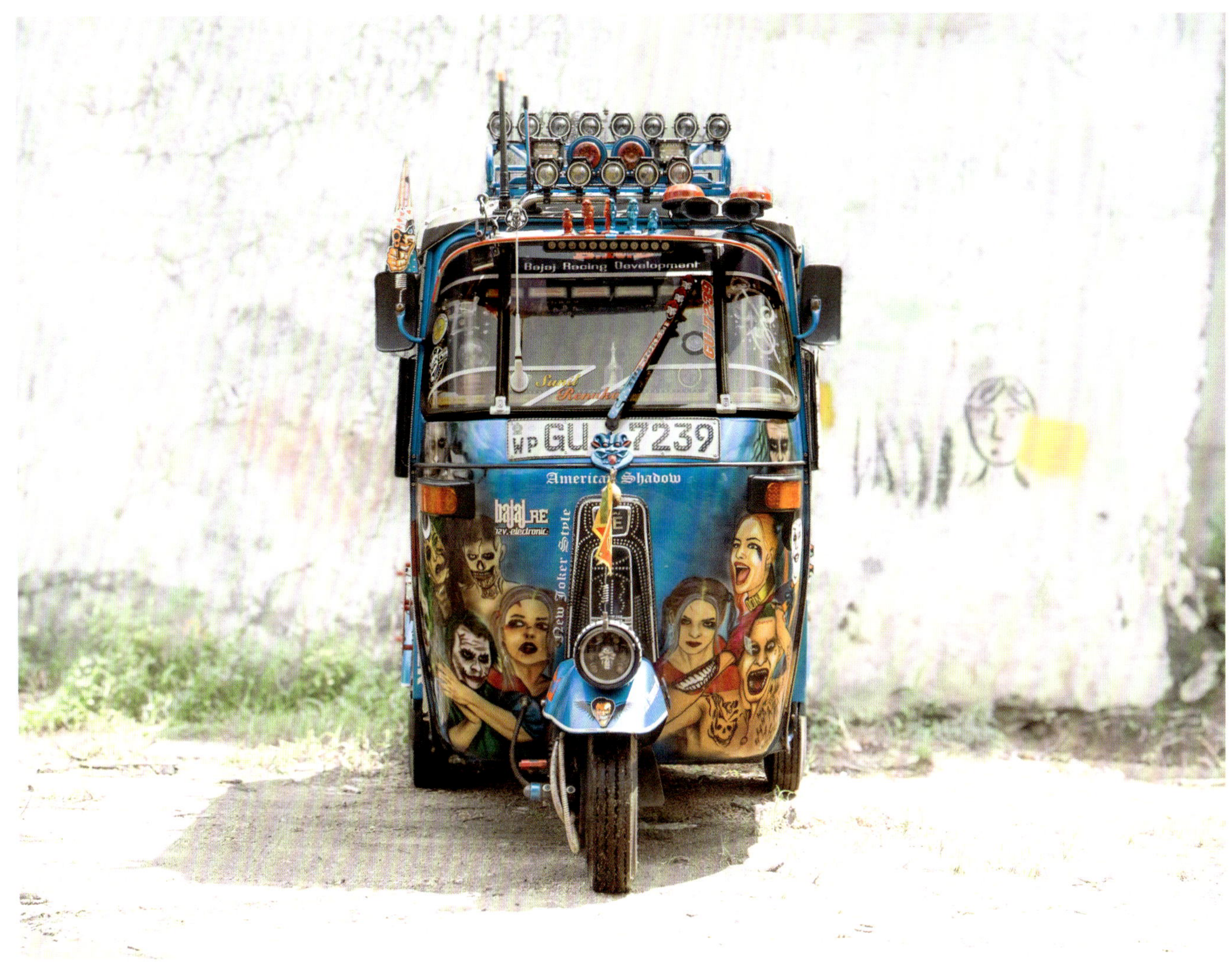

Bajaj Racing Development
WP GU 7239
American Shadow
bajaj RE
New Joker Style

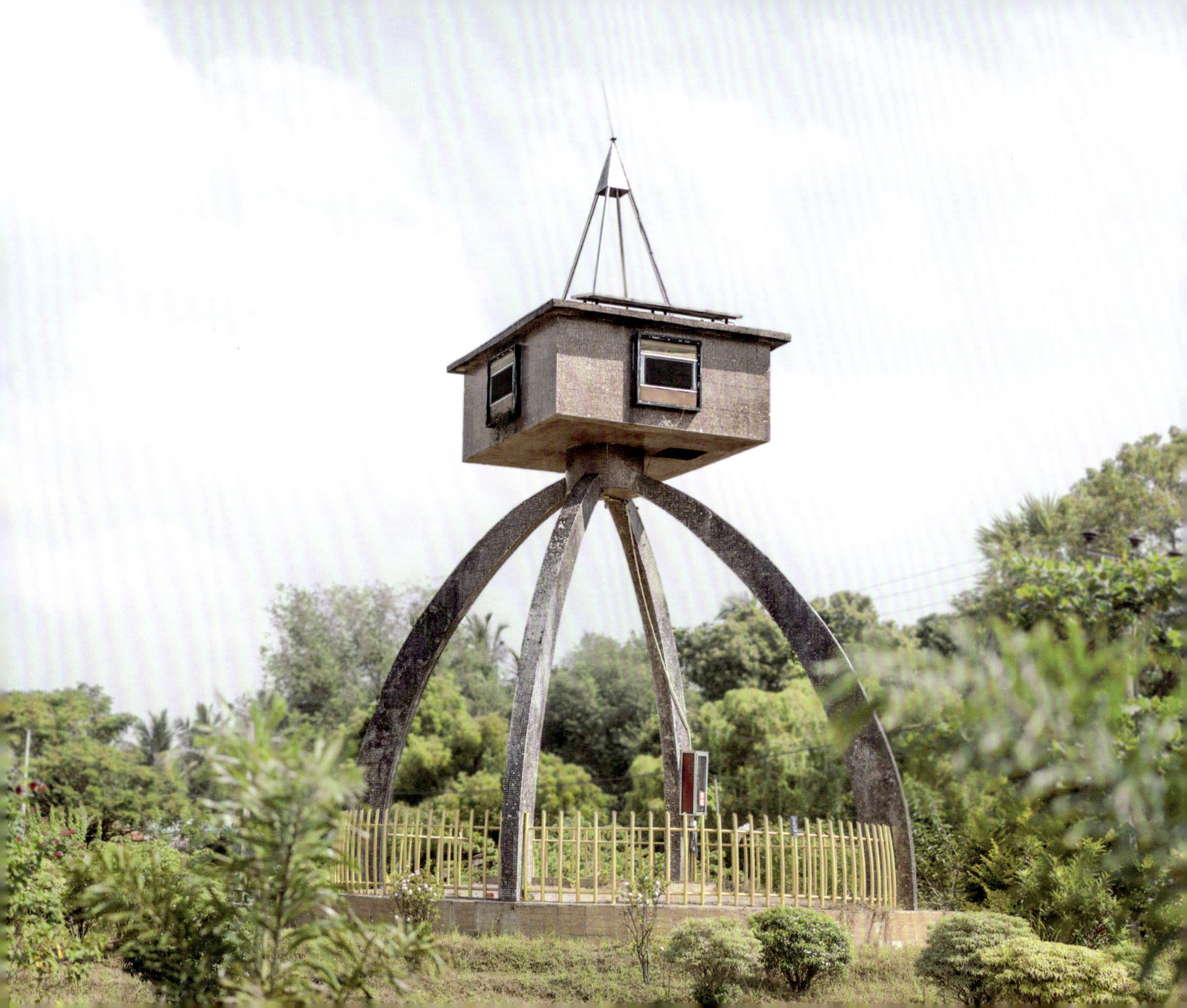

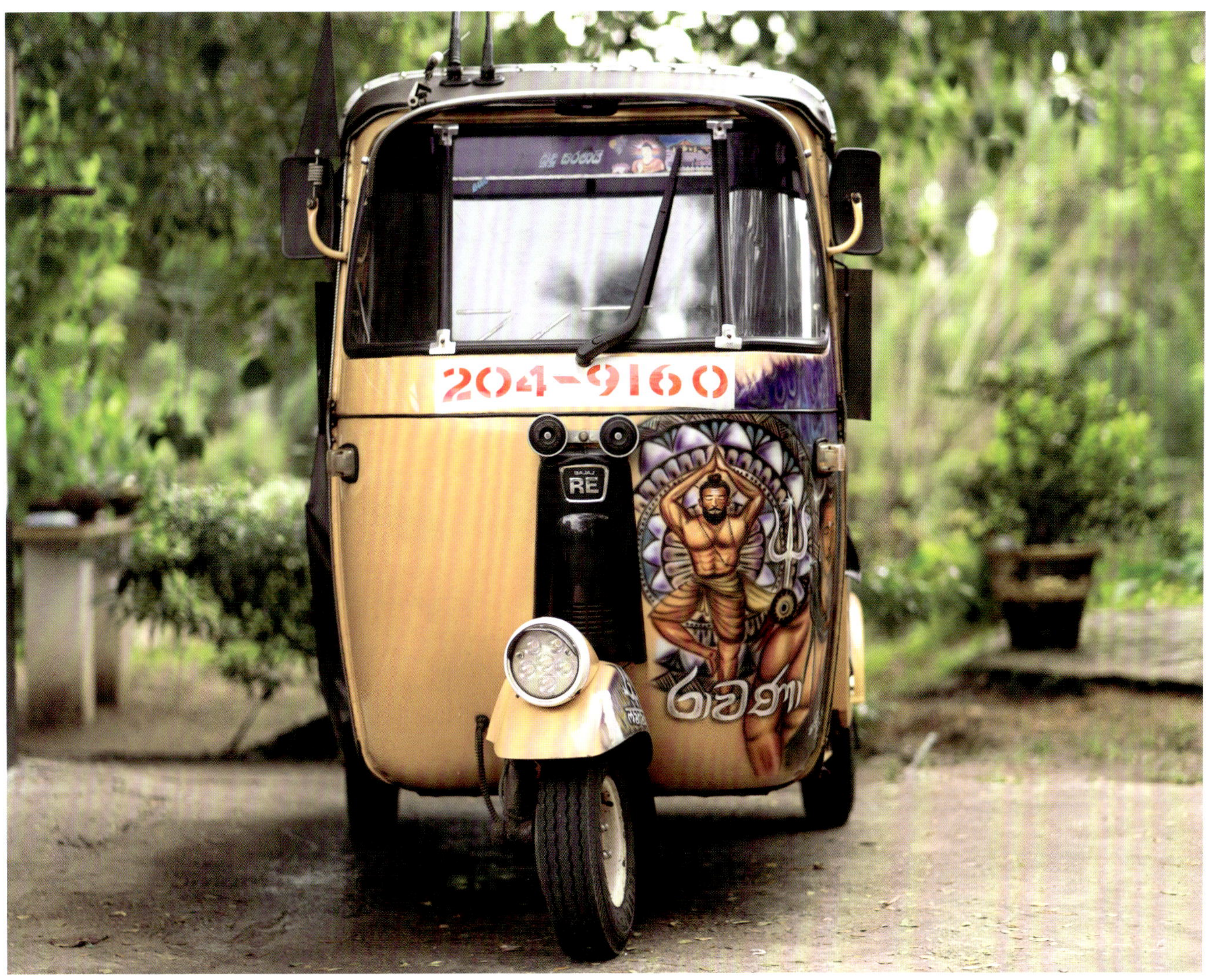

204-9160
BAJAJ RE

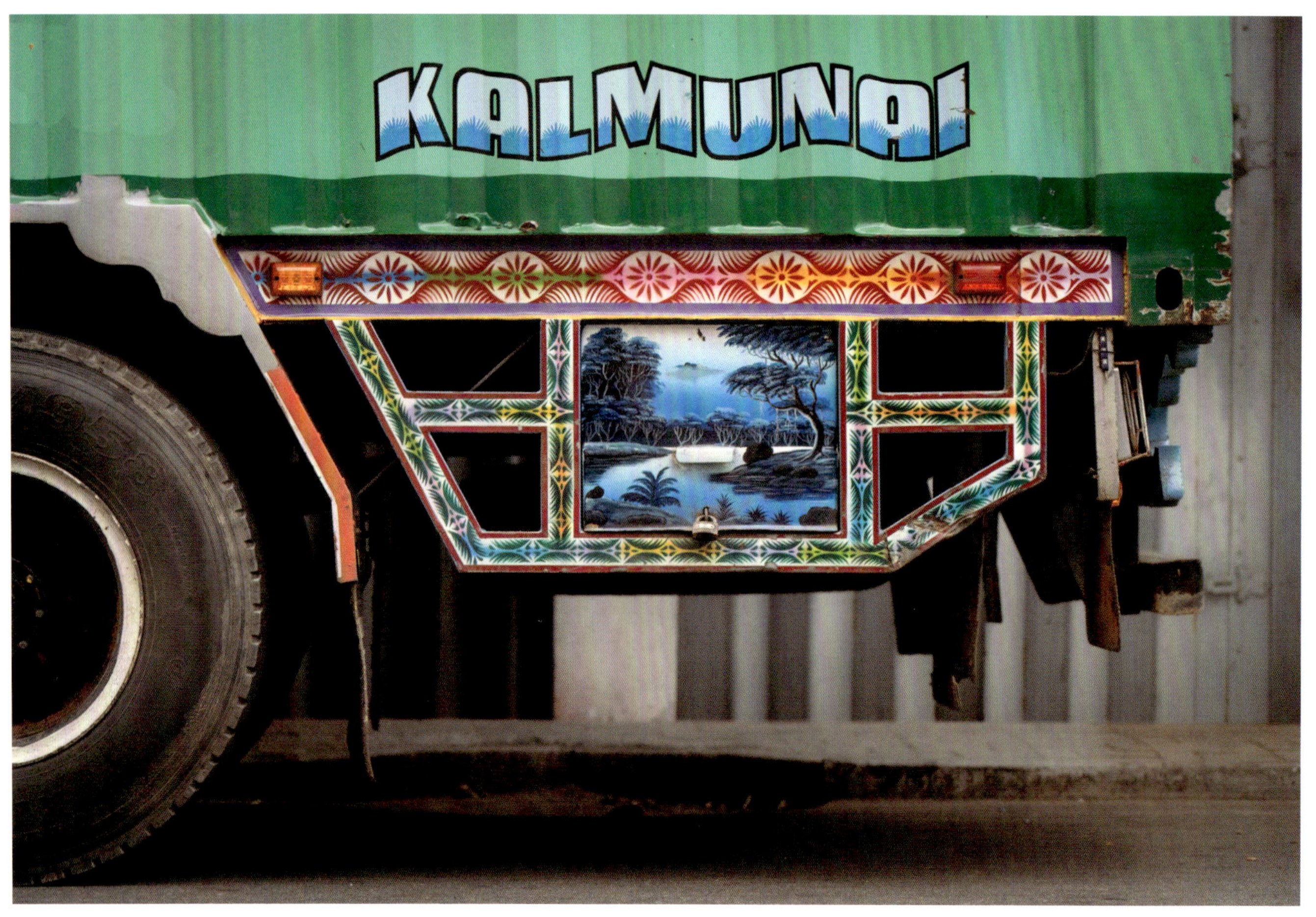

24–27: Colombo, SRI LANKA

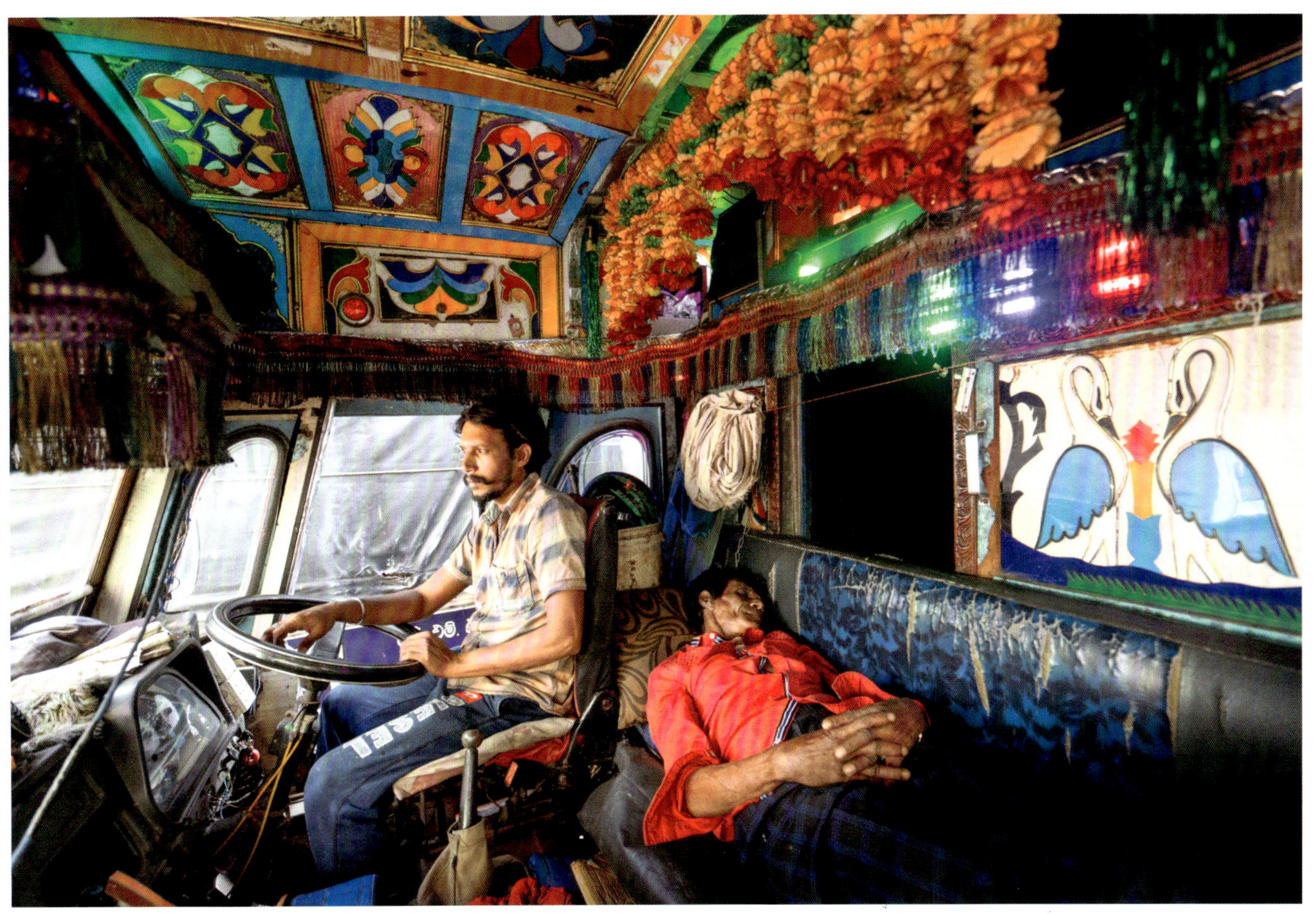

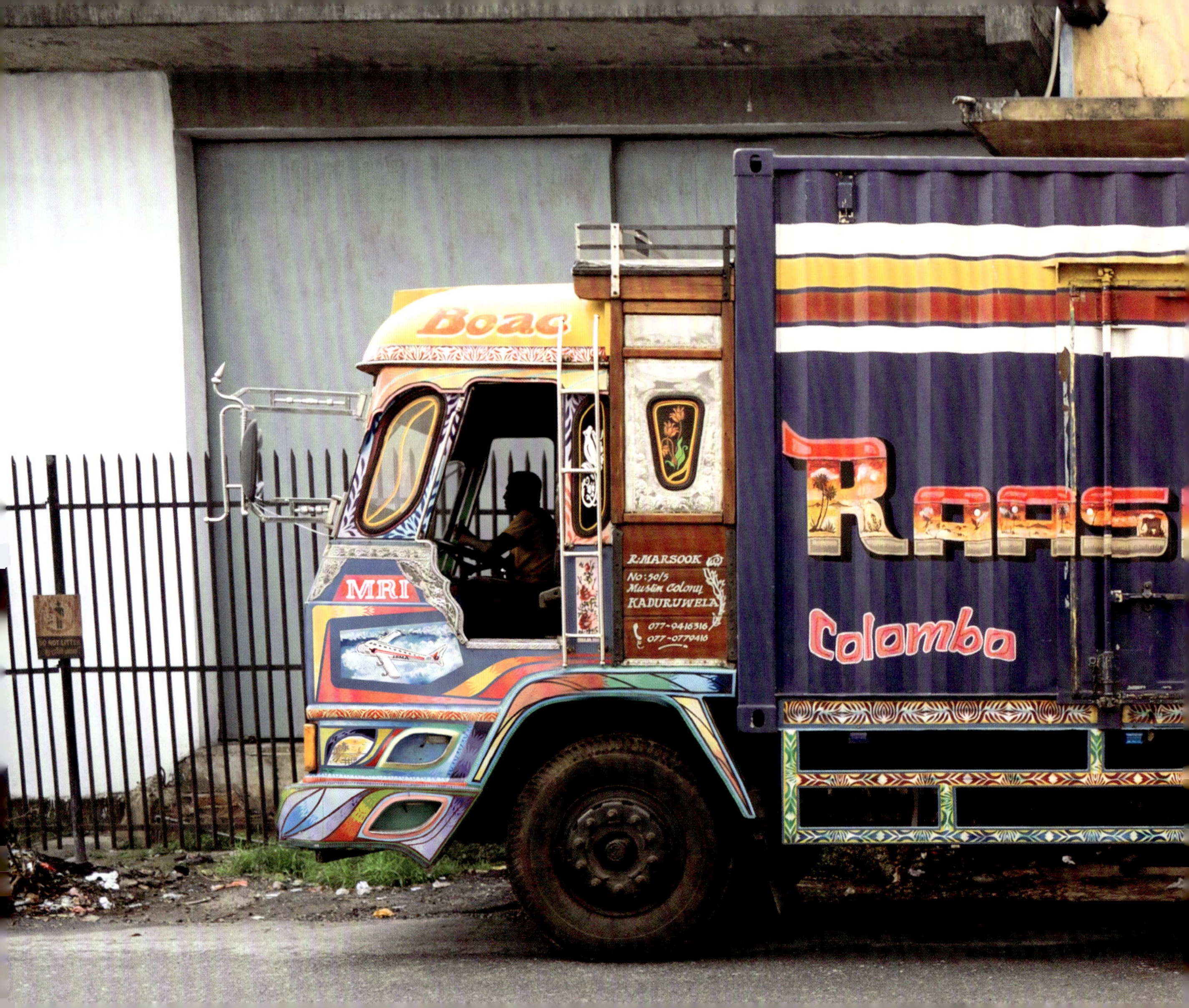

Boac
MRI
R.MARSOOK
No:50/5
Muslim Colony
KADURUWELA
077-9416316
077-0779416
RAAS
Colombo

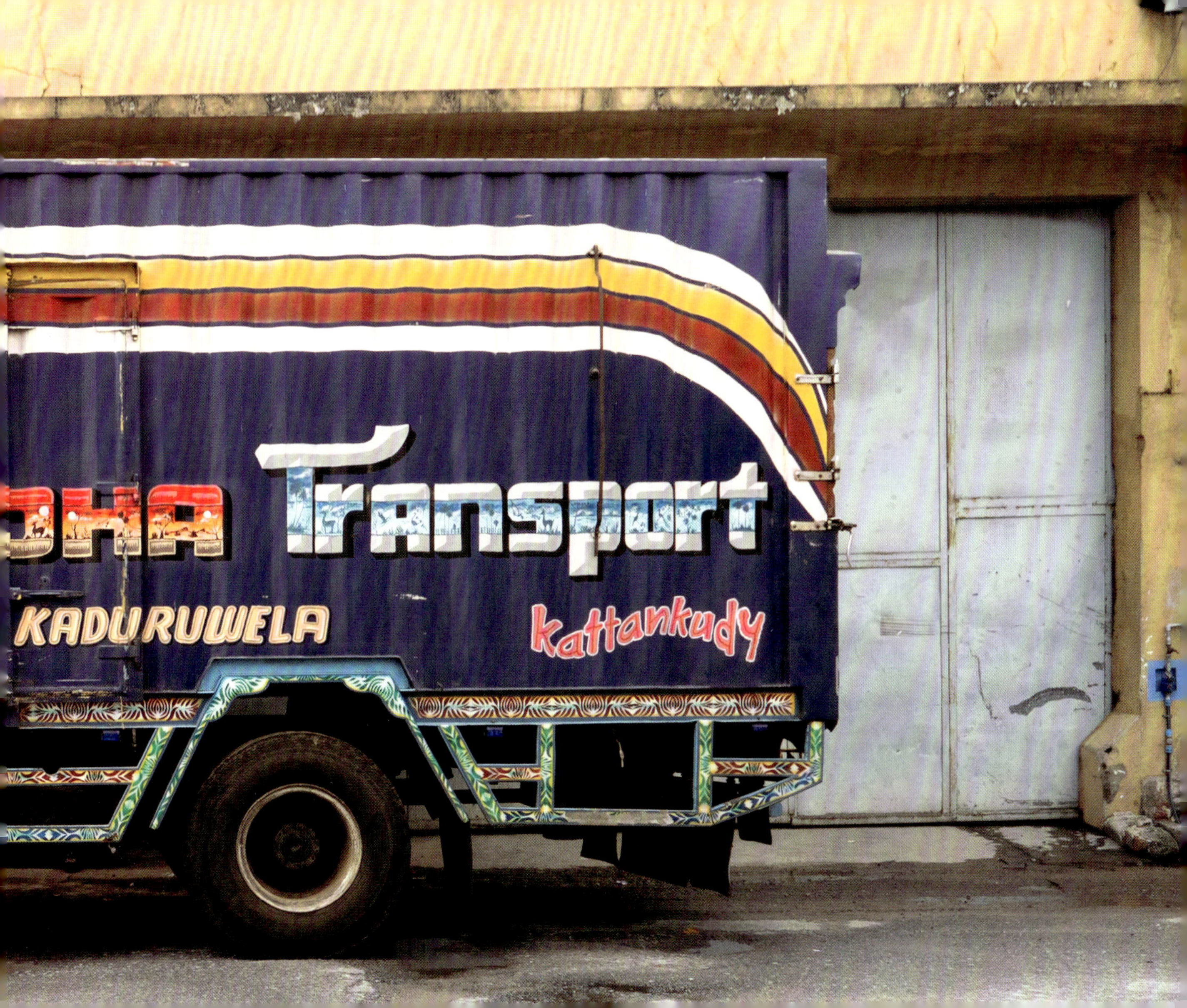
DHA Transport
KADURUWELA
Kattankudy

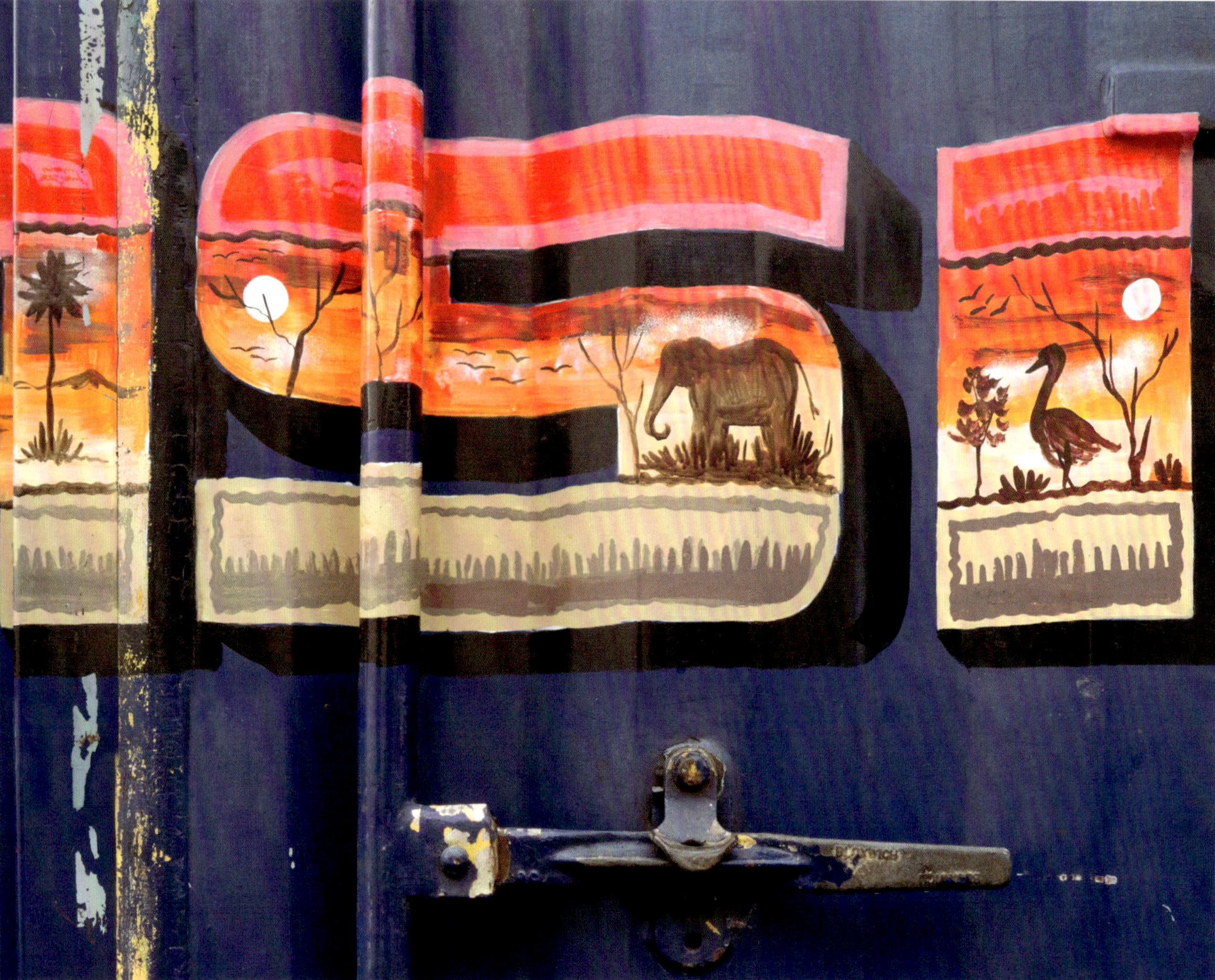

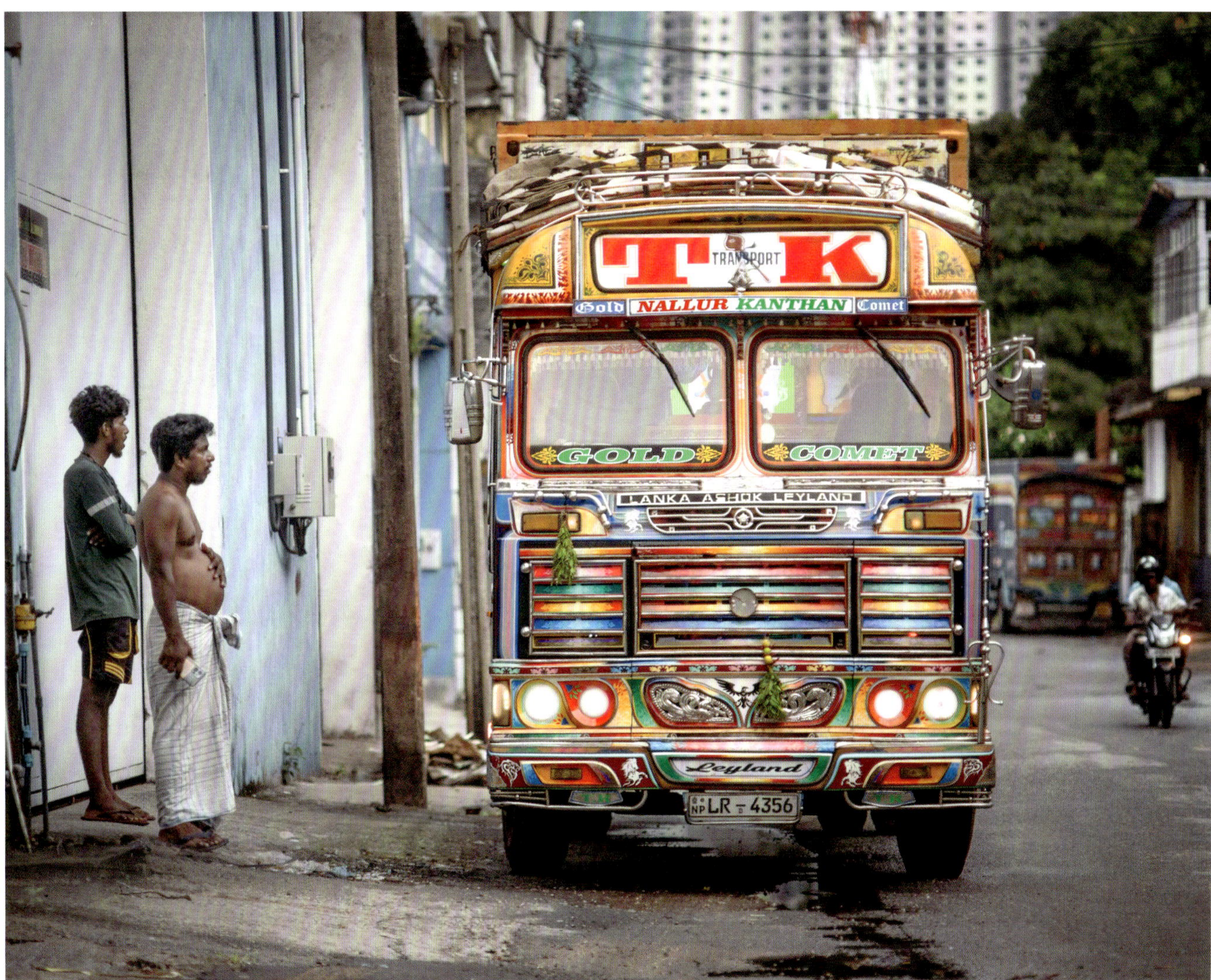
T K
TRANSPORT
Gold NALLUR KANTHAN Comet
GOLD COMET
LANKA ASHOK LEYLAND
Leyland
NP LR 4356

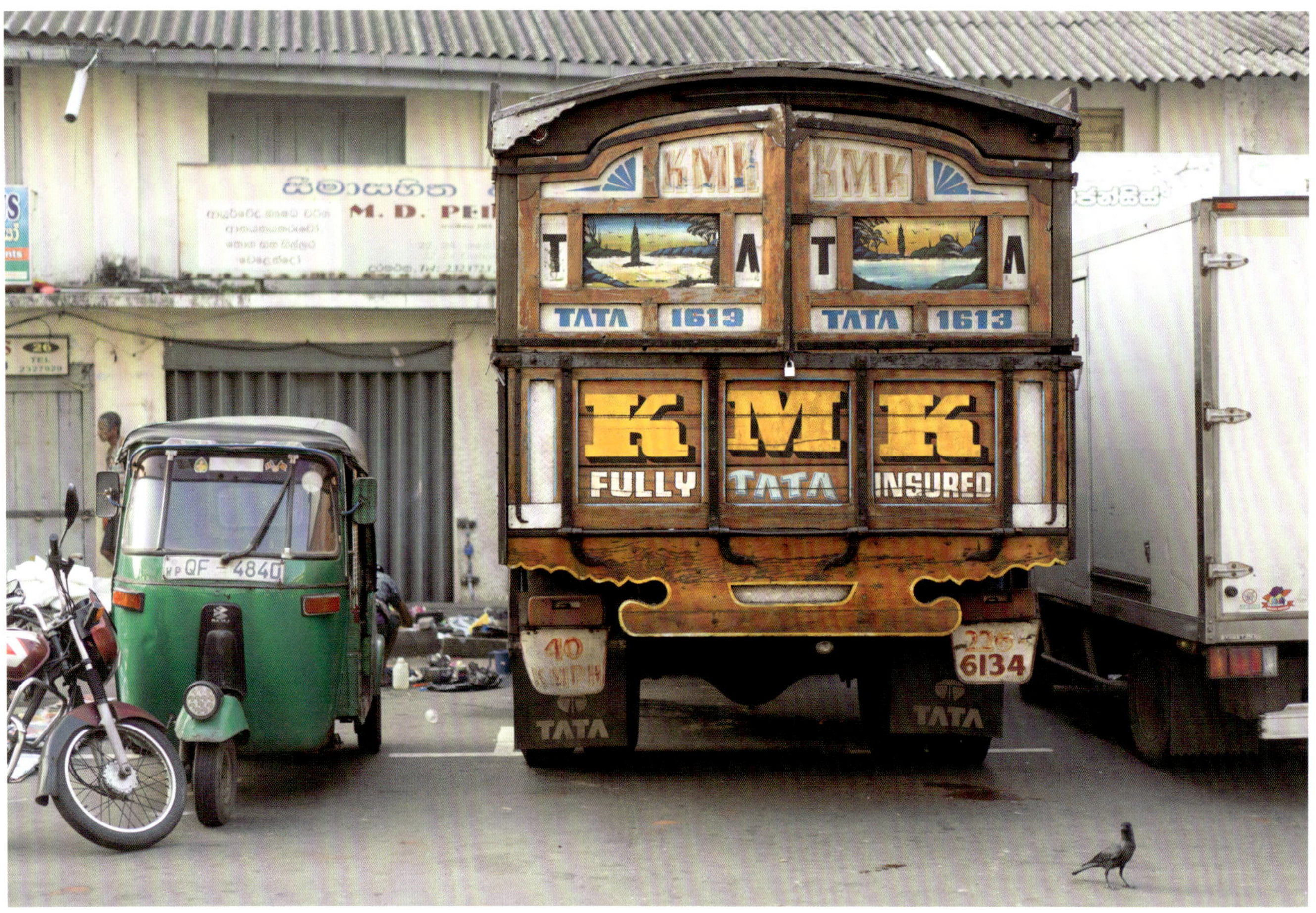

28   Colombo, SRI LANKA

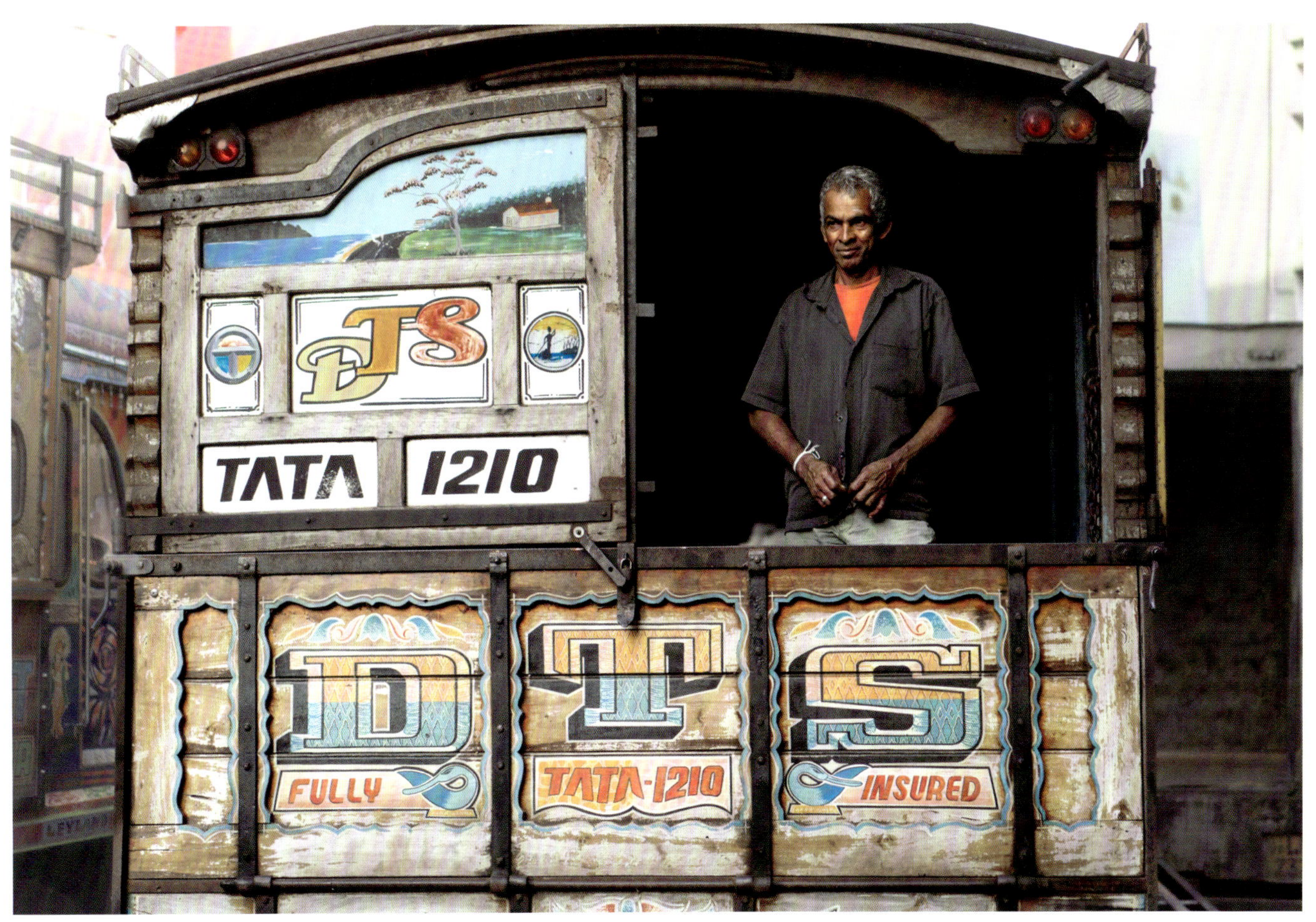

Colombo, SRI LANKA

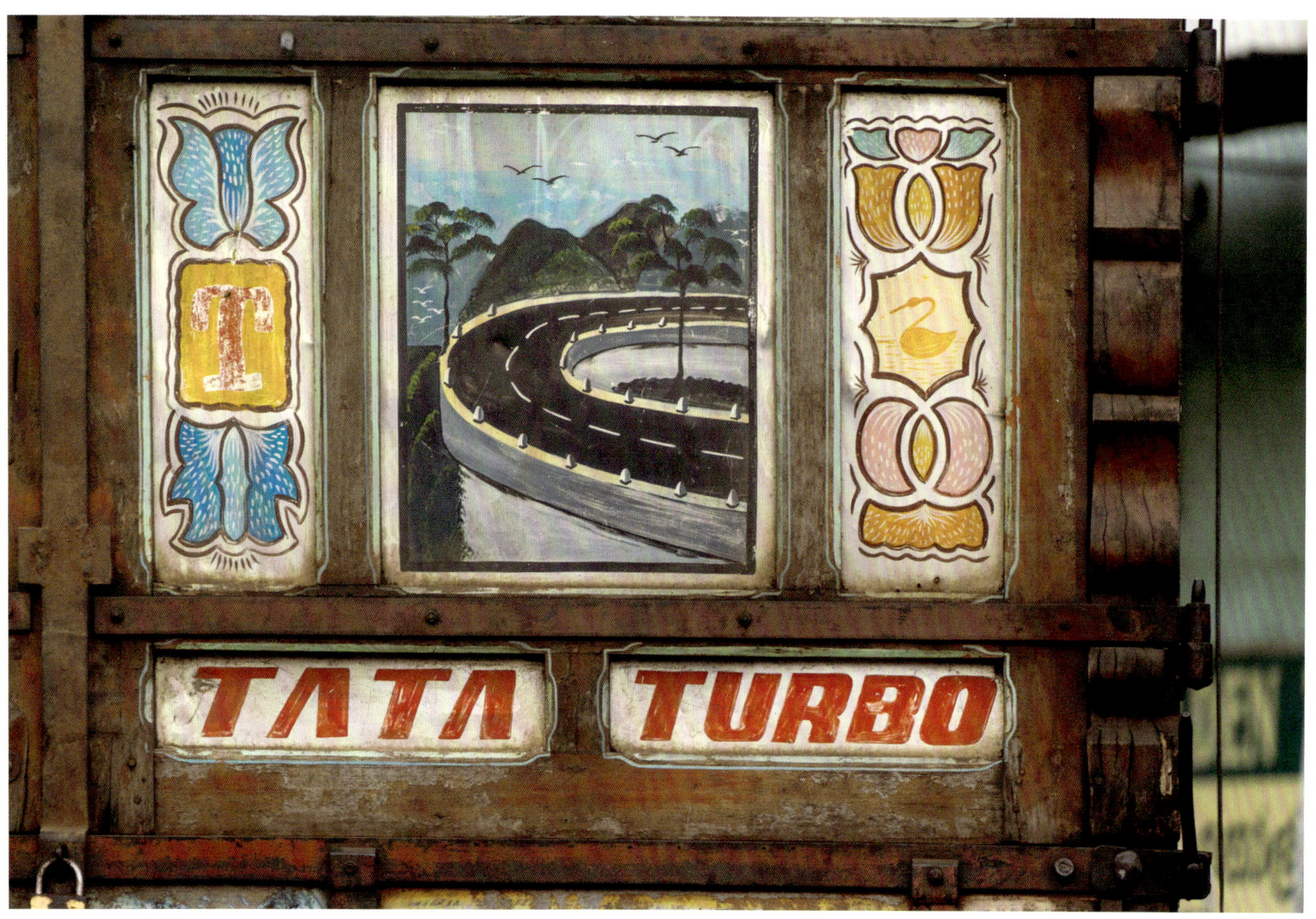

 Colombo, SRI LANKA

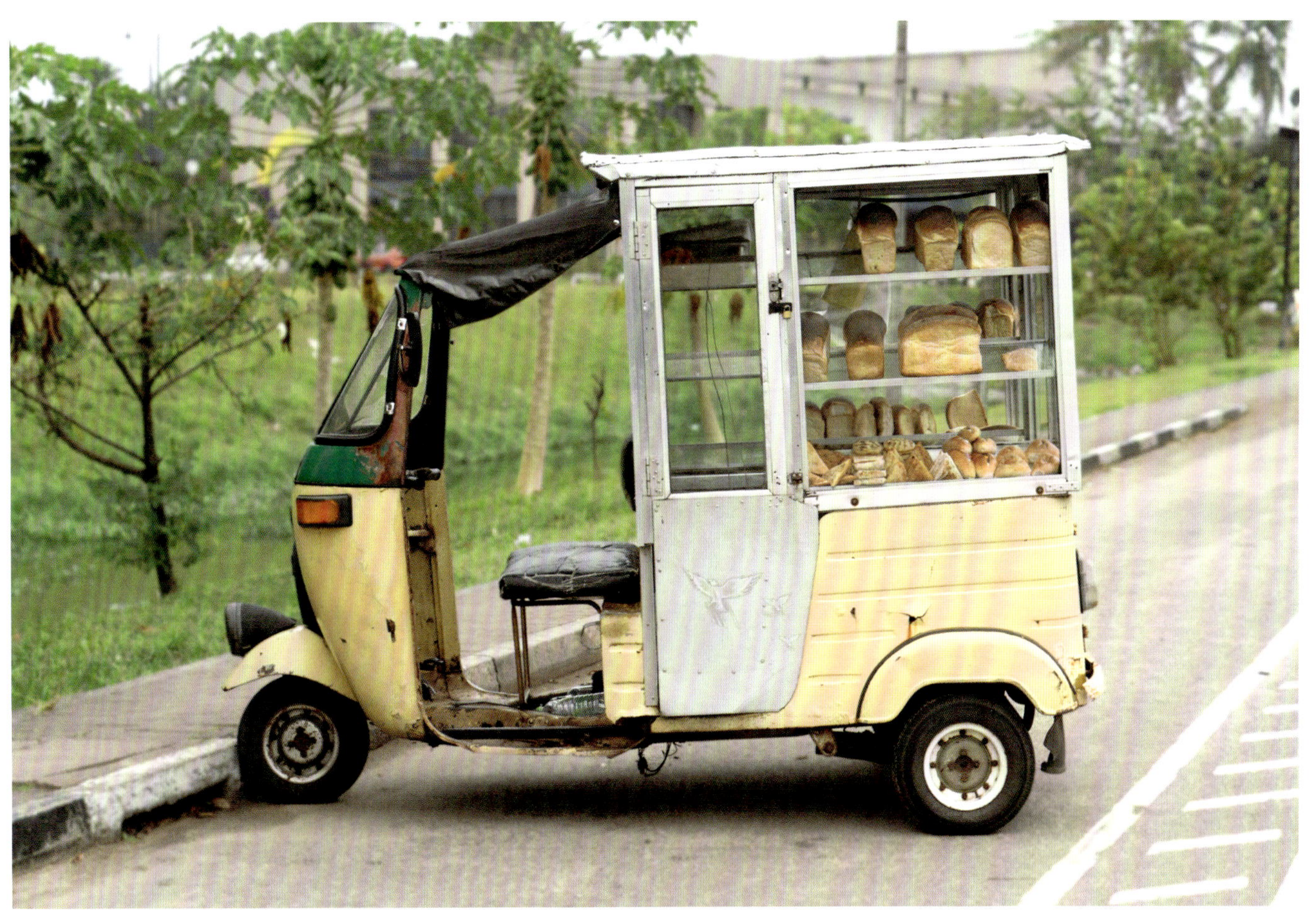

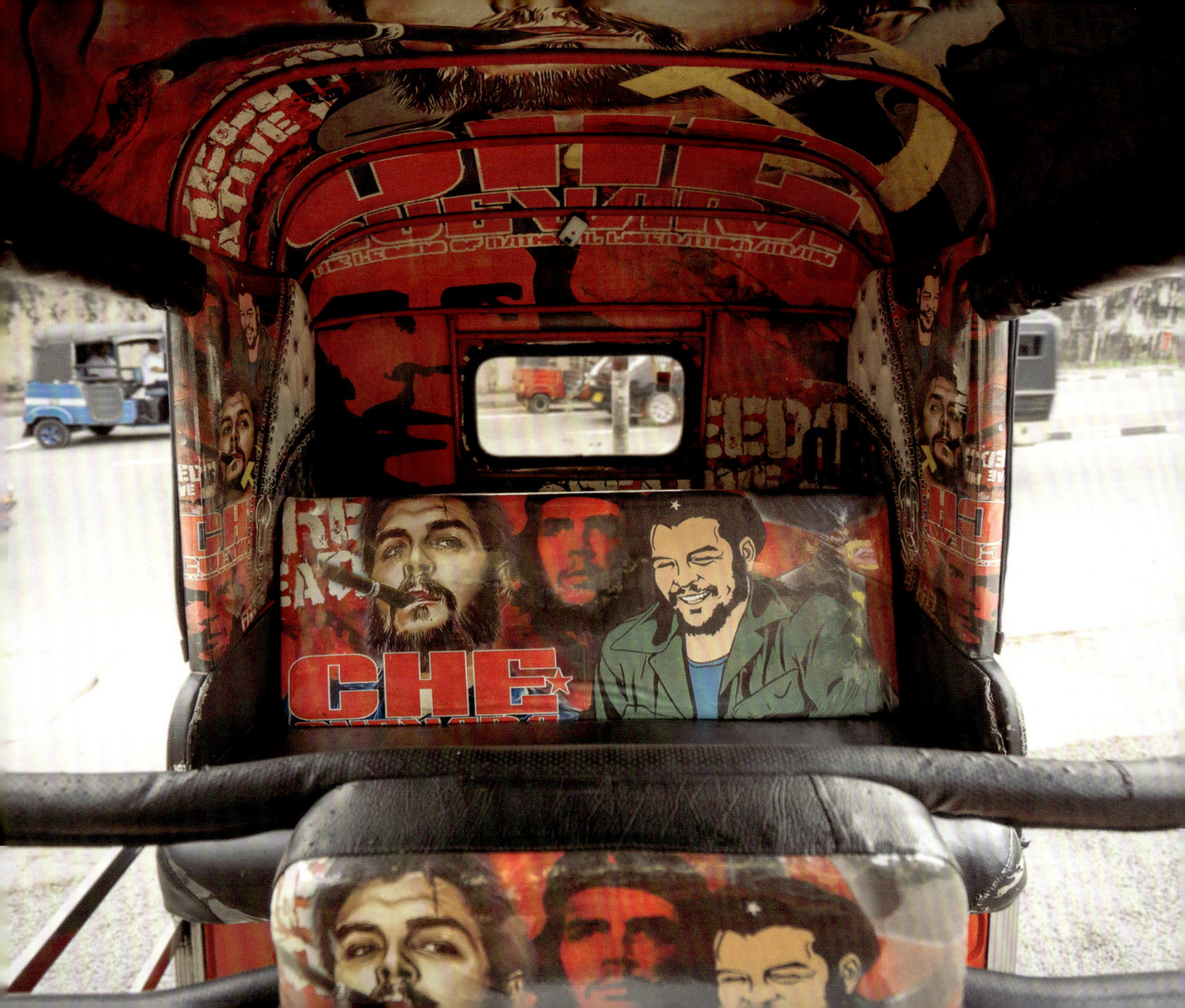
CHE

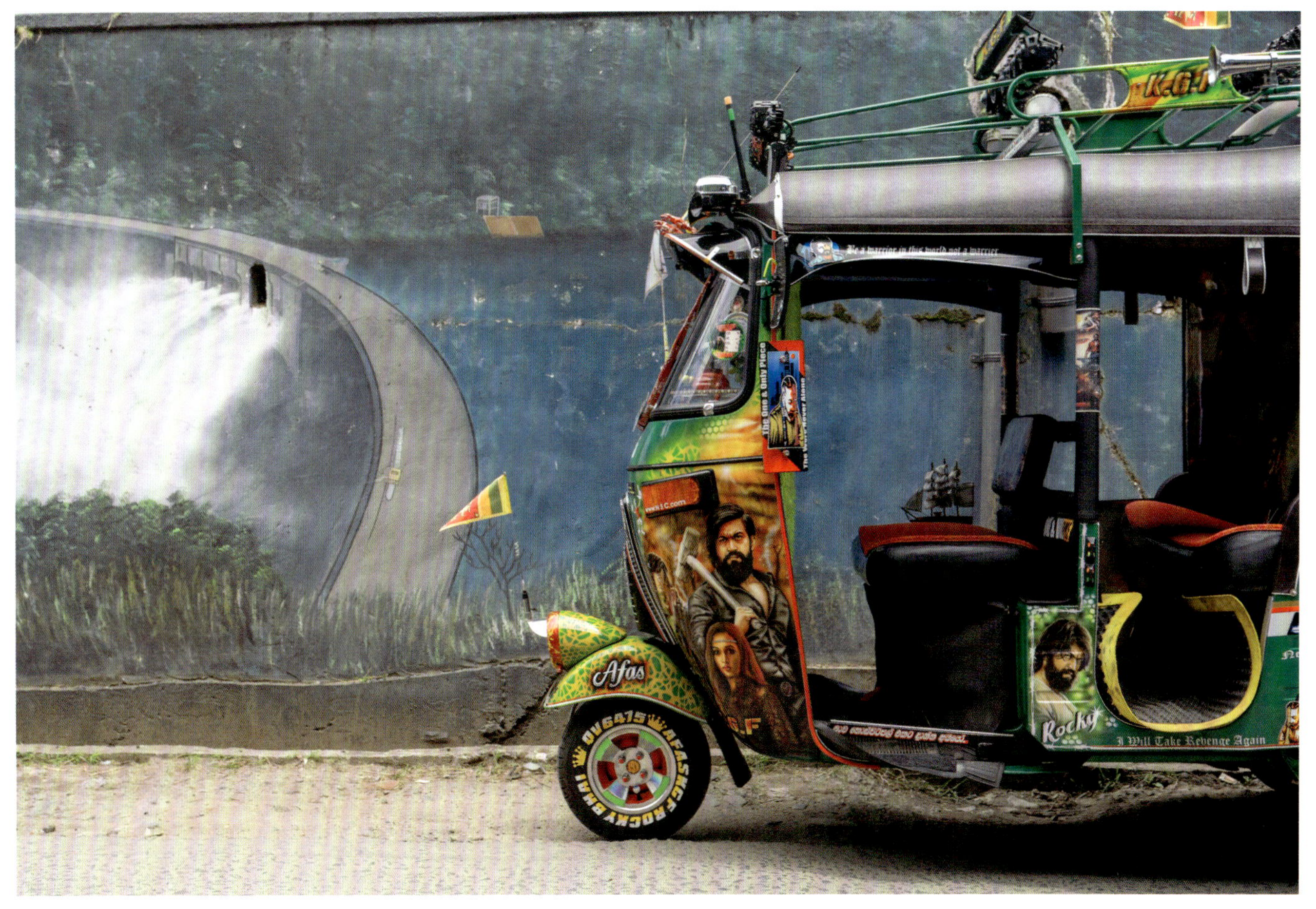

Battaramulla, SRI LANKA

Kegalle, SRI LANKA

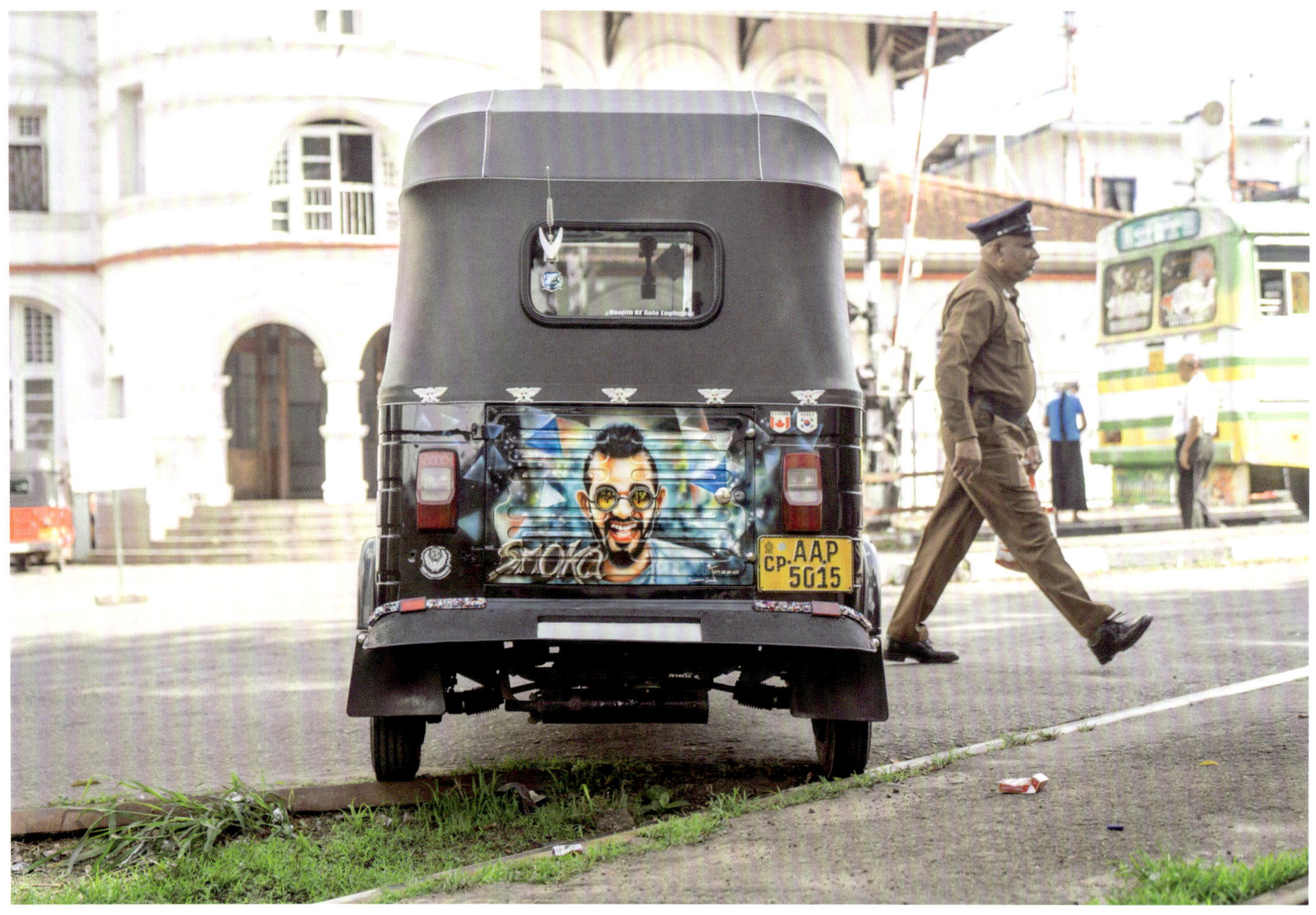

34   Kandy, SRI LANKA

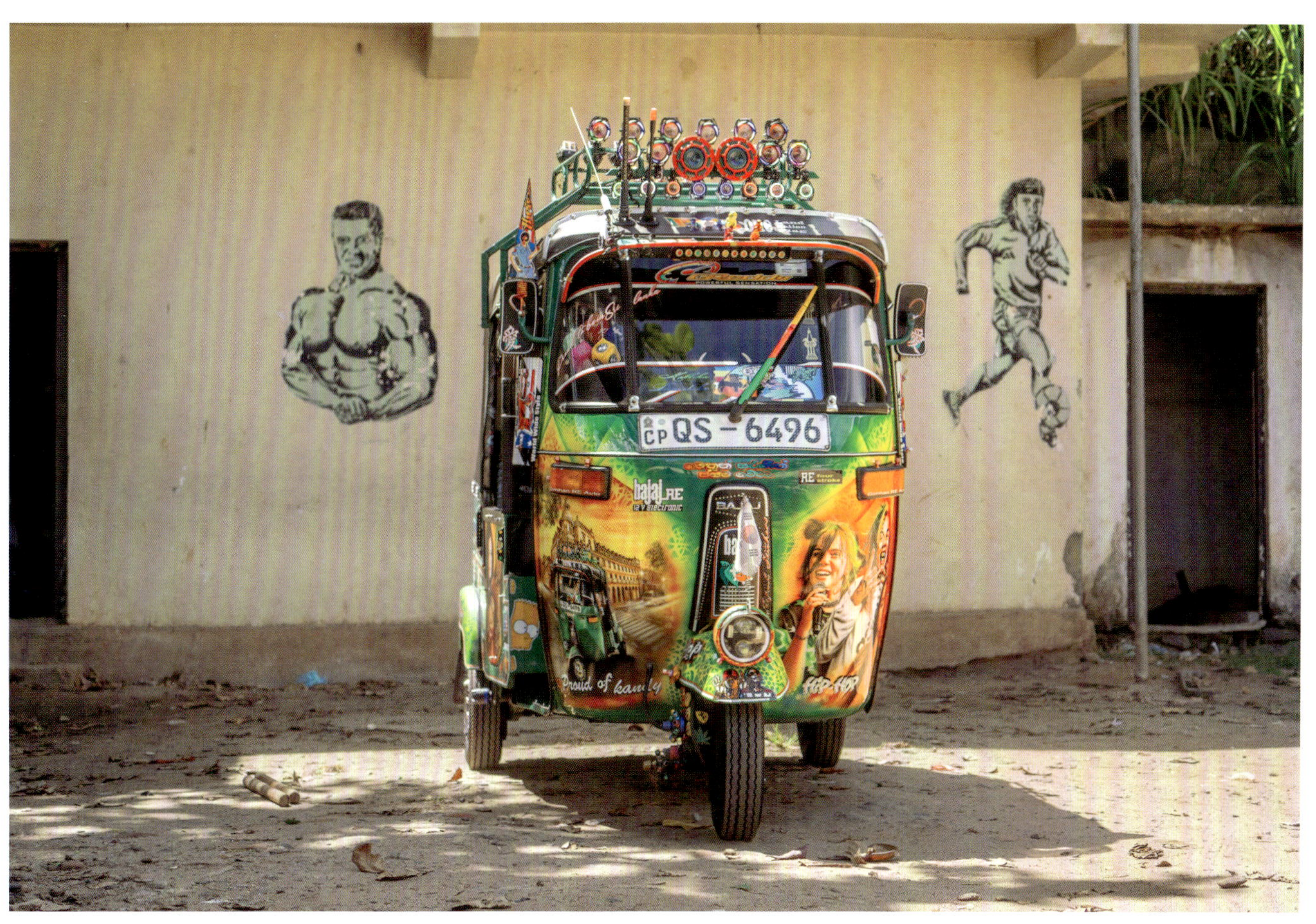

Kandy, SRI LANKA　35

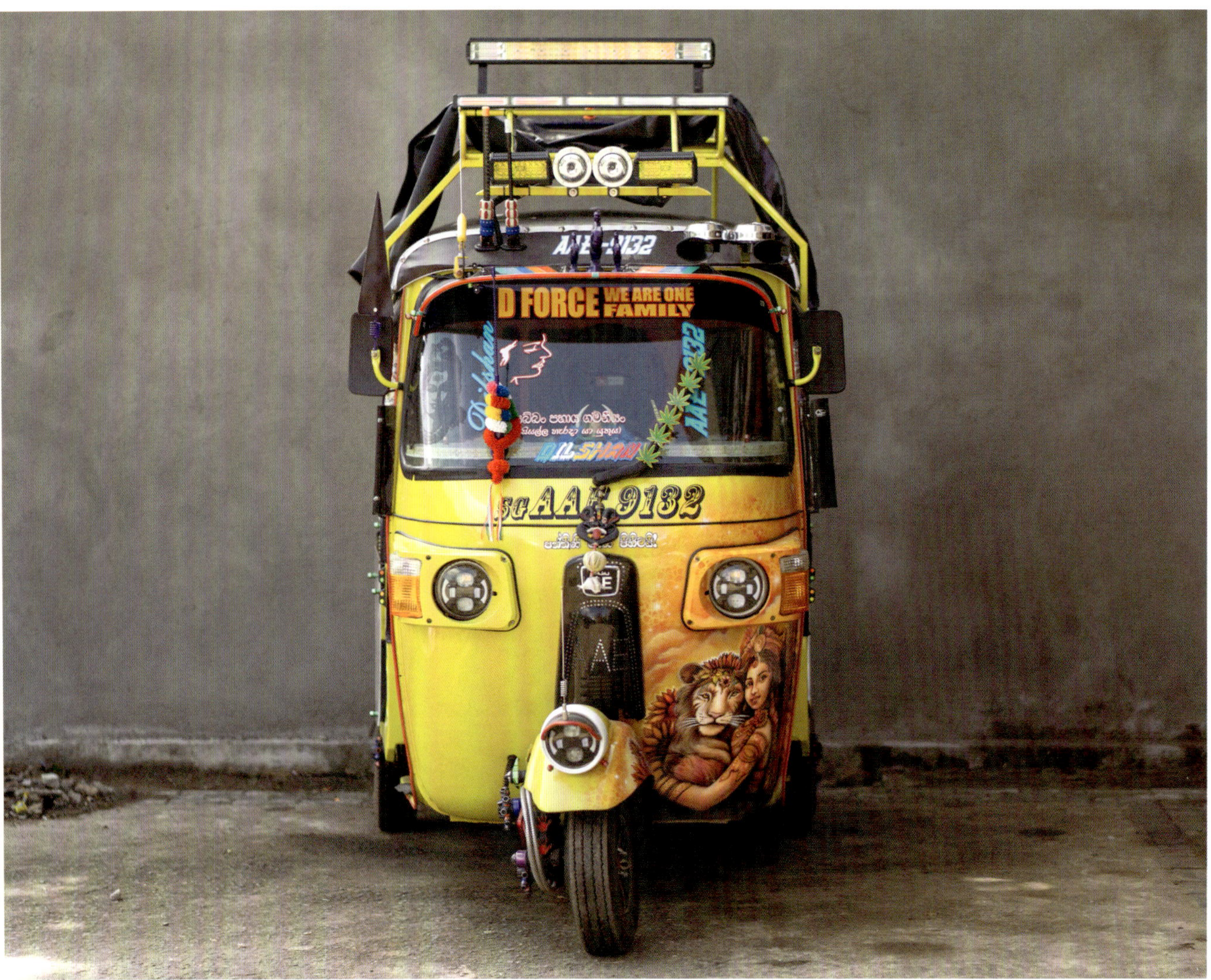
D FORCE WE ARE ONE FAMILY
D:shan
sc AAF 9132

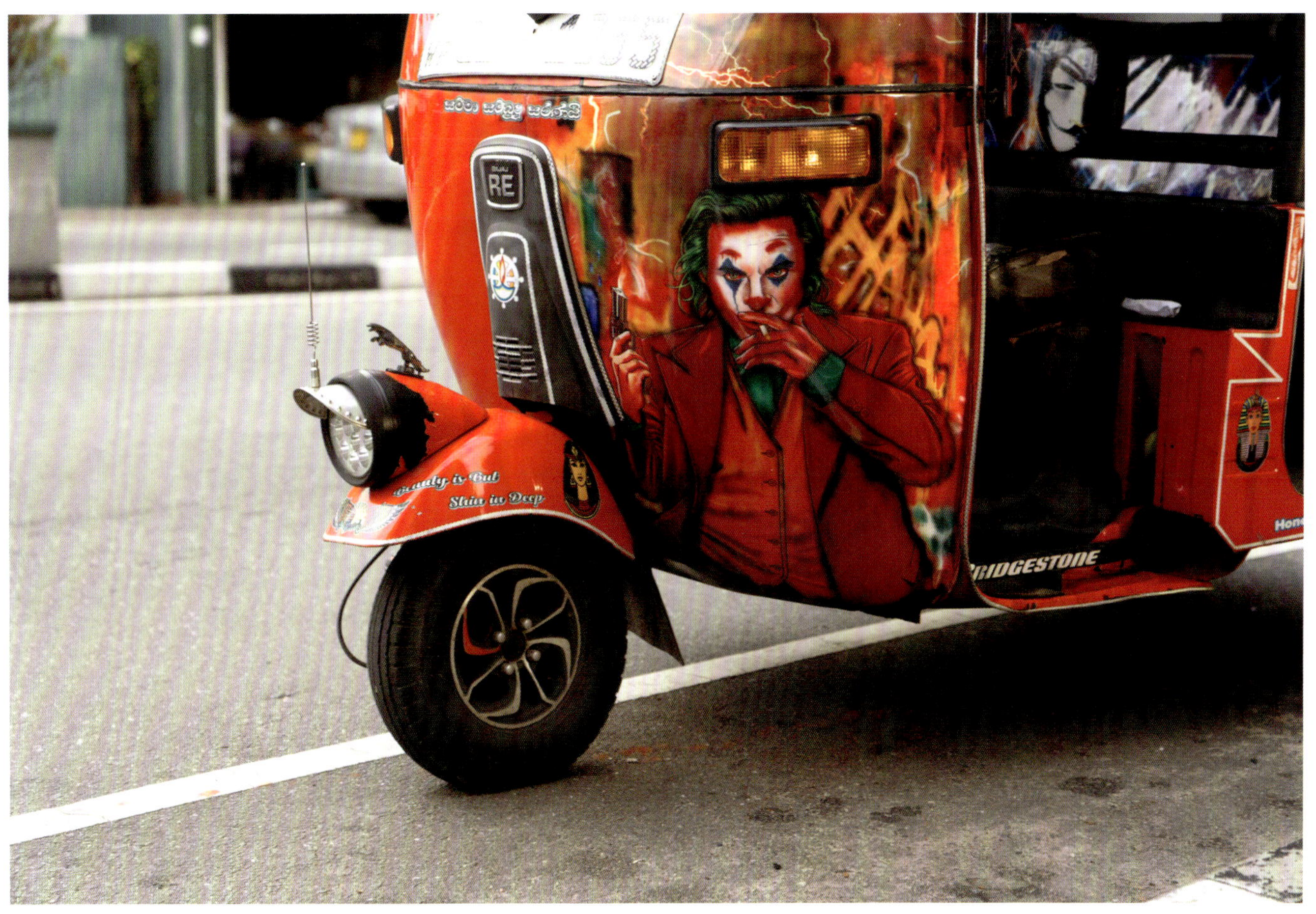

RE
Beauty is But
Skin in Deep
BRIDGESTONE

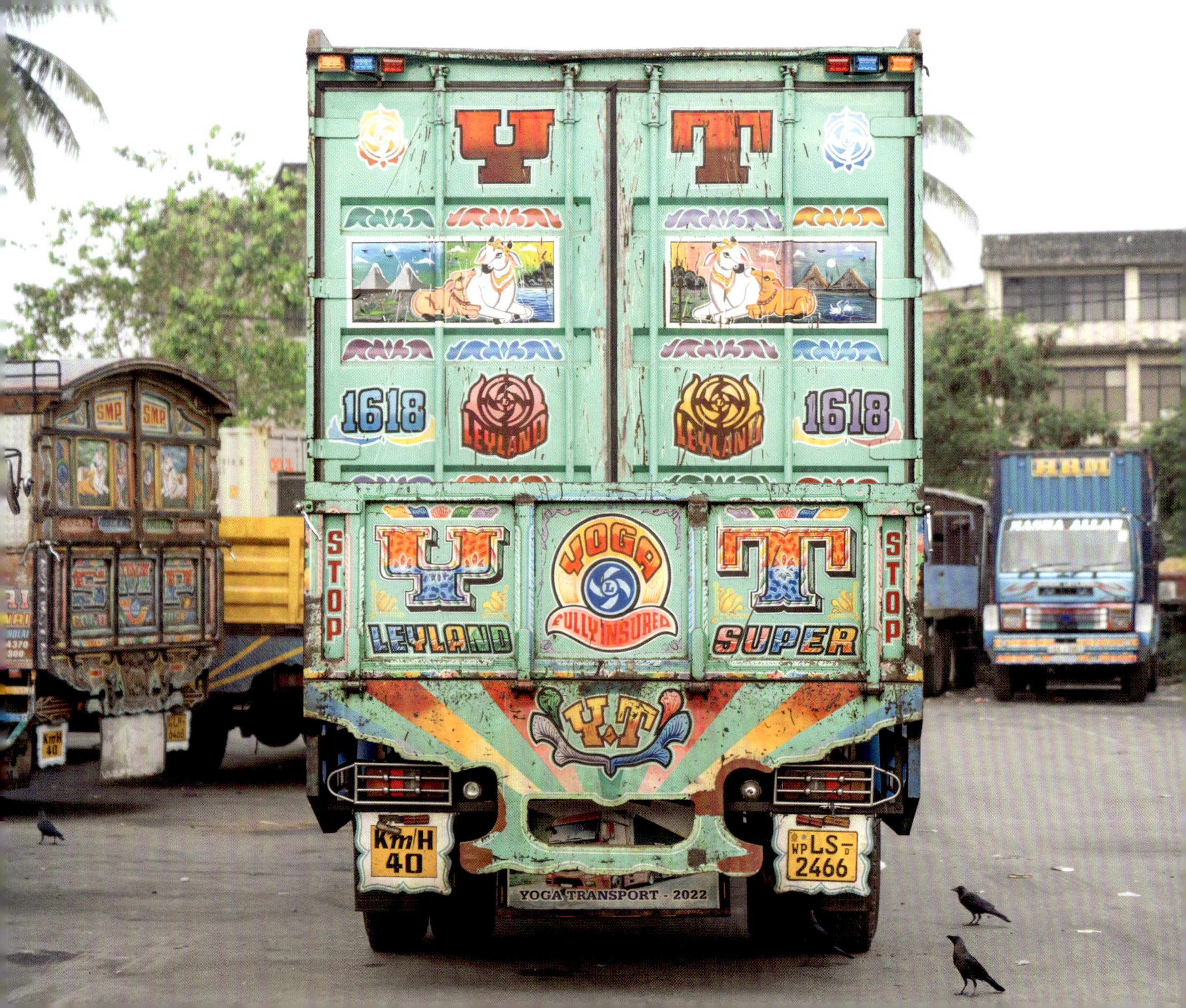
Y T
1618
LEYLAND
1618
STOP
U
LEYLAND
YOGA
FULLY INSURED
T
SUPER
STOP
Y-T
KmH
40
WP LS-
2466
YOGA TRANSPORT - 2022
SMP SMP
HBM
RAHBA ALLAH

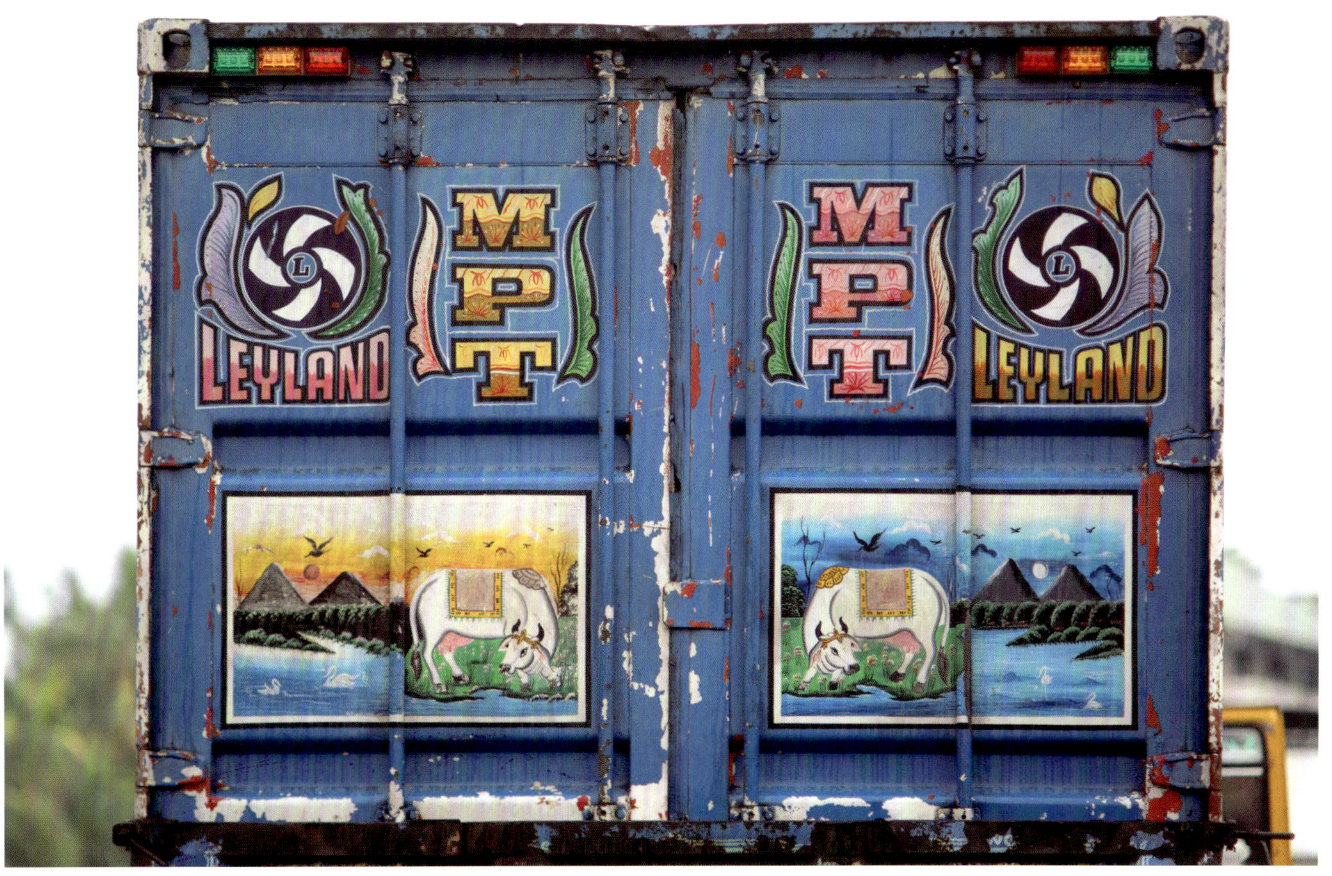

Colombo, SRI LANKA

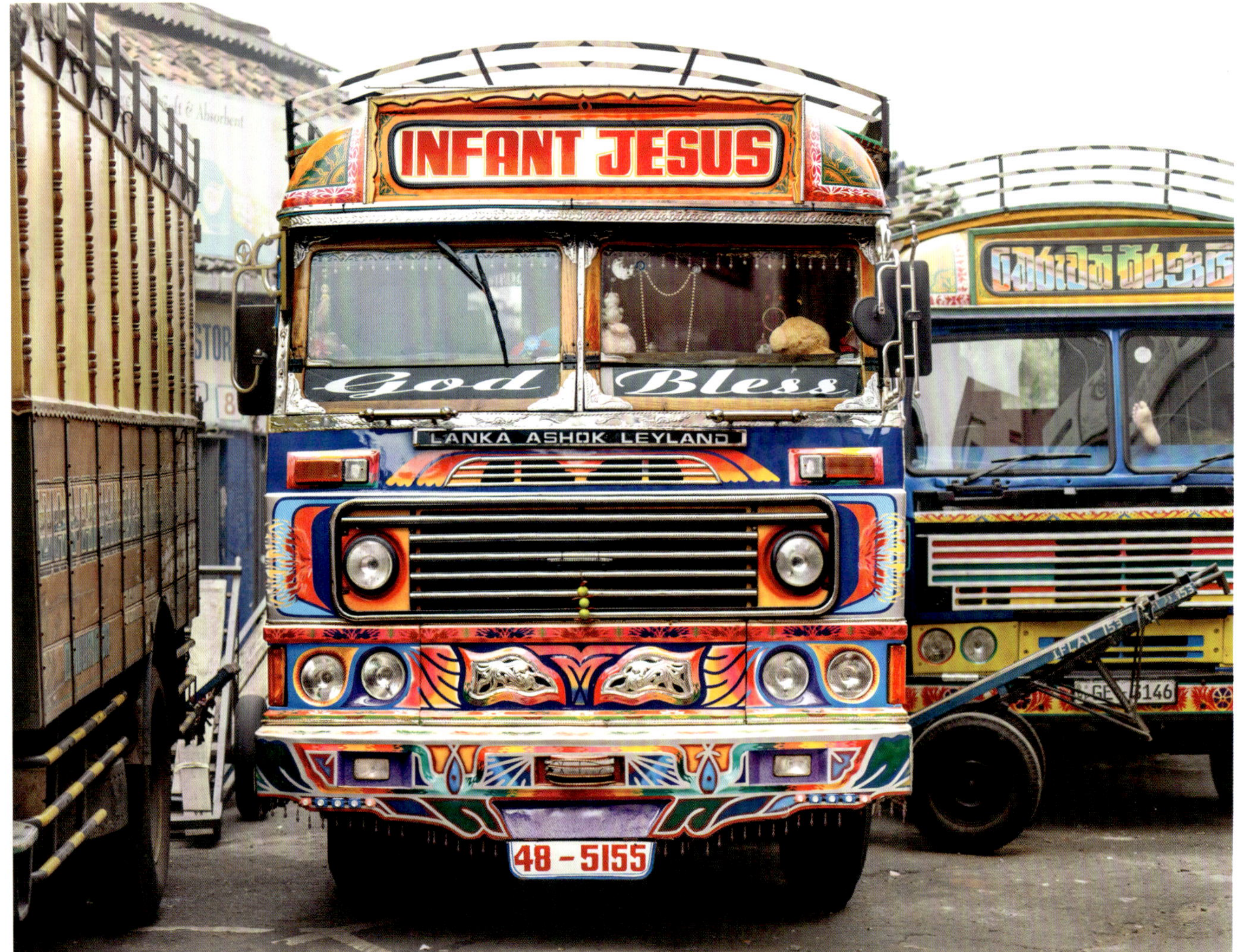

40   Colombo, SRI LANKA

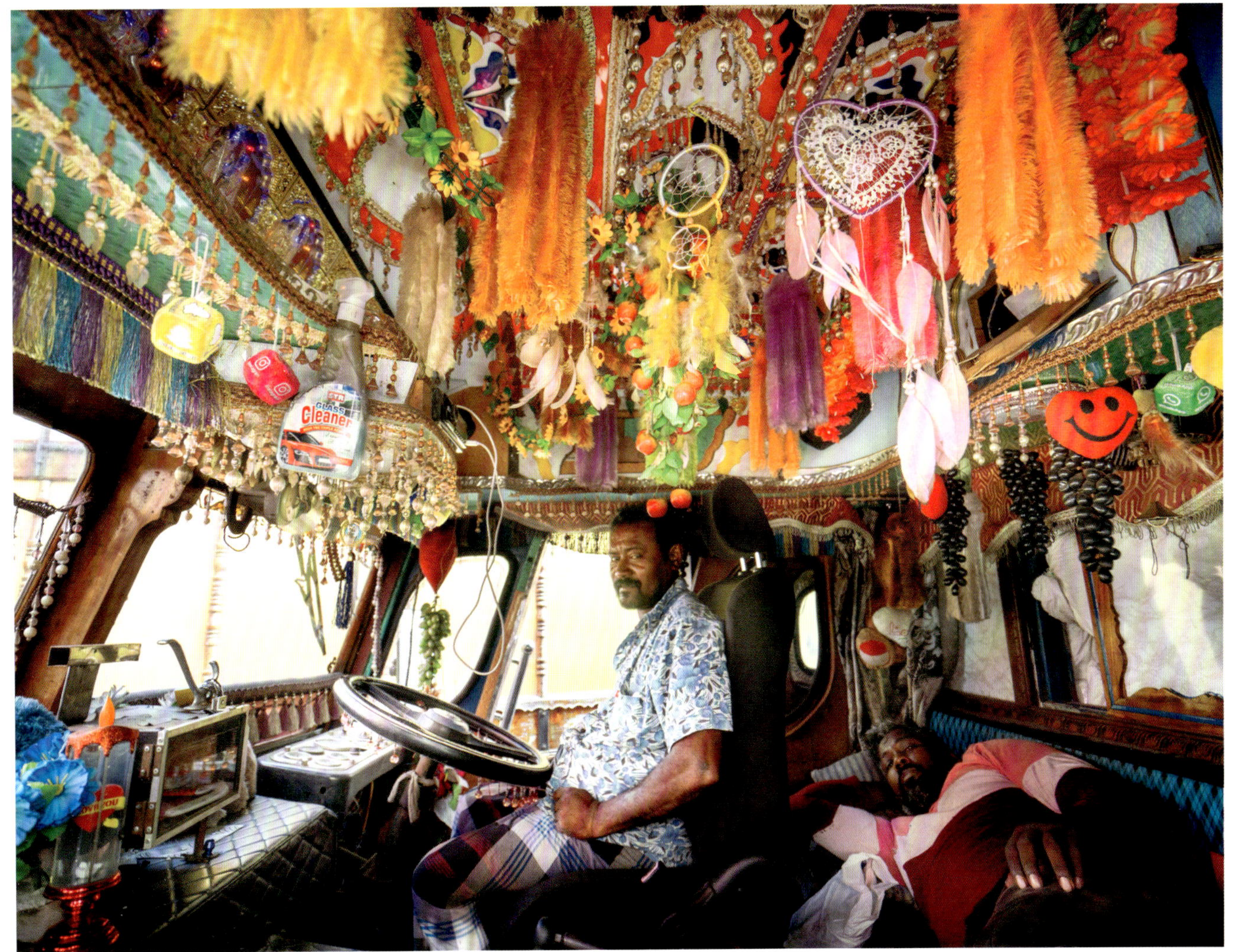

Colombo, SRI LANKA   41

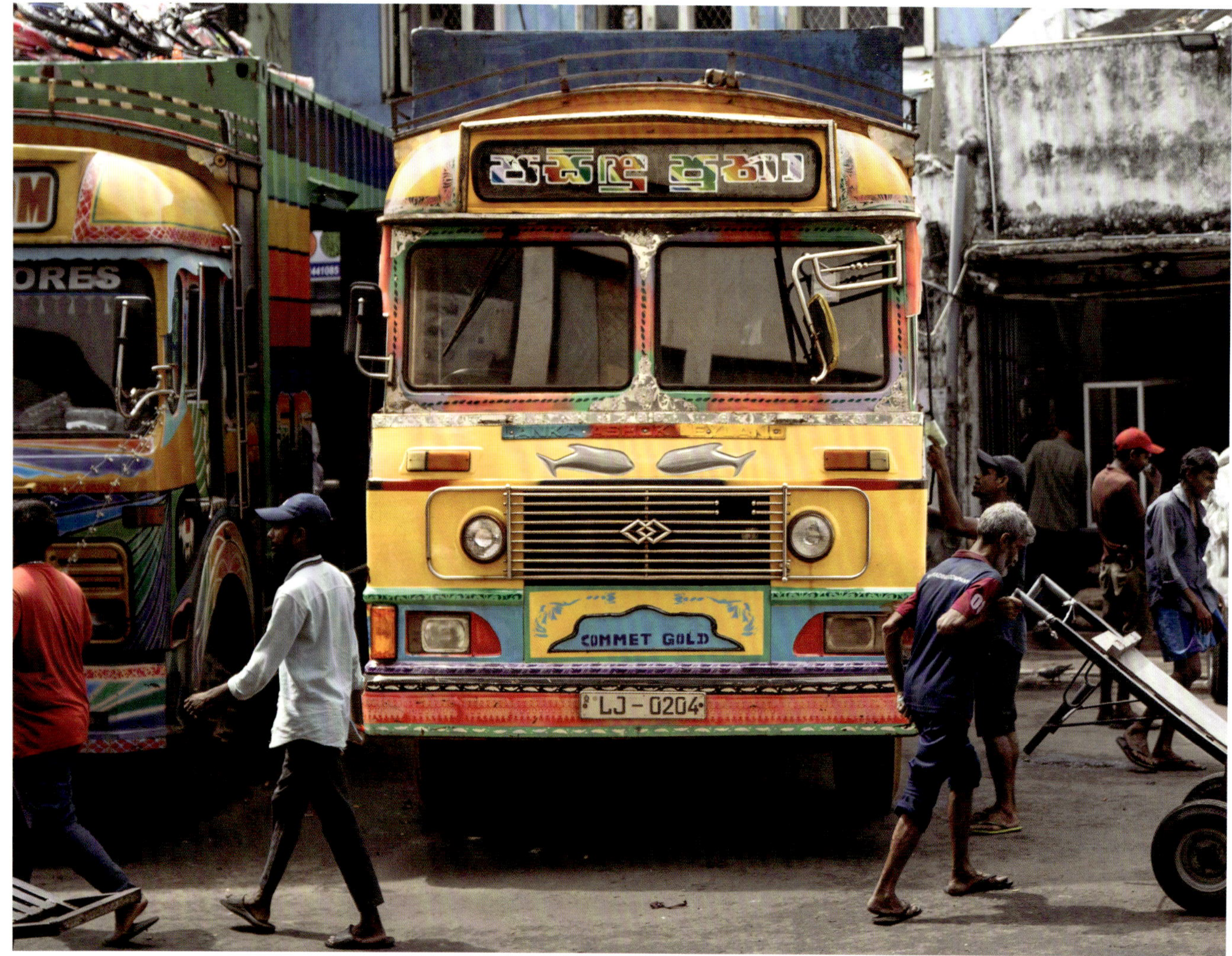

42   Colombo, SRI LANKA

overleaf: Ella, SRI LANKA

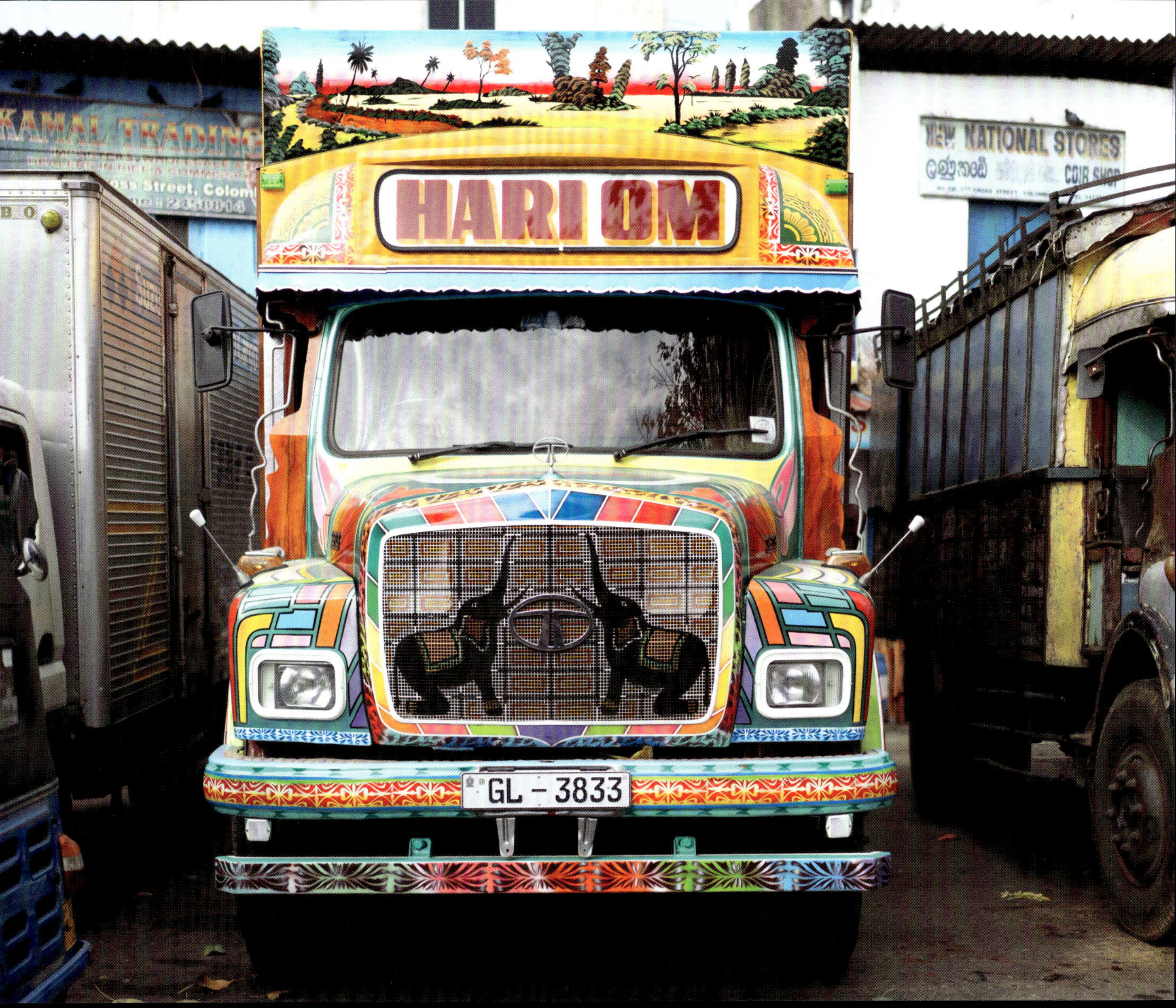
KAMAL TRADING
HARI OM
NEW NATIONAL STORES
COIR SHOP
GL - 3833

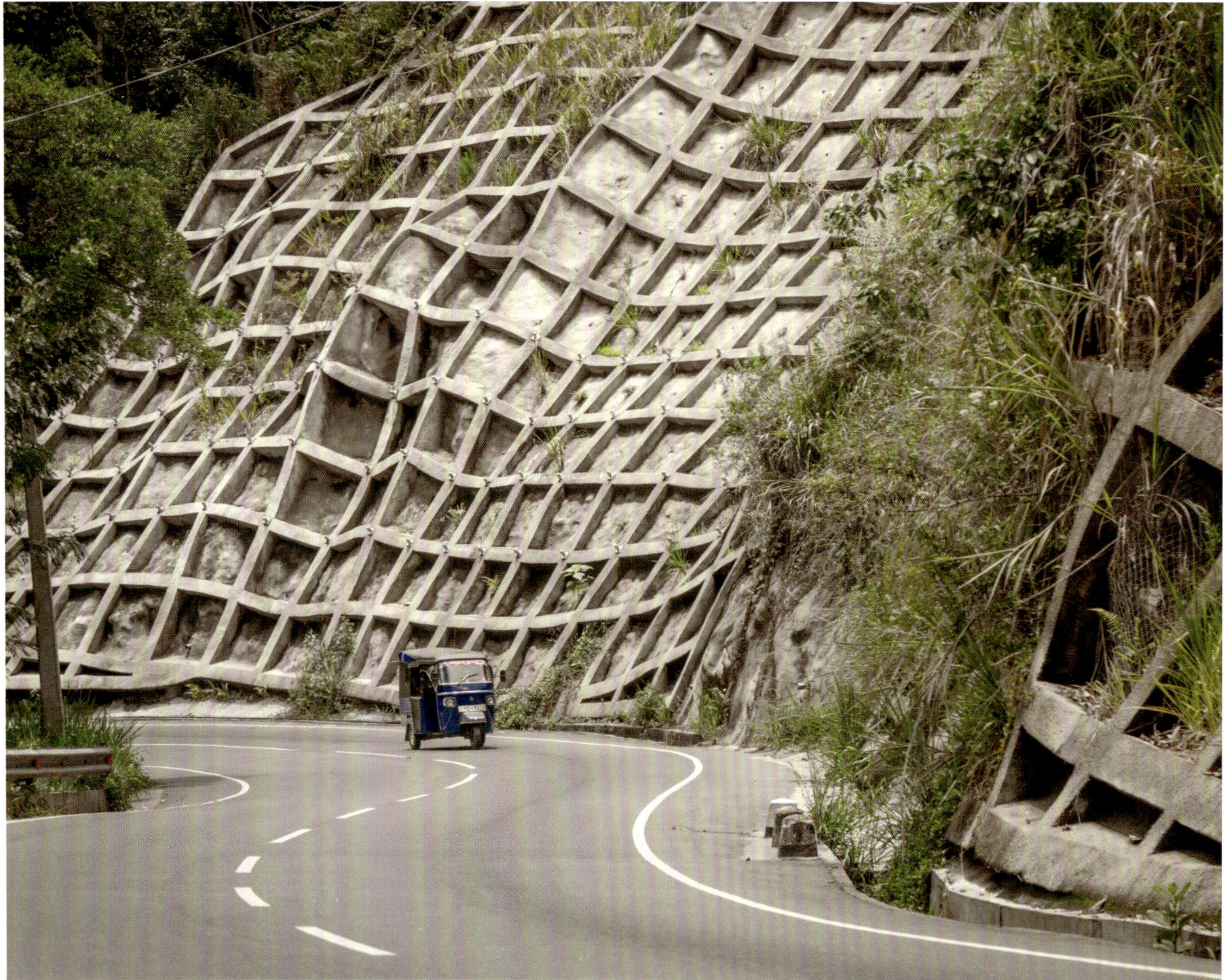

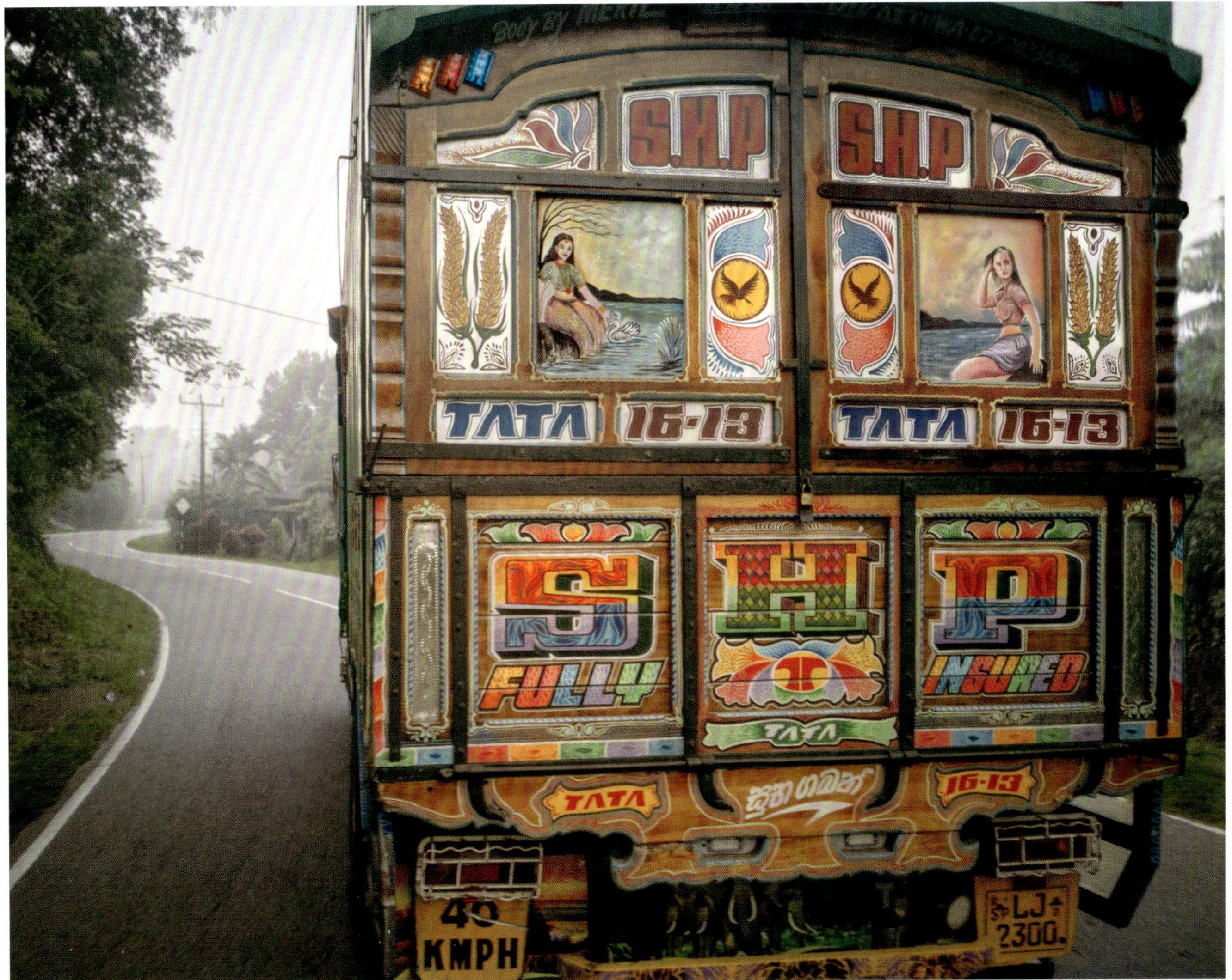
S.H.P
S.H.P
TATA 16-13
TATA 16-13
S H P
FULLY
INSURED
TATA
16-13
40
KMPH
LJ
2300

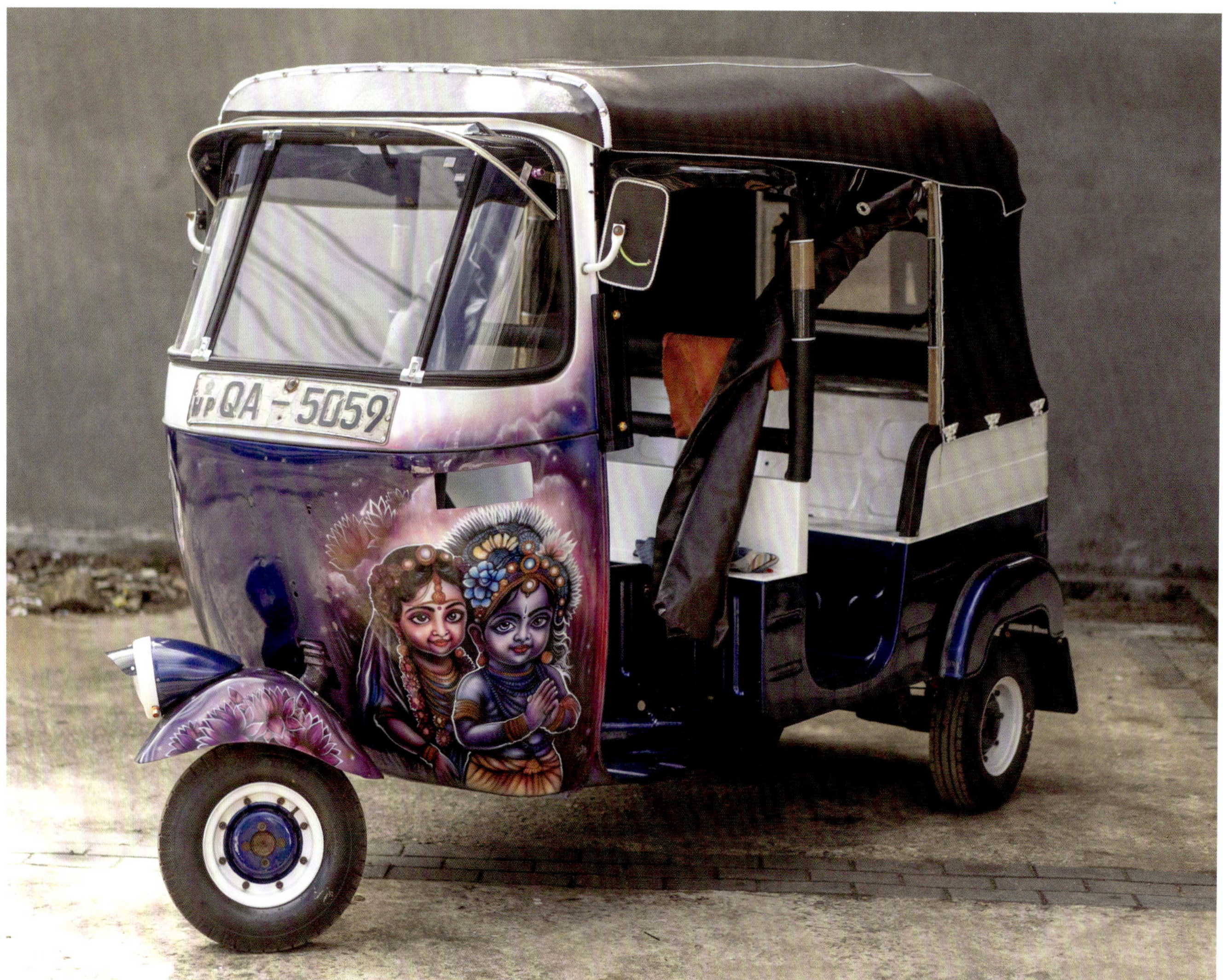

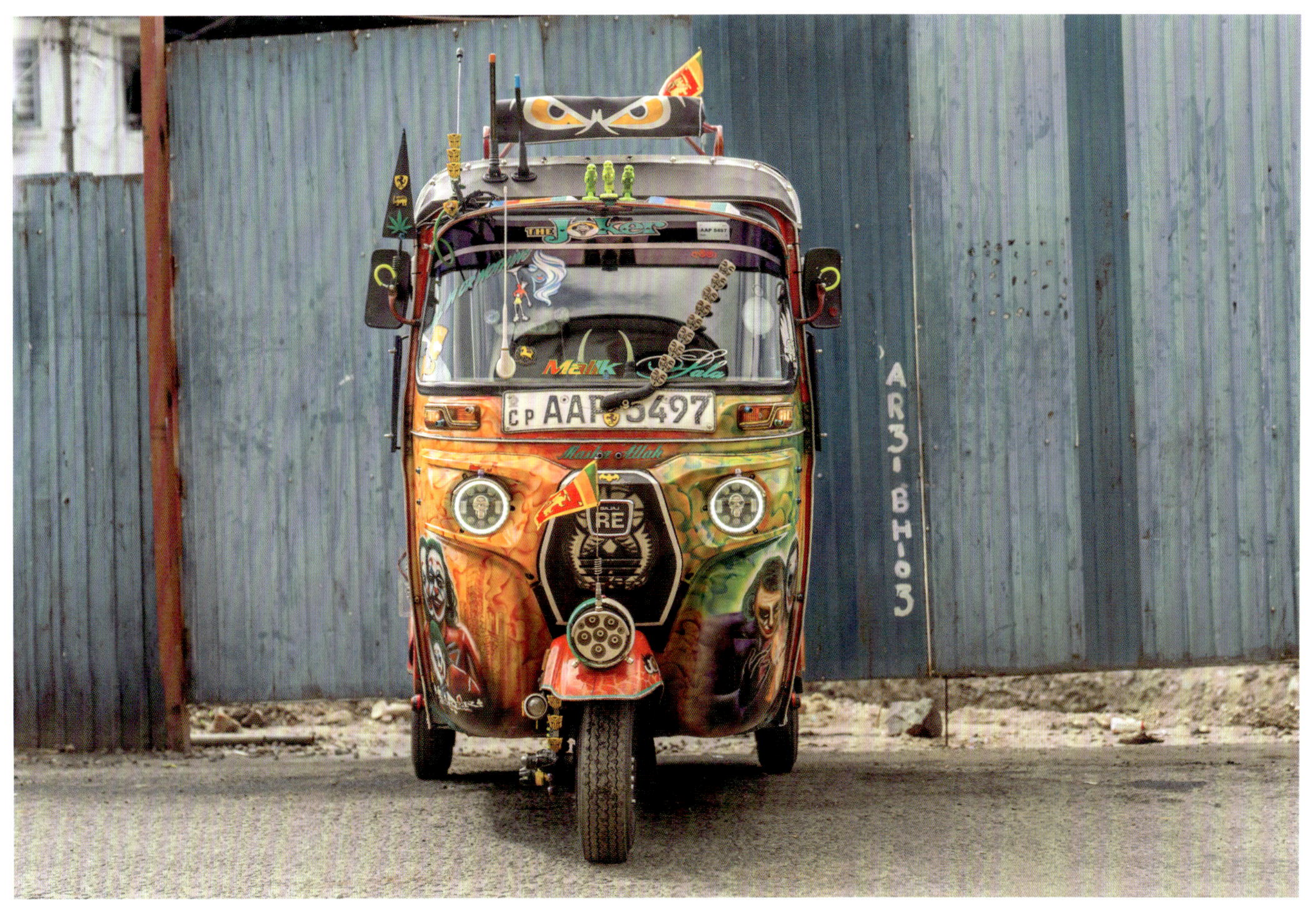

Ratnapura, SRI LANKA

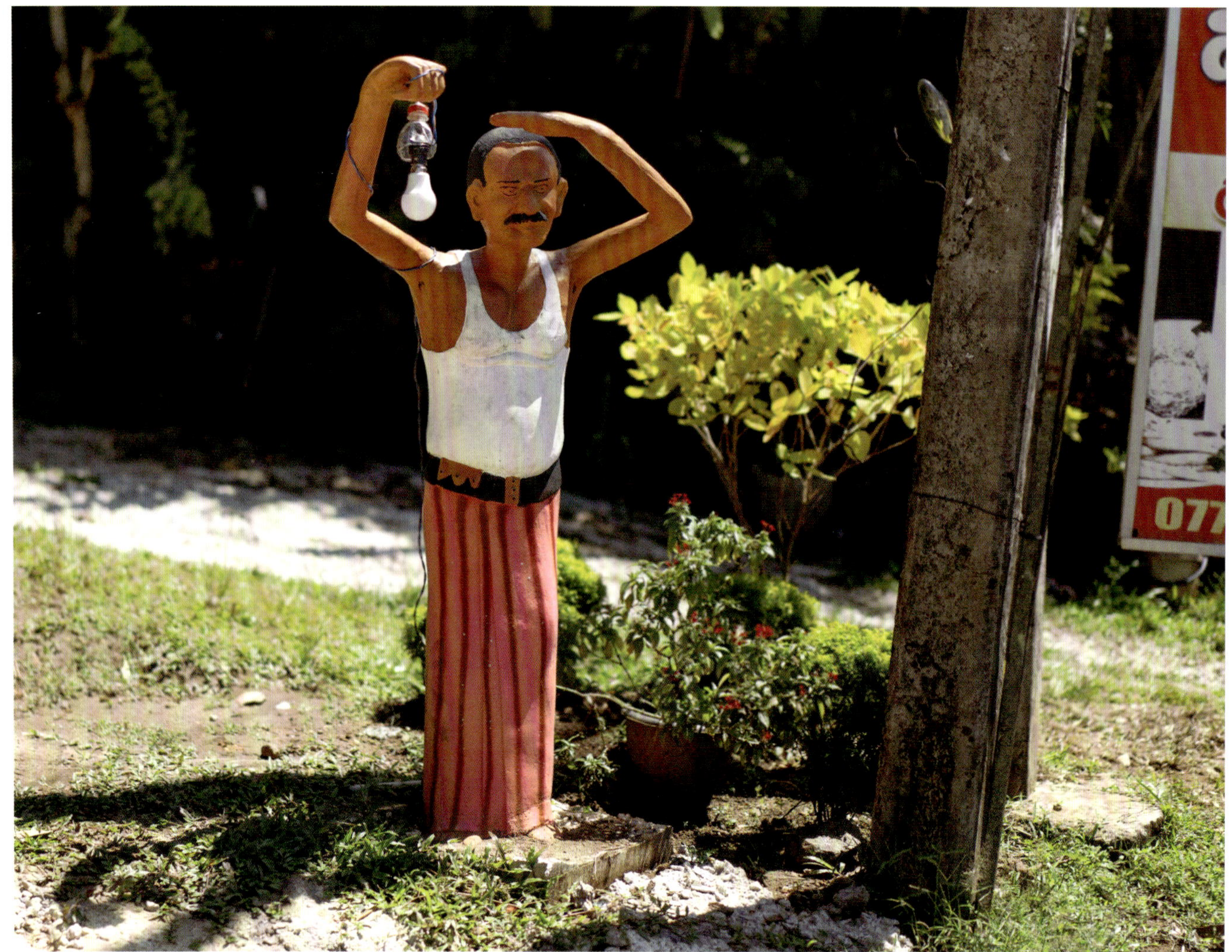

48   Ratnapura, SRI LANKA

overleaf: Ratnapura, SRI LANKA

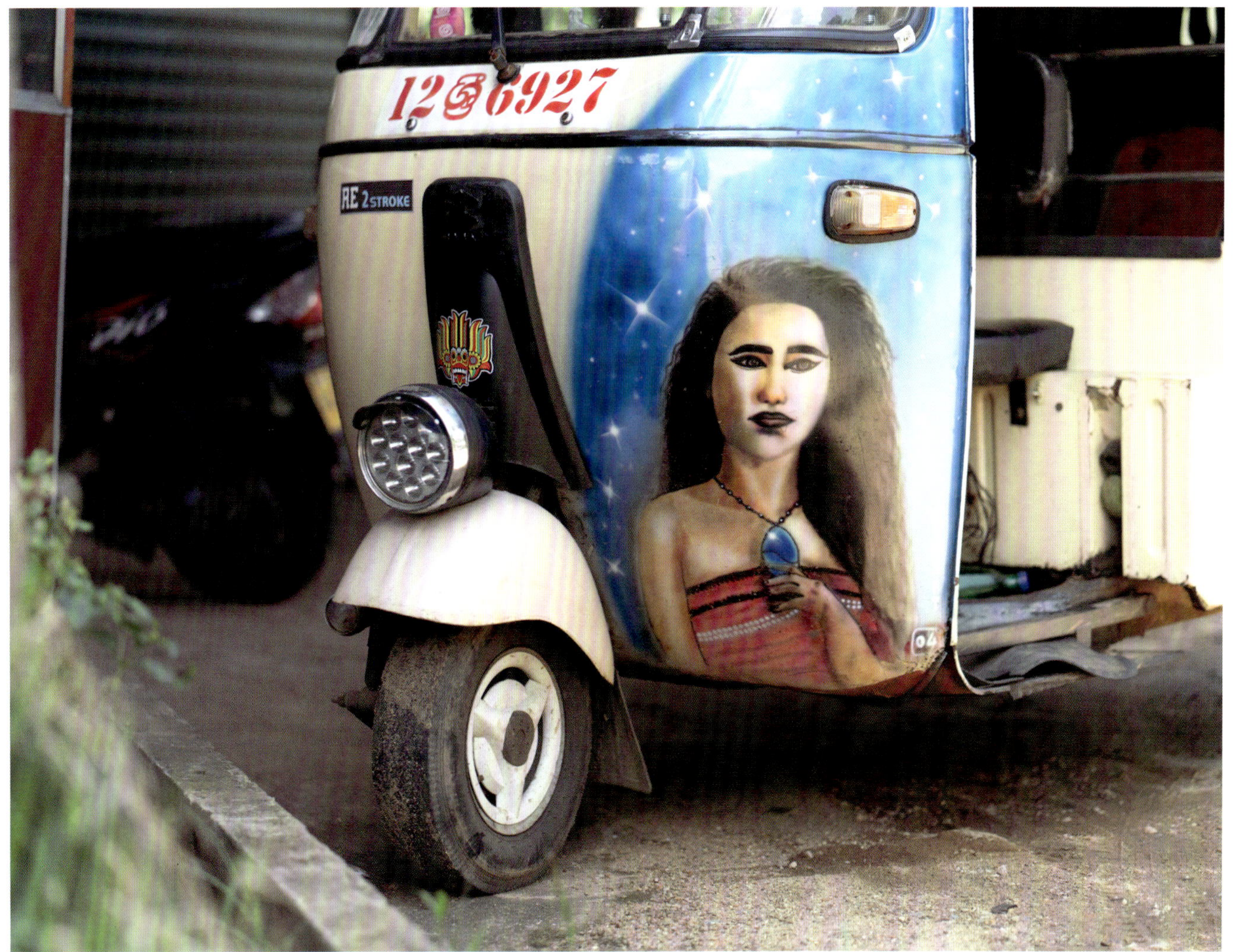

12 6927
RE 2STROKE

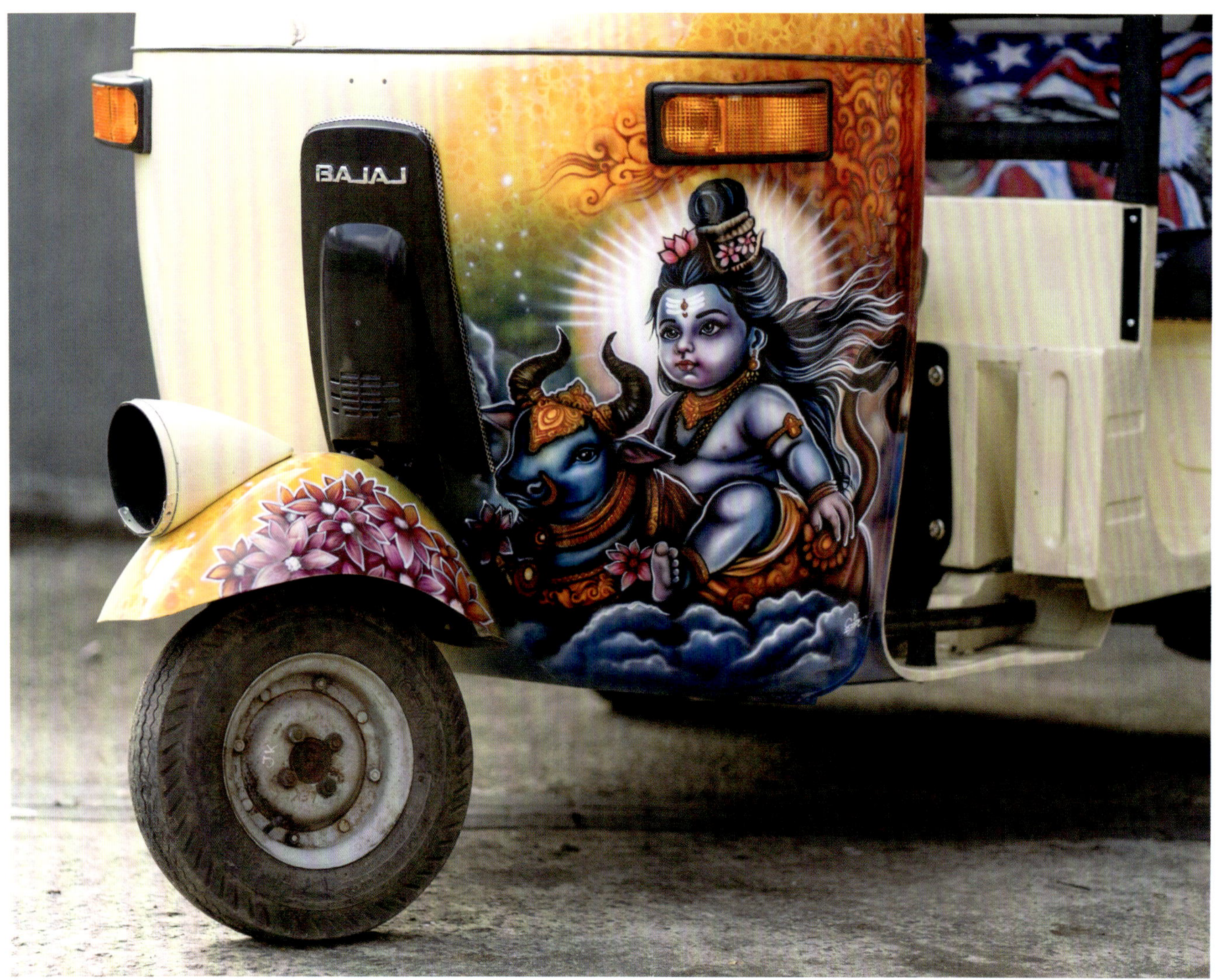

BAJAJ

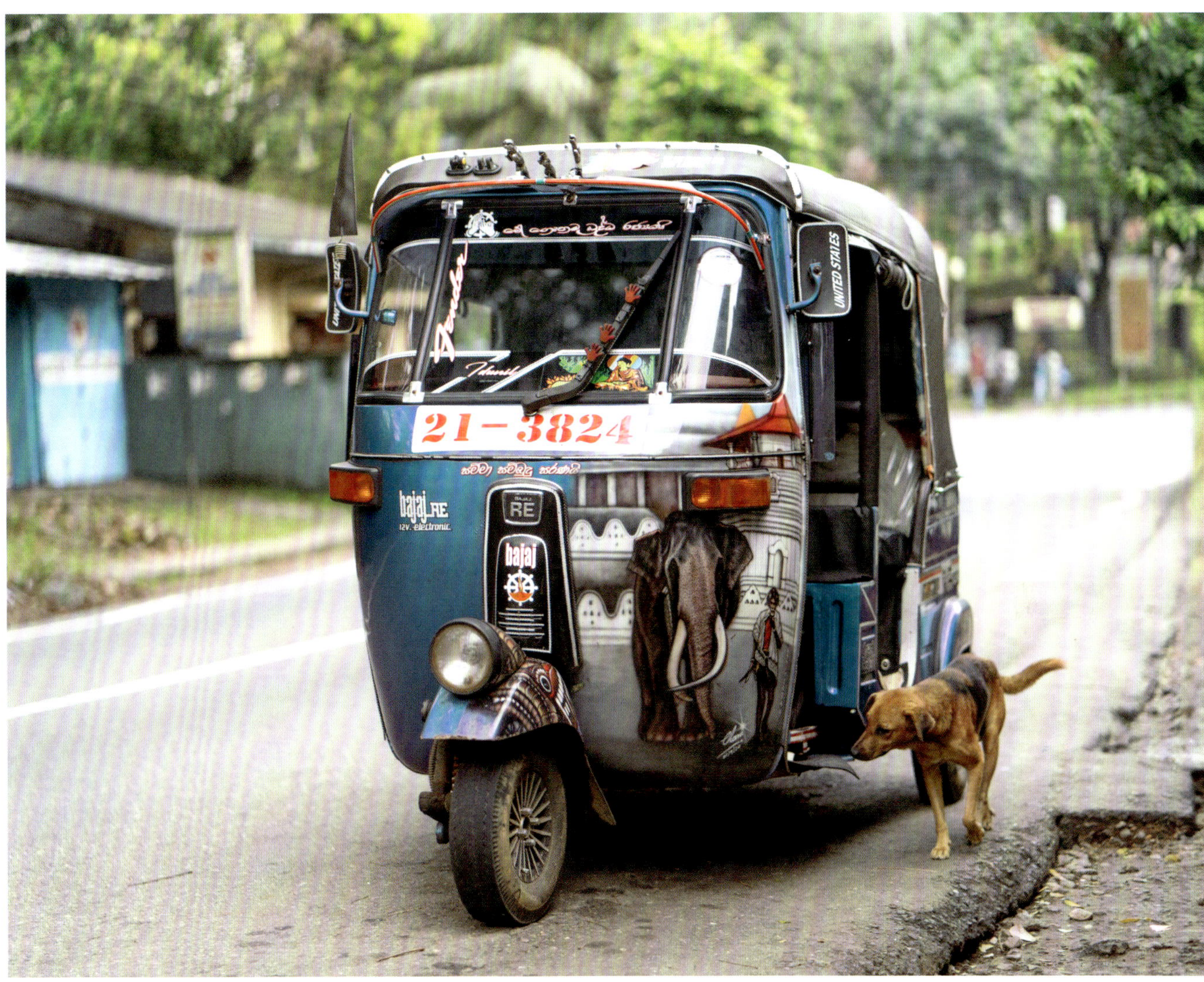

UNITED STATES
21-3824
bajaj RE
12v. electronic
RE
bajaj

INDIA

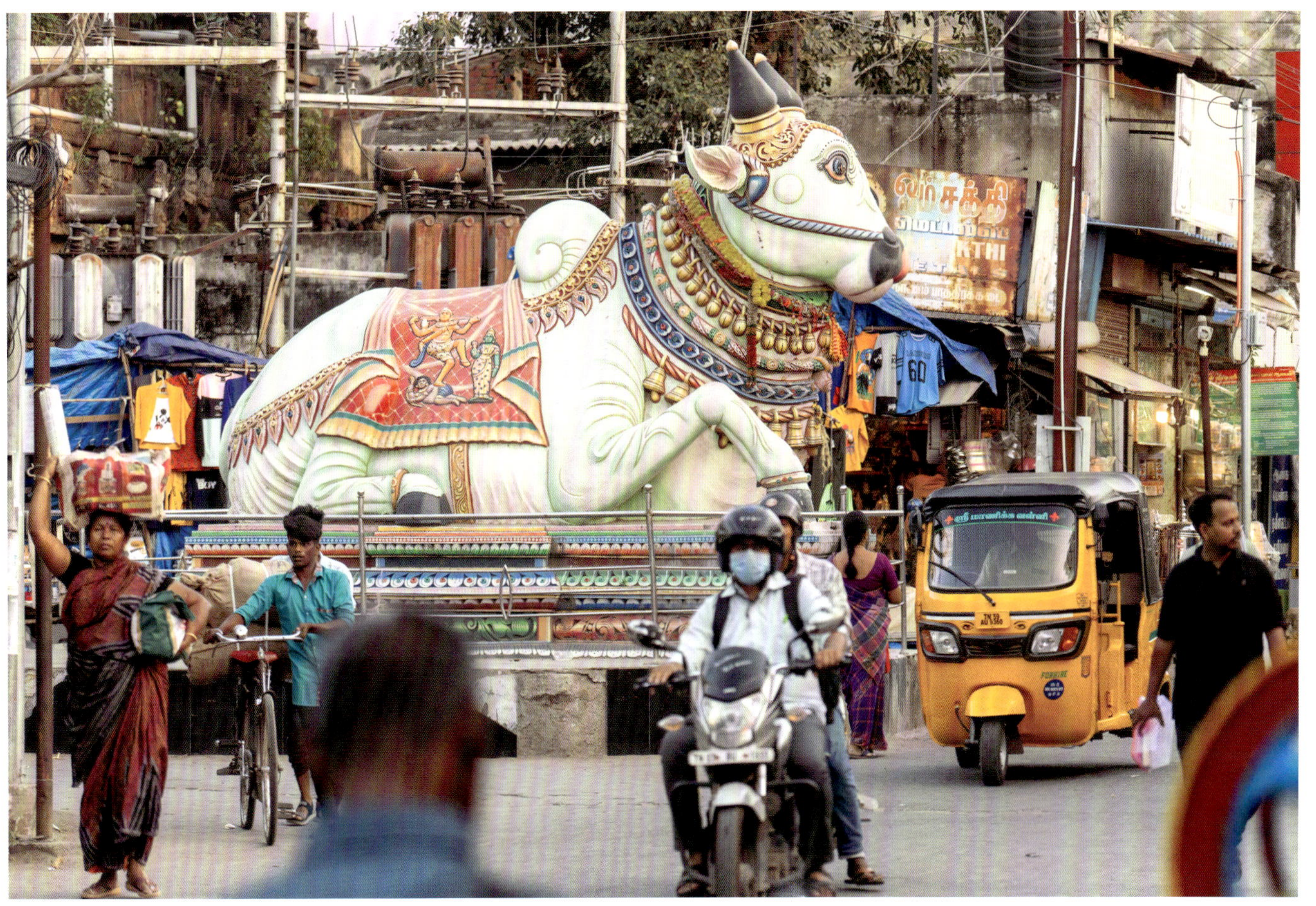

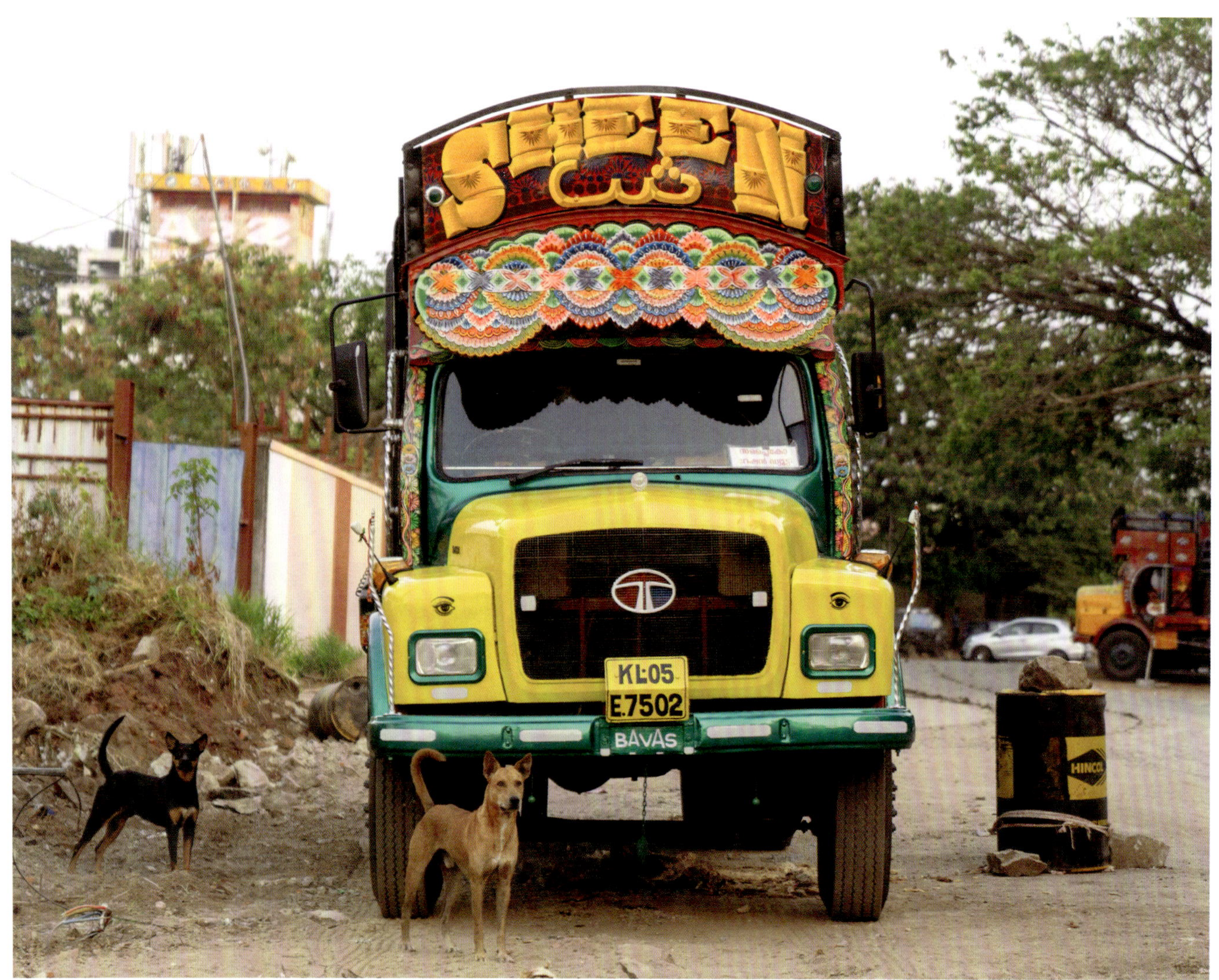

SHEEN
TATA
KL05
E.7502
BAVAS
HINCO

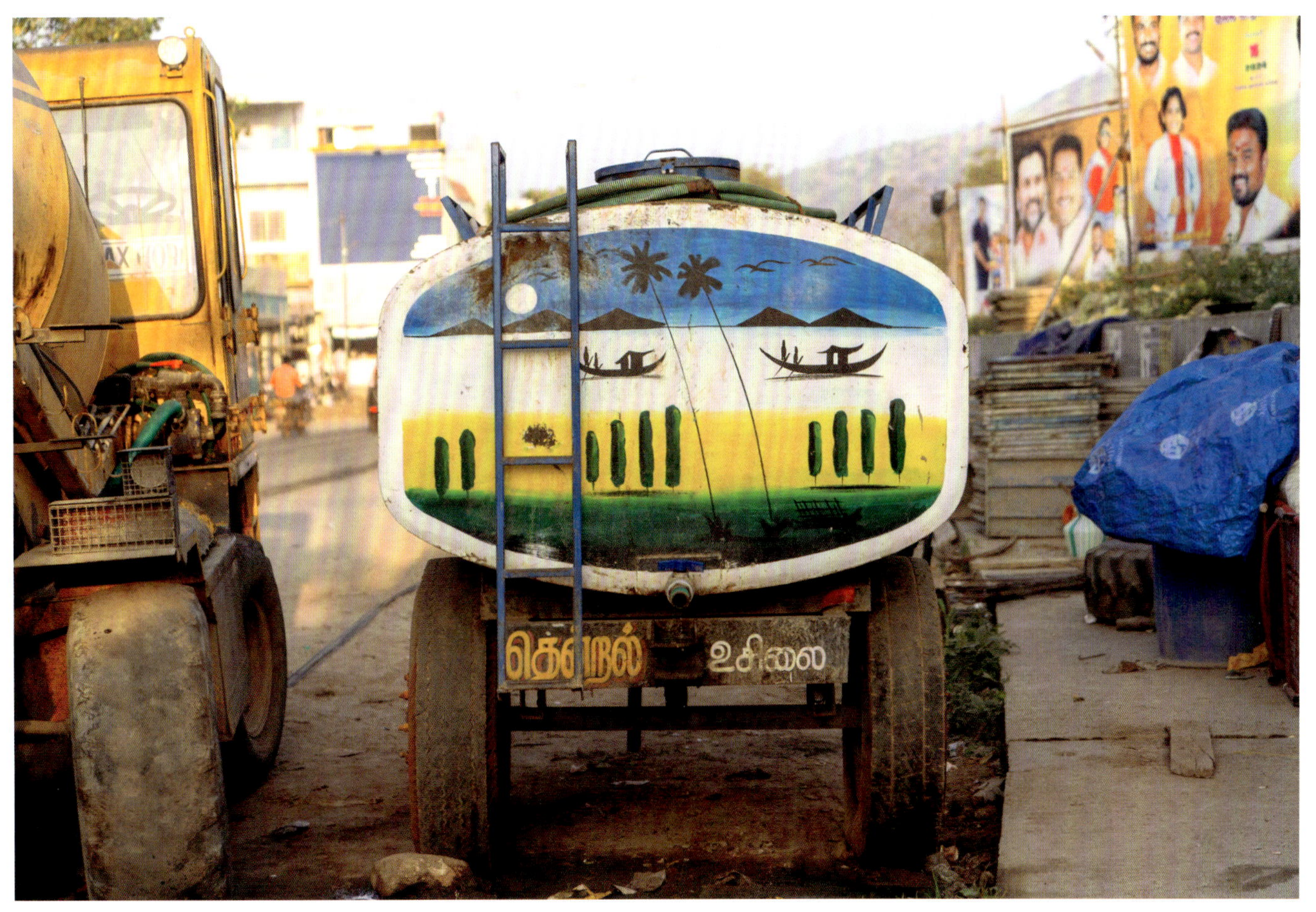

Kochi, INDIA

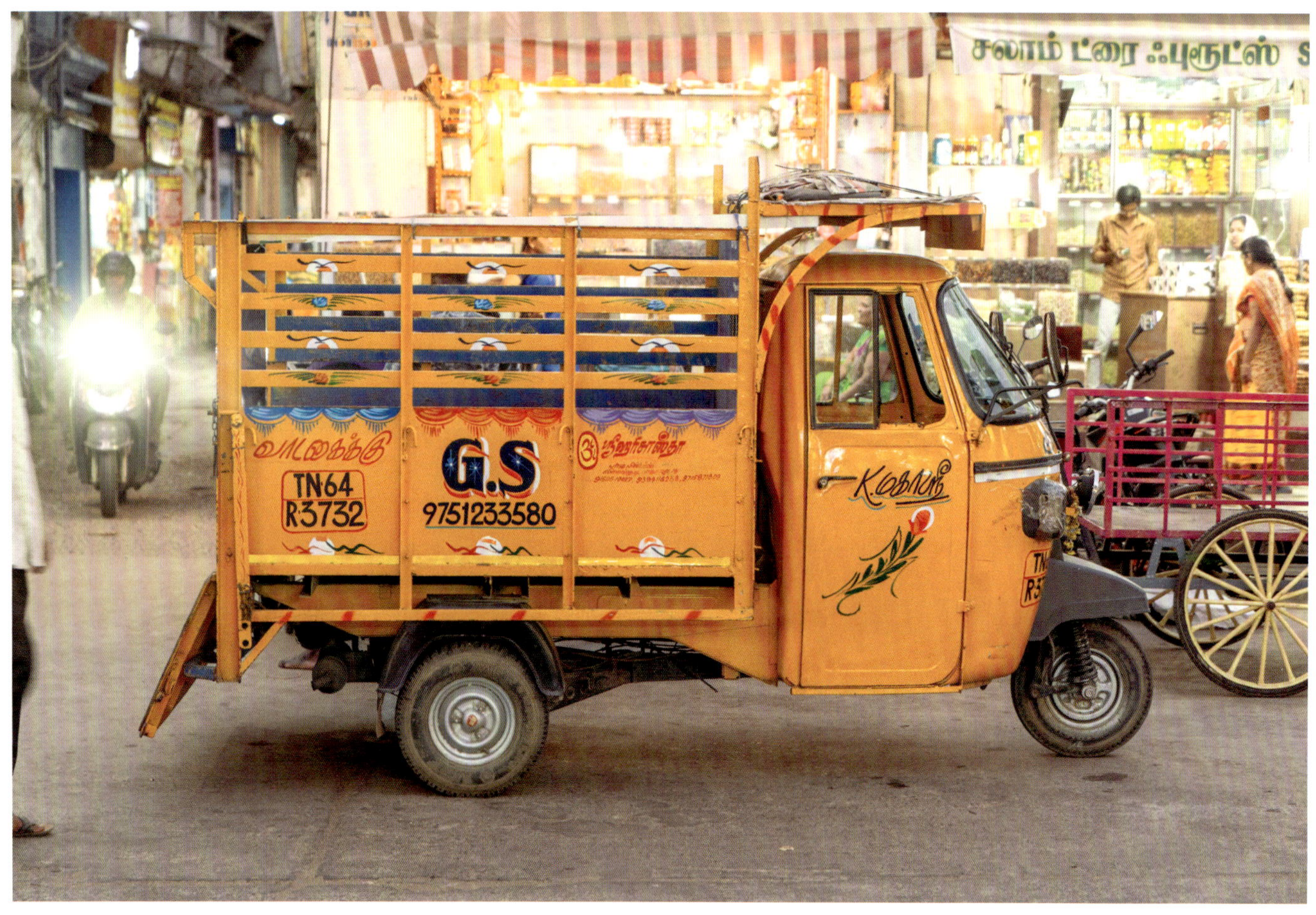

G.S
TN64
R3732
9751233580
K.

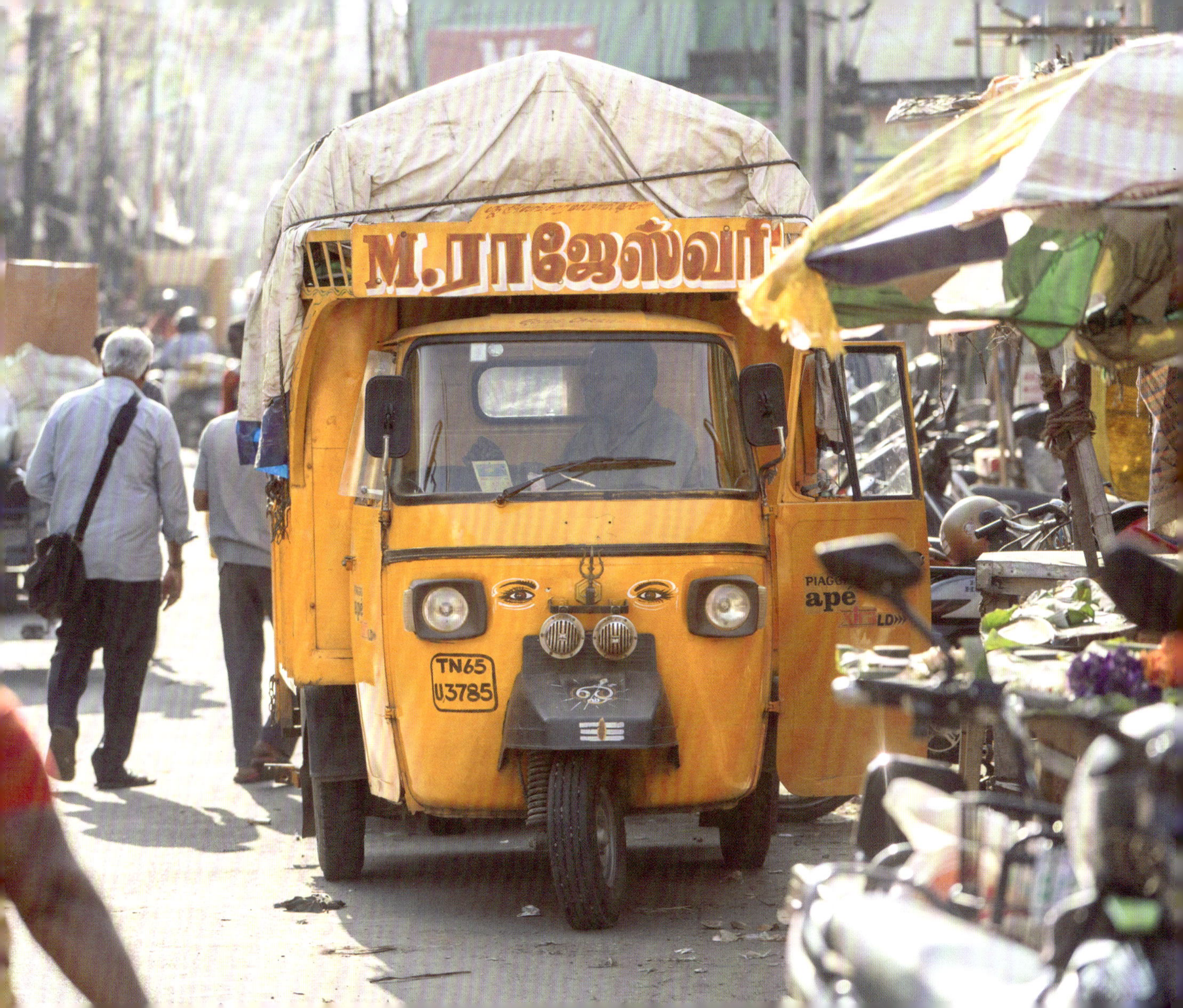

M.ராஜேஸ்வரி
TN65
U 3785
PIAGGIO
ape

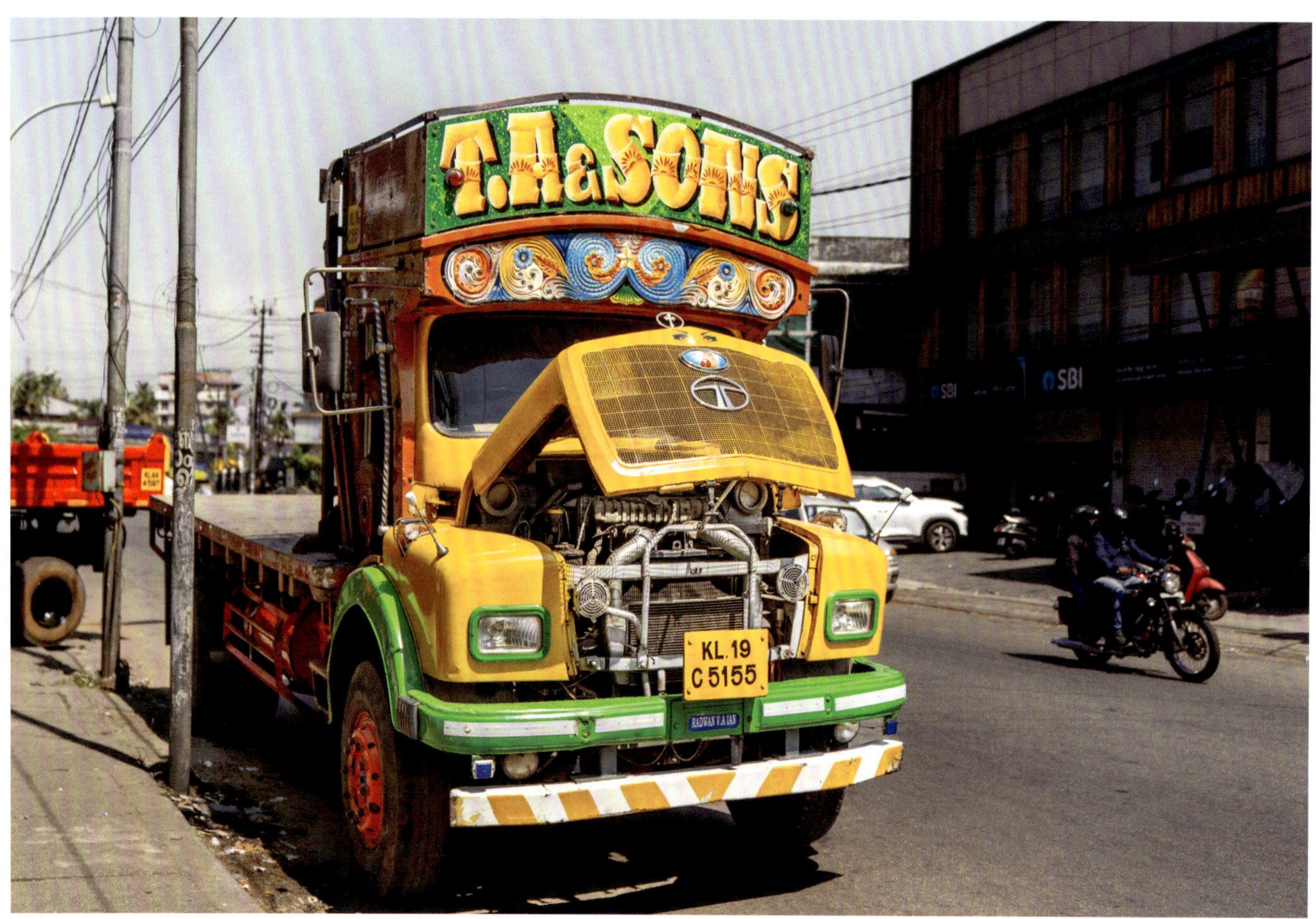

  Sreekrishnapuram, INDIA

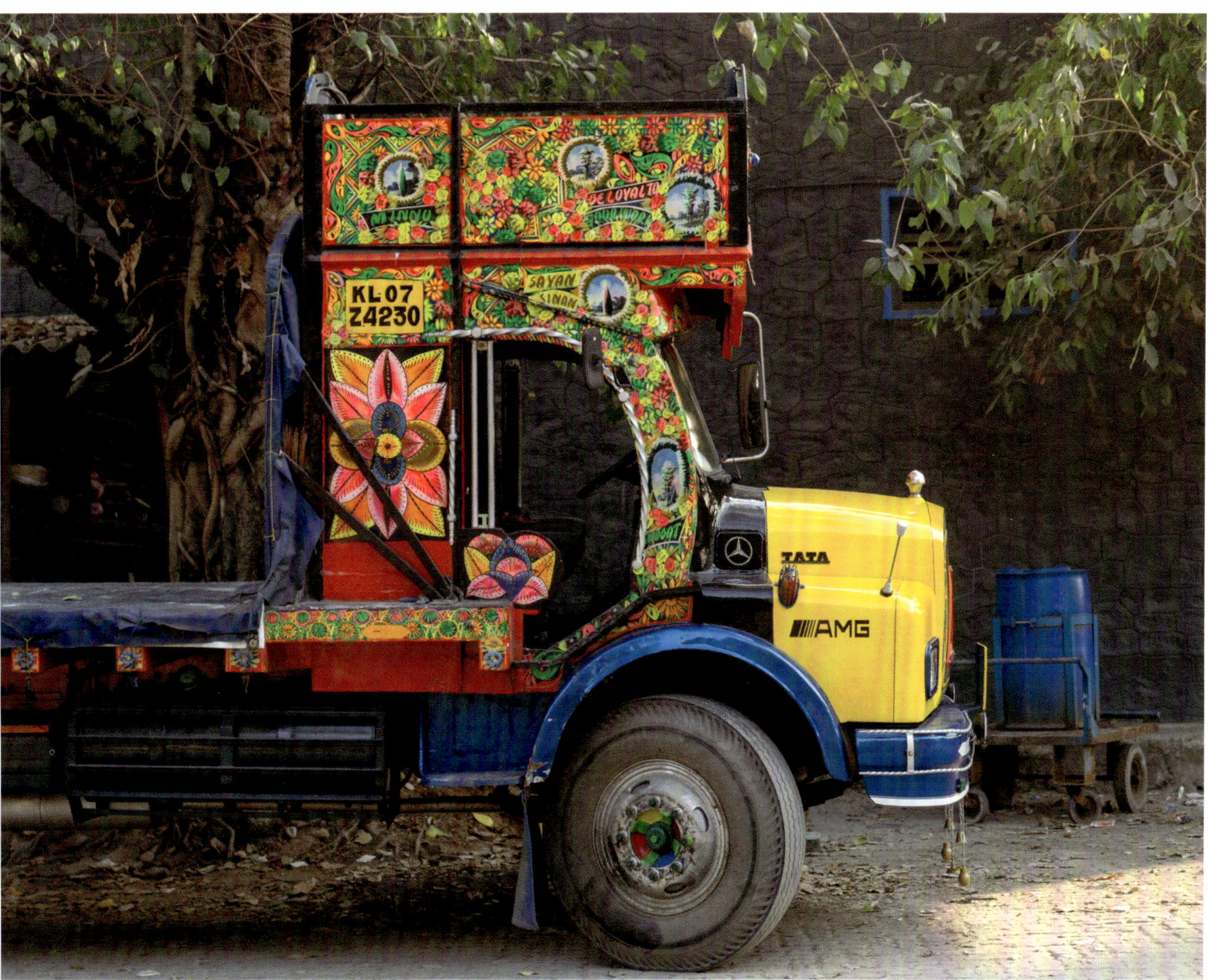

KL 07
Z4230
SAYAN
SINAN
TATA
AMG

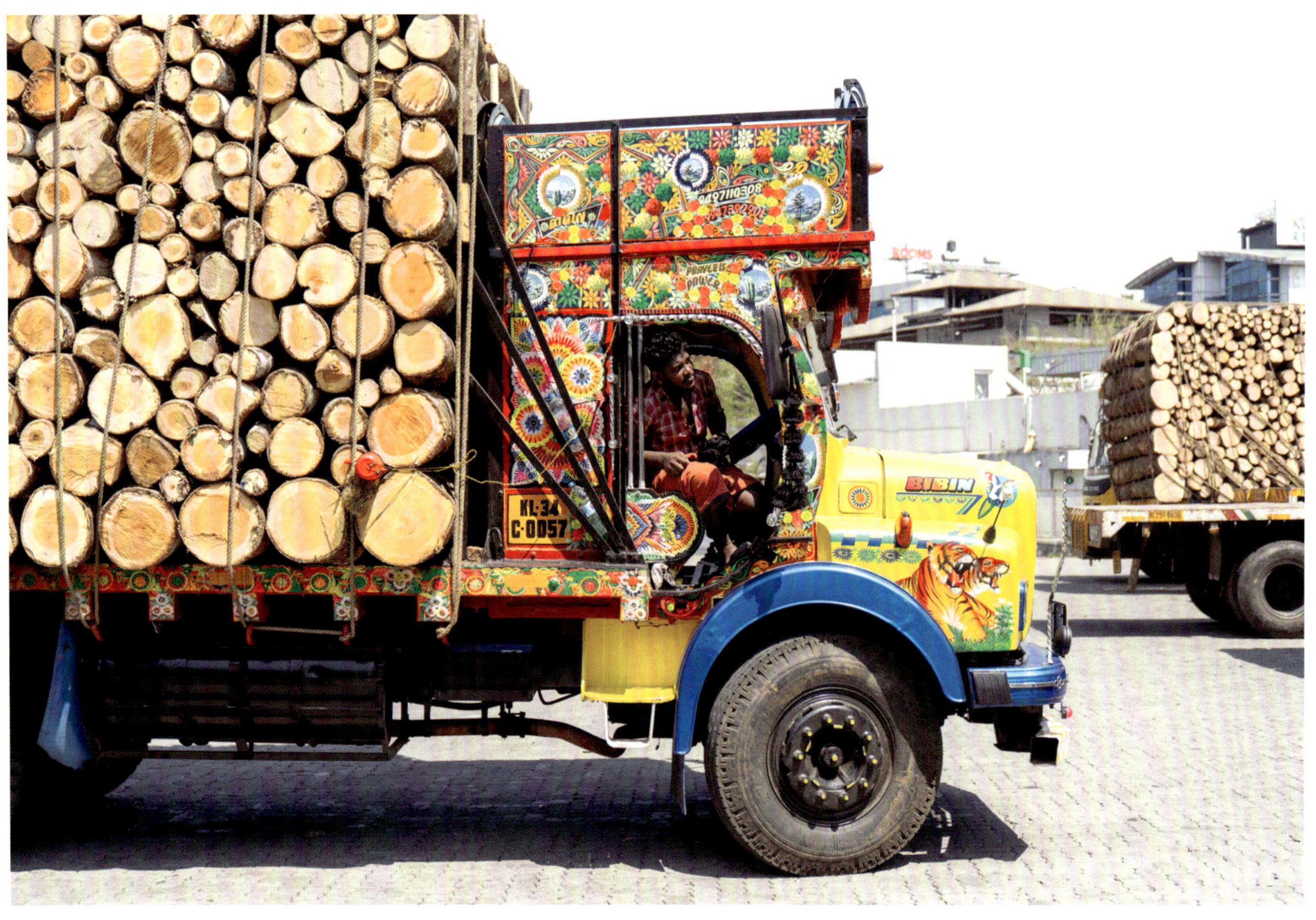

Kochi, INDIA

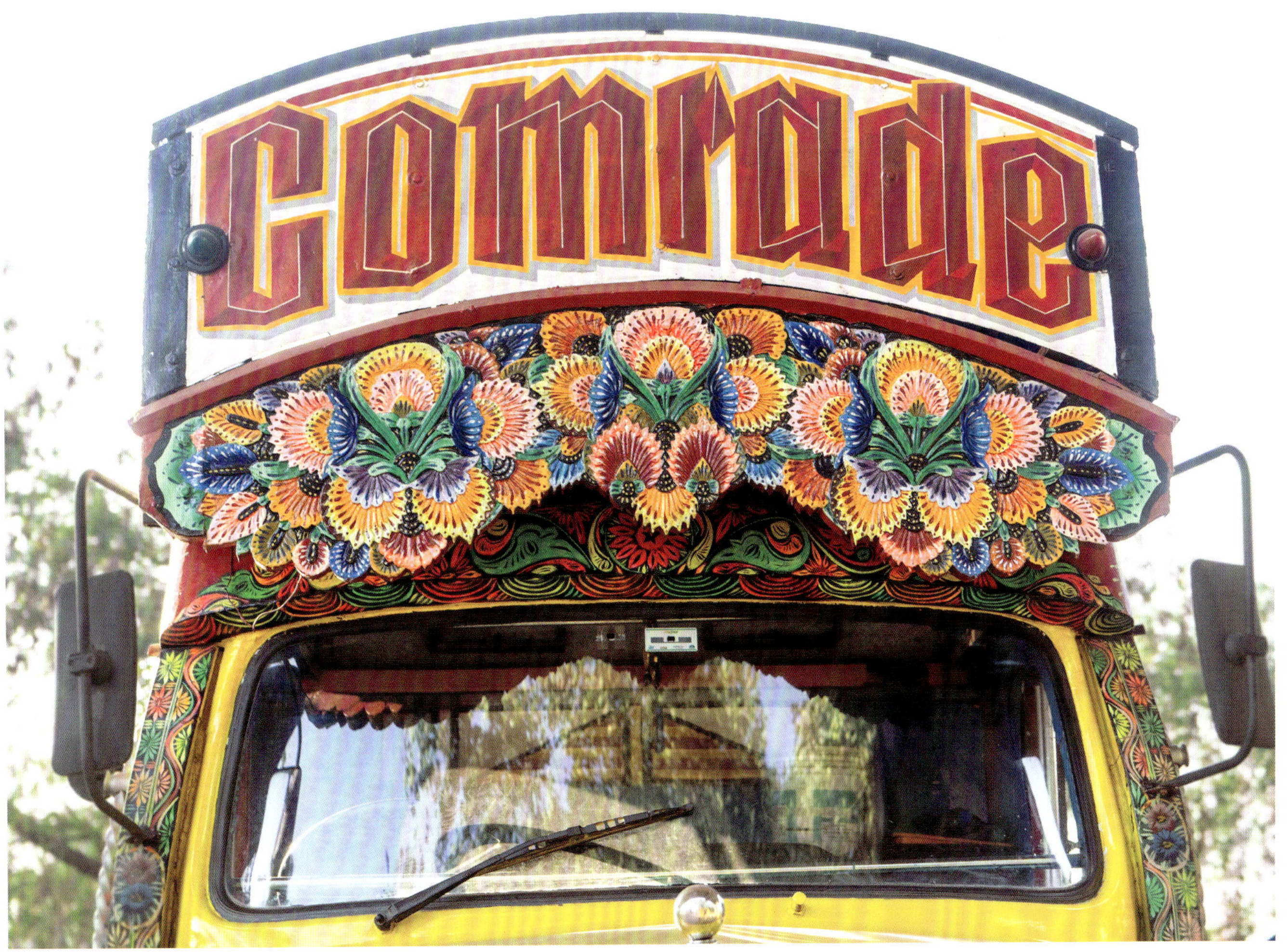

comrade

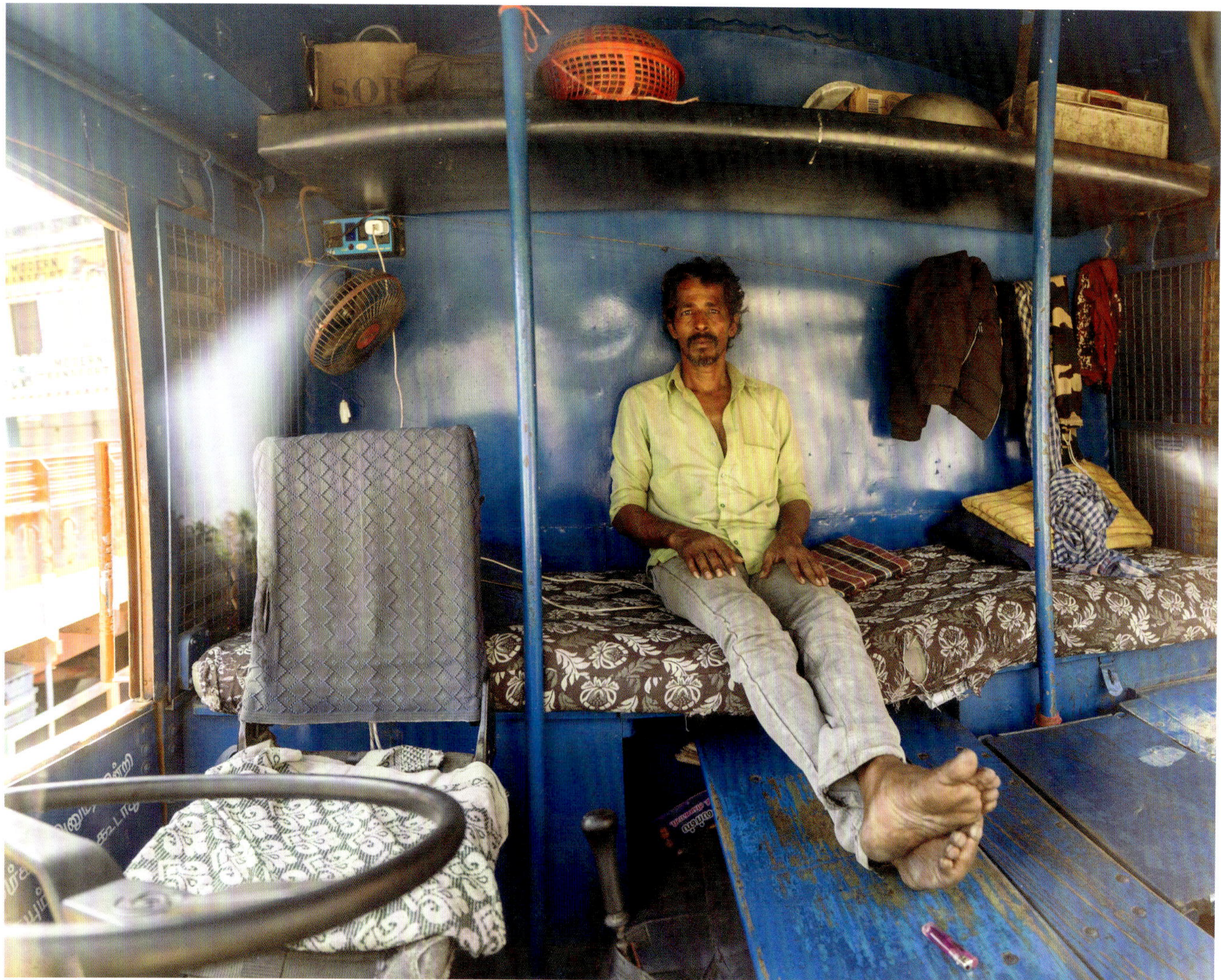

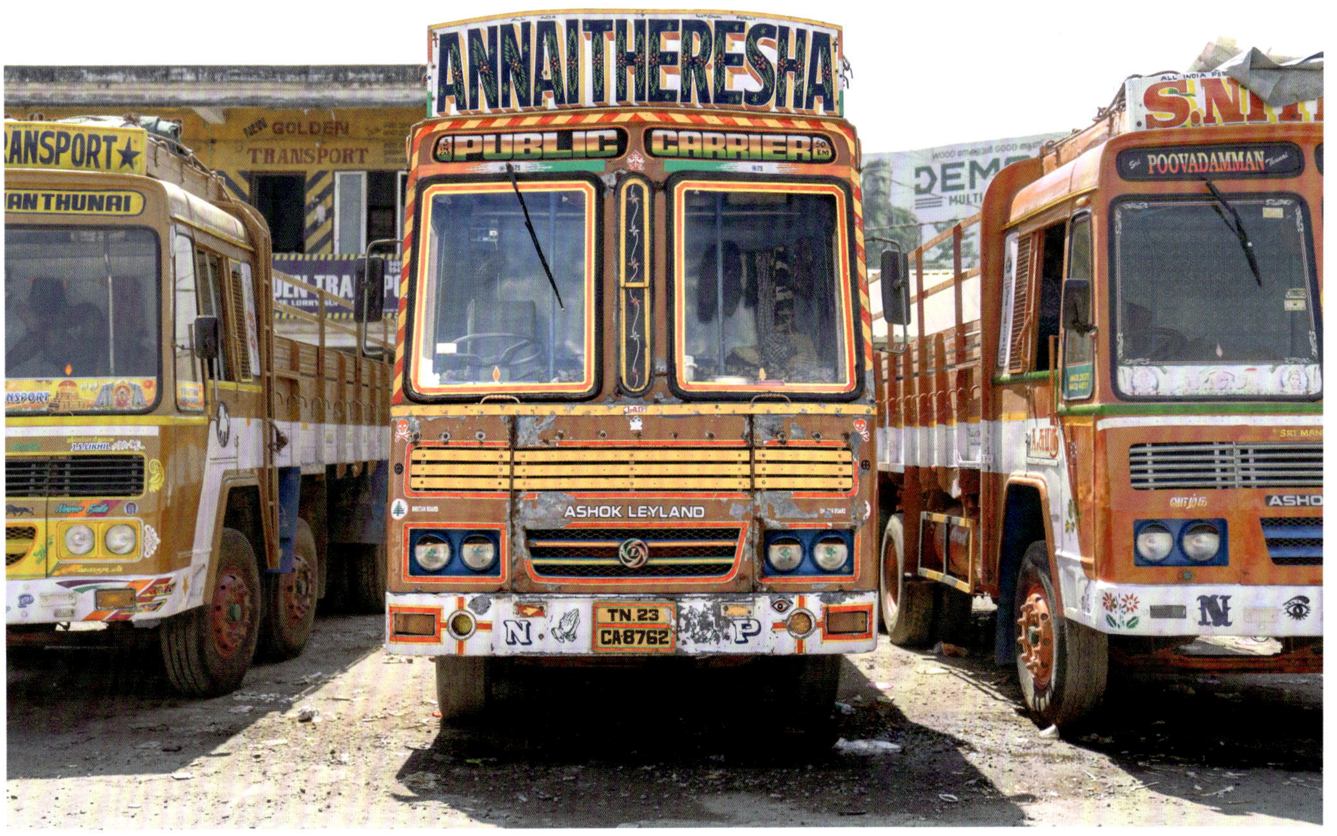

ANNAITHERESHA
PUBLIC CARRIER
ASHOK LEYLAND
TN.23
CA 8762
N
P
TRANSPORT
GOLDEN
TRANSPORT
AN THUNAI
Sri POOVADAMMAN
S.N
DEM
N

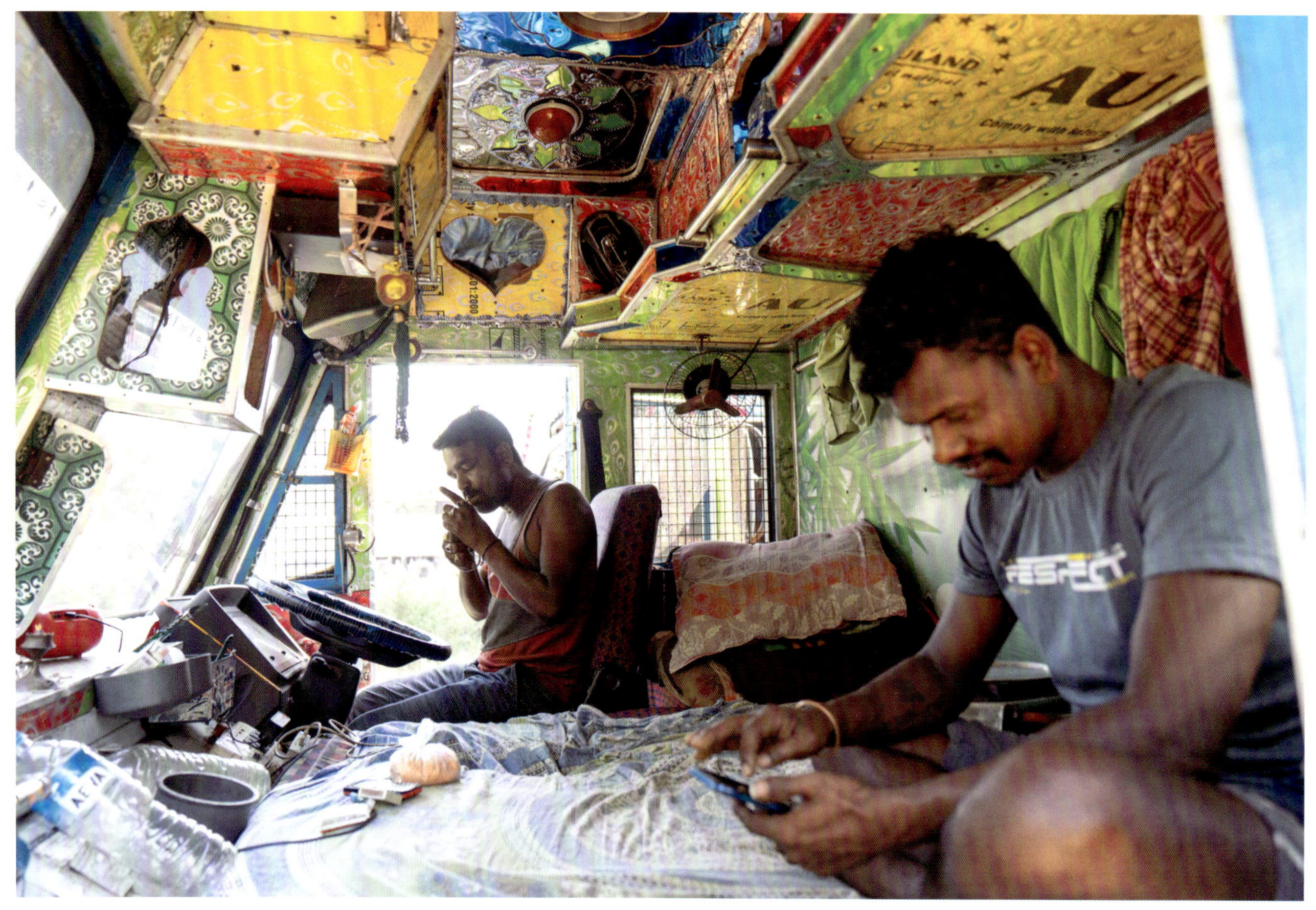

    Kochi, INDIA

Jaipur, INDIA

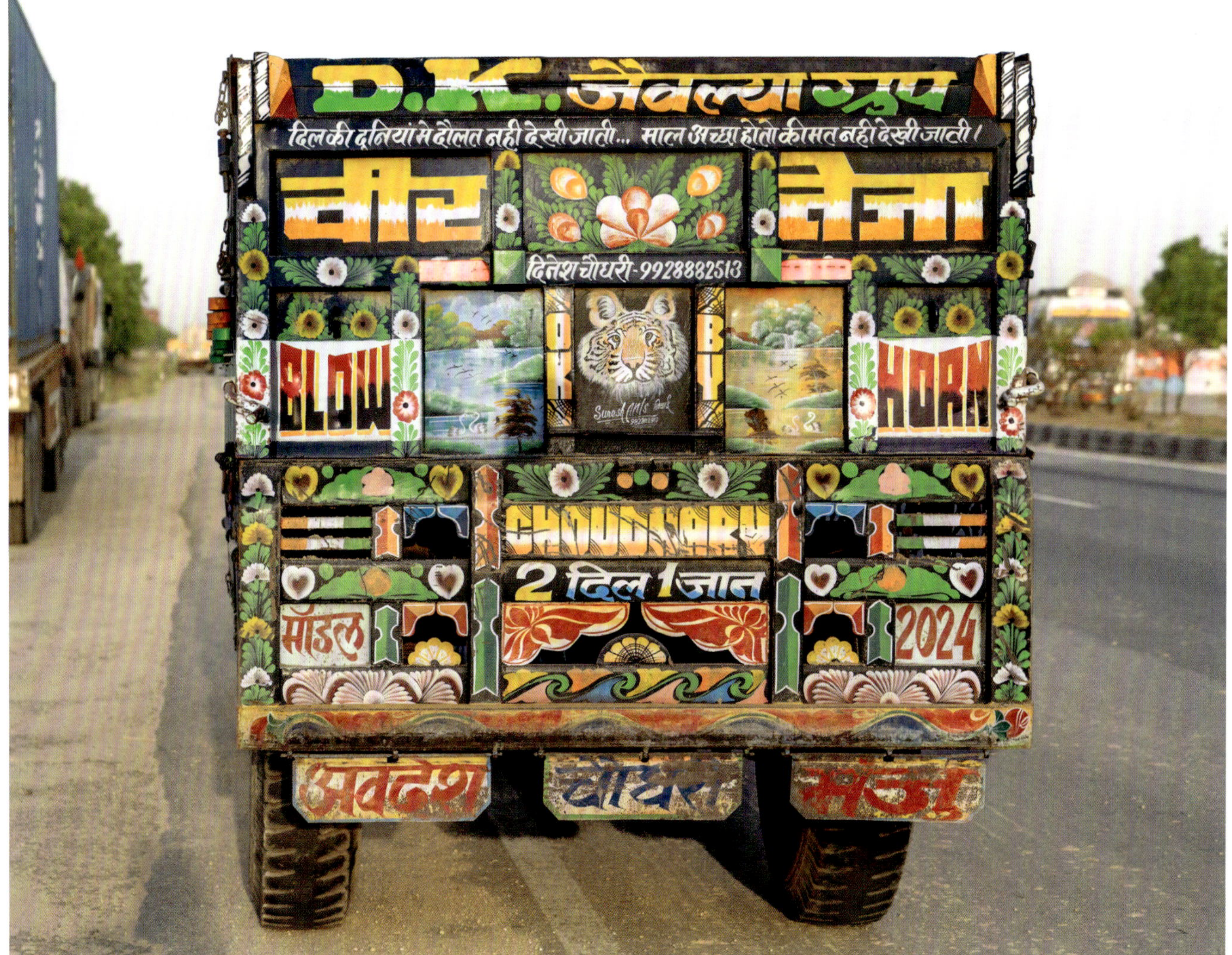

D.K. जैवल्या ग्रुप
दिल की दुनियां मे दौलत नही देखी जाती... माल अच्छा हो तो कीमत नही देखी जाती !
वीर
नेता
दिनेश चौधरी-9928882513
BLOW
HORN
CHOUDHARY
2 दिल 1 जान
मॉडल
2024

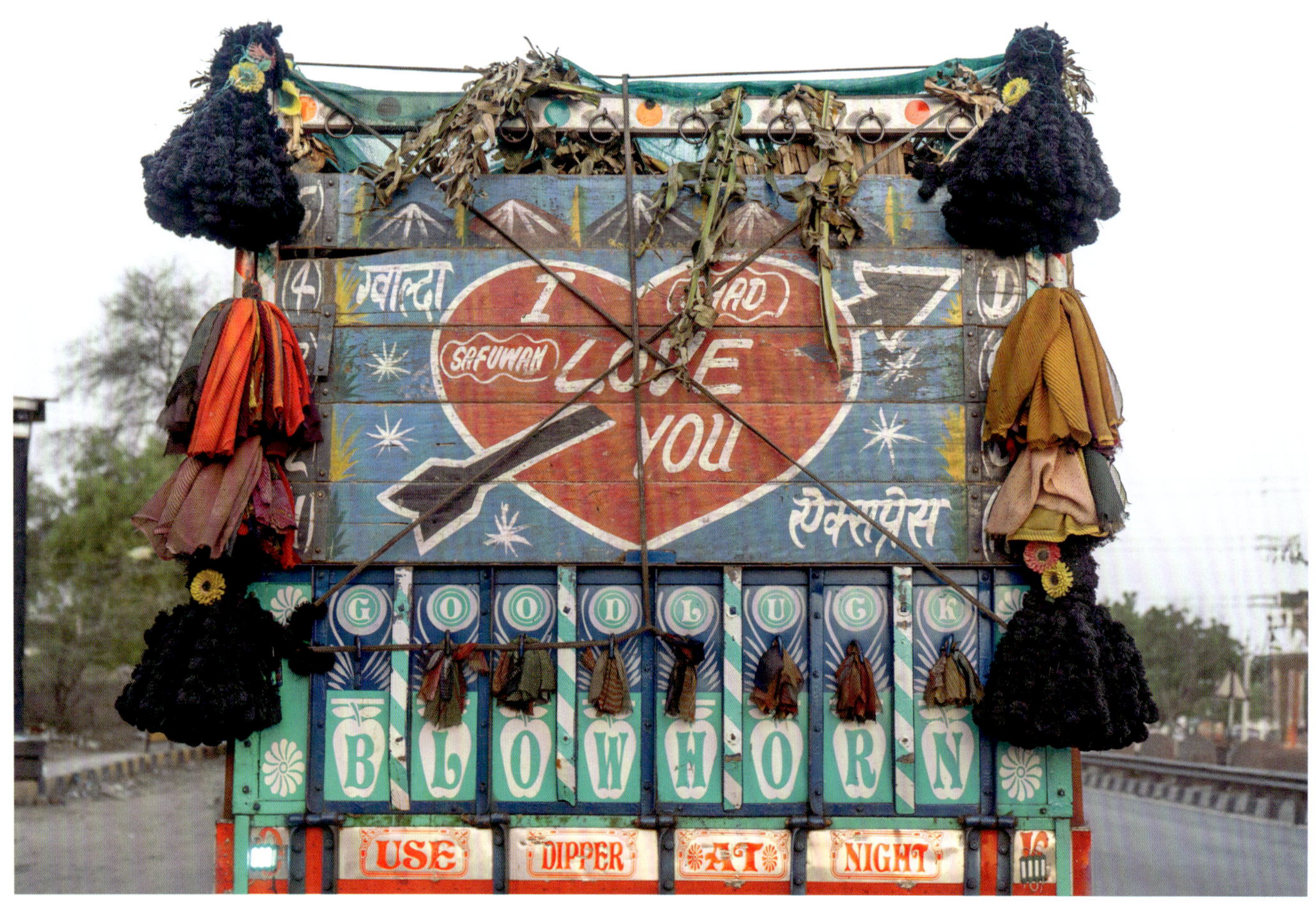
I LOVE YOU
SAFUWAN
GOOD LUCK
BLOW HORN
USE DIPPER AT NIGHT

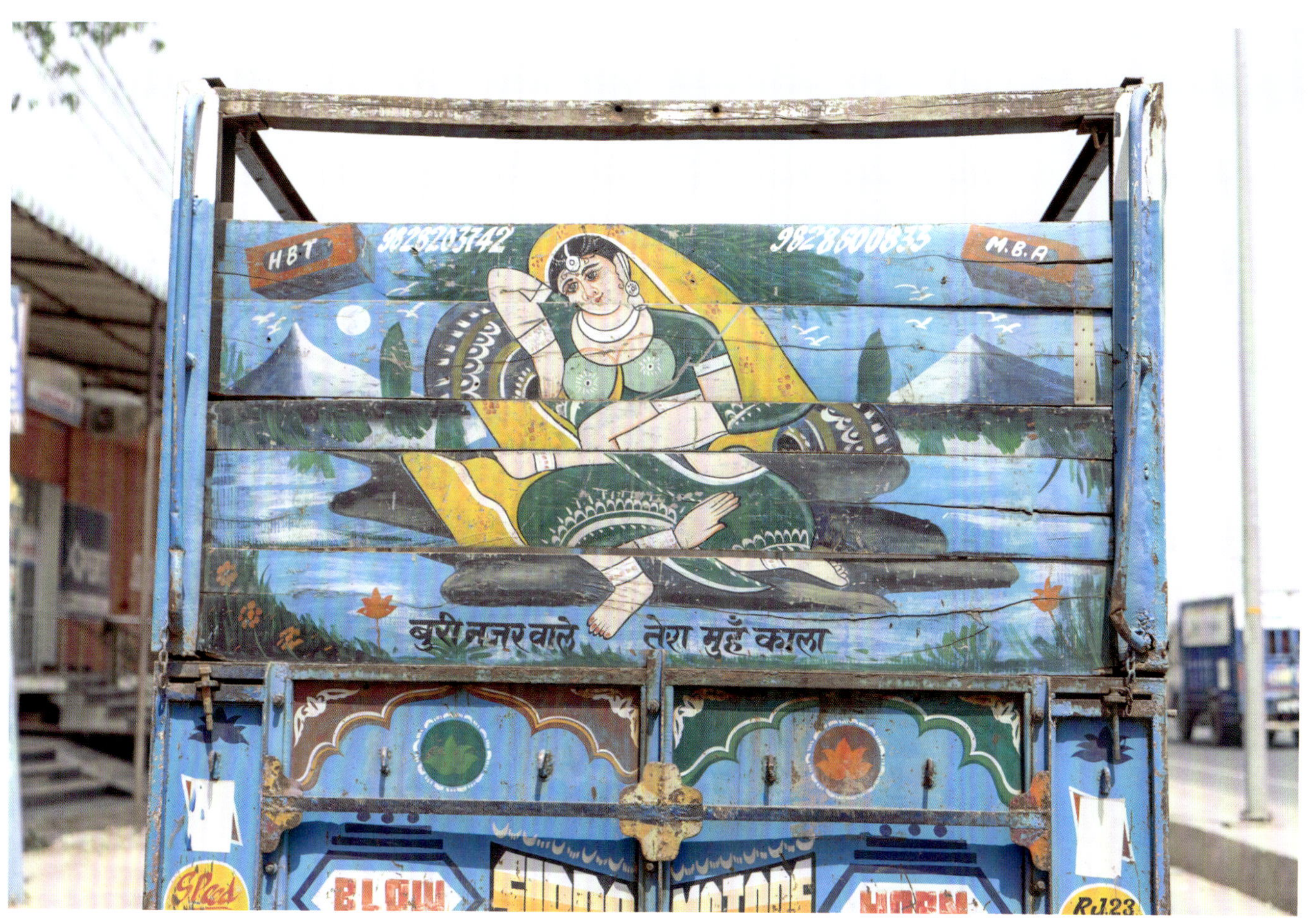
HBT
9828203742
9828600833
M.B.A
बुरी नजर वाले   तेरा मूँह काला
RJ.23

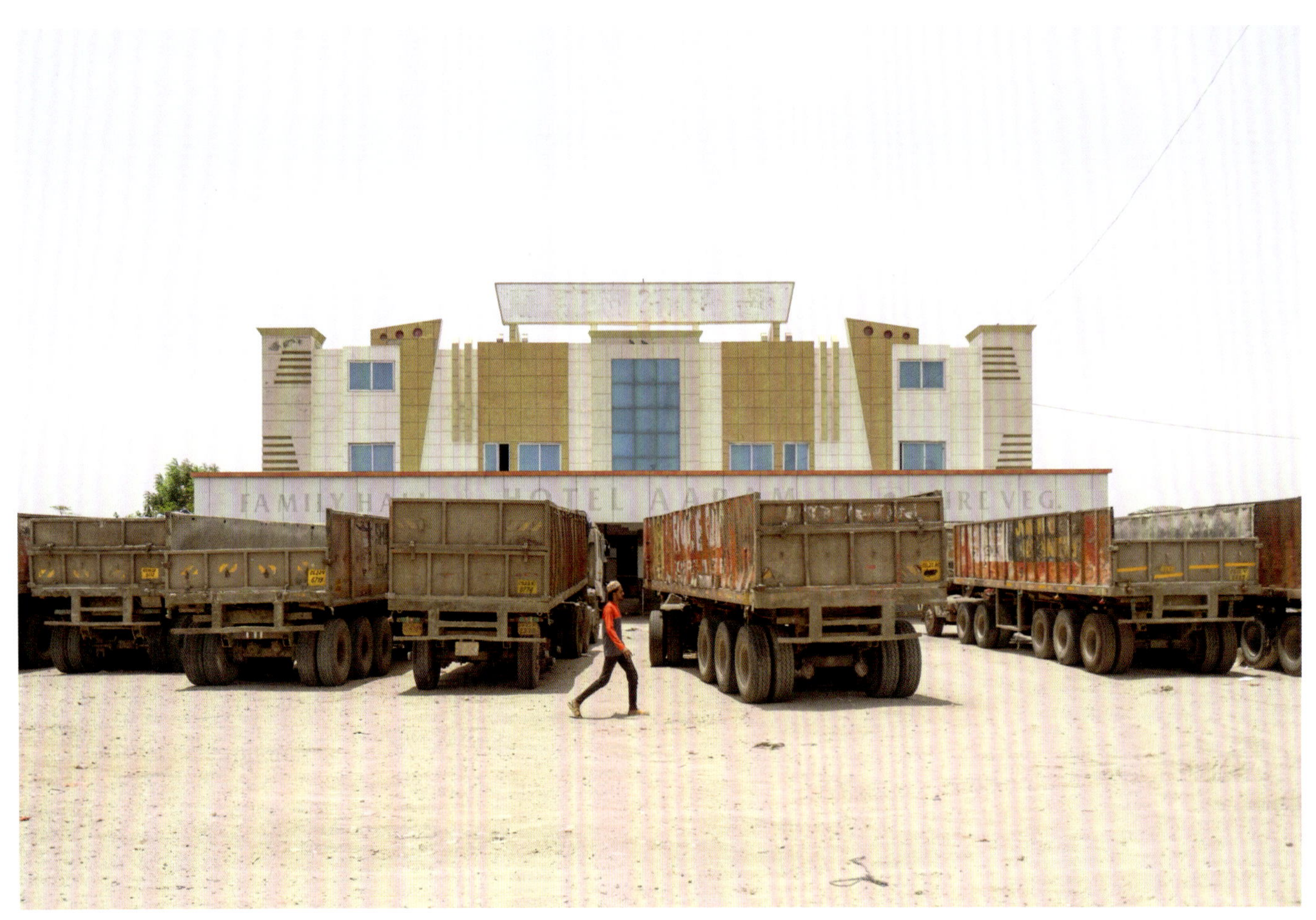

overleaf: Jaipur, INDIA

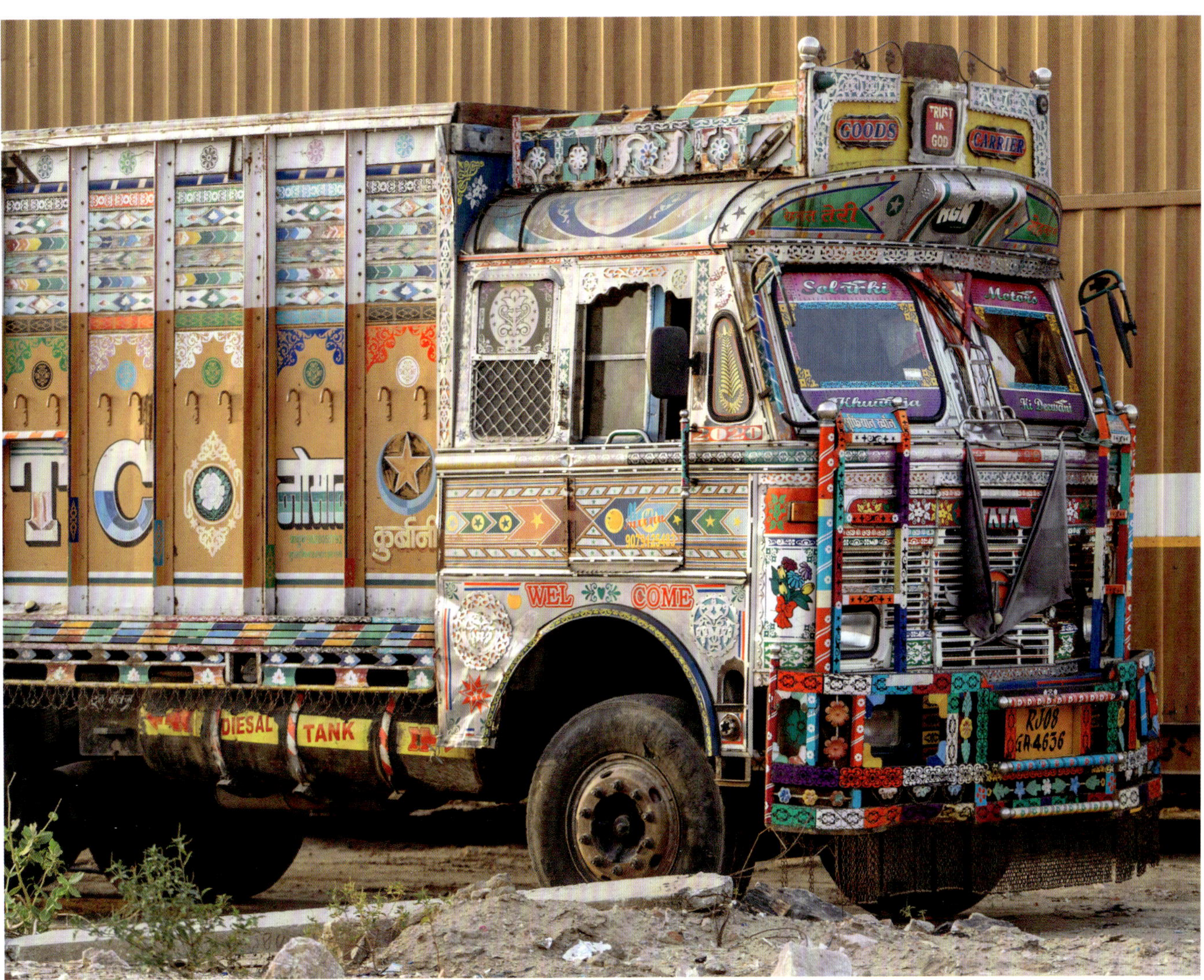

GOODS
TRUST IN GOD
CARRIER
Sol ti ki
Motors
Khutija
Ki Deundni
WEL COME
DIESAL TANK
TATA
RJ08
GA 4636
T C

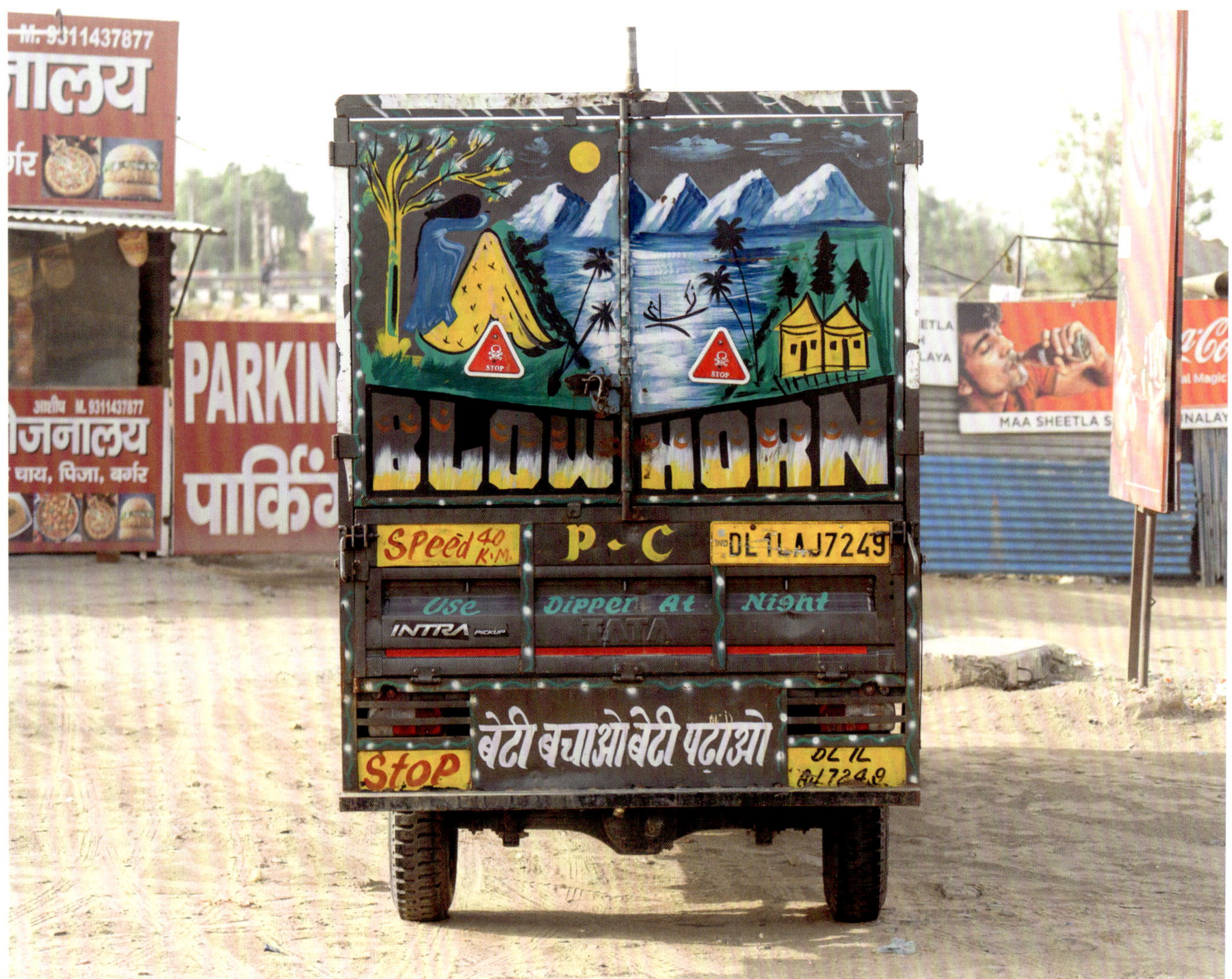
M. 9311437877
नालय
PARKIN
आशीष M.9311437877
जनालय
चाय, पिजा, बर्गर
पार्किंग
BLOW HORN
STOP
STOP
Speed 40 K.M.
P-C
IND DL 1LAJ 7249
Use Dipper At Night
INTRA PICKUP
TATA
STOP
बेटी बचाओ बेटी पढ़ाओ
DL 1L
AJ 7249
ETLA
LAYA
MAA SHEETLA S
NALAYA
Coca-Cola

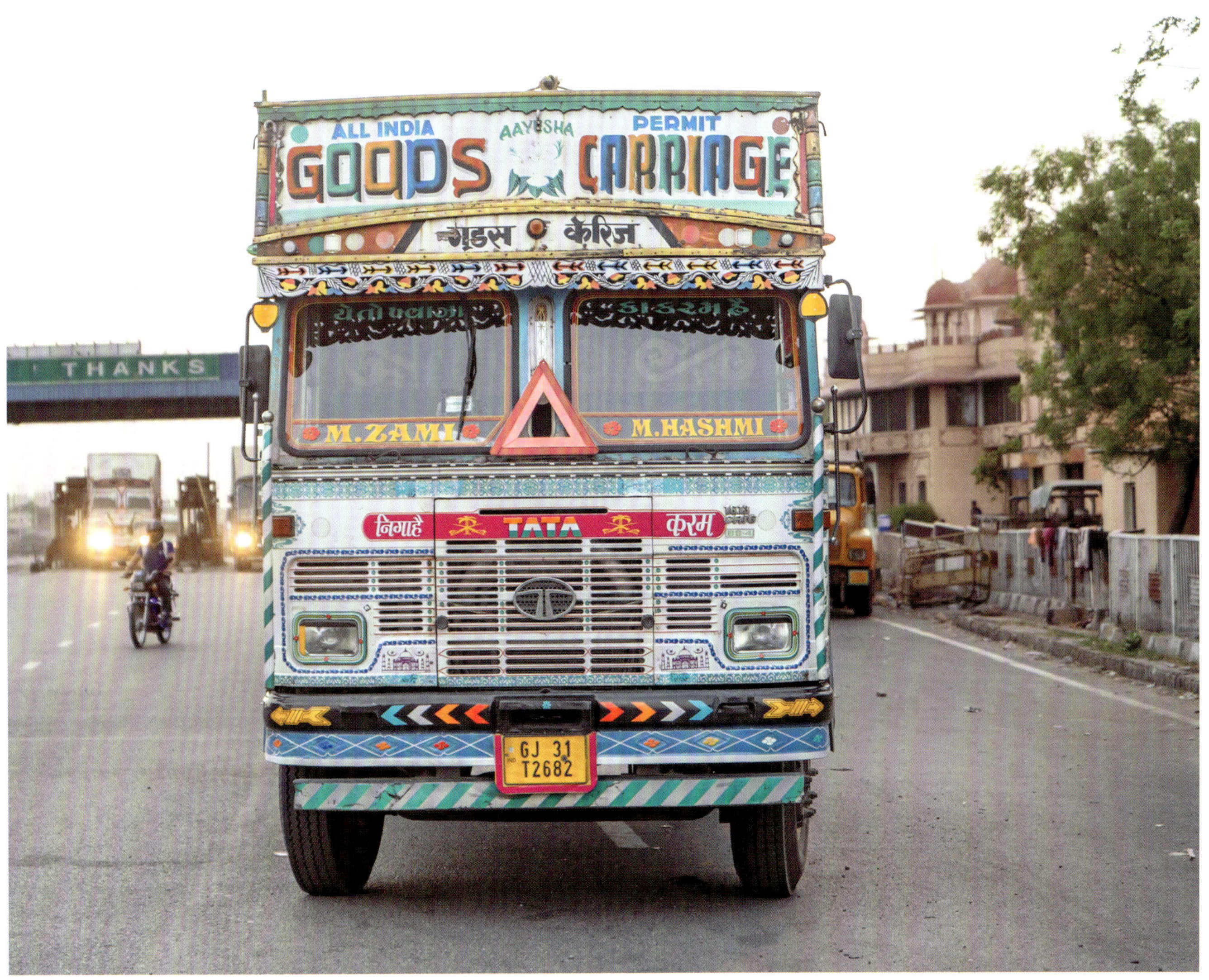

ALL INDIA
AAYBSHA
PERMIT
GOODS CARRIAGE
गूड्स ॰ केरिज
M. ZAMI
M. HASHMI
निगहै
TATA
करम
GJ 31
T2682
THANKS

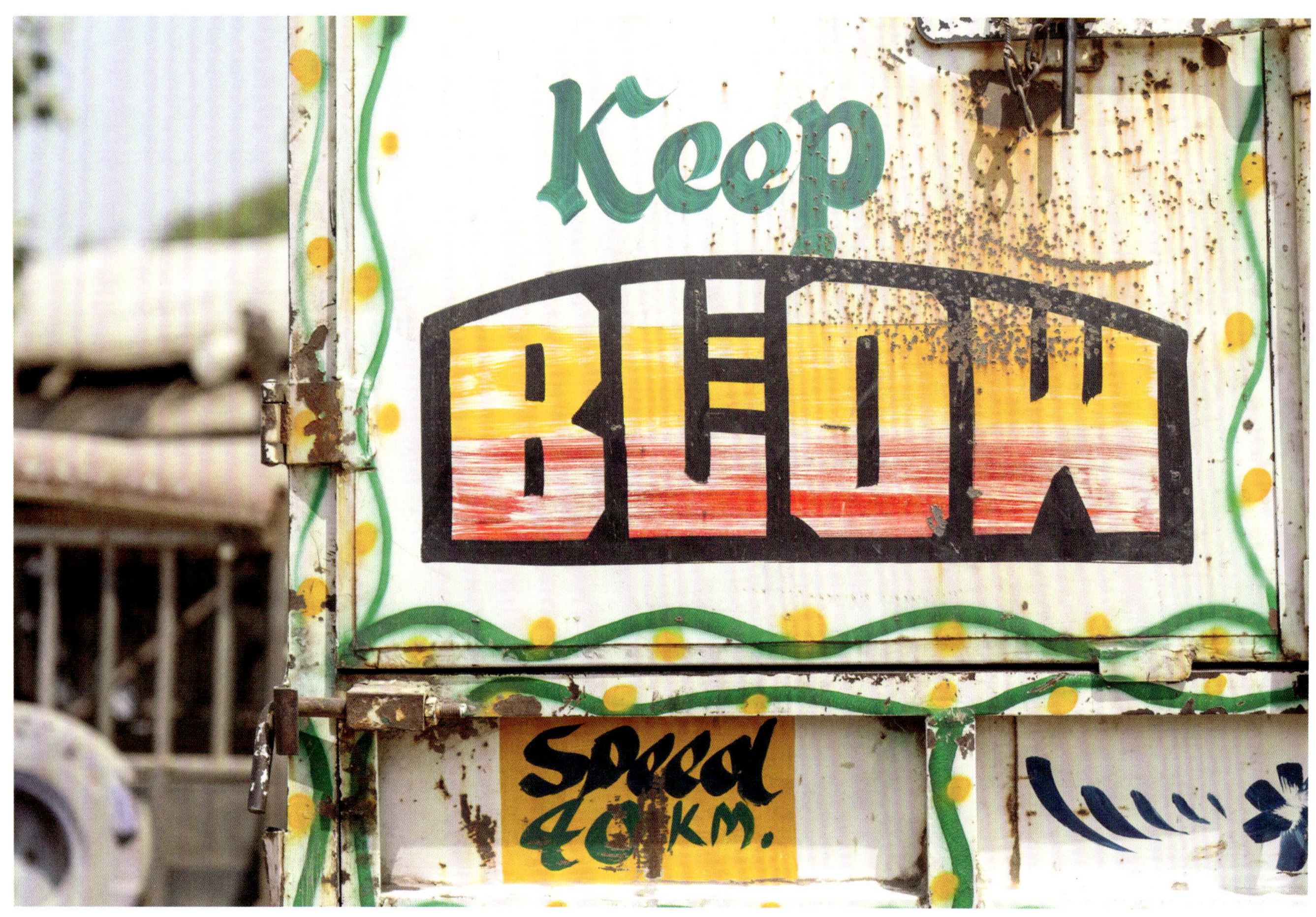

73–75: Jaipur, INDIA

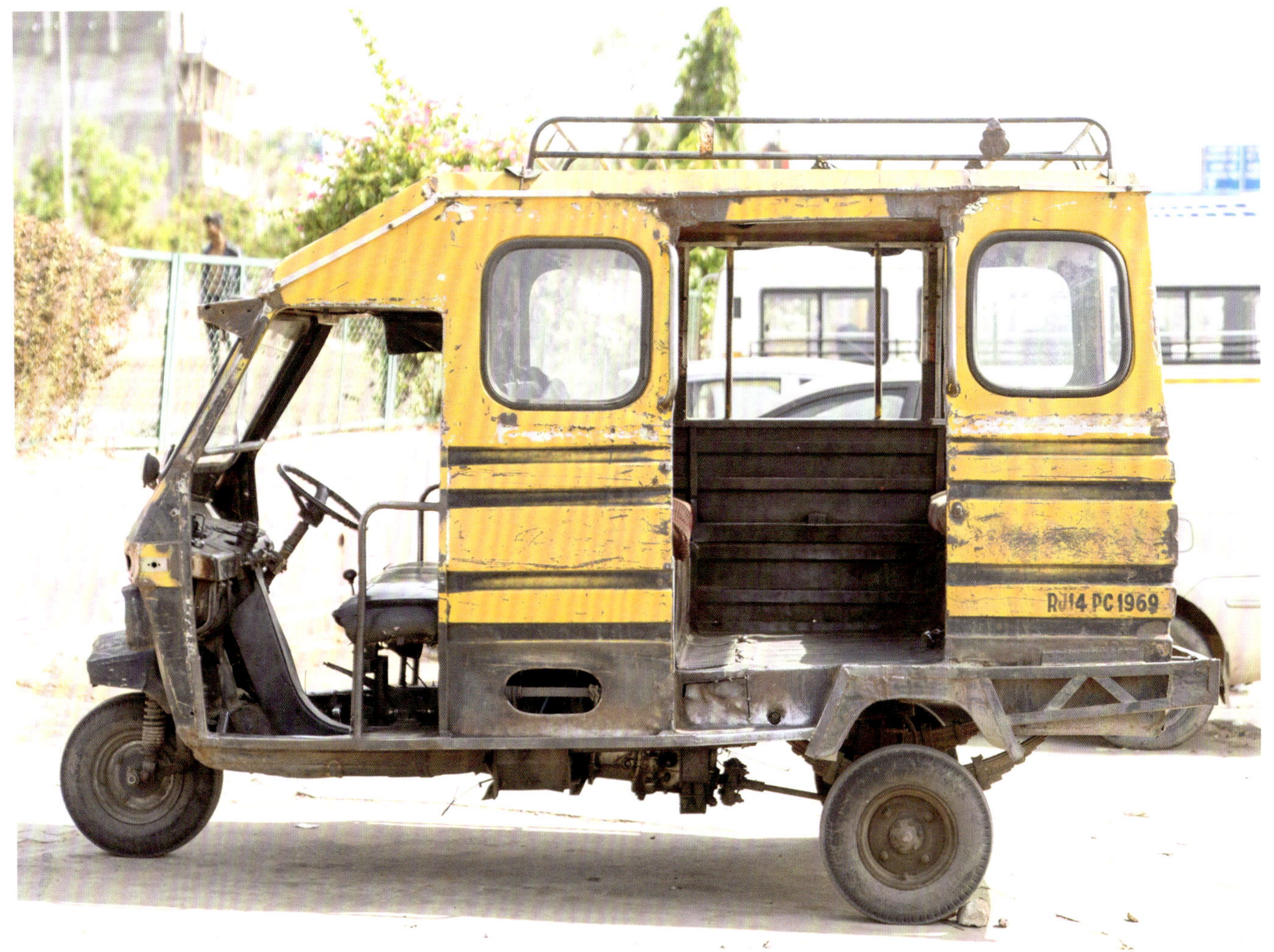
RJ14 PC 1969

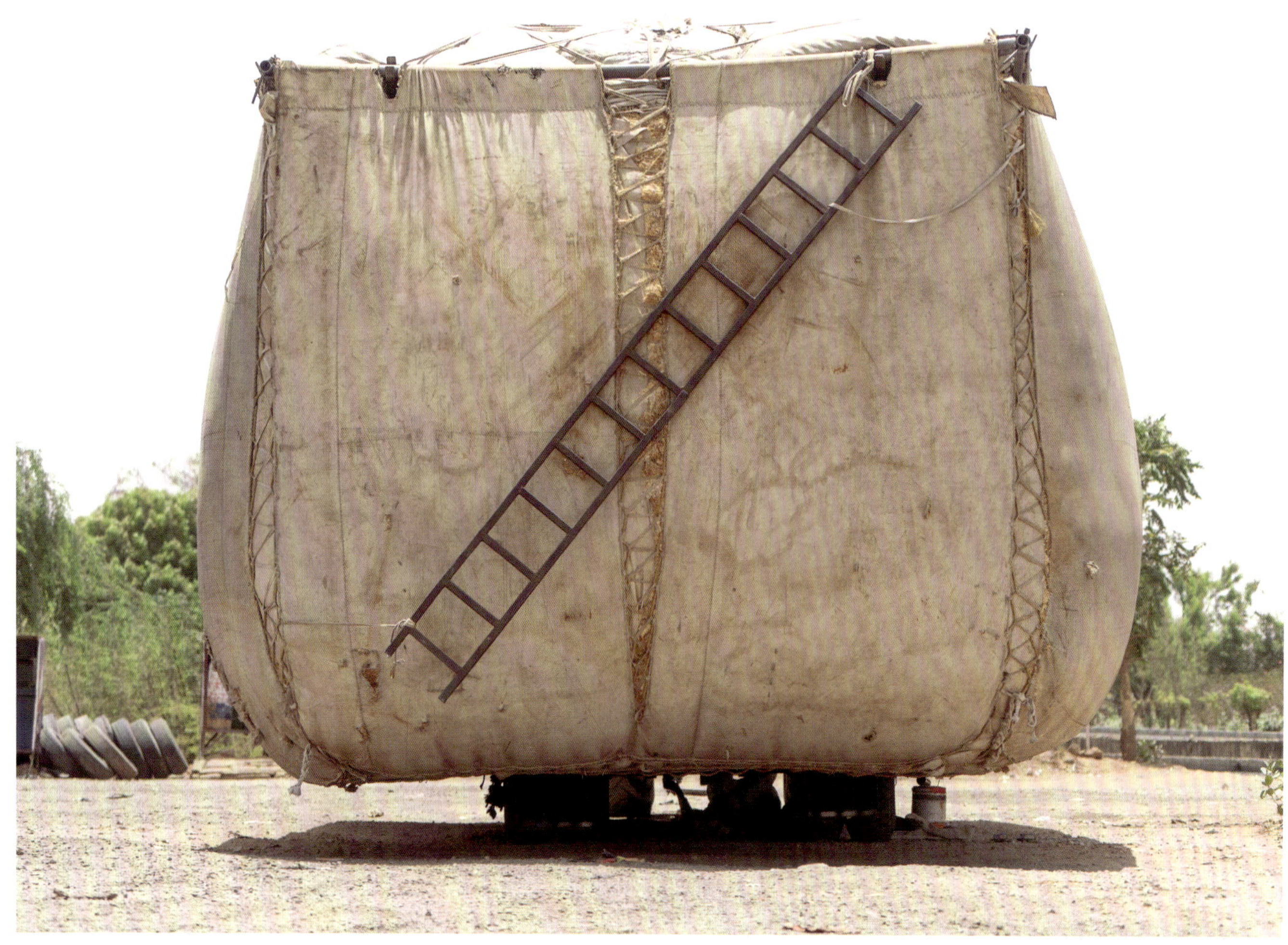

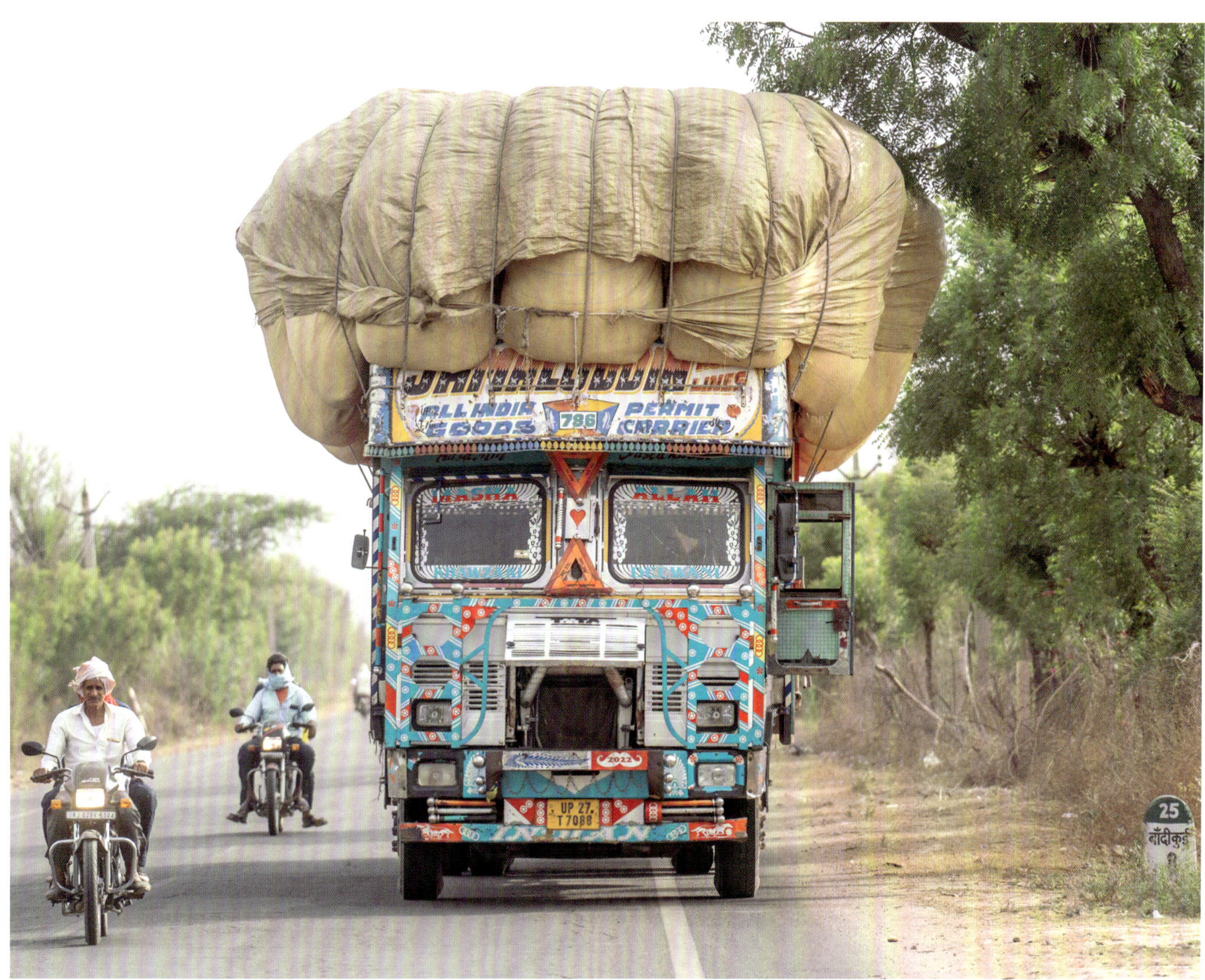

ALL INDIA PERMIT
GOODS 786 CARRIER
2022
UP 27
T 7088

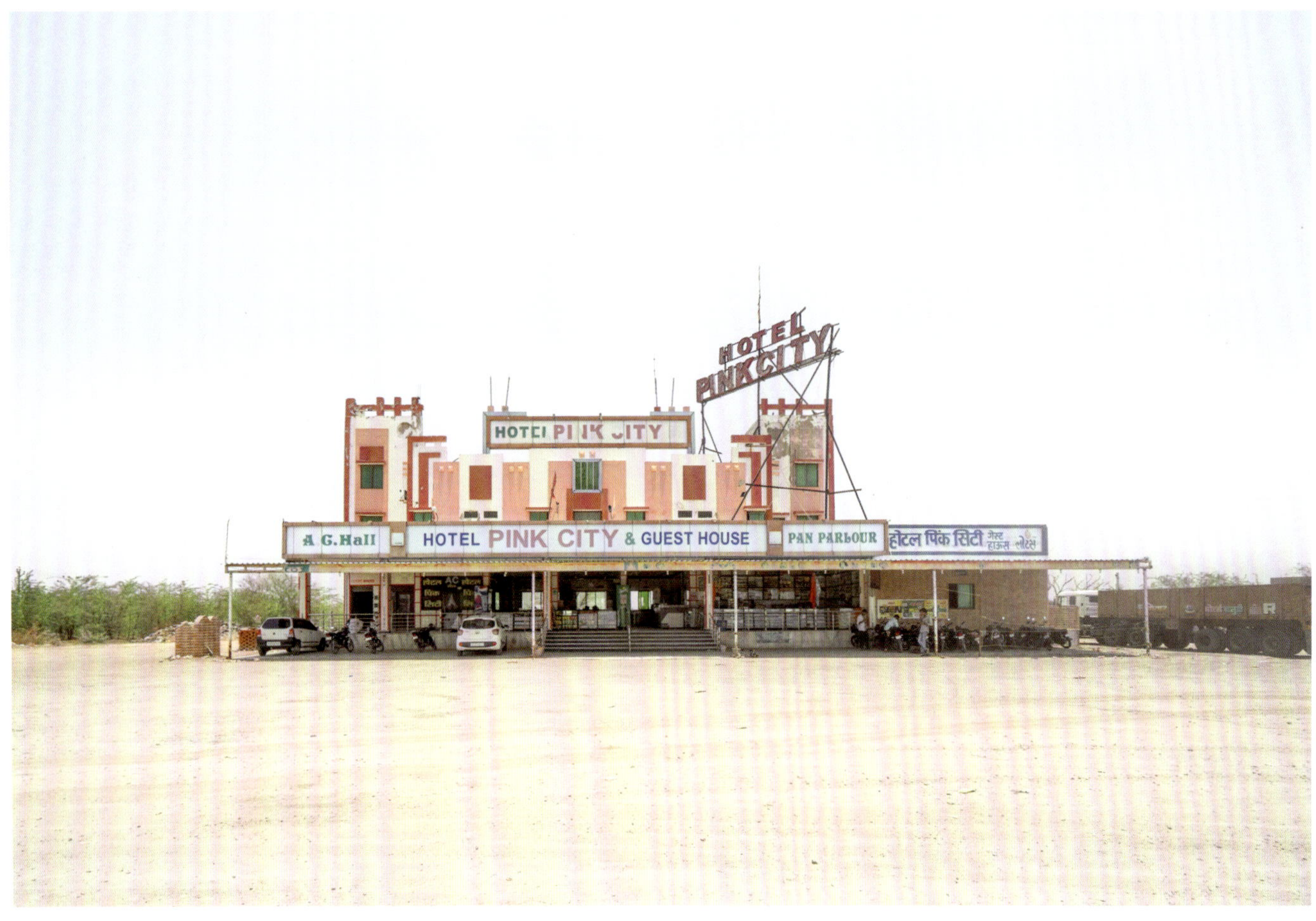

76   Jaipur, INDIA

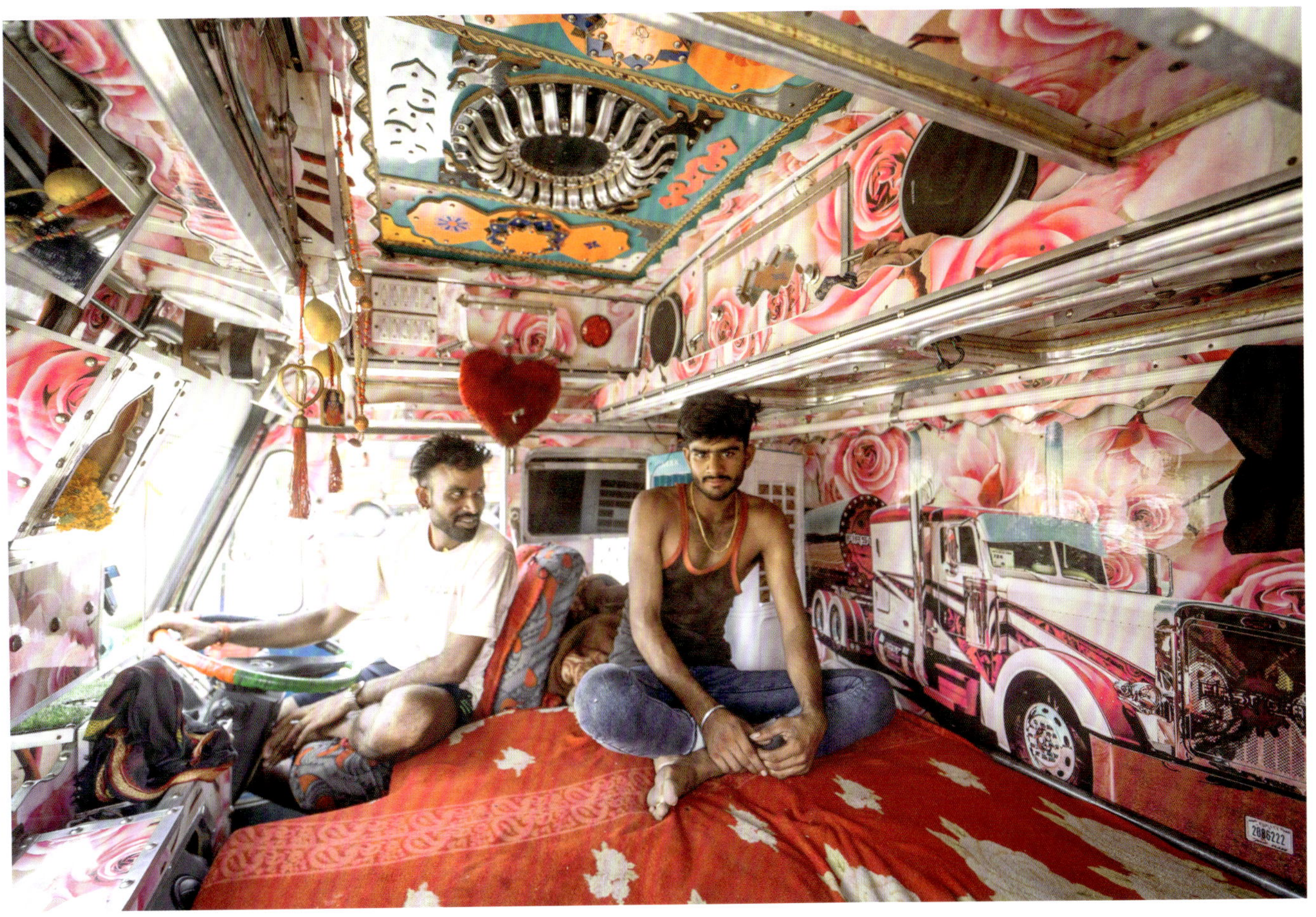

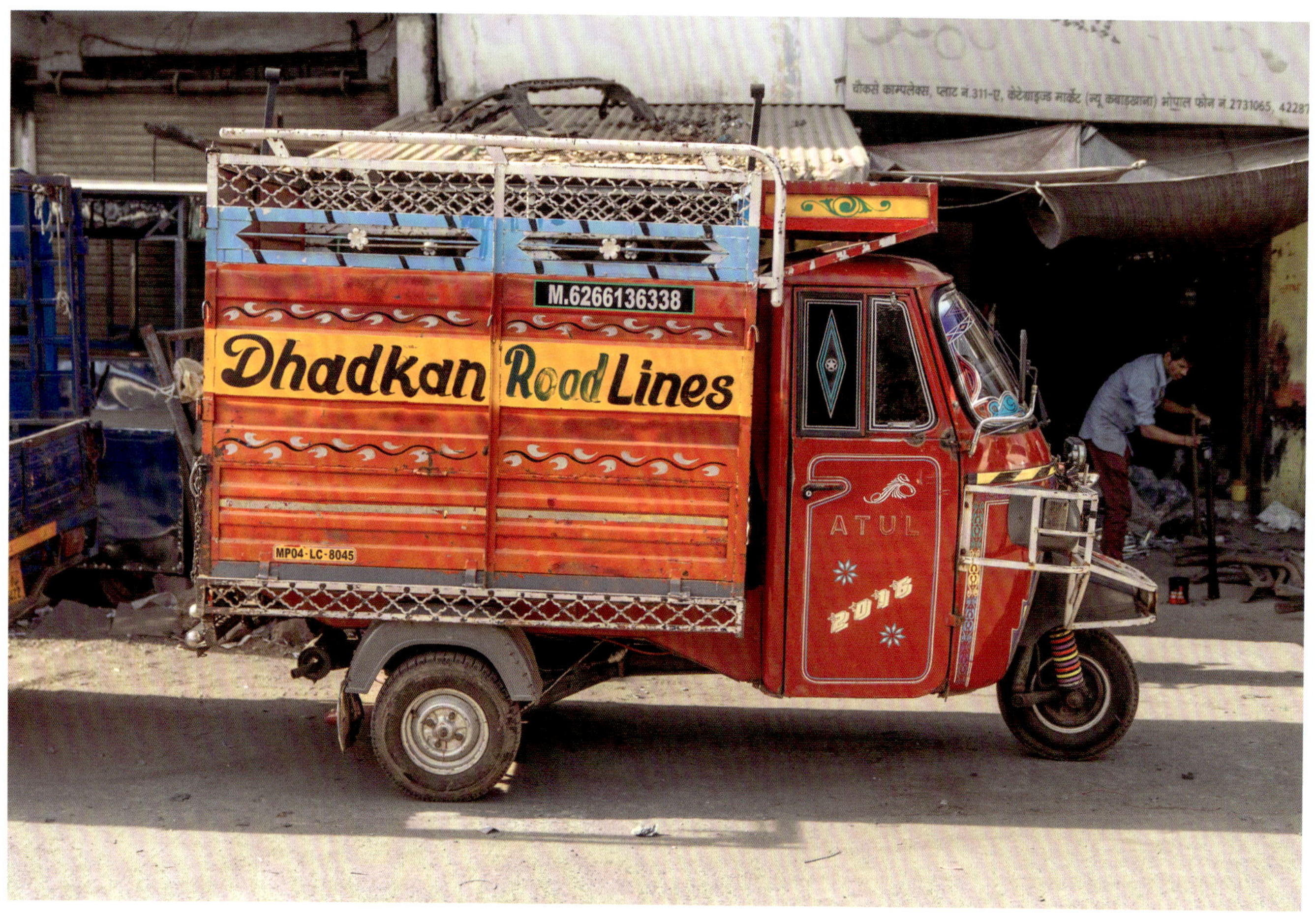

Jaipur, INDIA

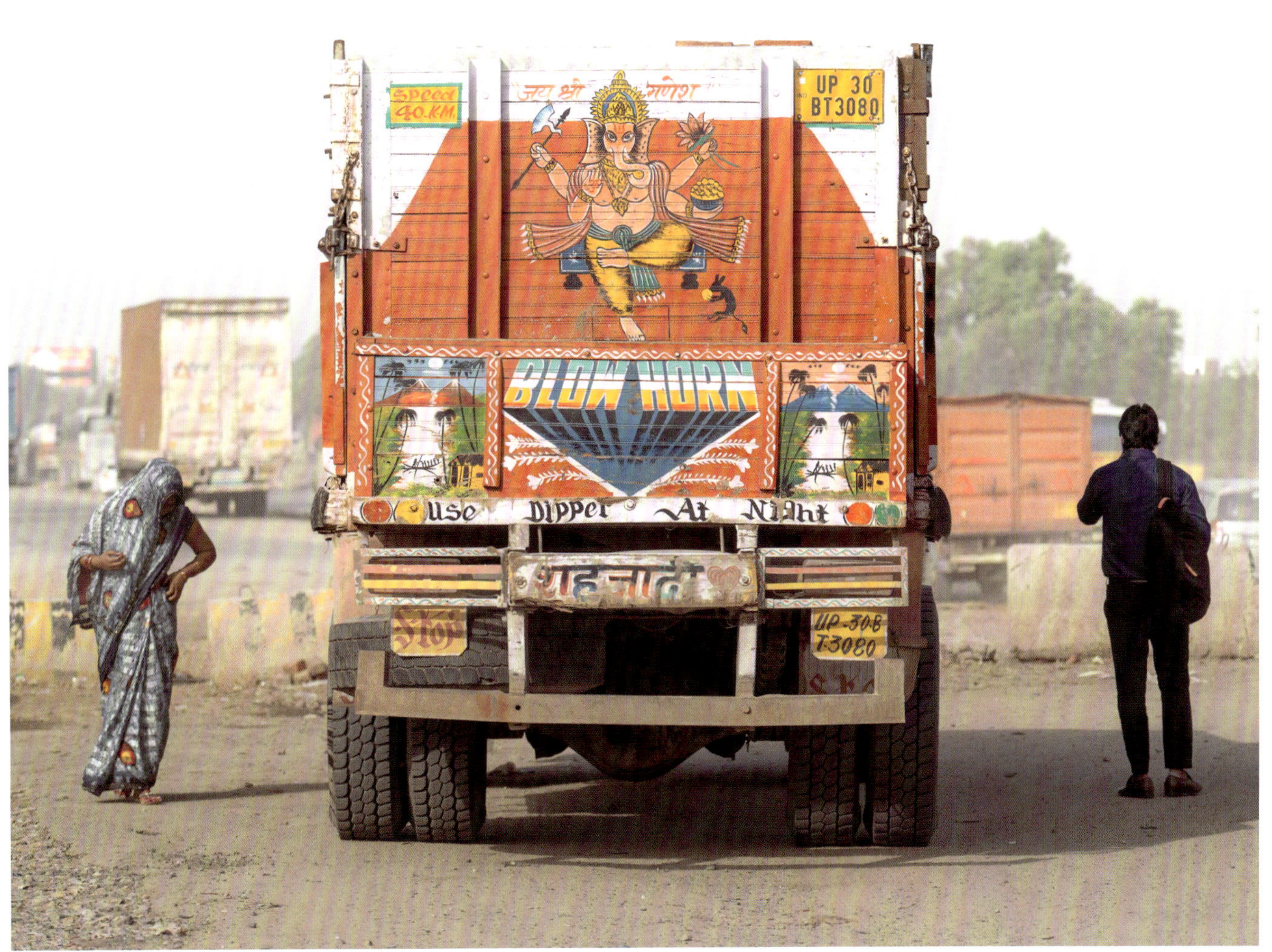
Speed 40.KM
जय श्री गणेश
UP 30 BT3080
BLOW HORN
use DIPPER At Night
गूहनाद
Stop
UP-30B T3080

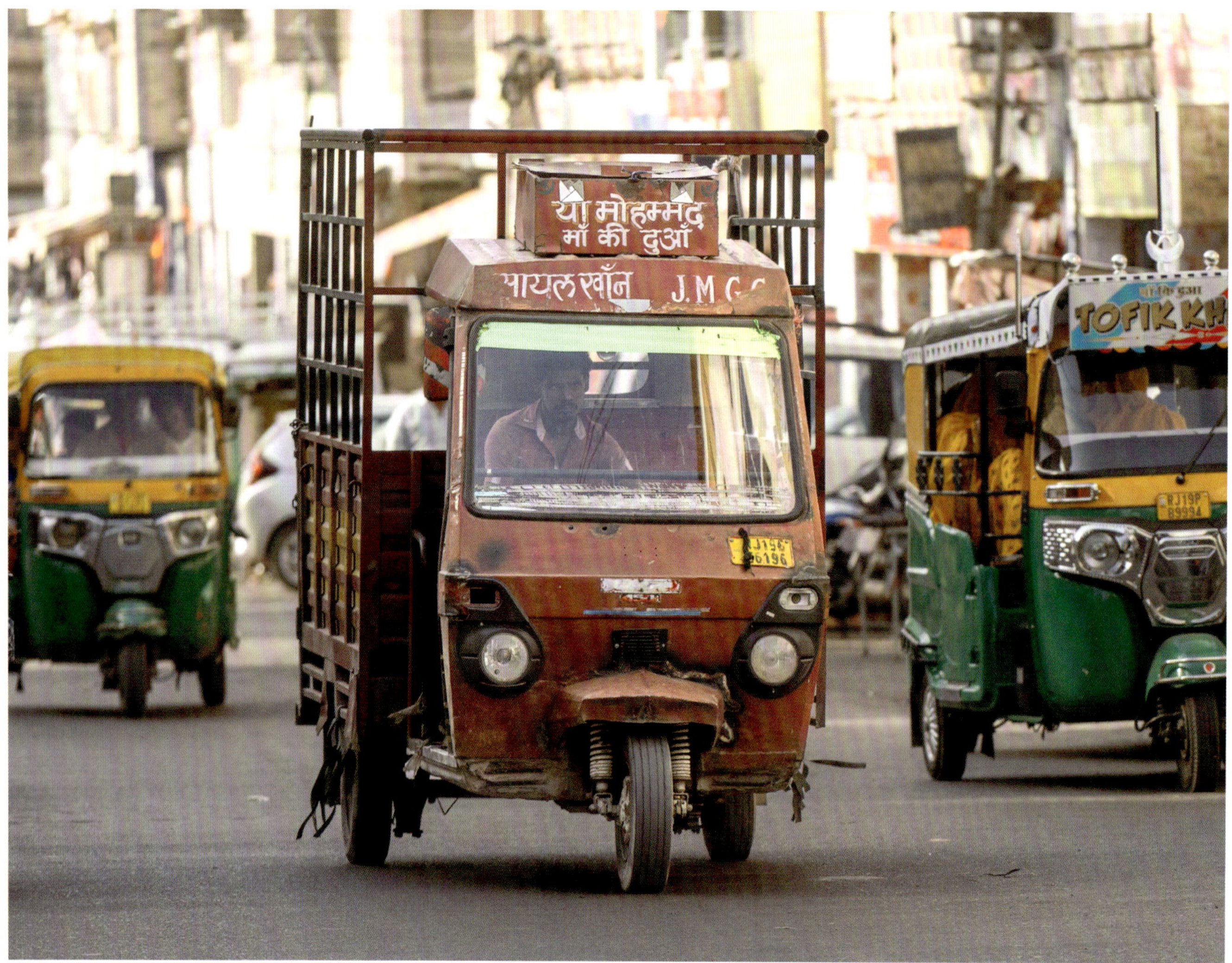
या मोहम्मद
माँ की दुआ
पायल खाँन   J.M.G.
TOFIK KH
RJ19P
8994
JJ19
6196

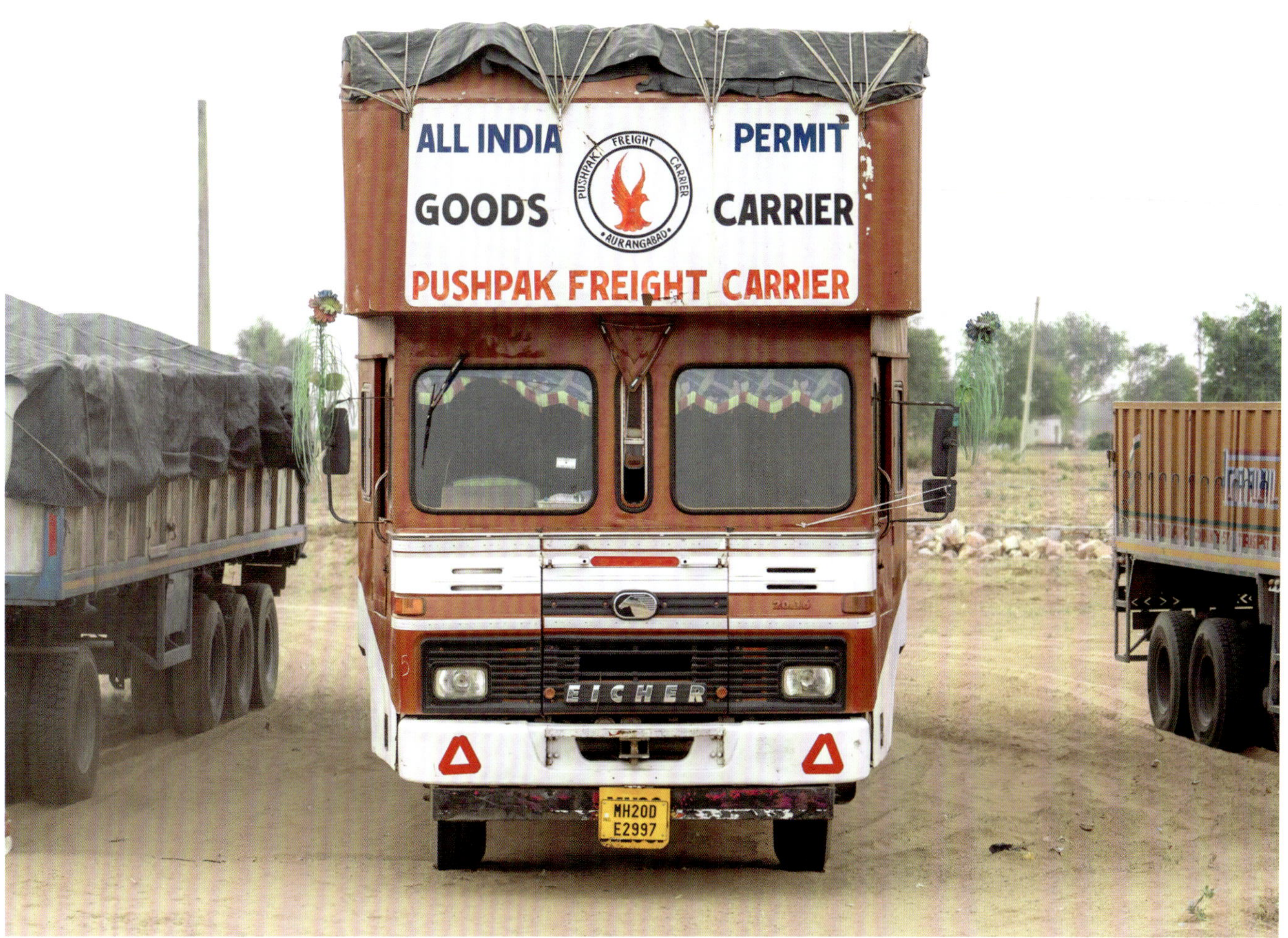

ALL INDIA
PERMIT
GOODS
CARRIER
PUSHPAK FREIGHT CARRIER
AURANGABAD
PUSHPAK FREIGHT CARRIER
EICHER
MH20D
E2997

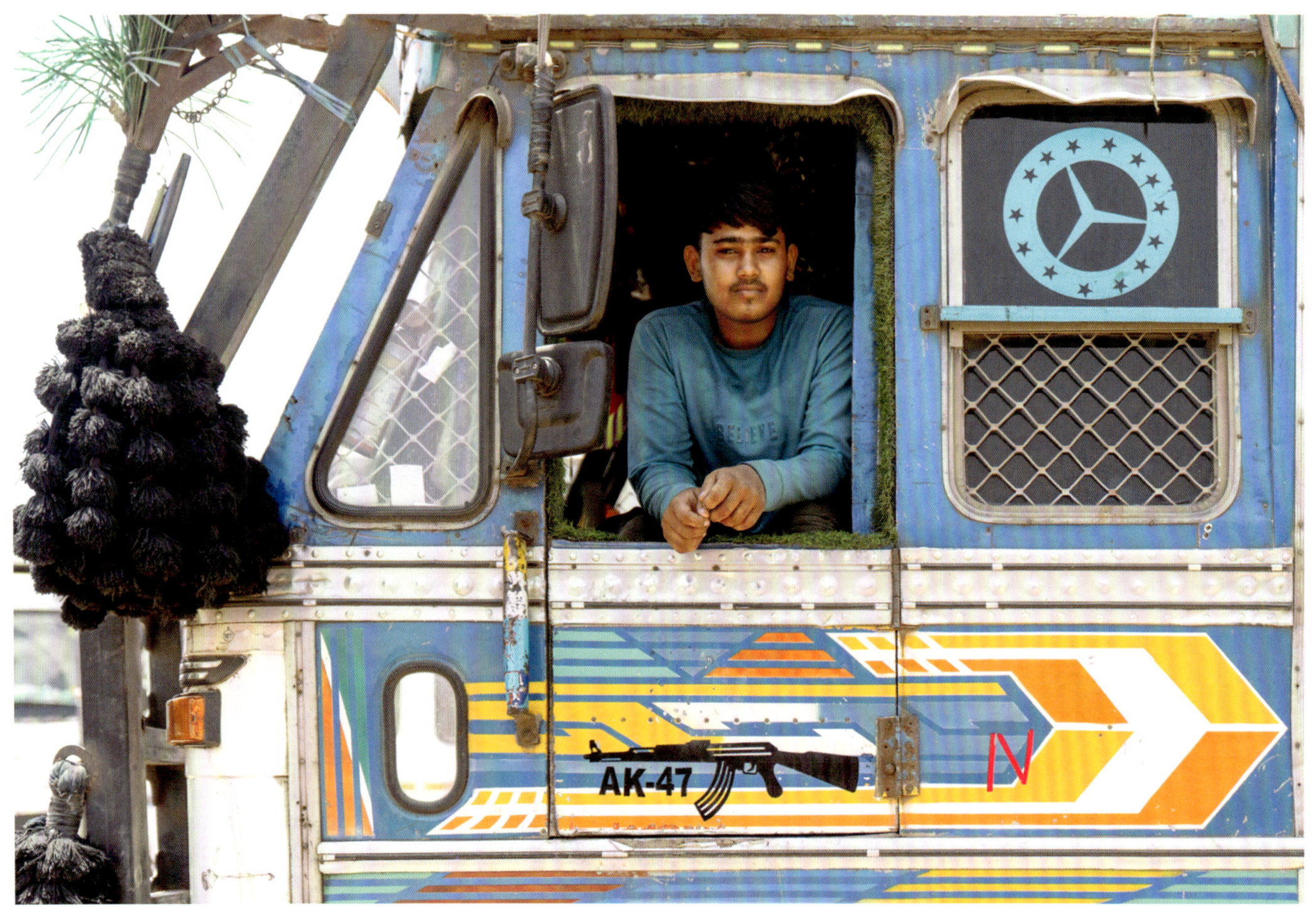

 Dehli, INDIA

overleaf: Indore, INDIA

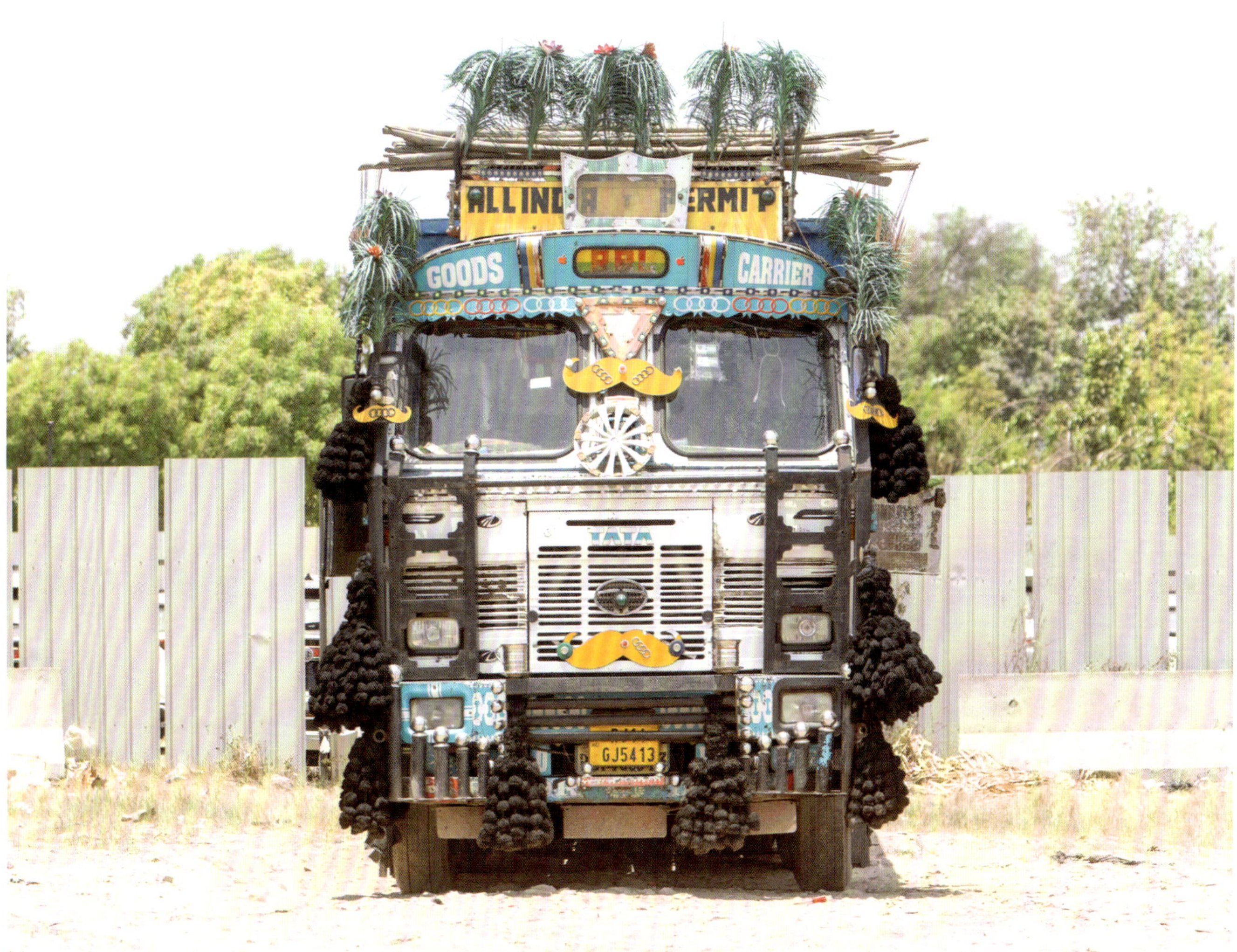

ALL INDIA PERMIT
GOODS
CARRIER
TATA
GJ5413

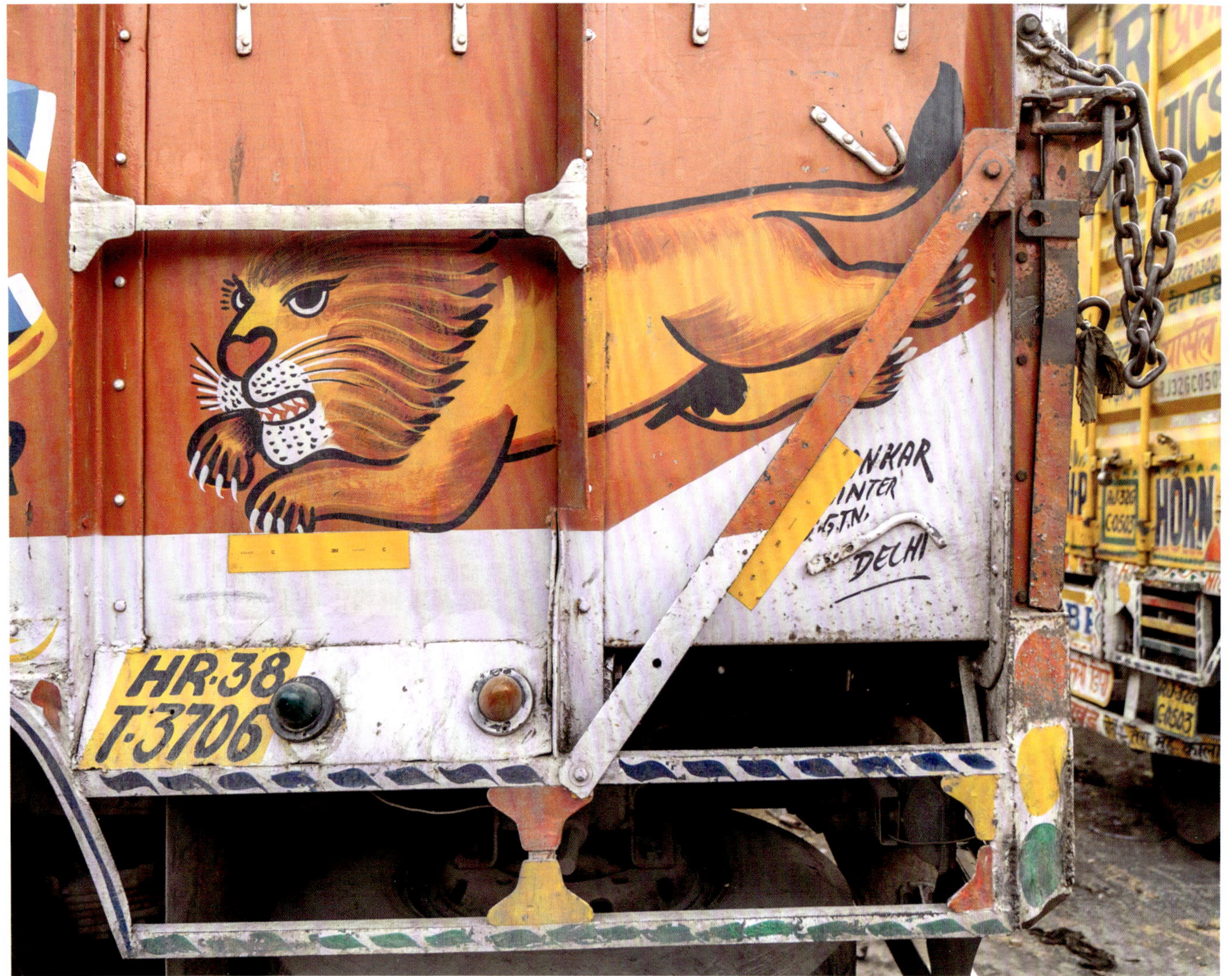

ONKAR
INTER
G.T.N.
DELHI
HR·38
T·3706

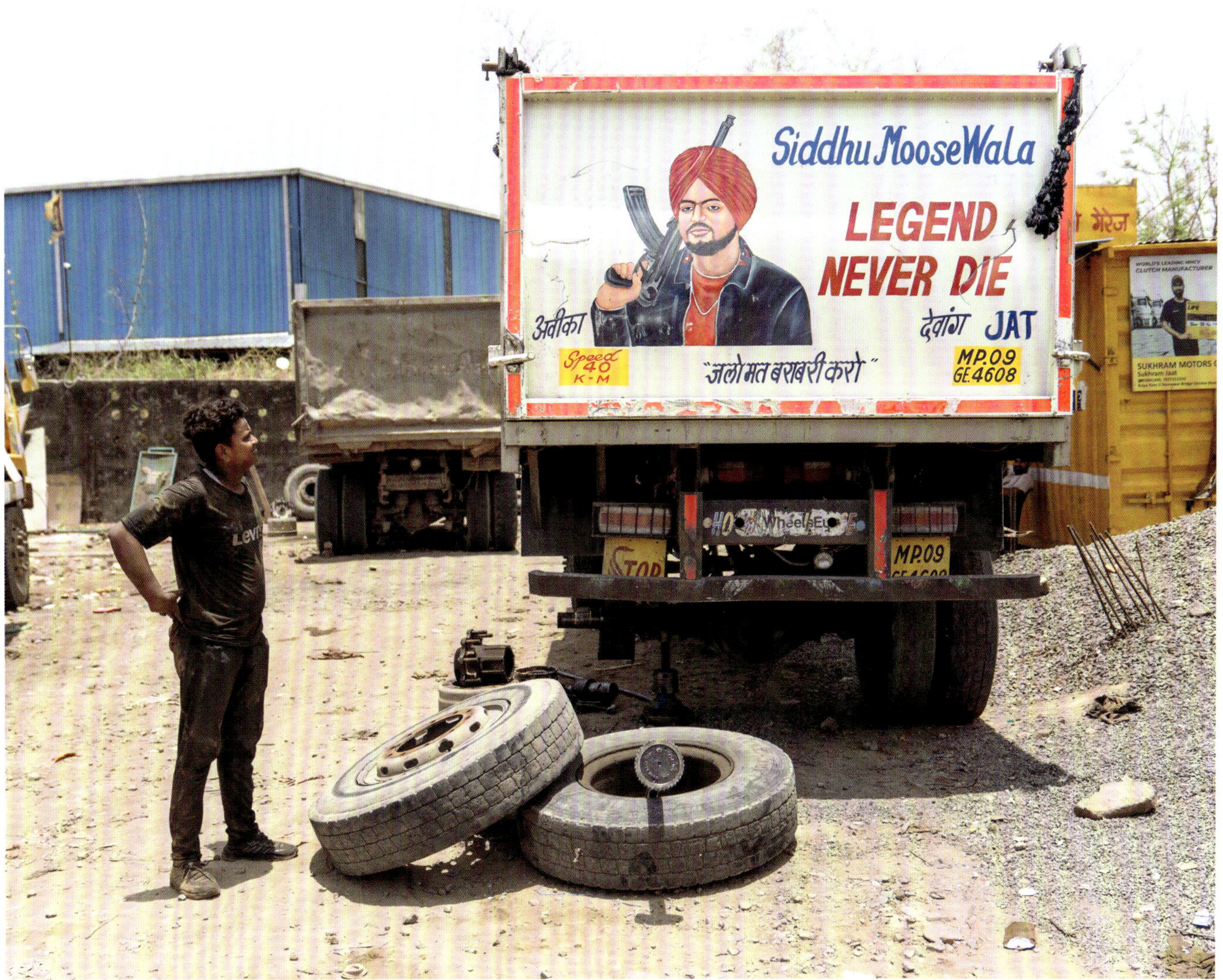

Siddhu MooseWala
LEGEND
NEVER DIE
अवीका
देवांग JAT
Speed 40 K·M
"जलो मत बराबरी करो"
MP.09 GE.4608
MP.09
SUKHRAM MOTORS
WORLD'S LEADING MHCV
CLUTCH MANUFACTURER
Levi's

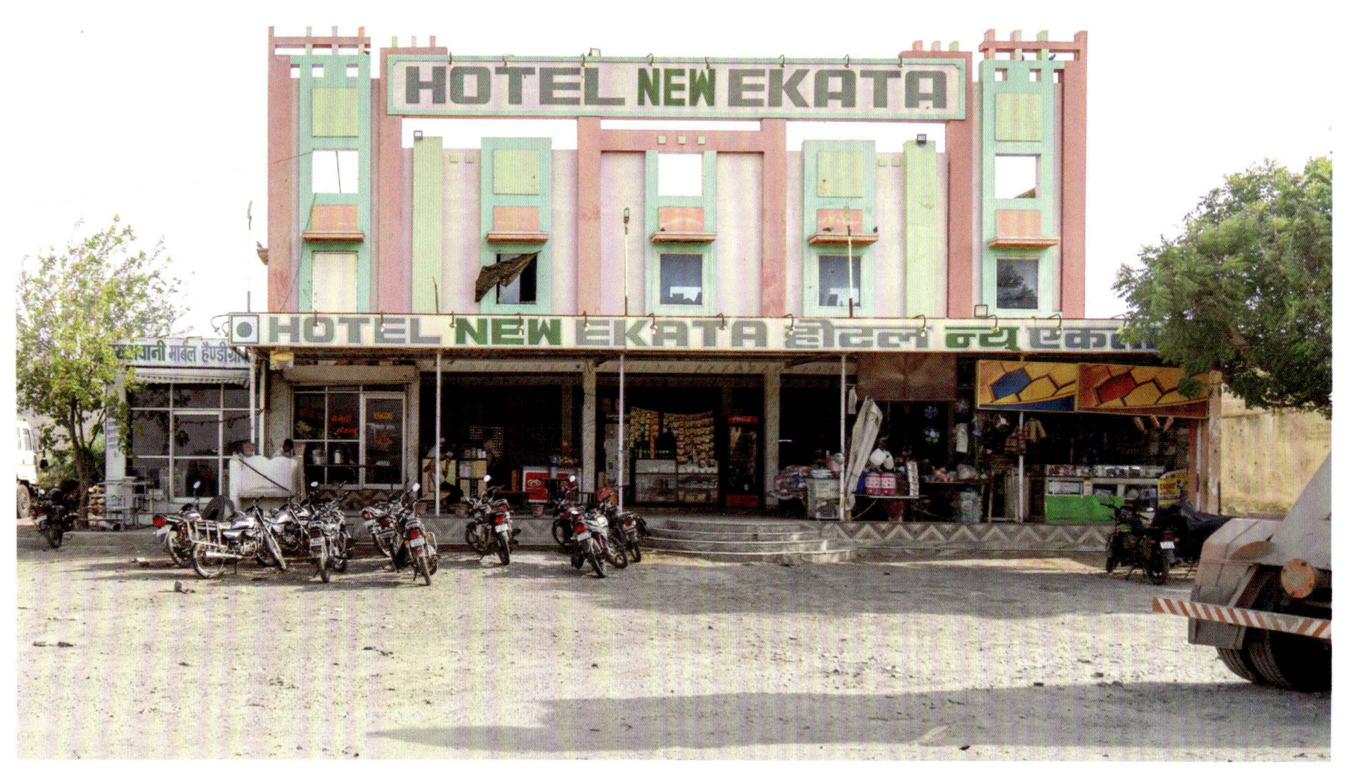

87–90: Jodhpur, INDIA

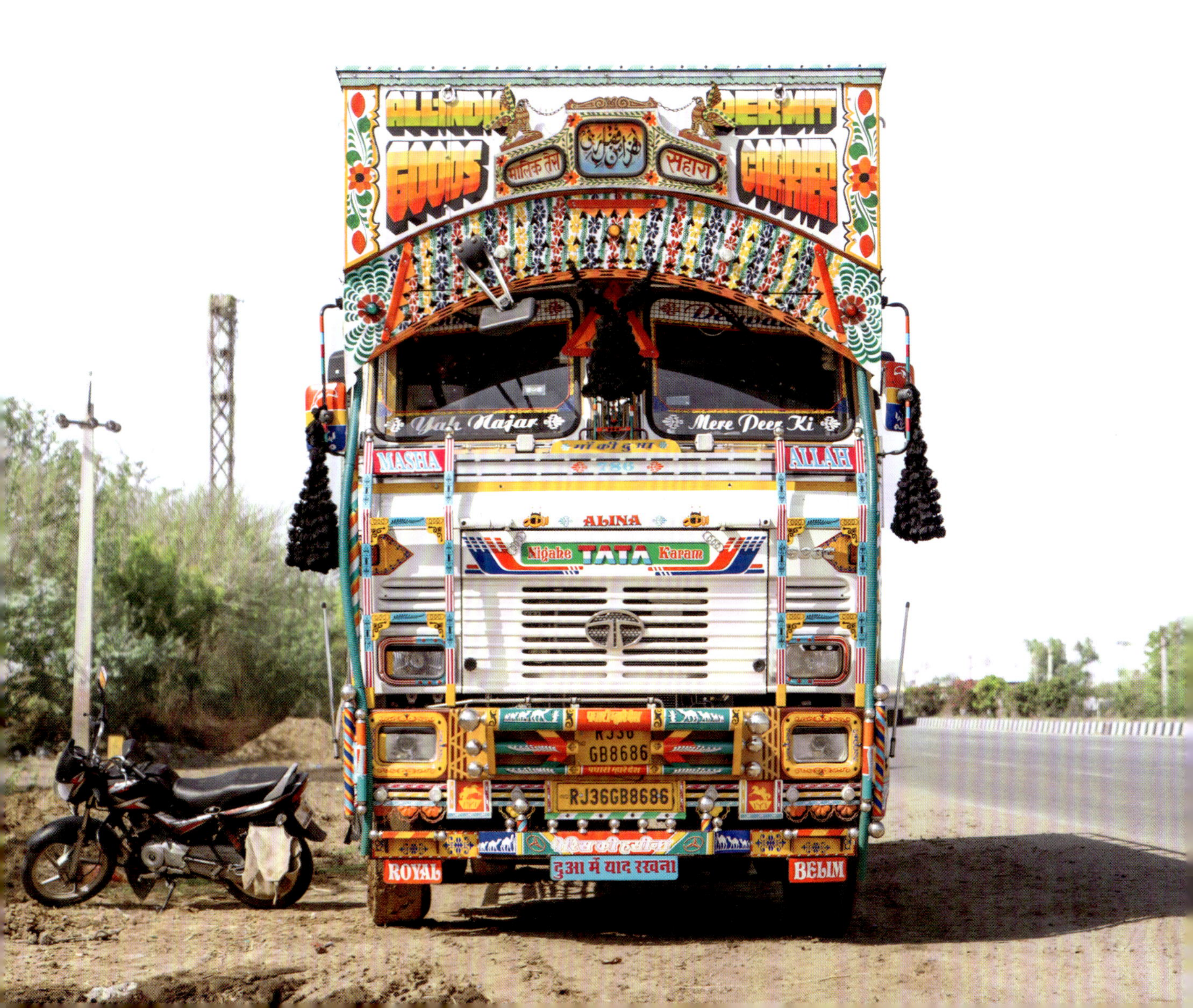

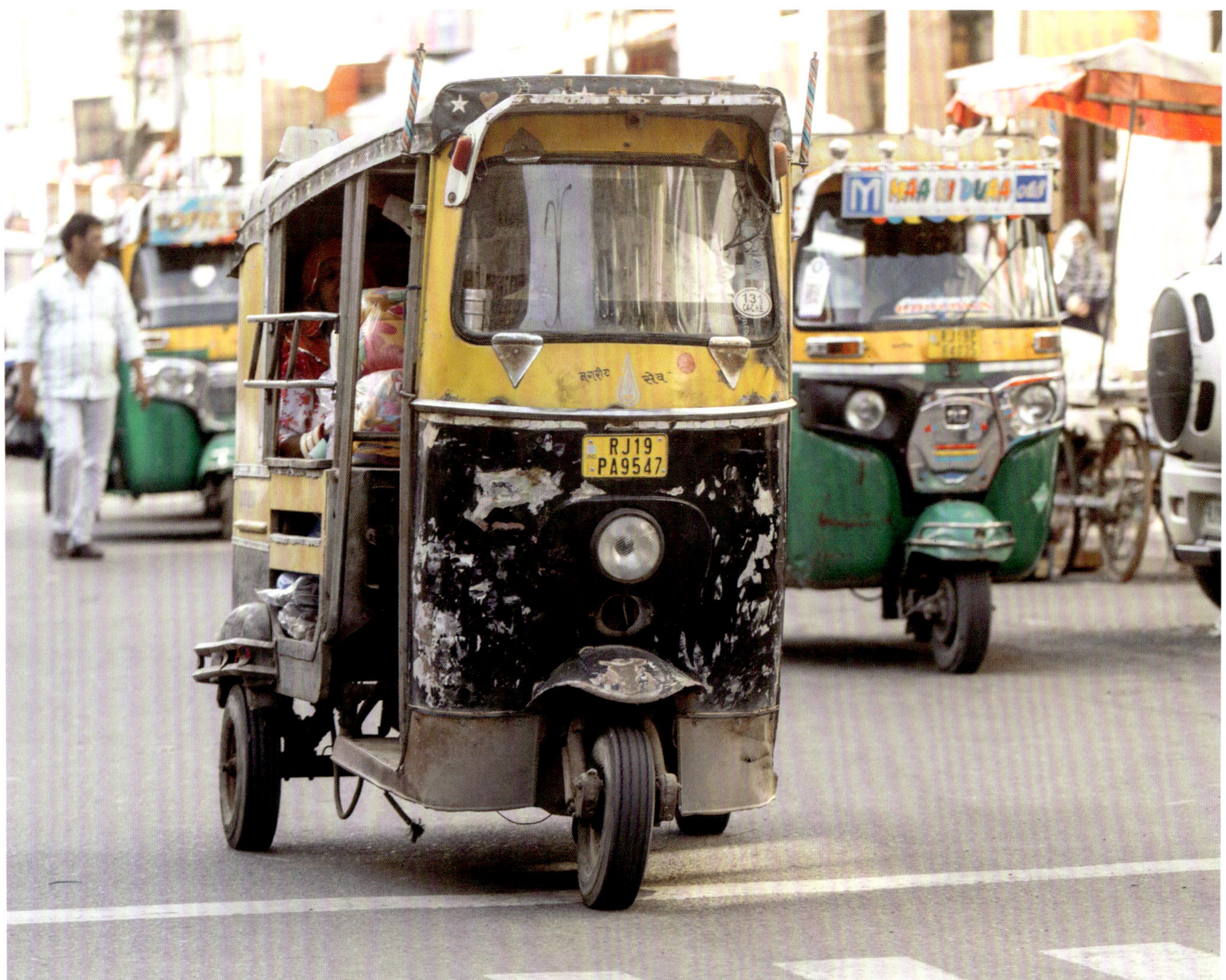

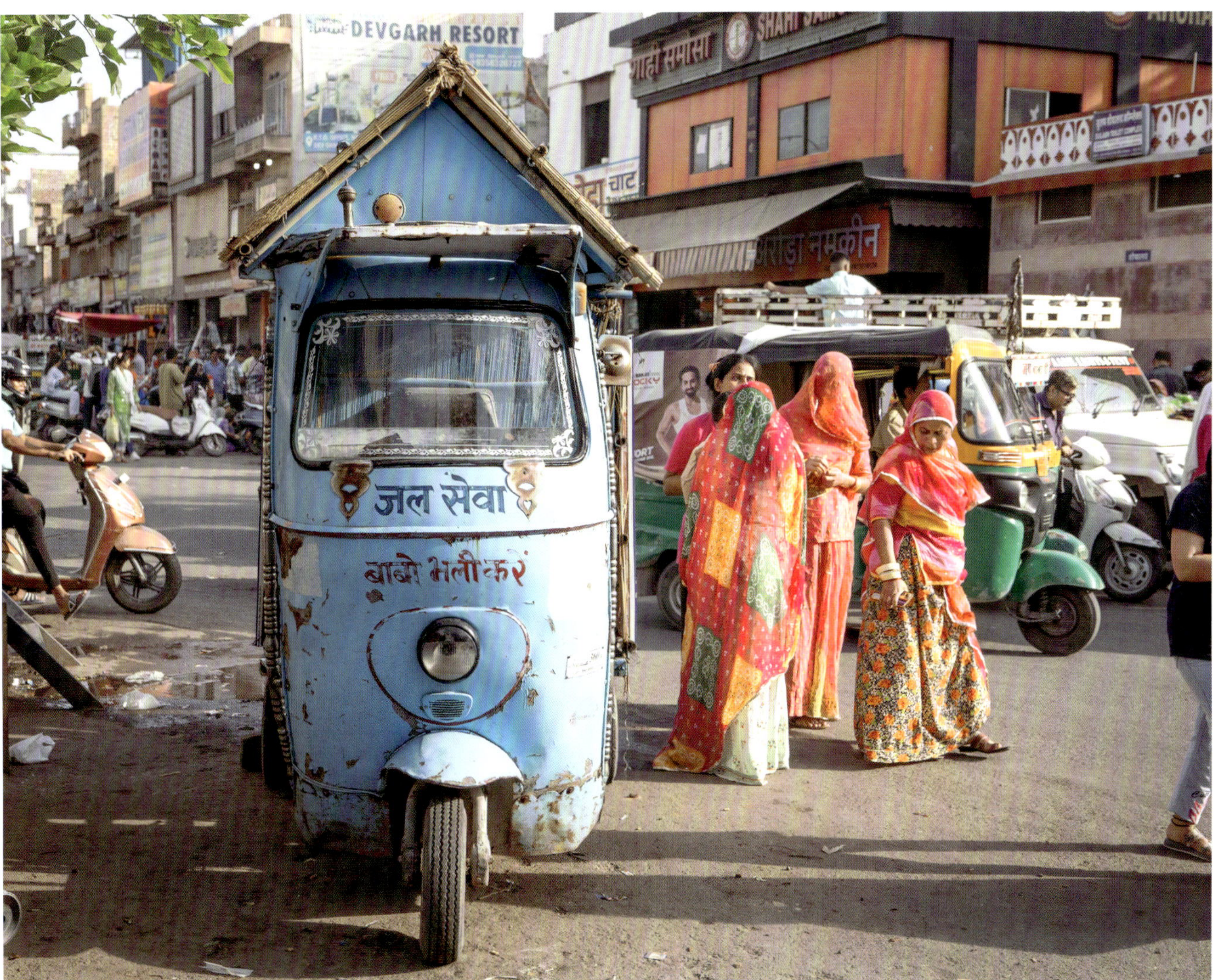

DEVGARH RESORT
SHAHI SAMOSA
जल सेवा
बाबो भली करें

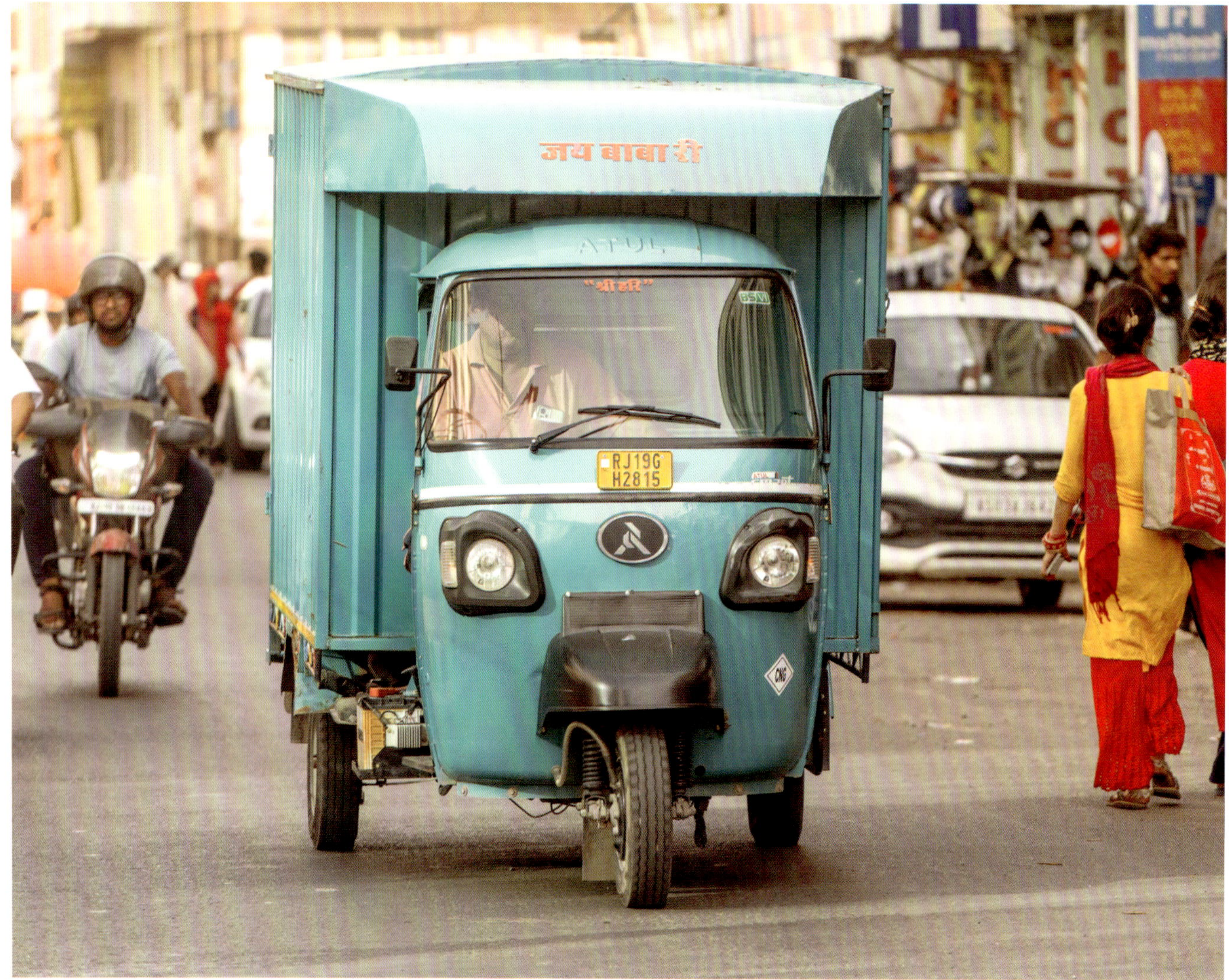

जय बाबा री
ATUL
"श्री हरि"
BSVI
RJ19G
H2815
CNG

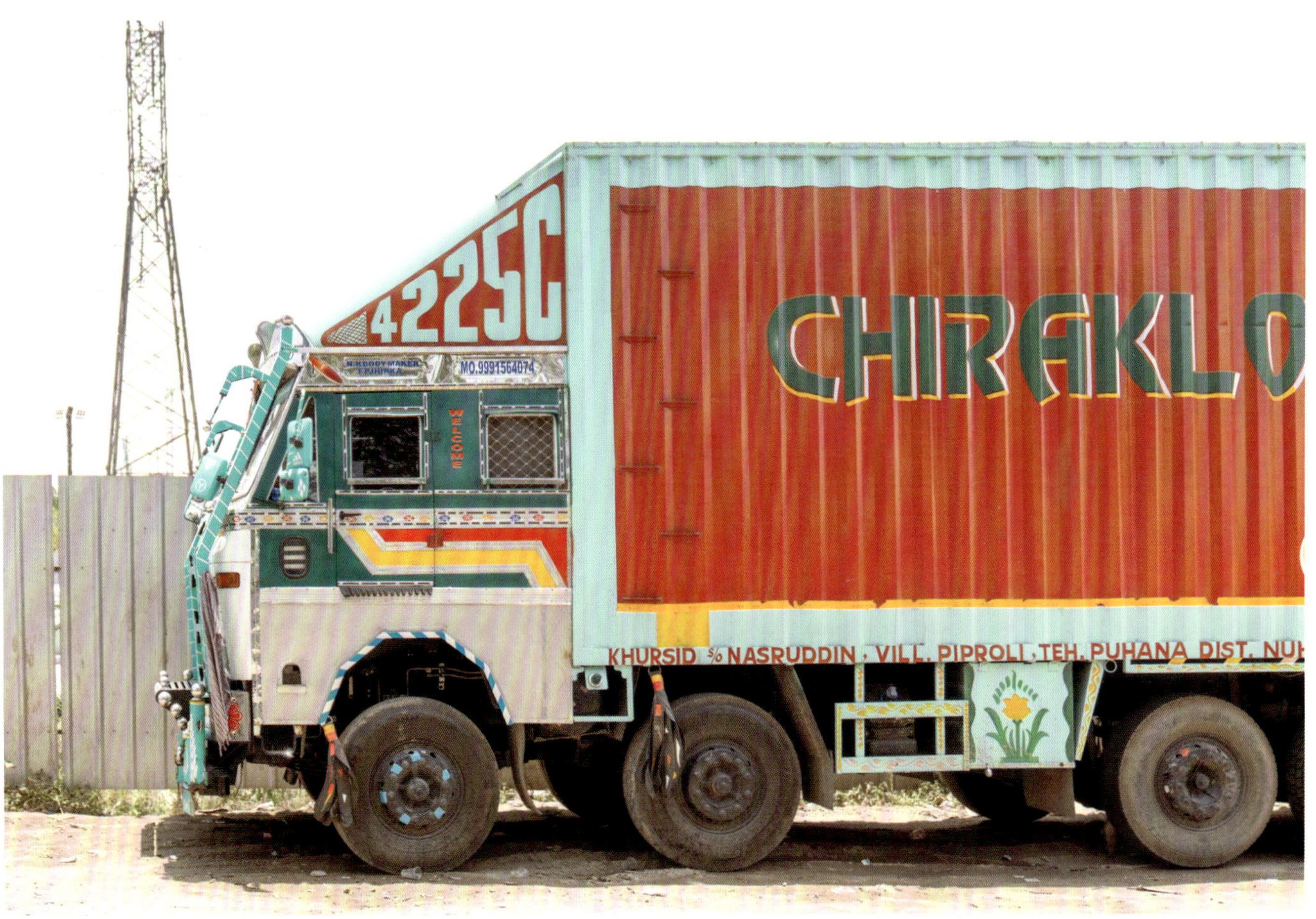
4225C
CHIRAKLO
WELCOME
MO.9991564074
KHURSID S/o NASRUDDIN, VILL. PIPROLI, TEH. PUHANA DIST. NUH

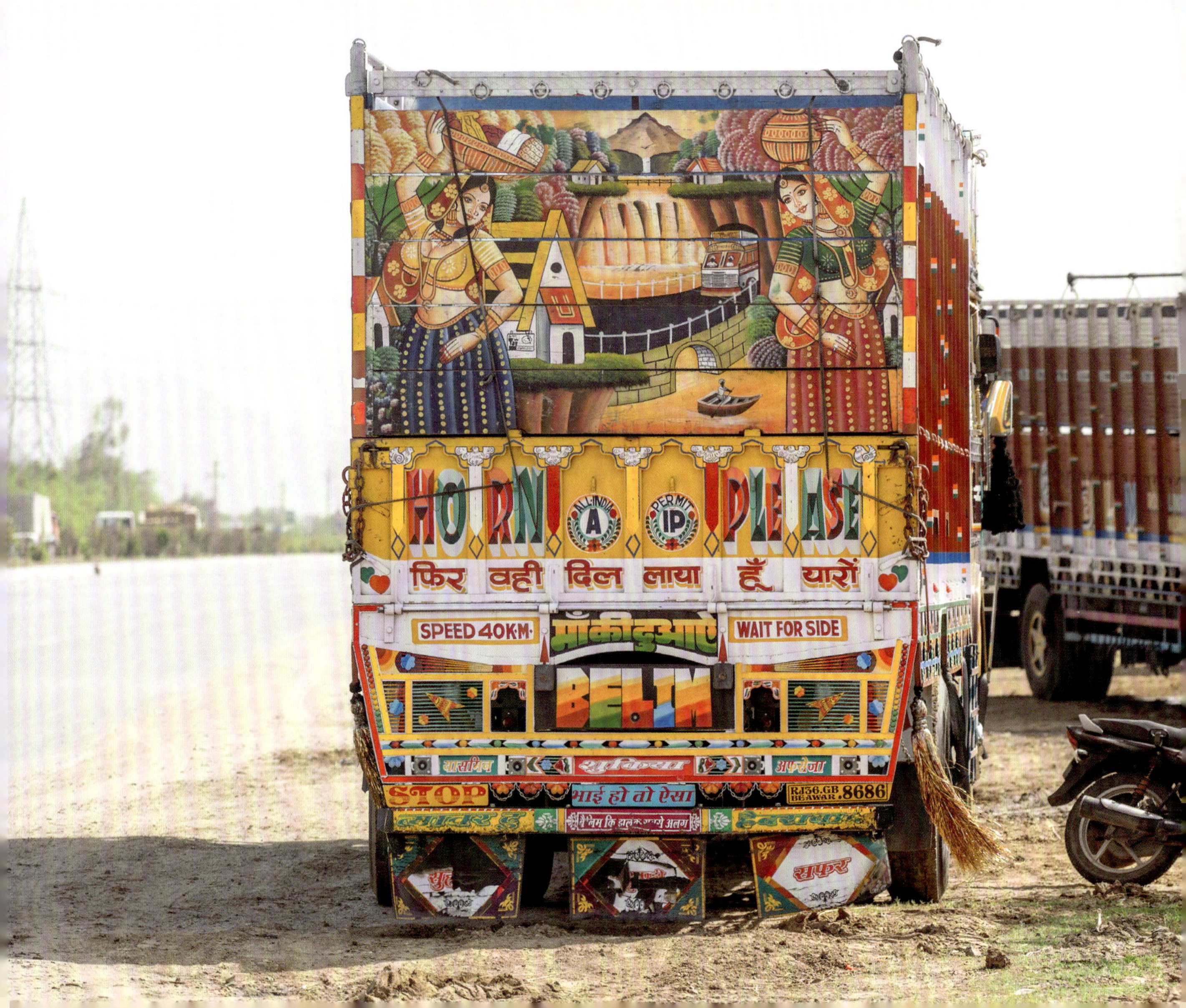
HORN PLEASE
ALL INDIA
A
PERMIT
IP
फिर वही दिल लाया हूँ यारों
SPEED 40 KM.
WAIT FOR SIDE
माँ की दुआऐ
BELTM
STOP
भाई हो तो ऐसा
RJ36.GB 8686
BEAWAR

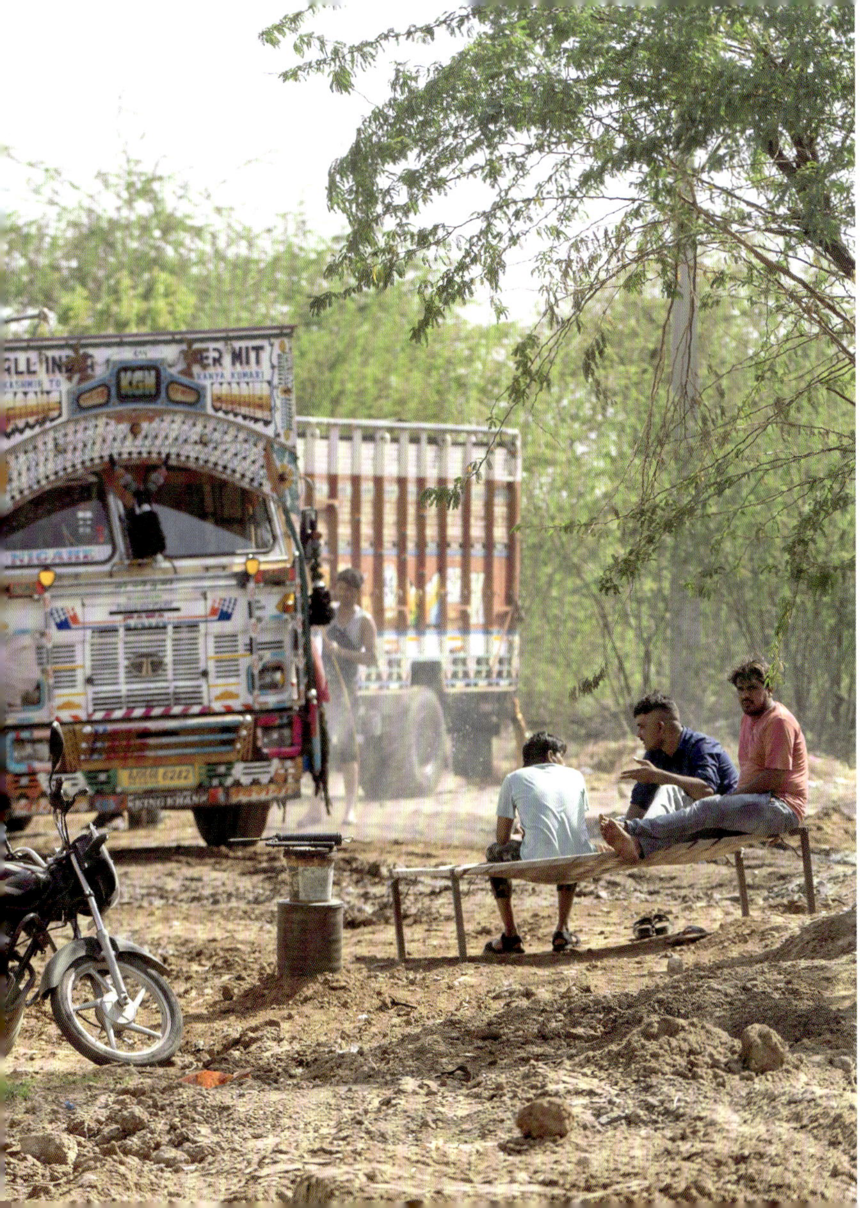

Jodhpur, INDIA   93

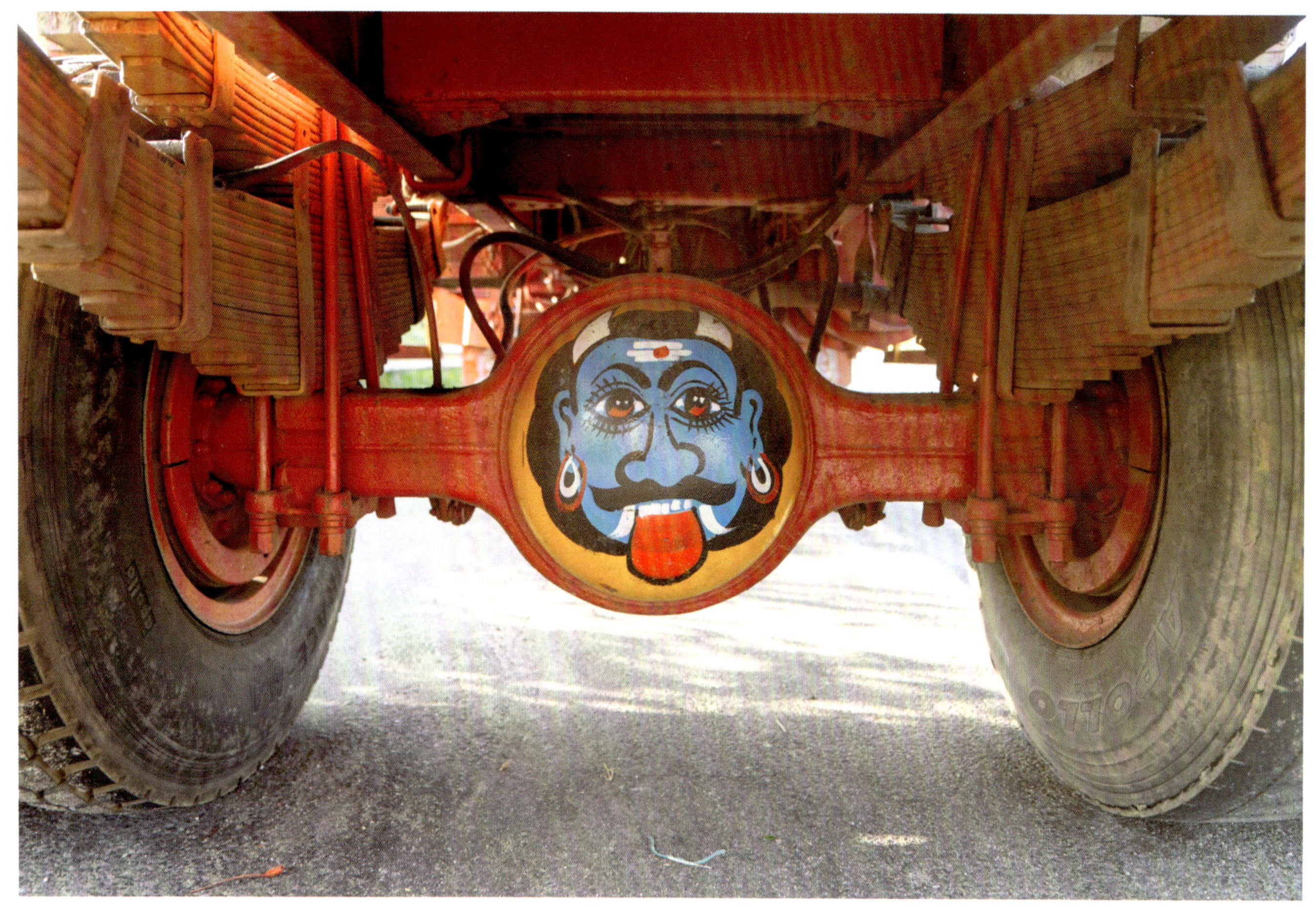

94   Jodhpur, INDIA

overleaf: Jodhpur, INDIA

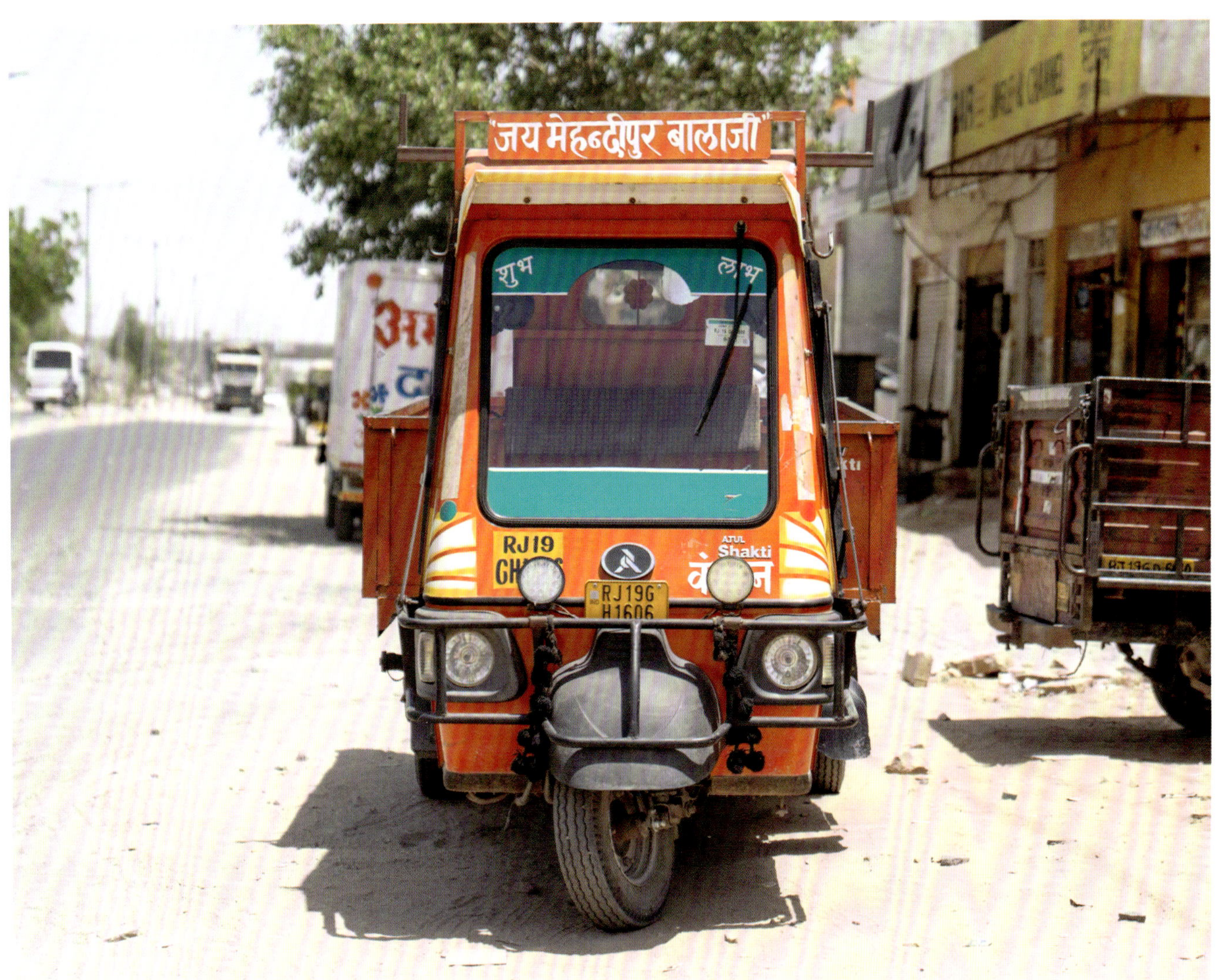
"जय मेहन्दीपुर बालाजी"
शुभ
लाभ
RJ19
GH
ATUL
Shakti
वेंजन
RJ19G
H1606

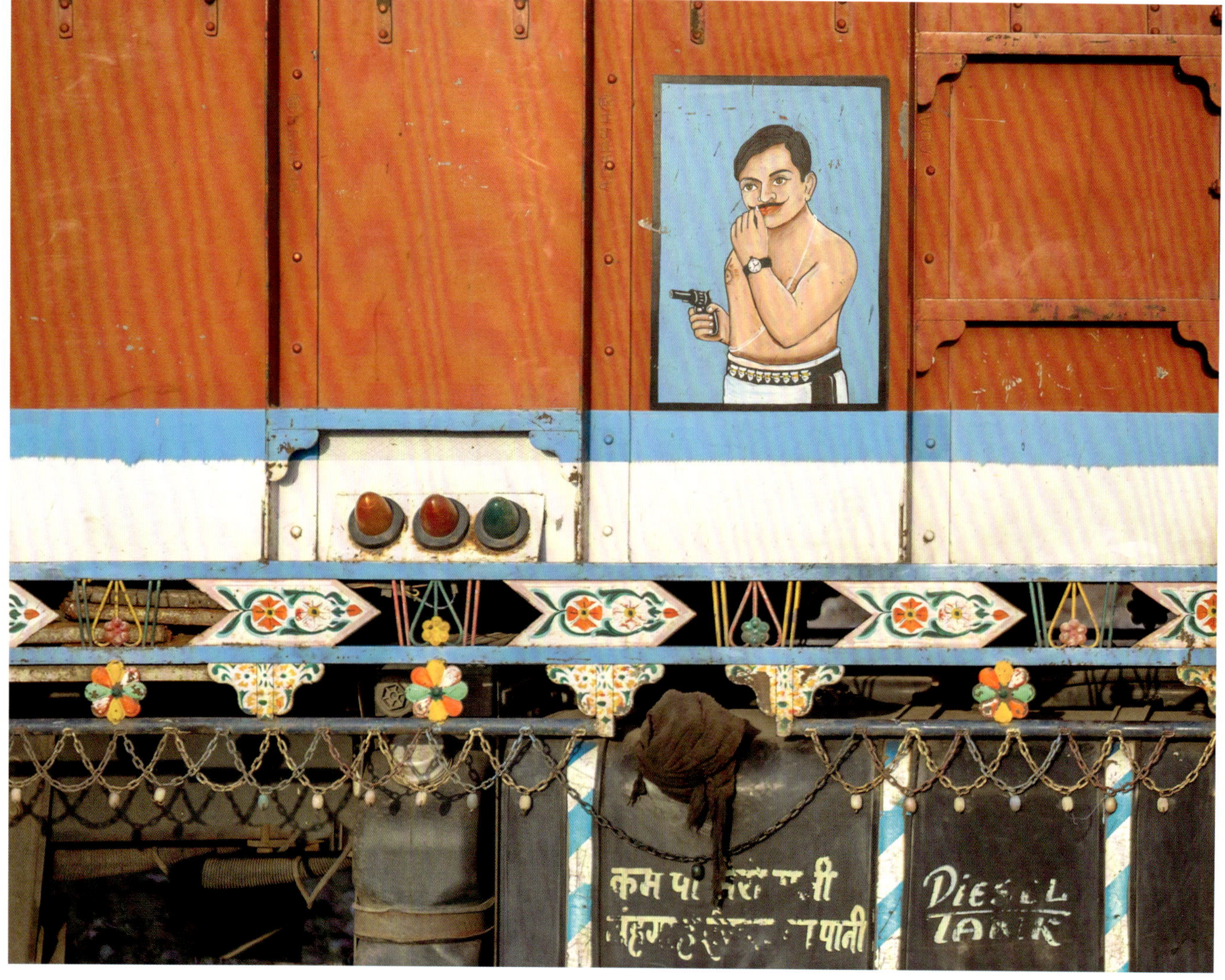

कम पा नी की
बहुत ... पानी
Diesel
TANK

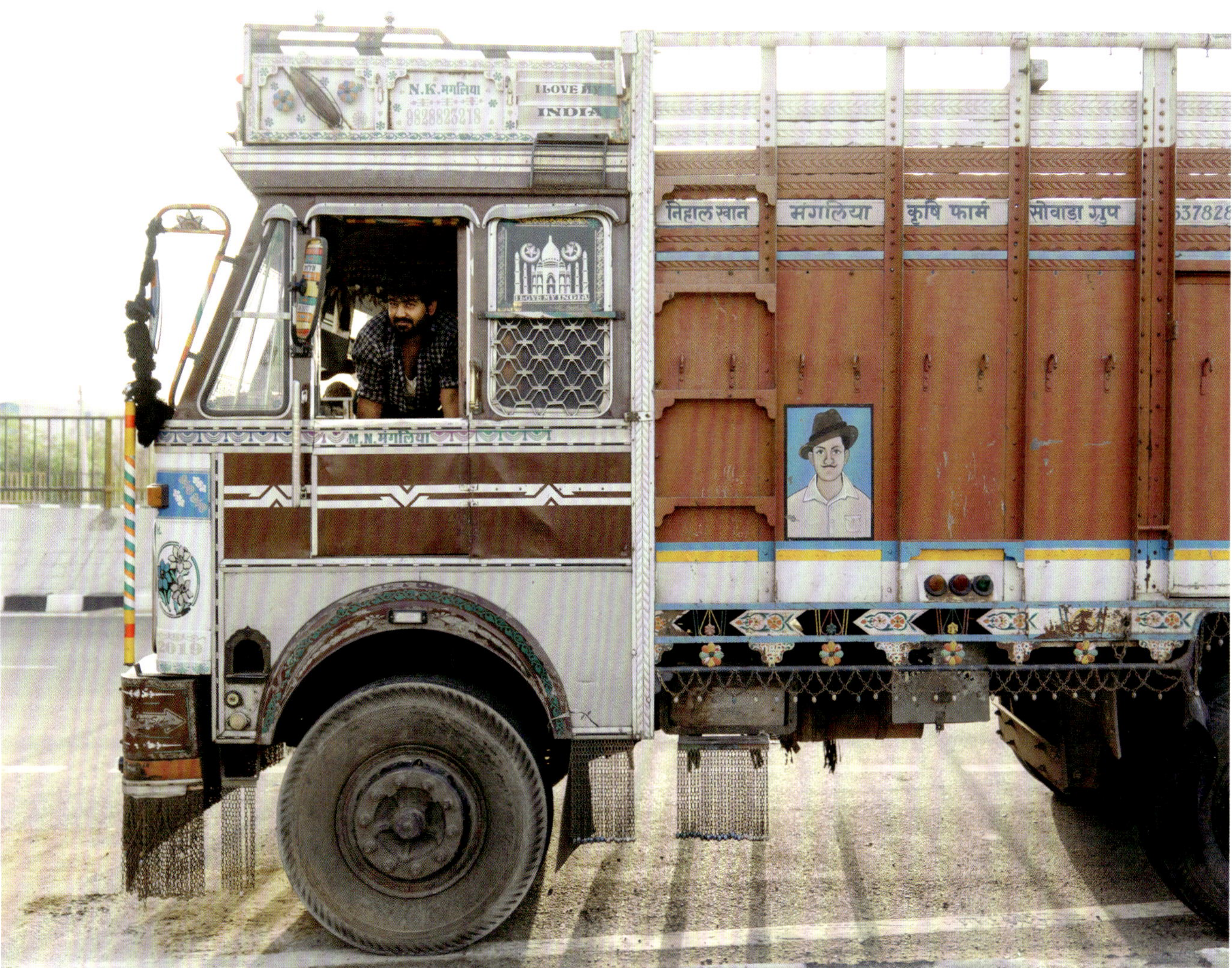
N.K. मगलिया
9828823218
I LOVE MY
INDIA
M.N. मगलिया
निहाल खान   मंगलिया   कृषि फार्म   सीवाड़ा ग्रुप
2019

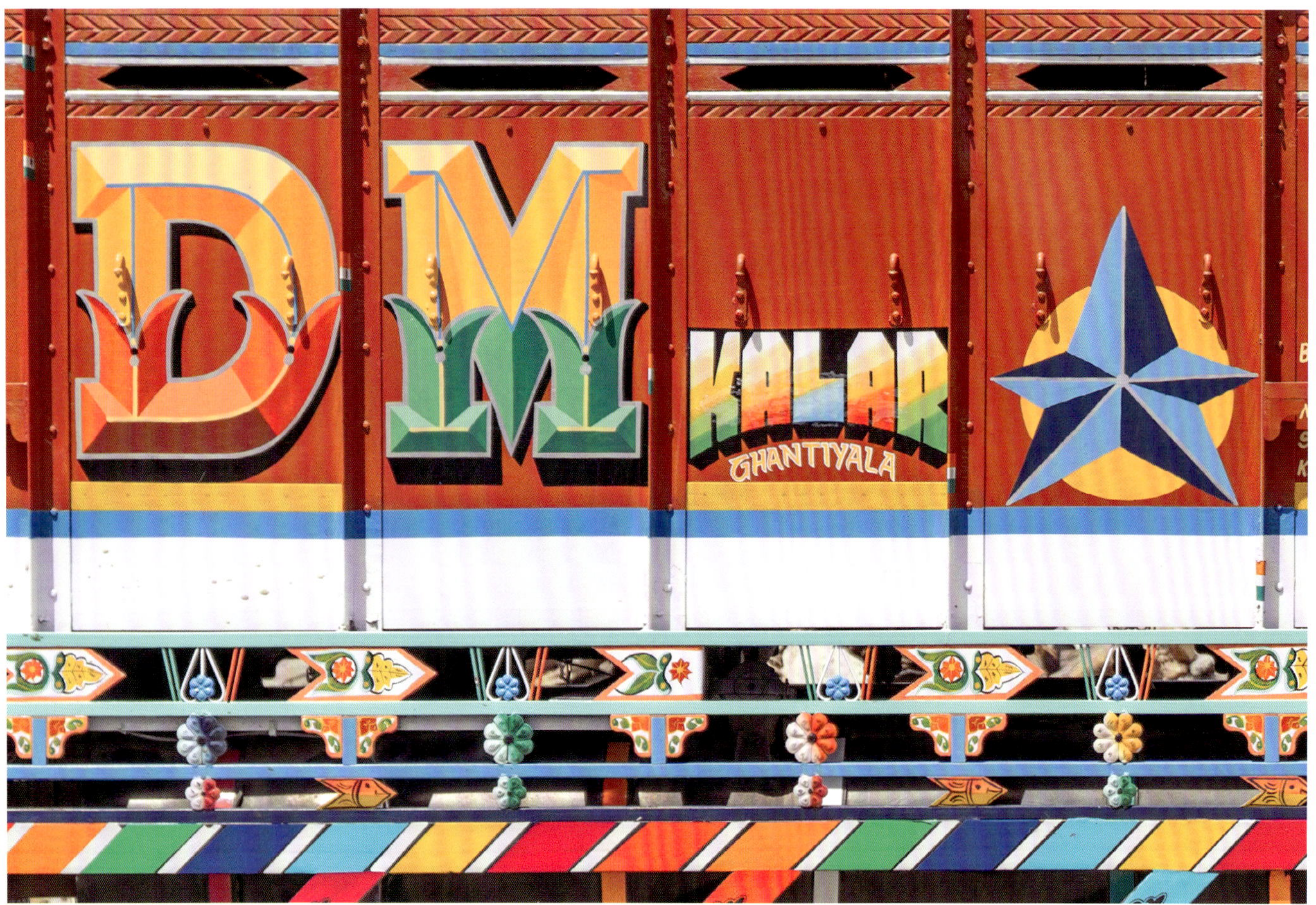

KALAR
GHANTIYALA

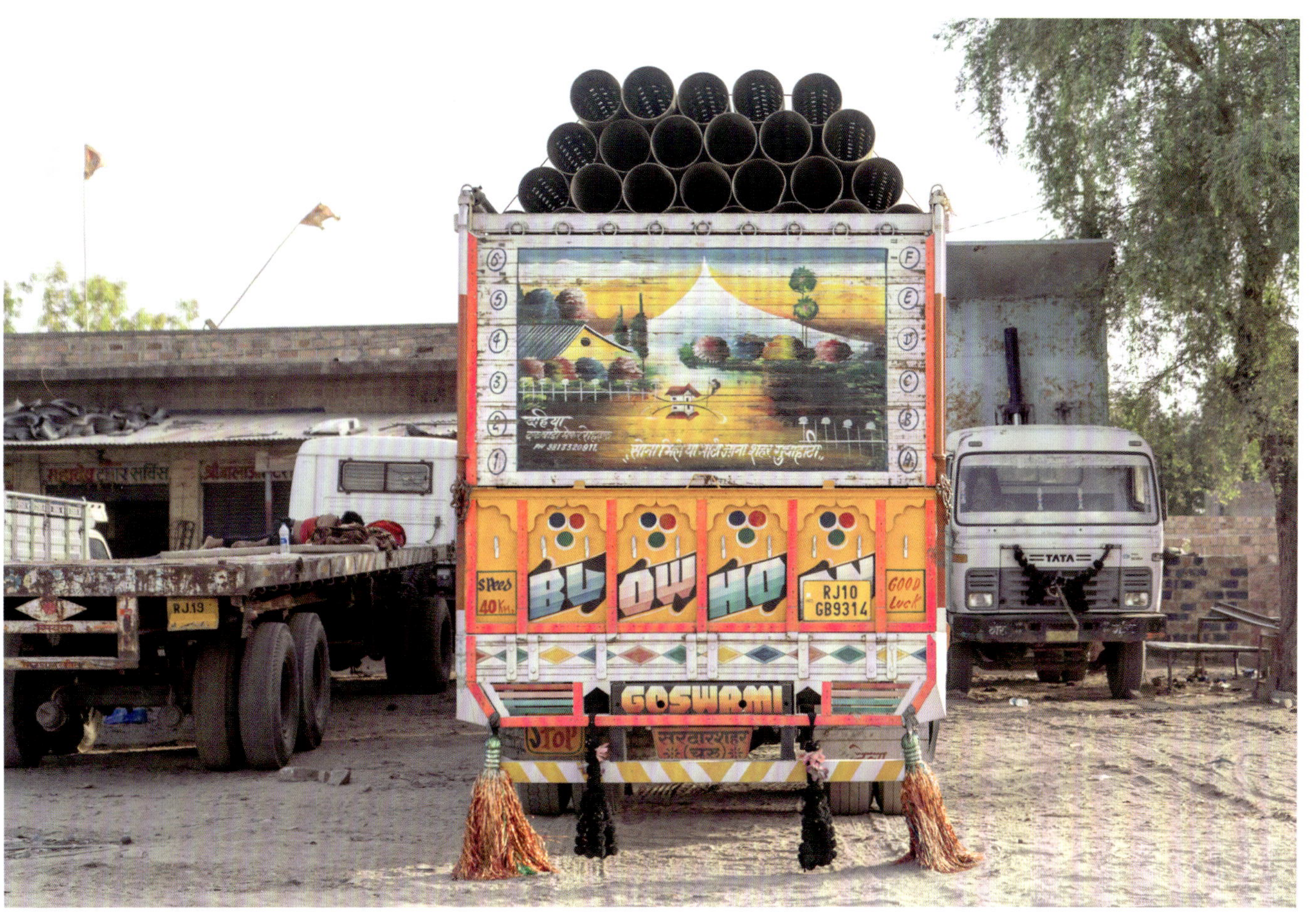

Jodhpur, INDIA 99

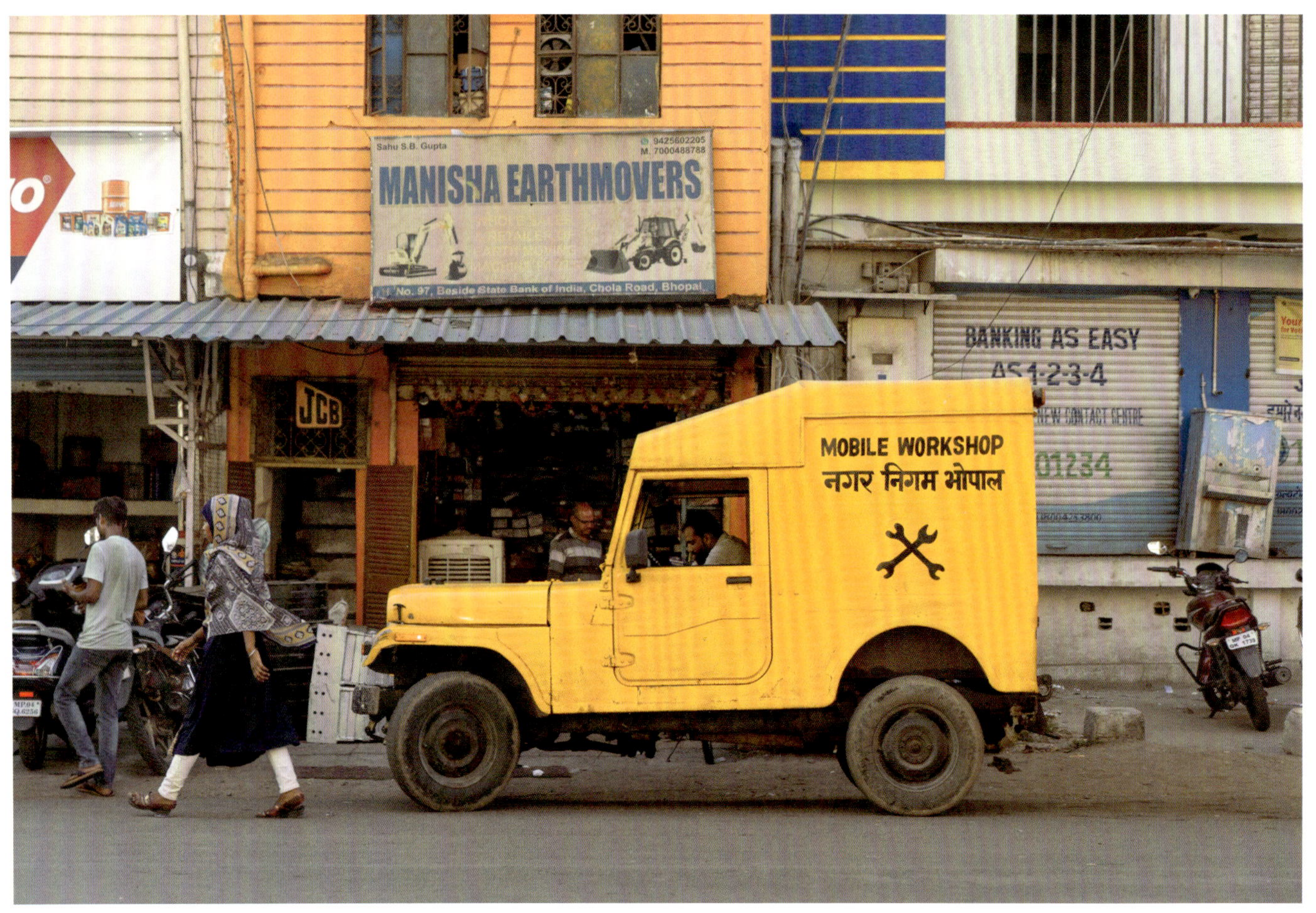

overleaf: Jodhpur, INDIA

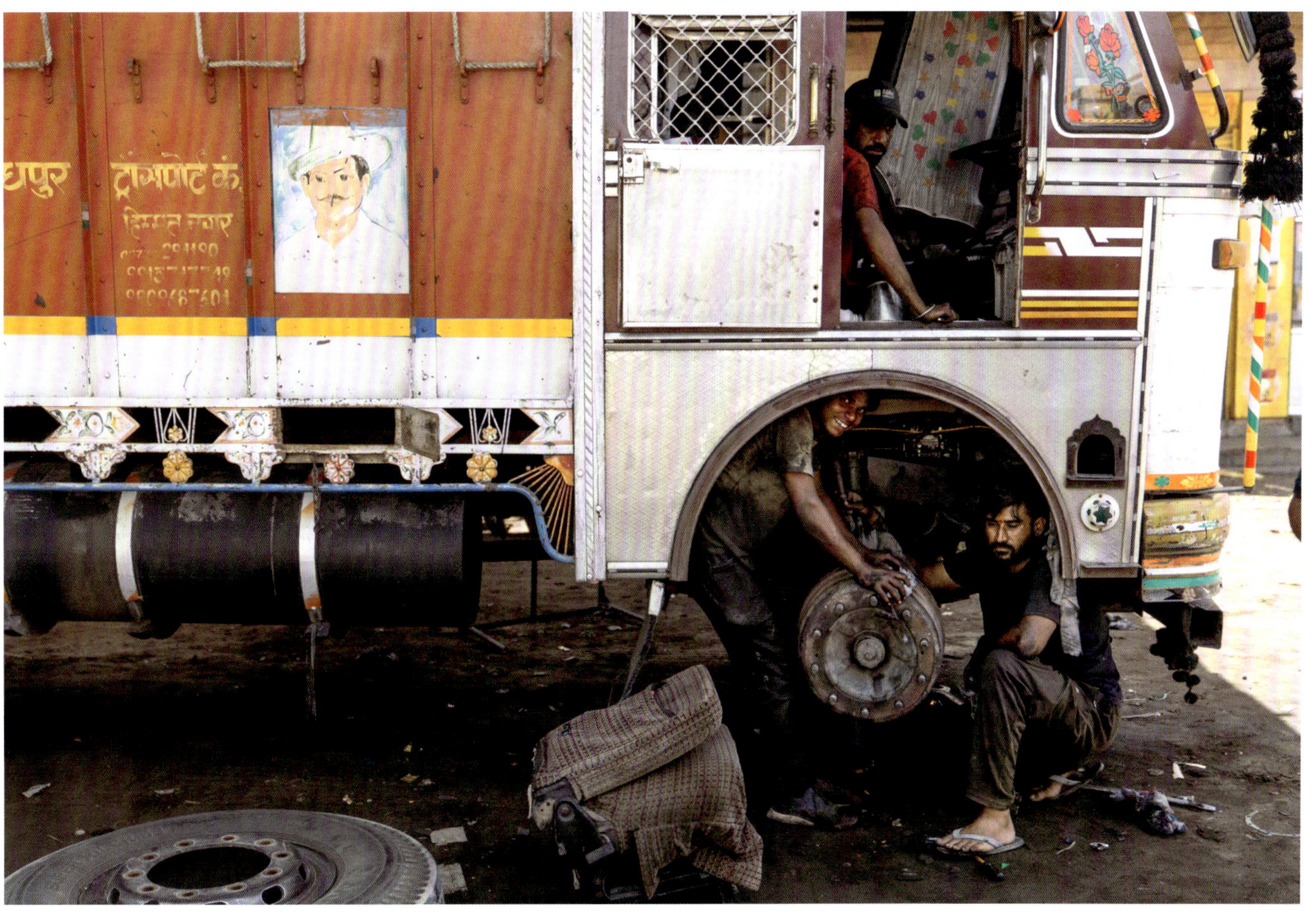

धपुर   ट्रांसपोर्ट कं.
हिरण नगर

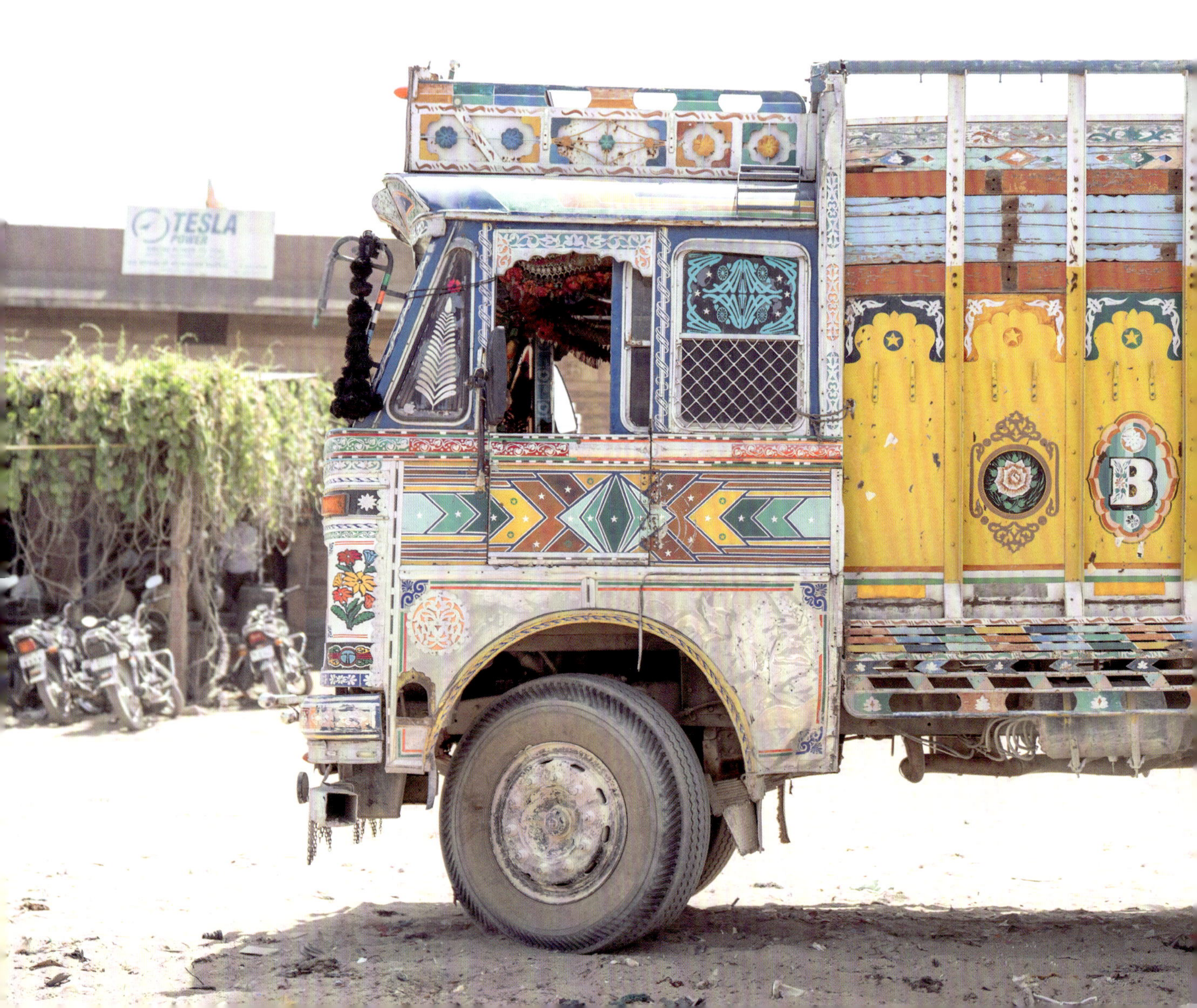
TESLA
POWER
B

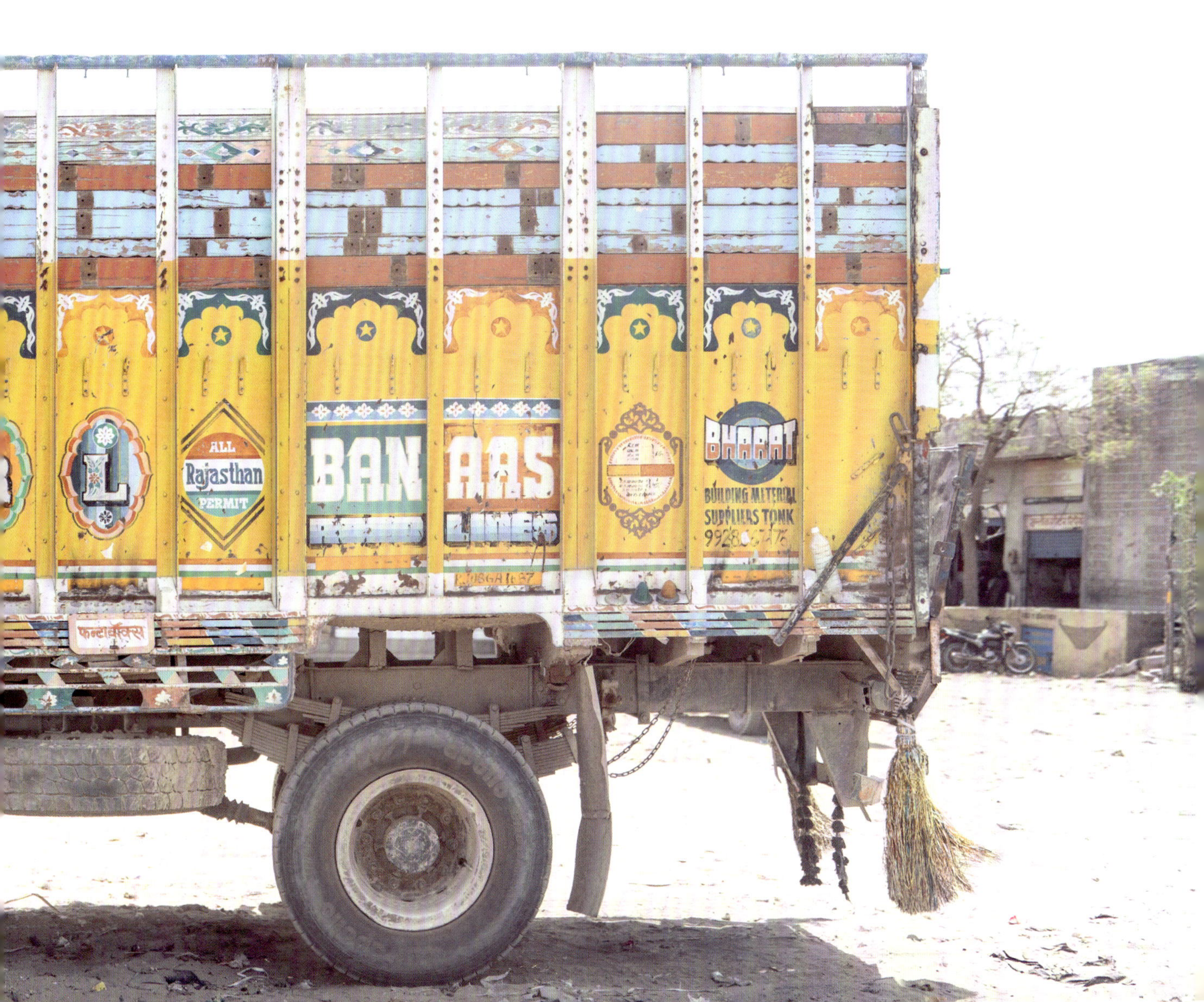
L
ALL
Rajasthan
PERMIT
BAN
AAS
BHARAT
BUILDING MATERIAL
SUPPLIERS TONK
9928067476

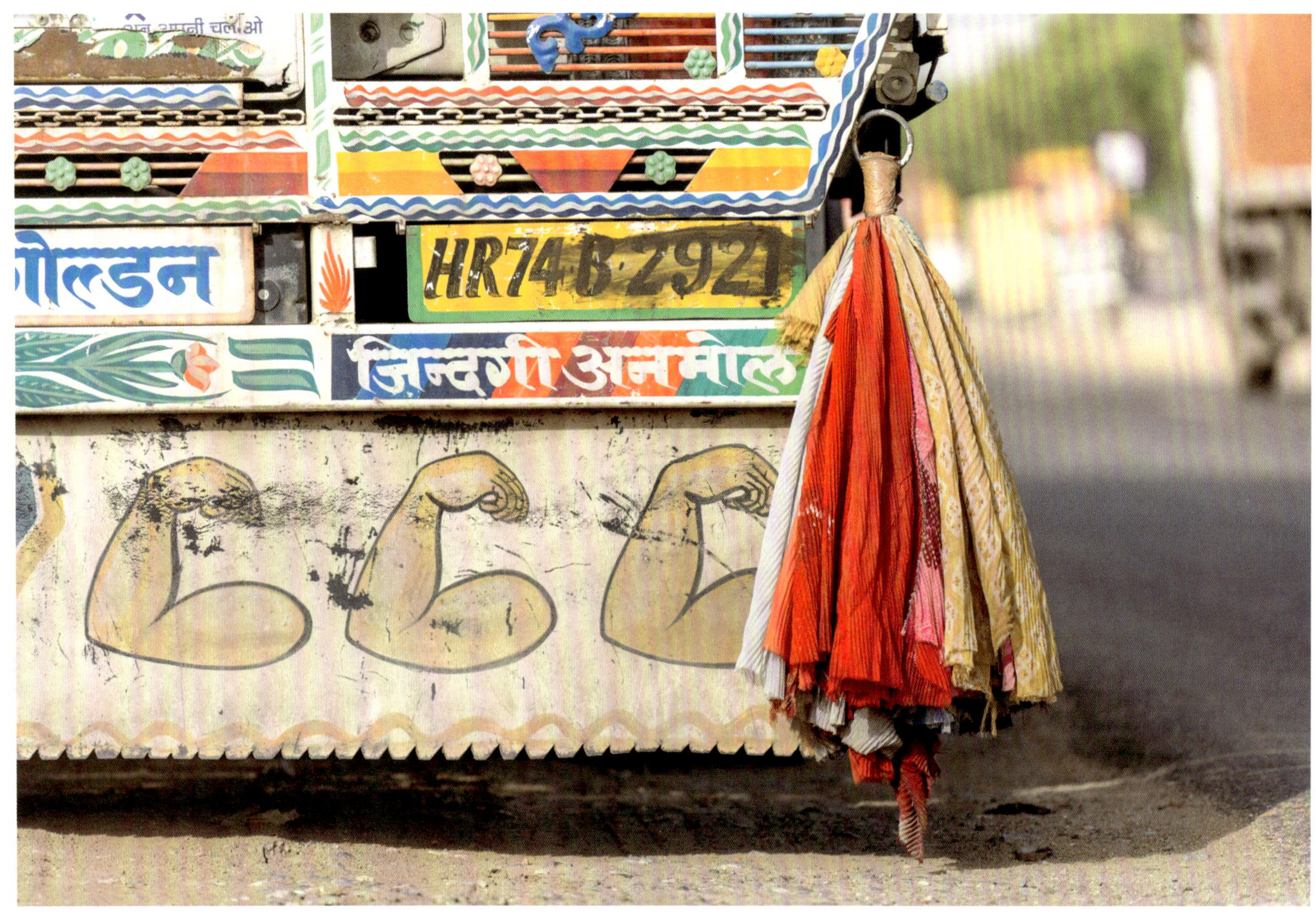

Indore, INDIA

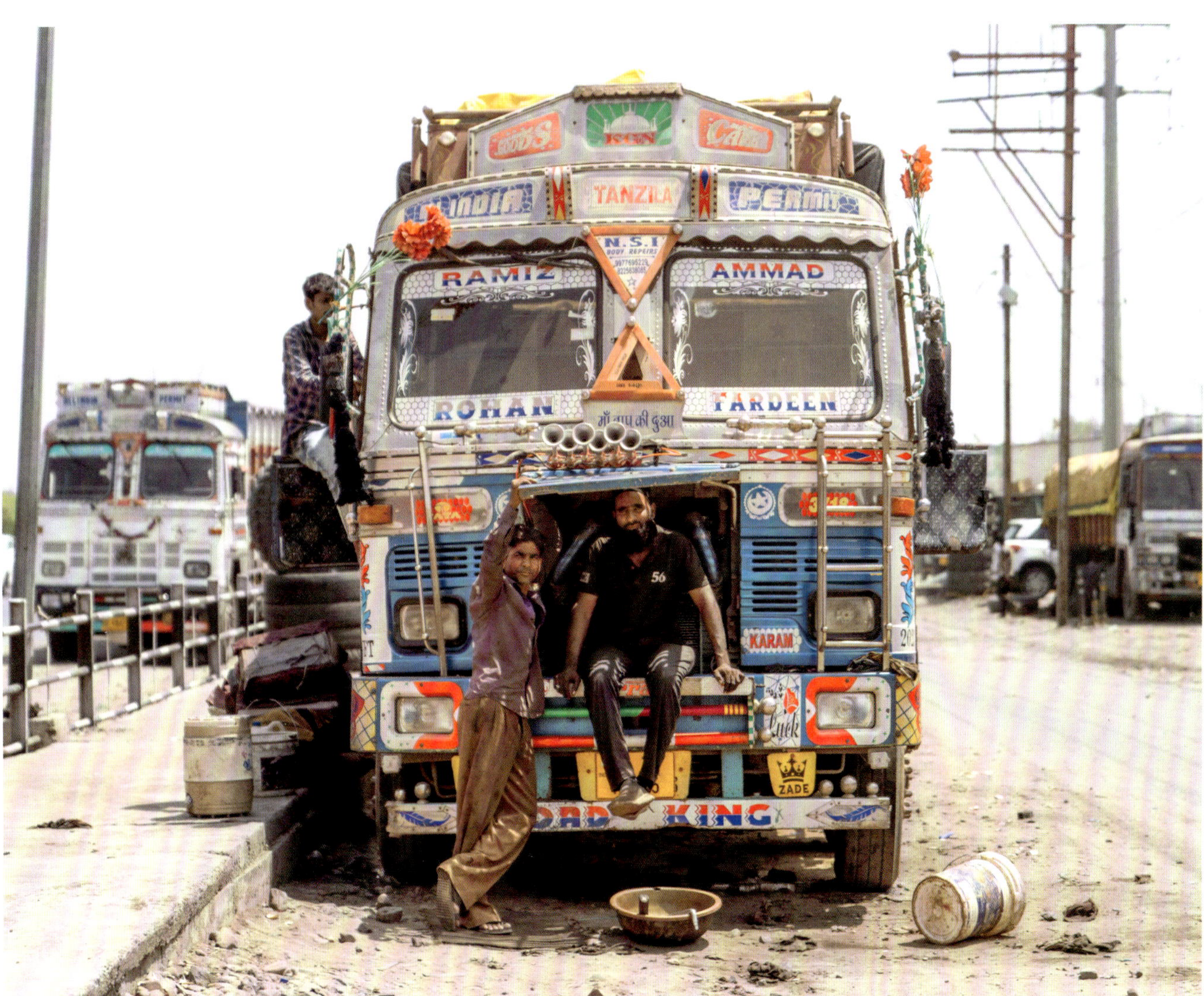
ISGN
TANZILA
INDIA
PERMIT
N.S.I
BODY REPAIRS
RAMIZ
AMMAD
ROHAN
FARDEEN
KARAM
ZADE
KING
PERMIT

PAKISTAN

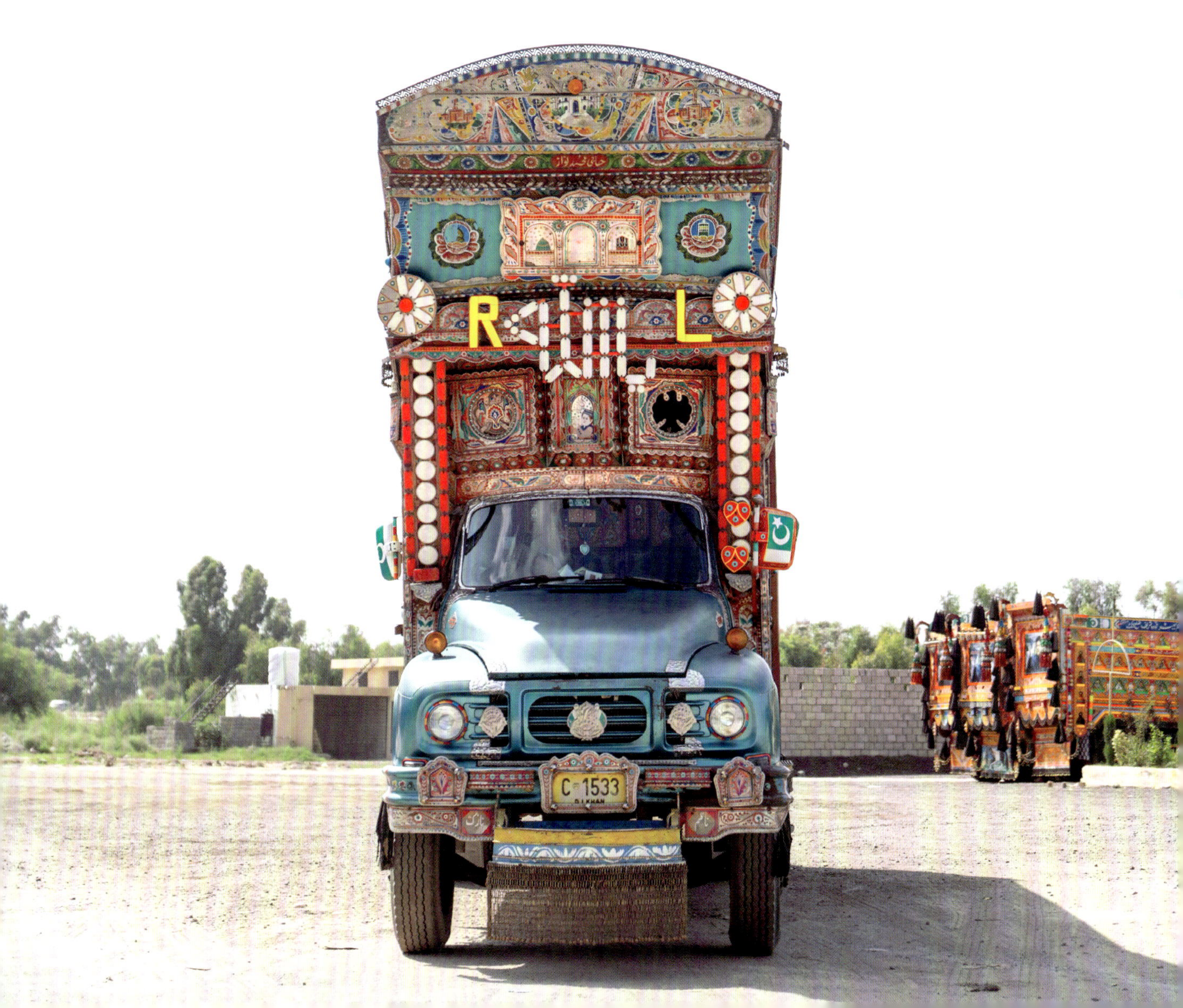

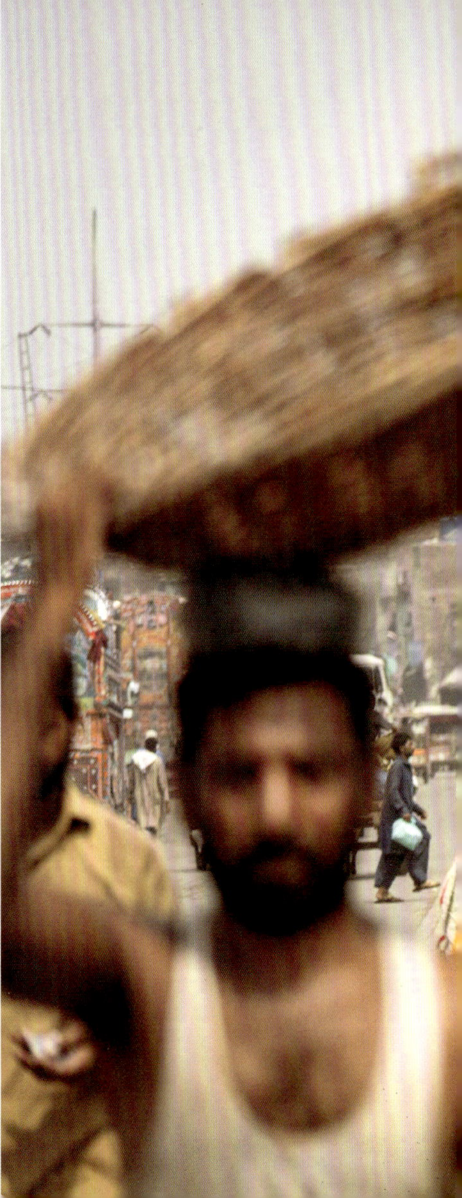

108   Lahore, PAKISTAN

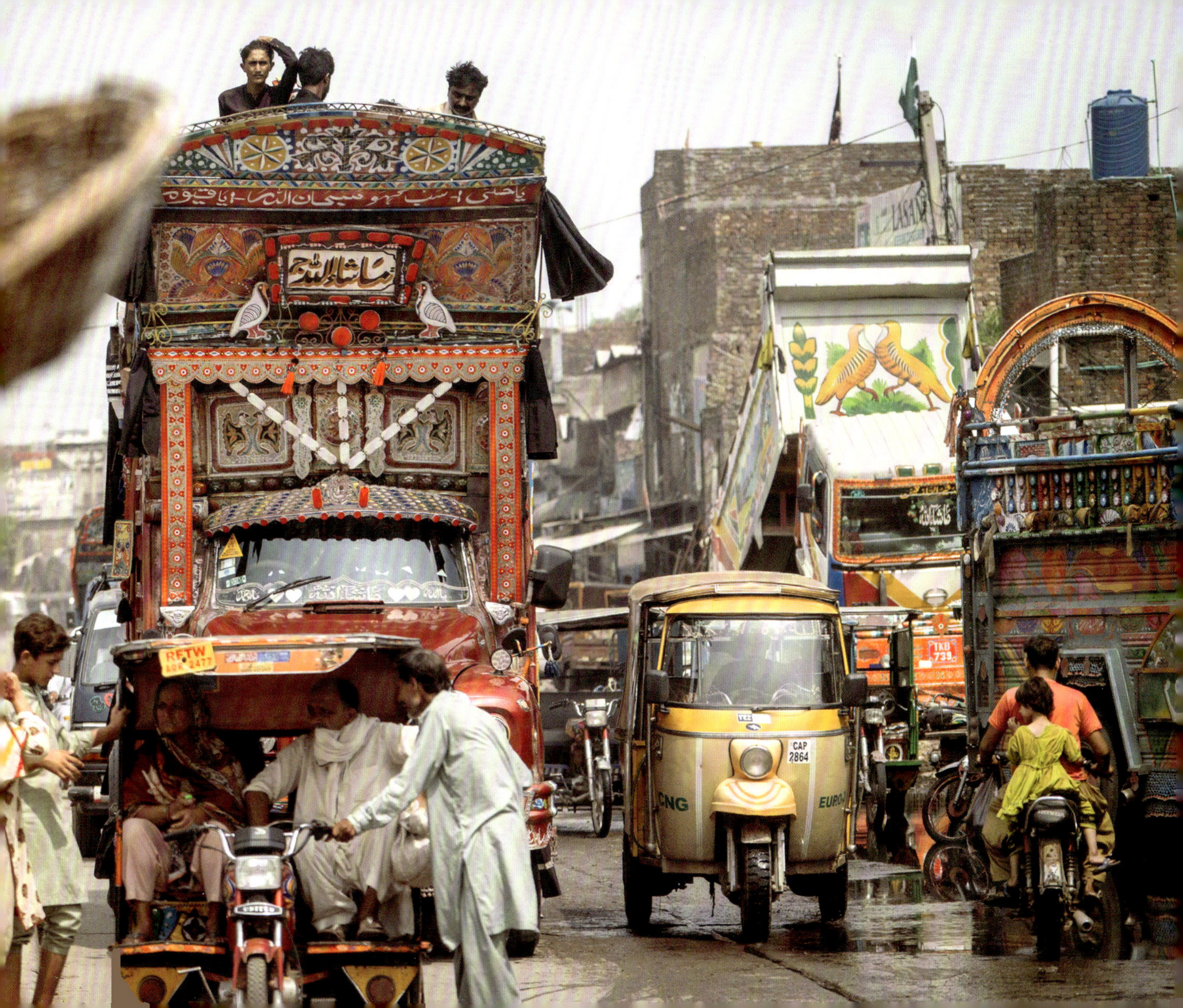

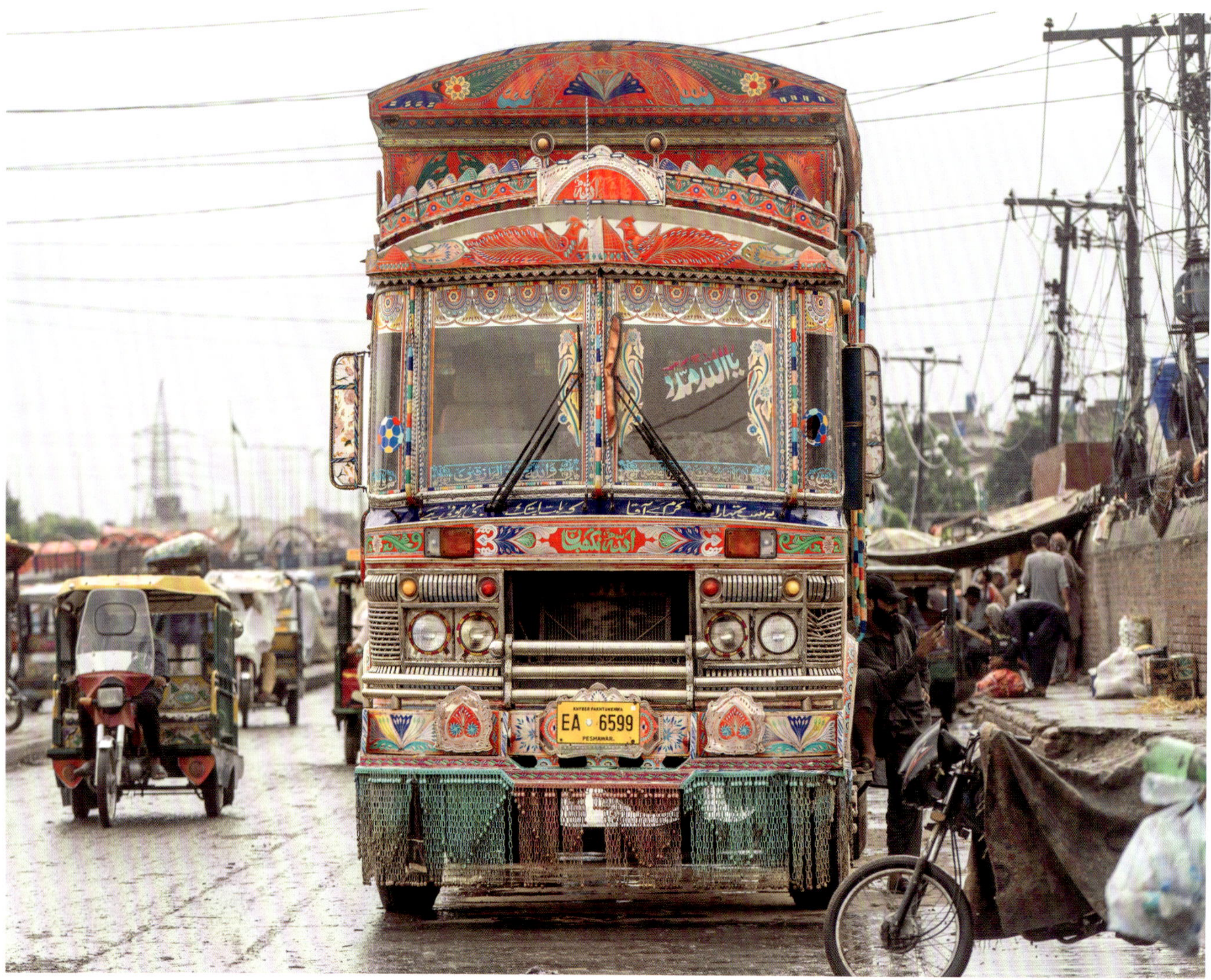

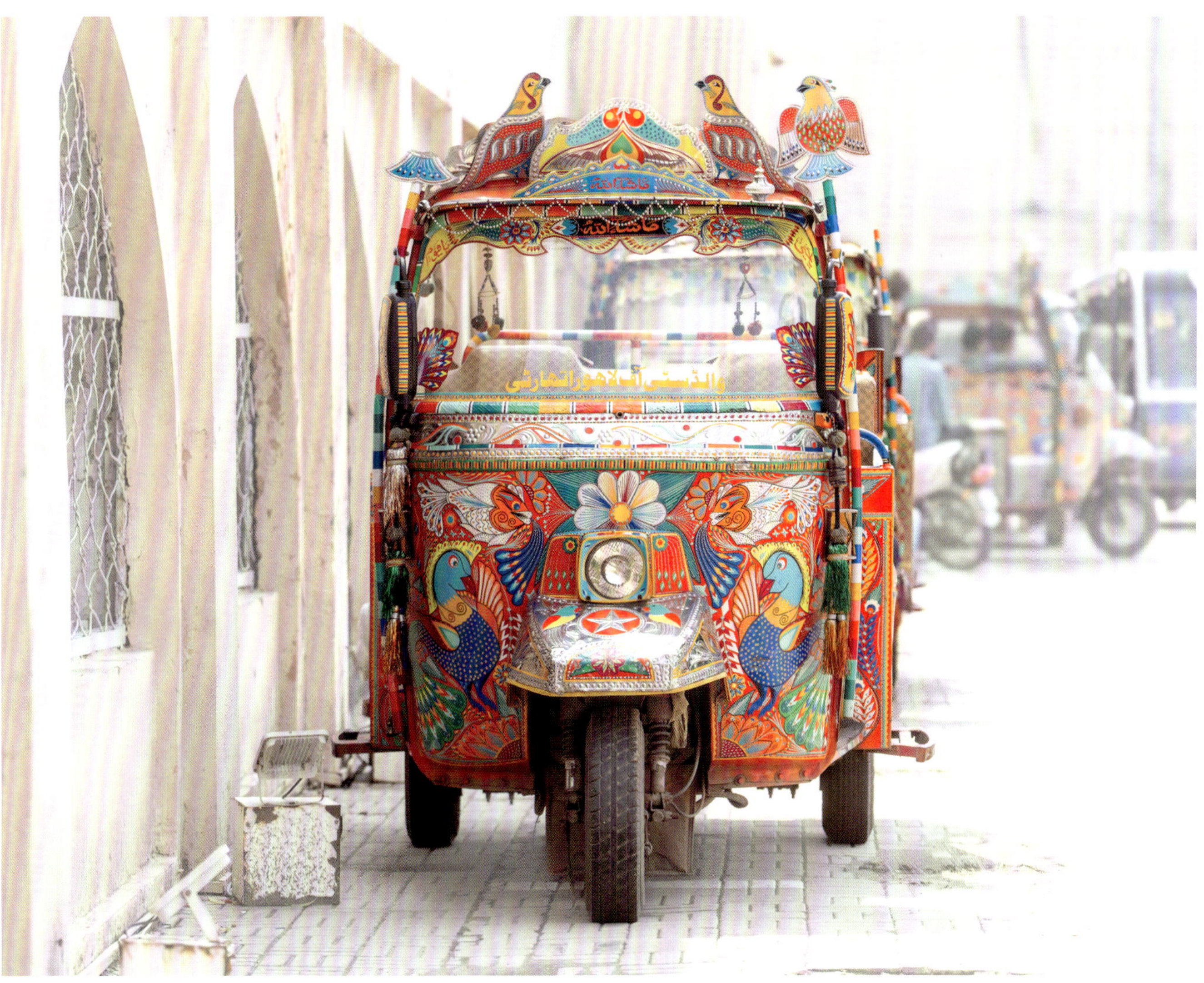

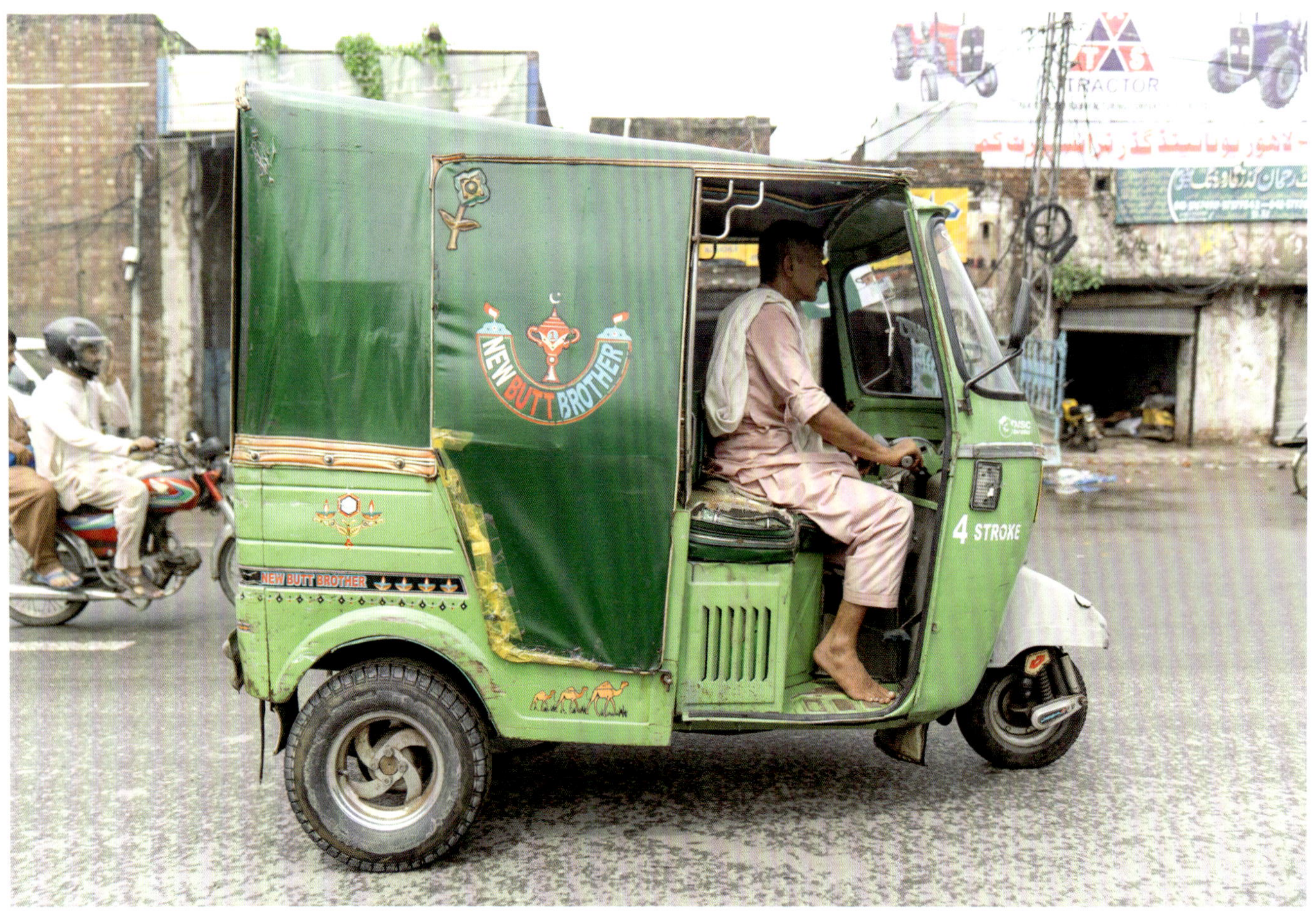

112   Lahore, PAKISTAN

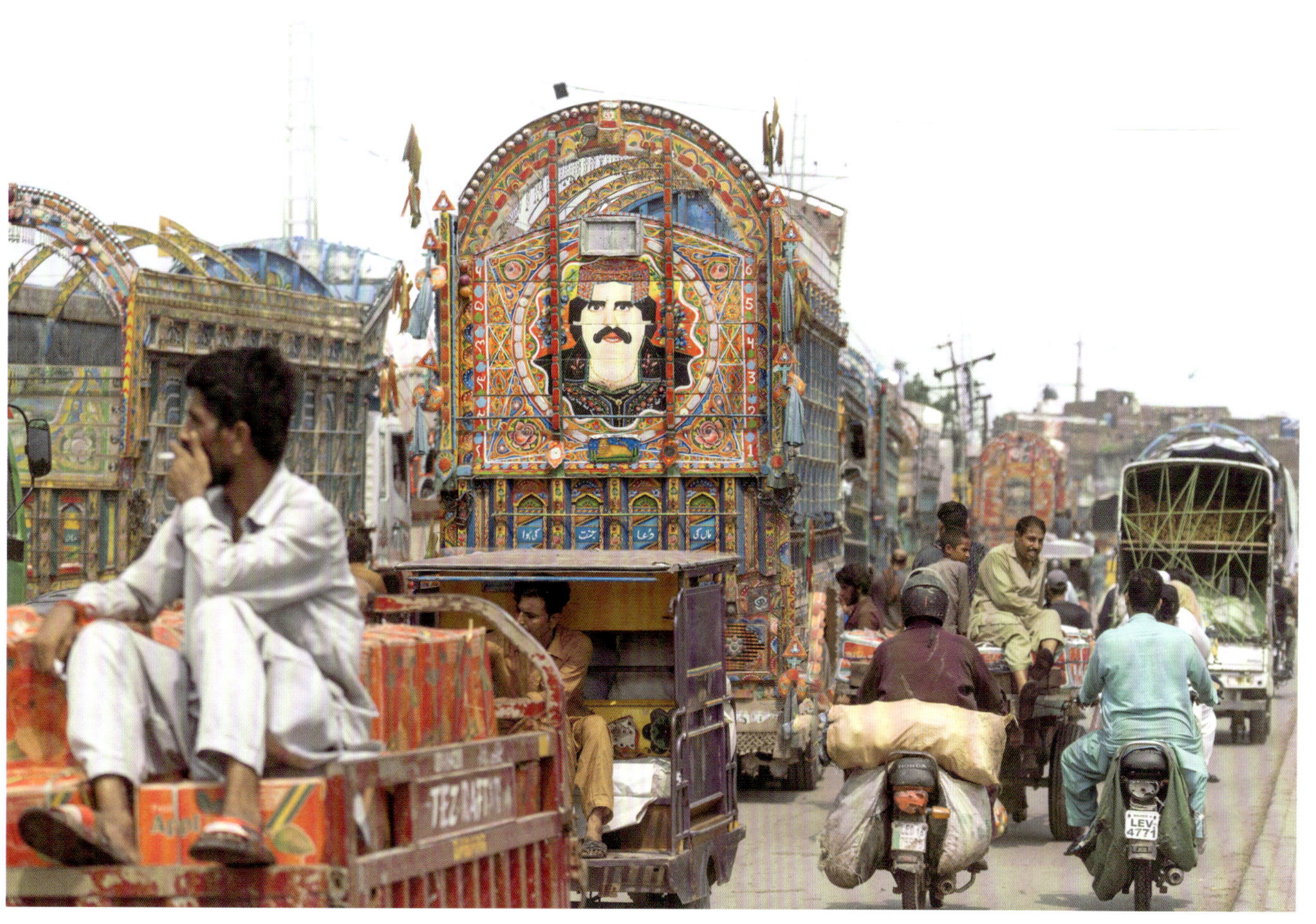

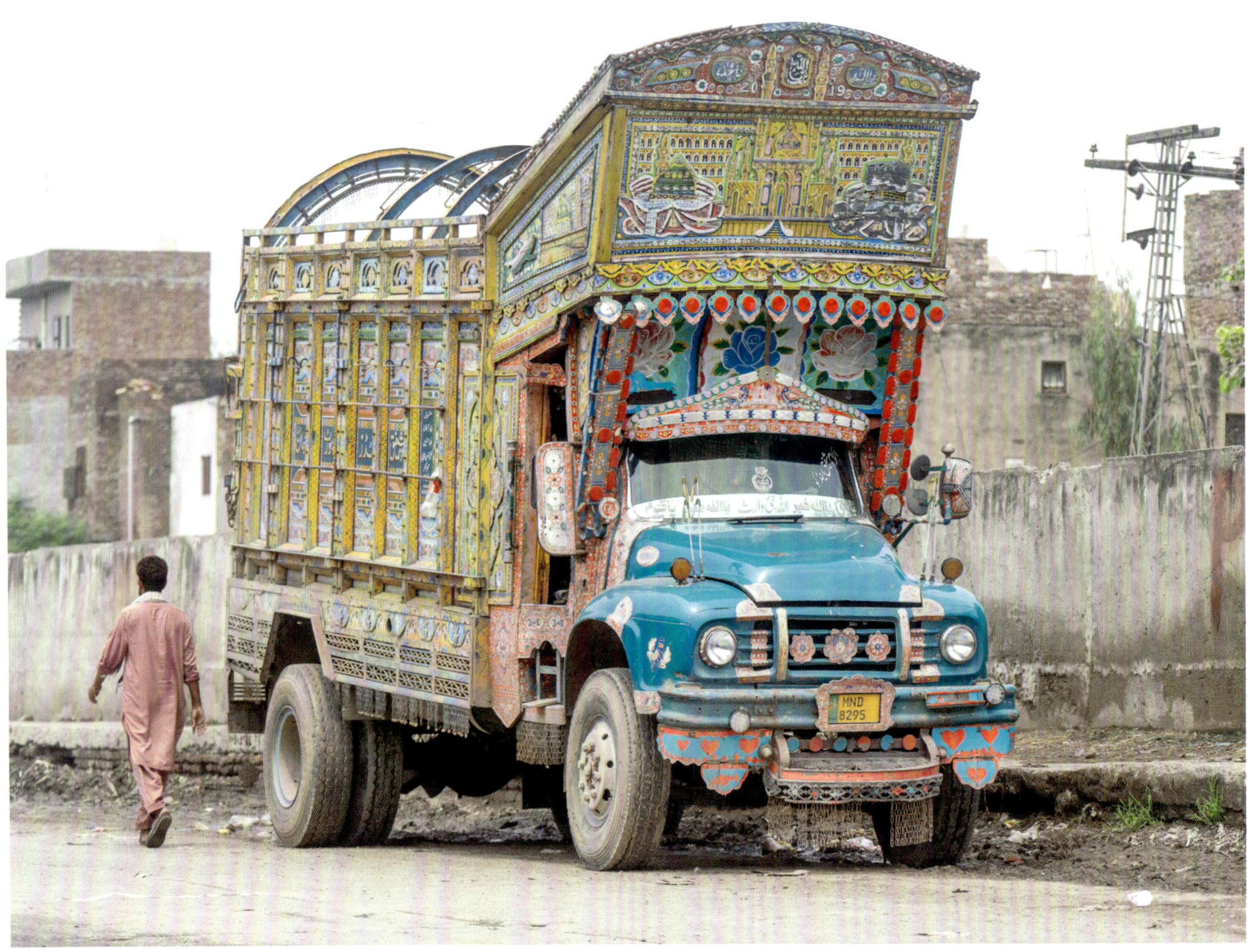

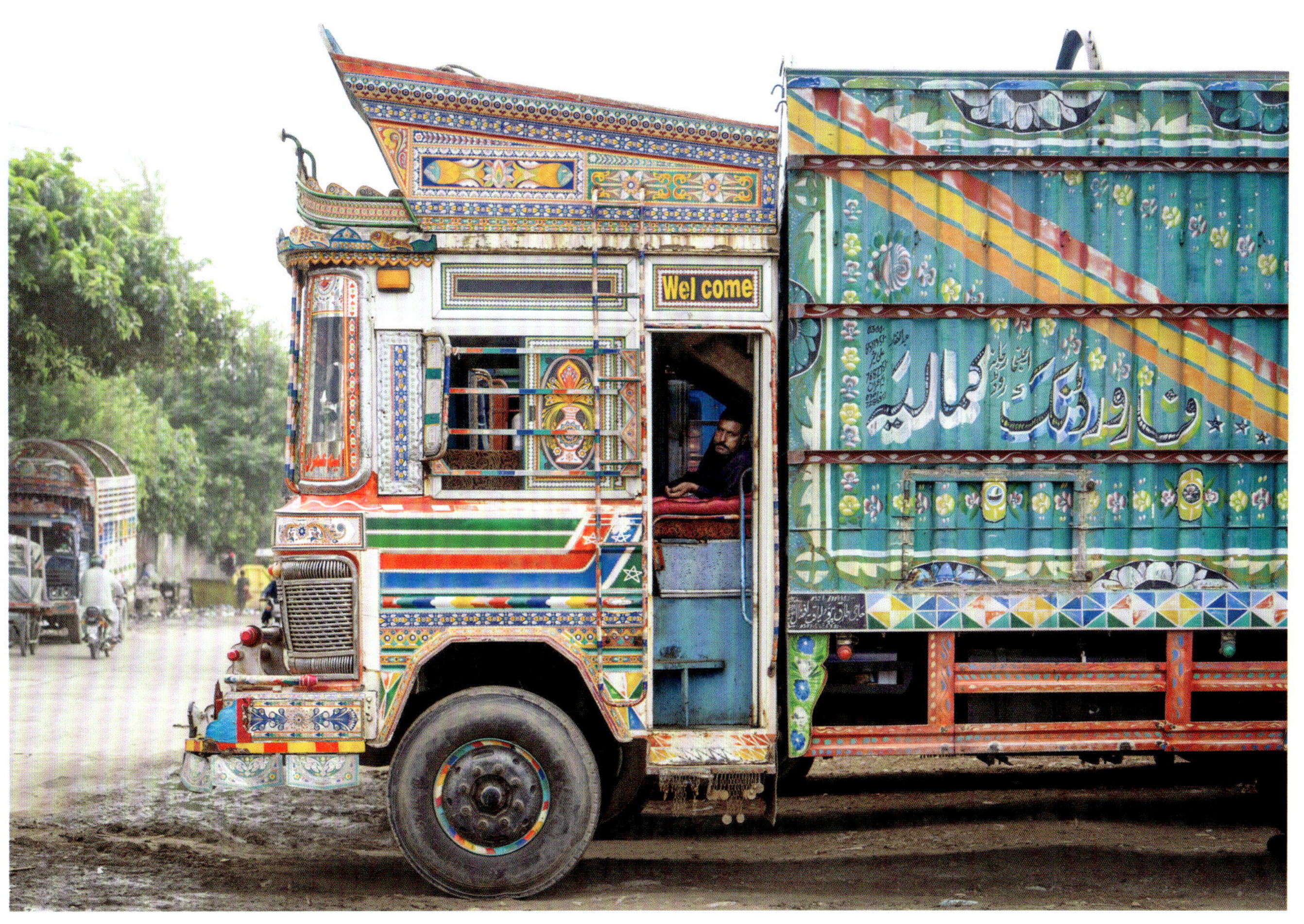

Wel come

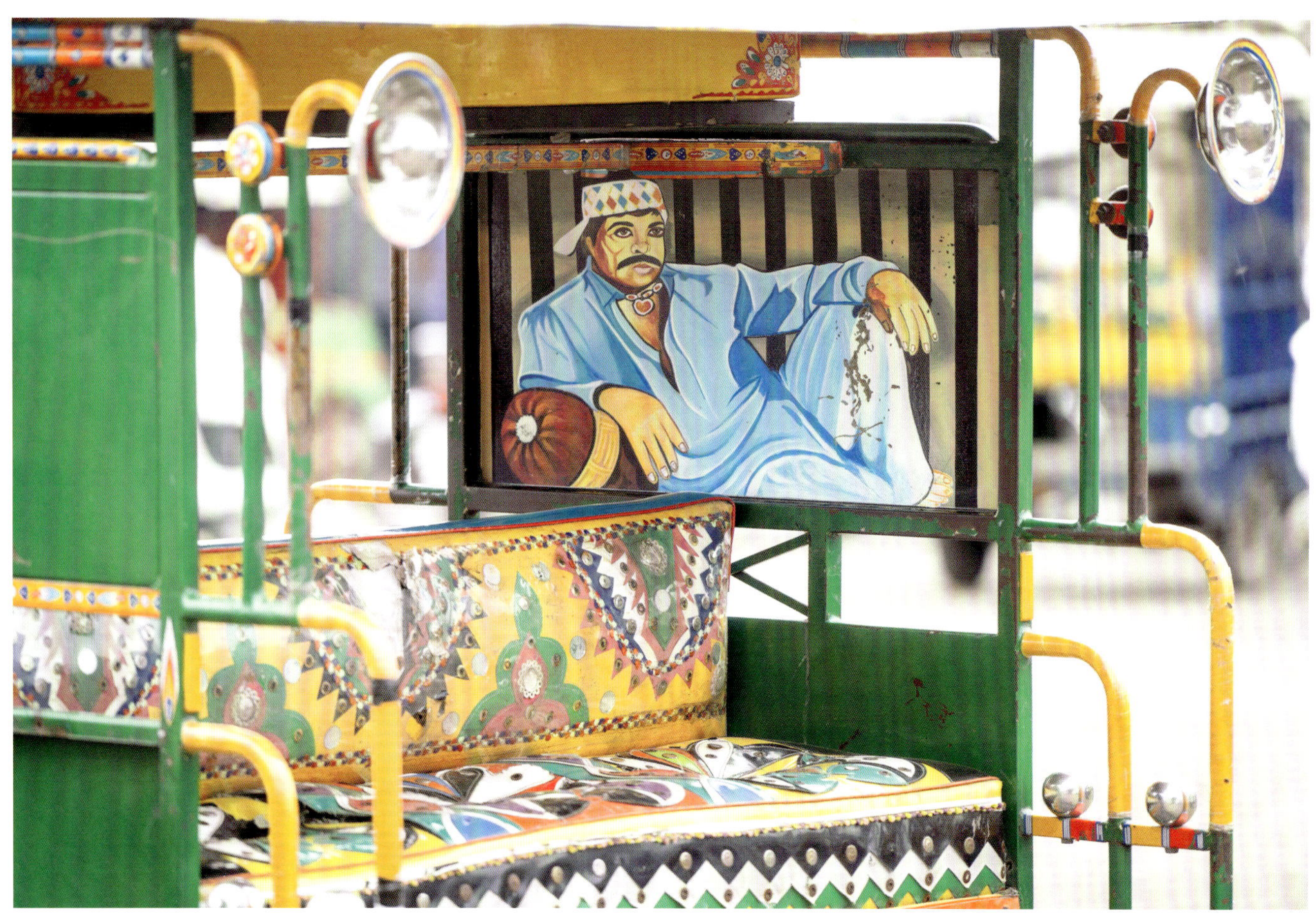

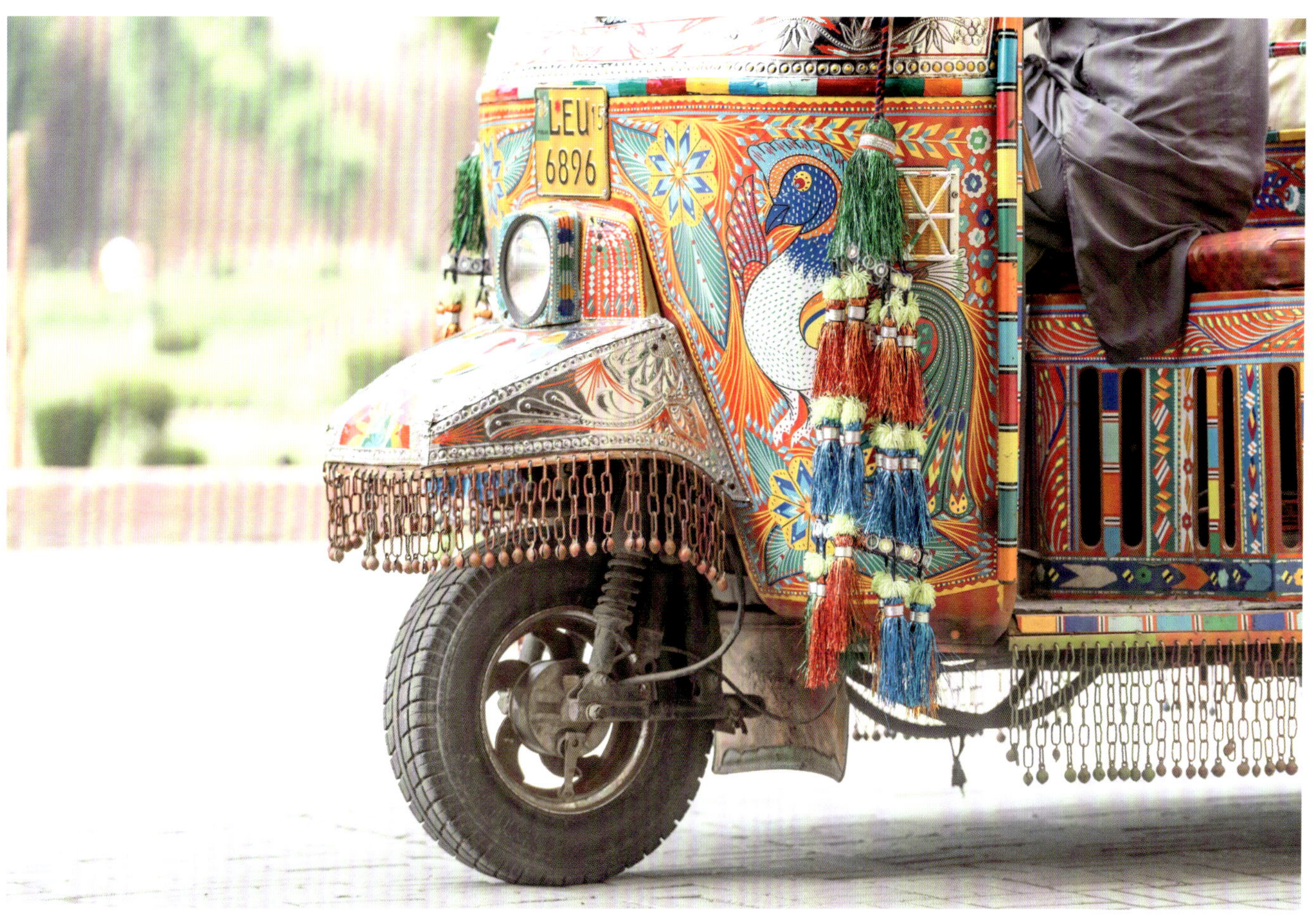

Lahore, PAKISTAN   117

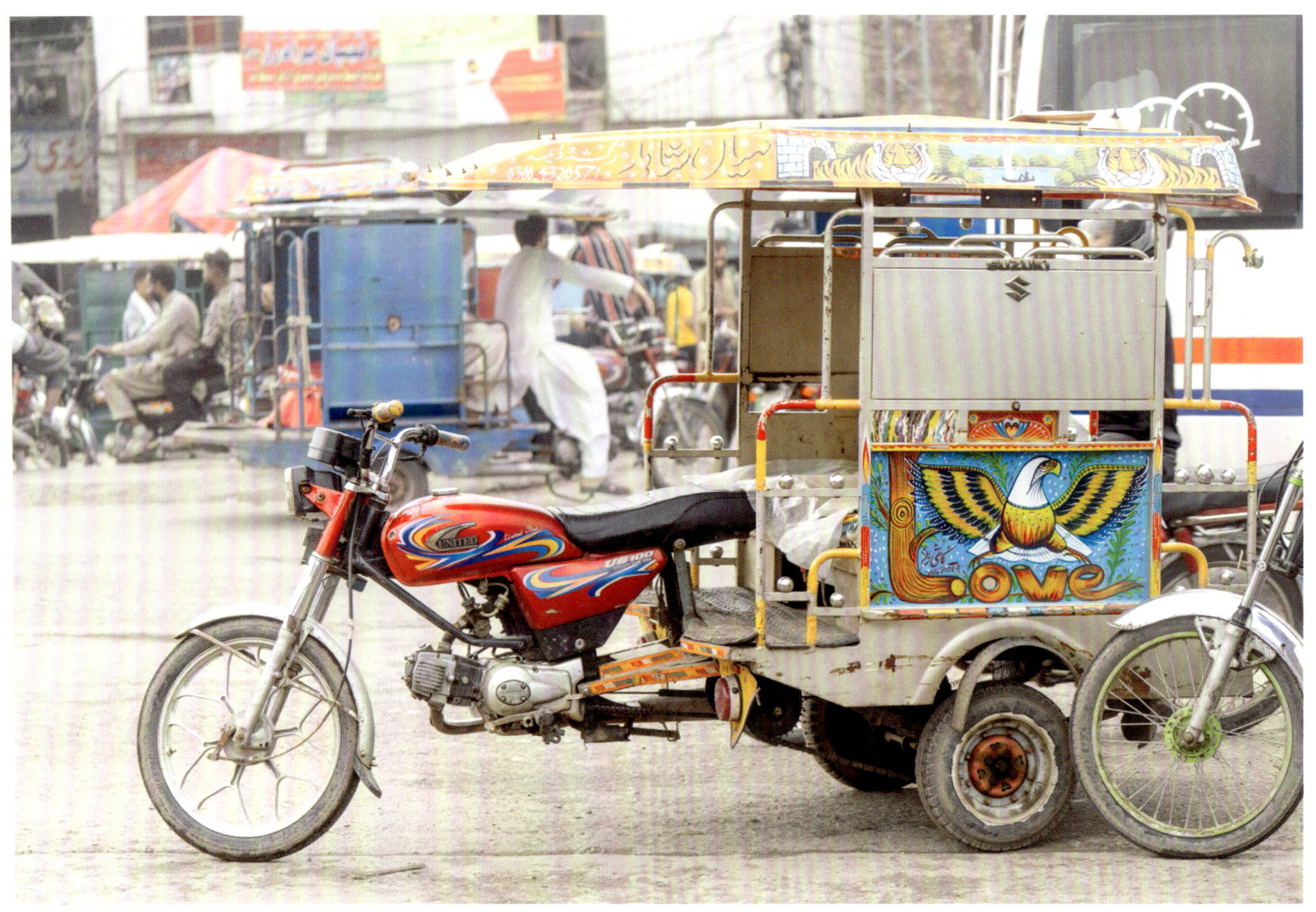

0300 4320571
SUZUKI
Love

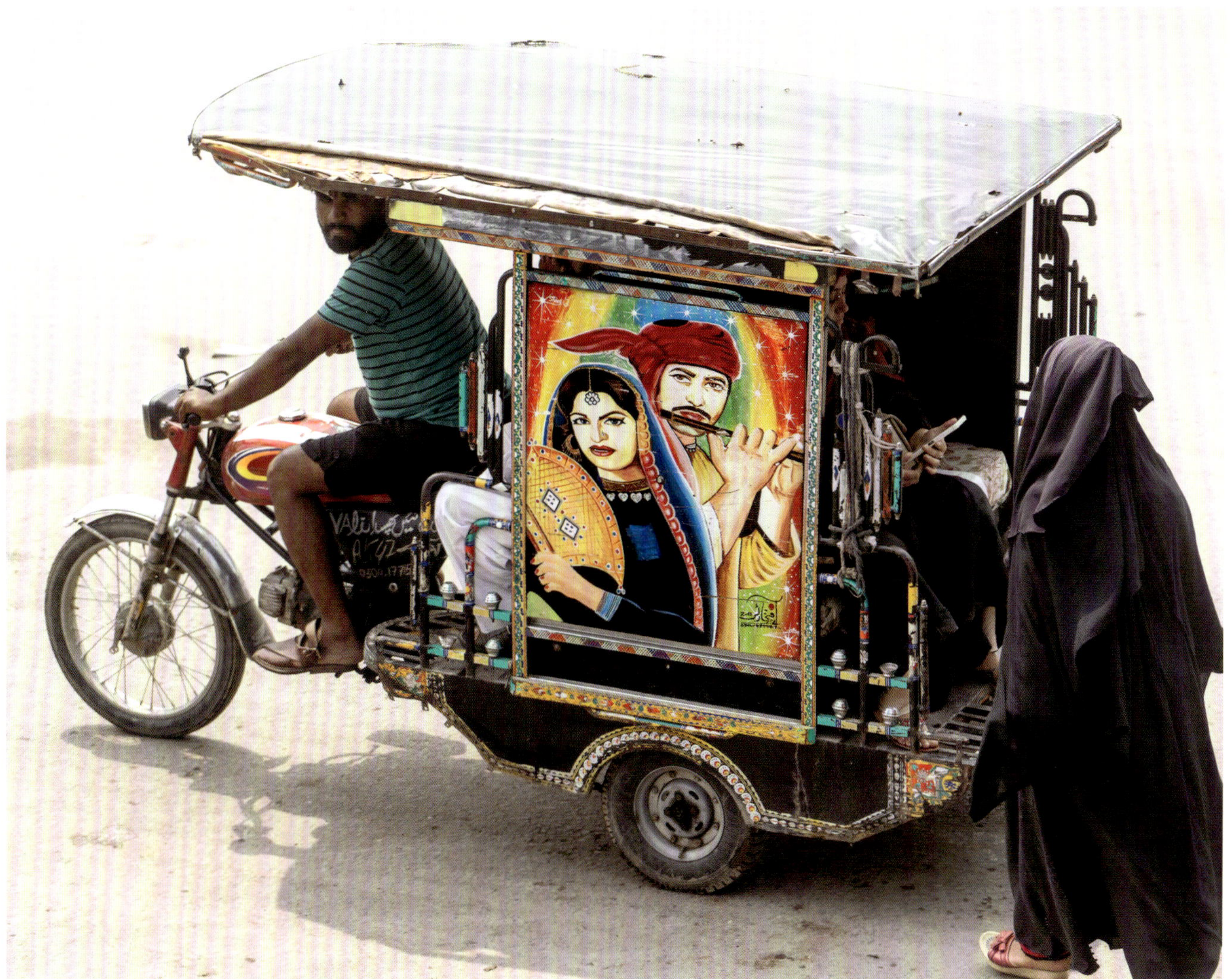

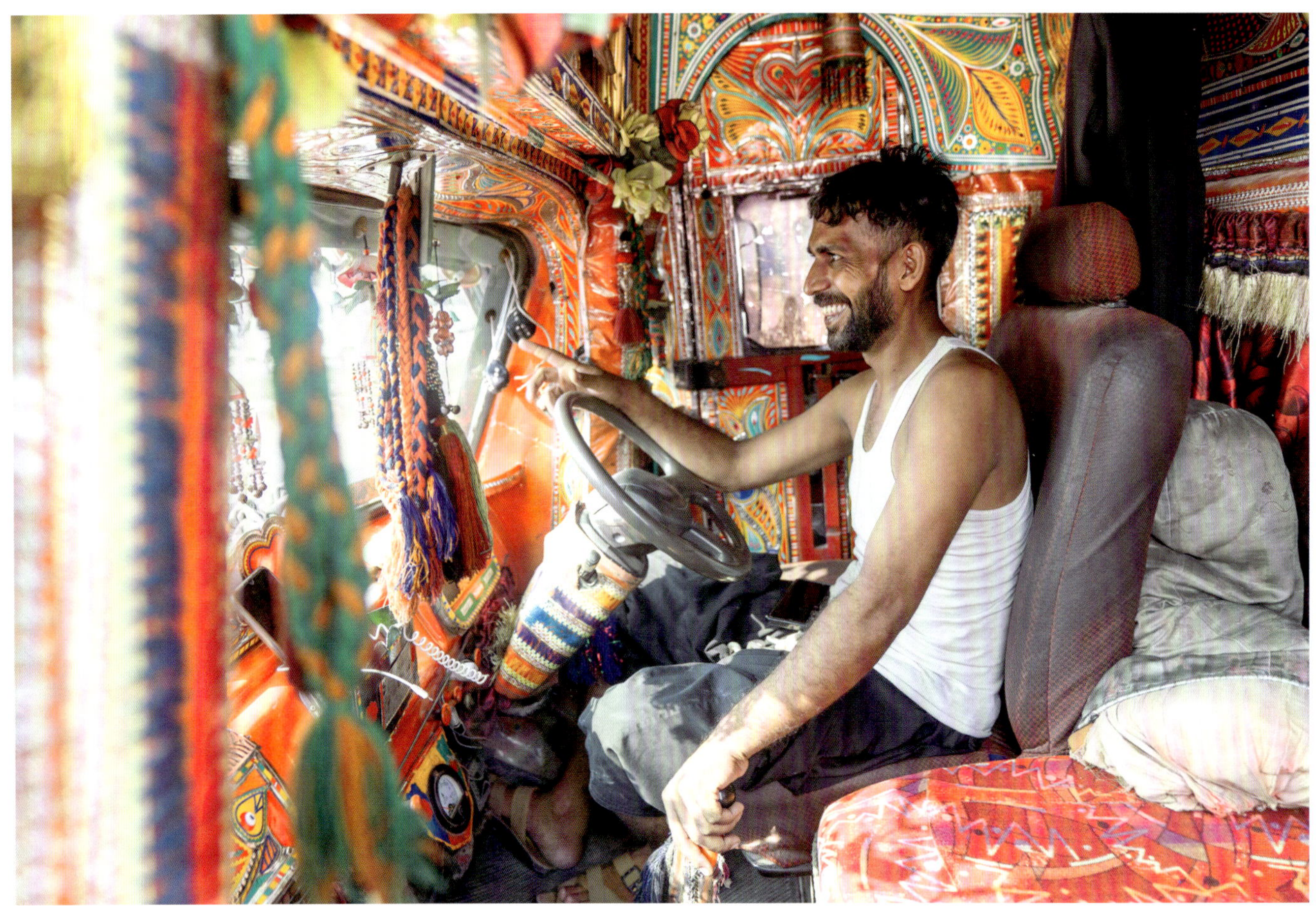

 Rawalpindi, PAKISTAN

overleaf: Gujranwala, PAKISTAN

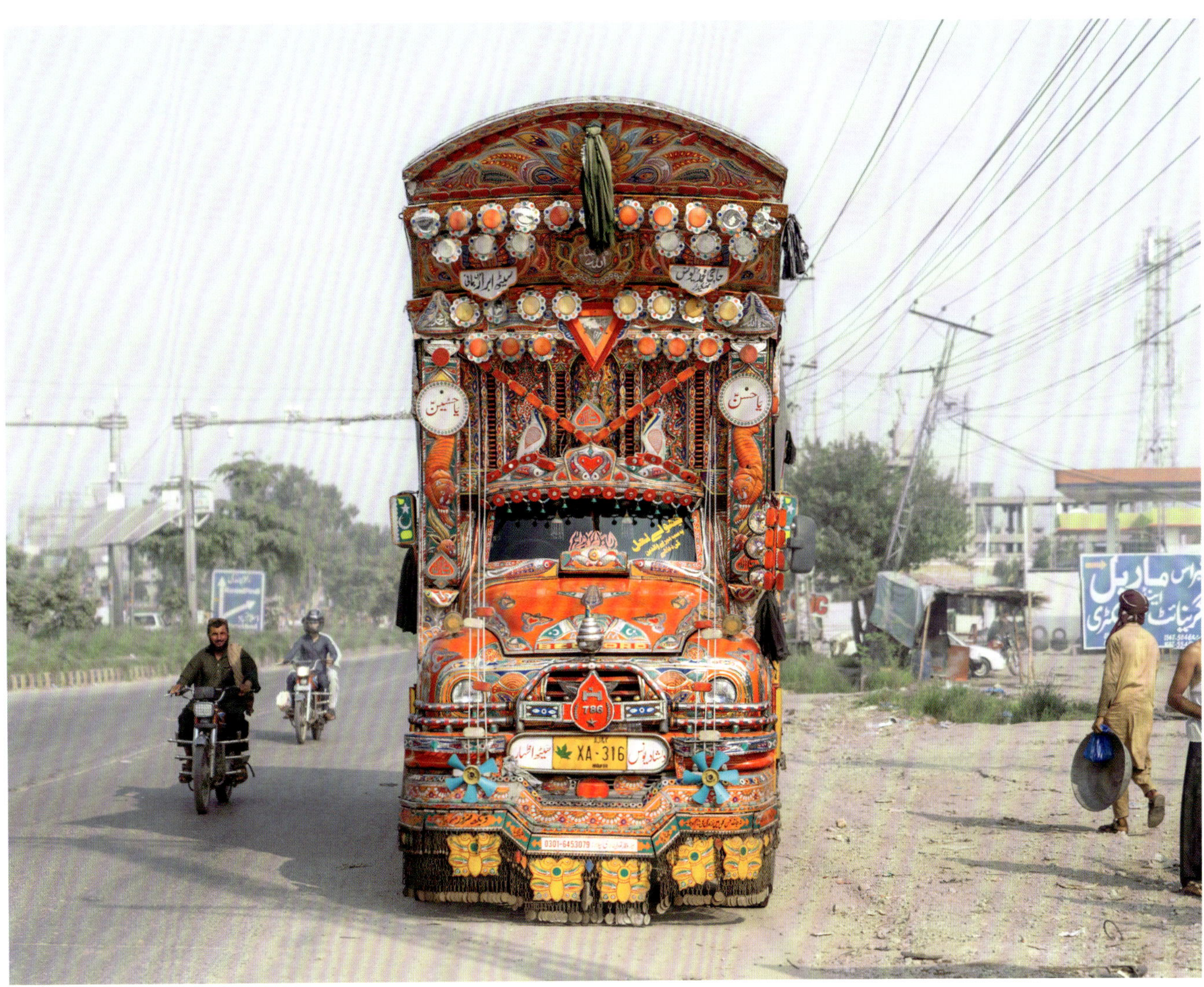

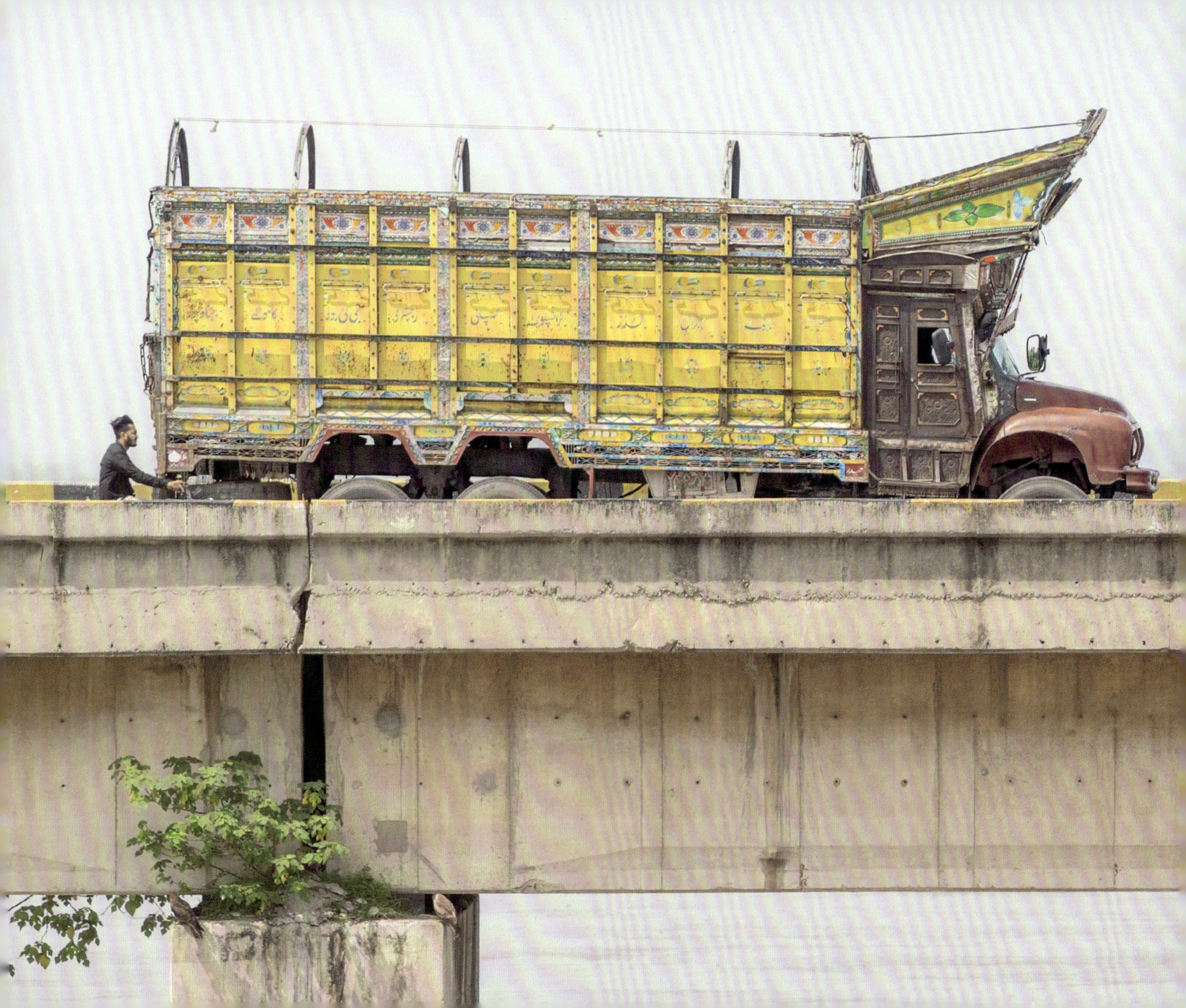

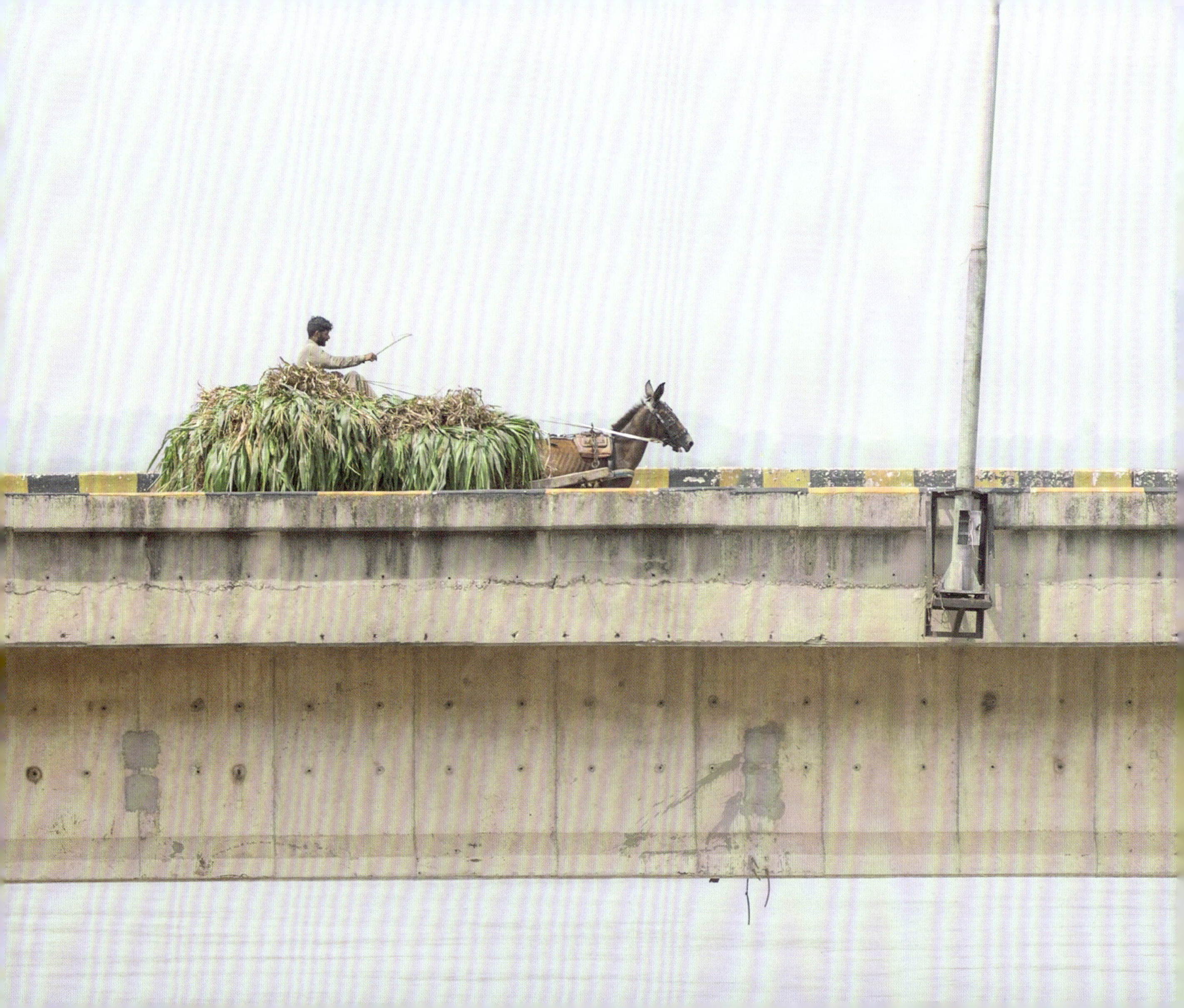

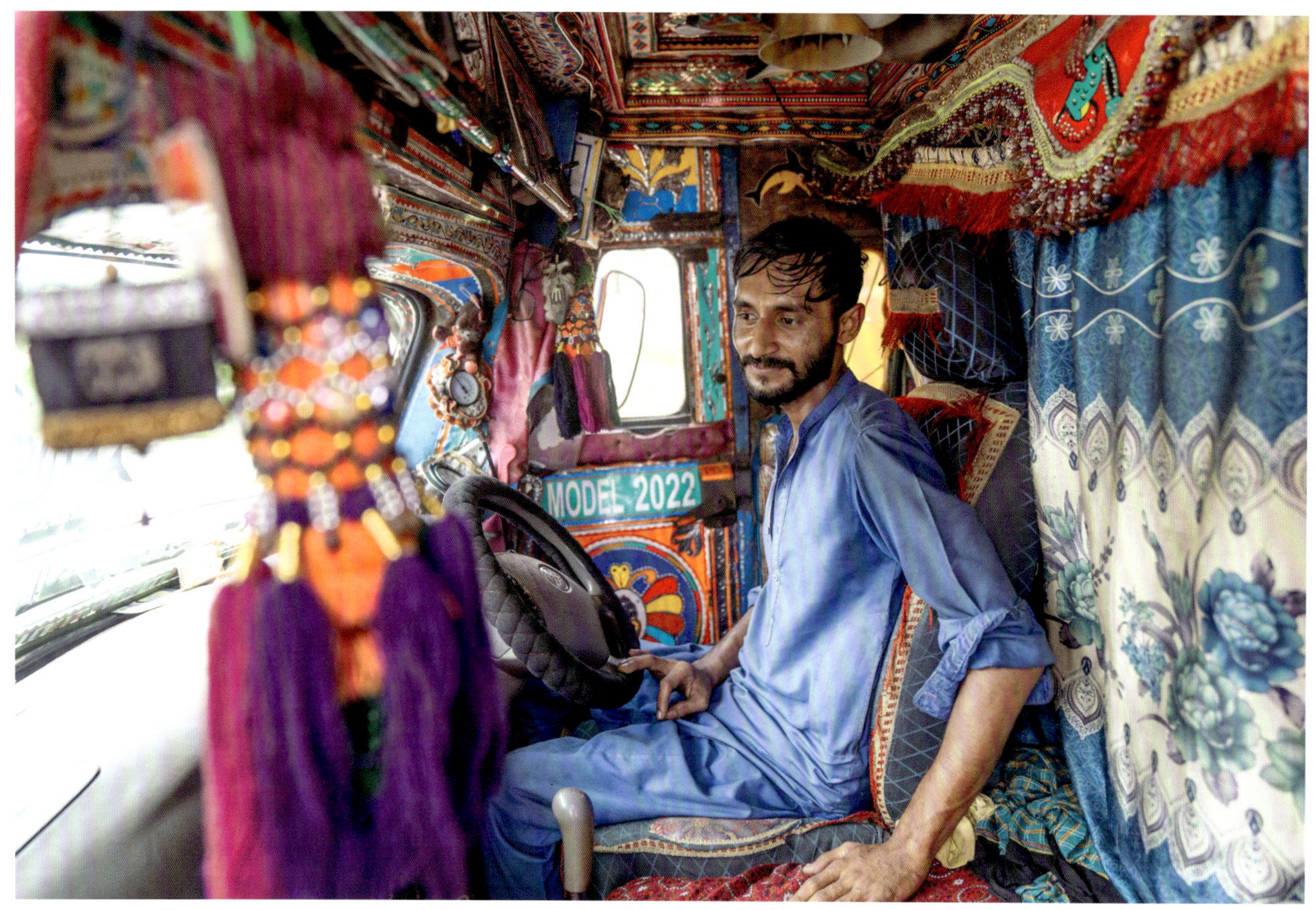

overleaf: Taxila, PAKISTAN

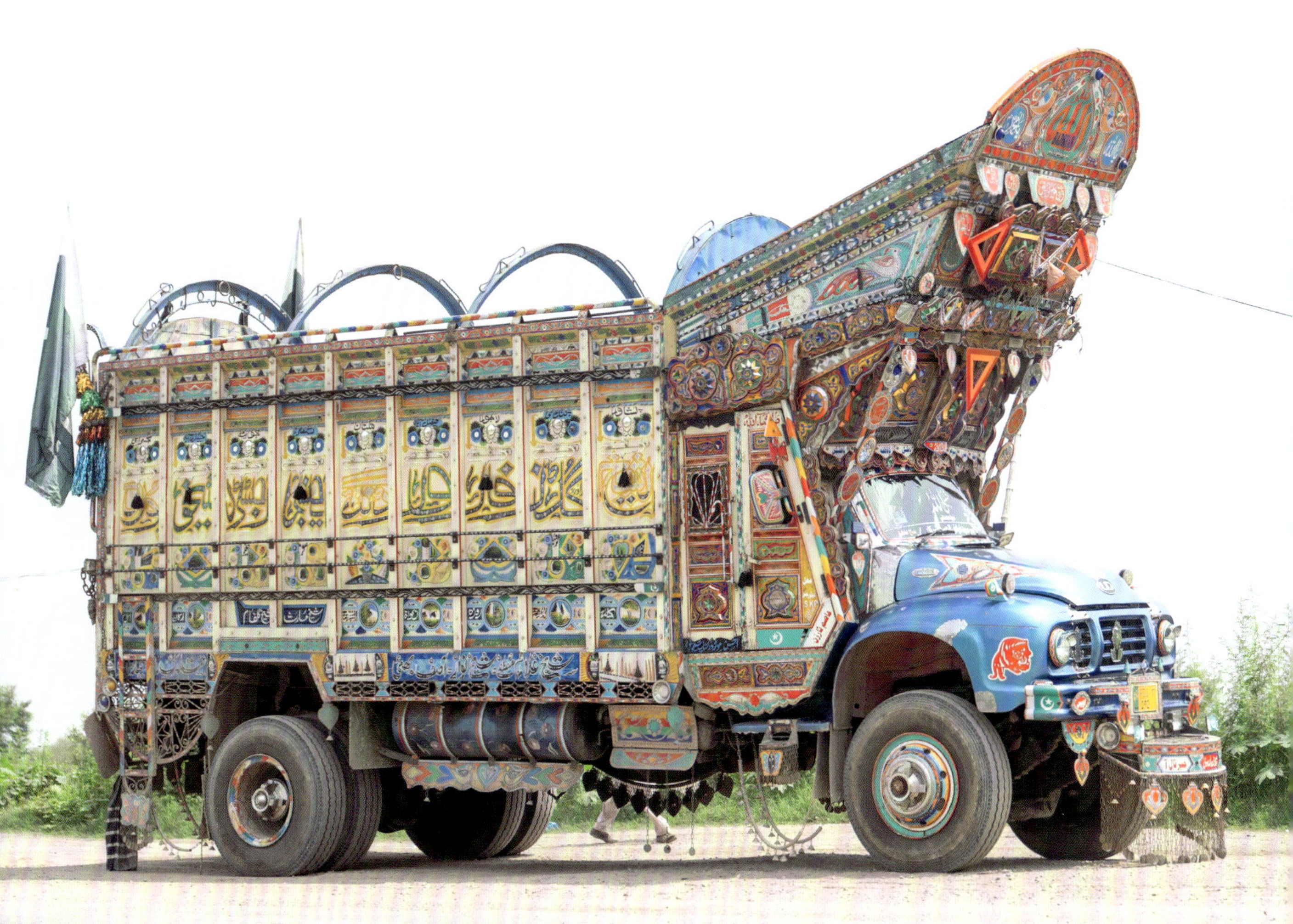

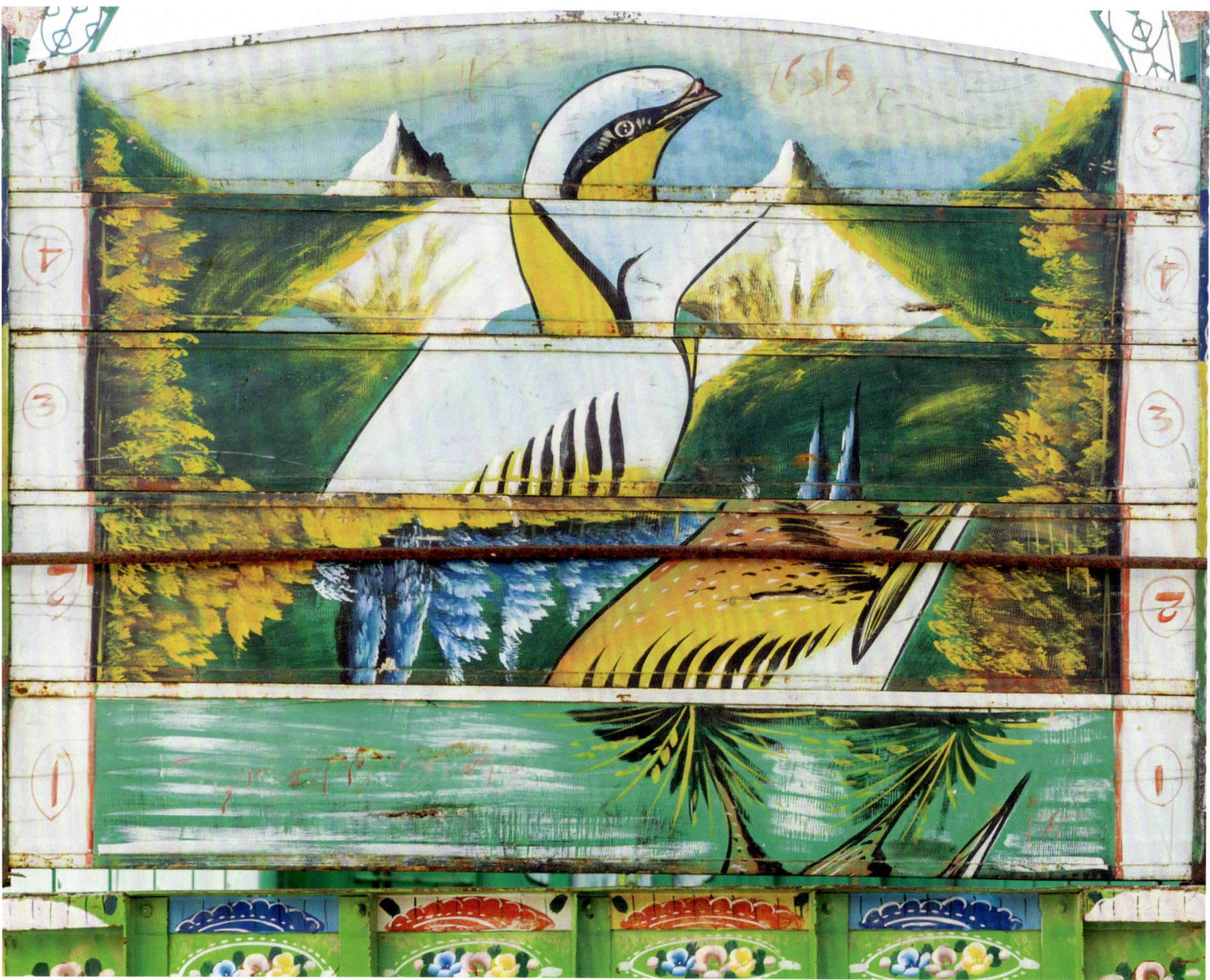
واوی

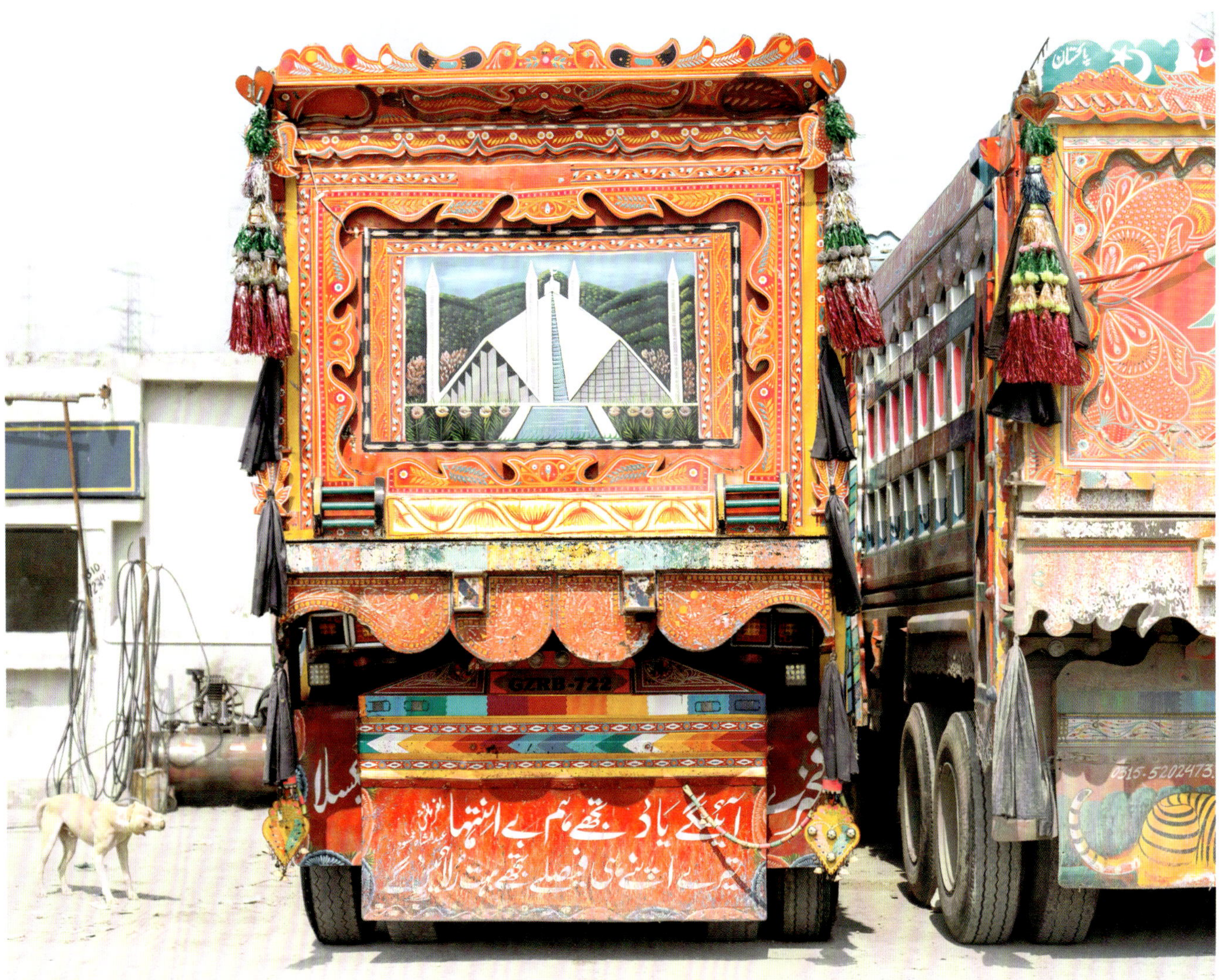

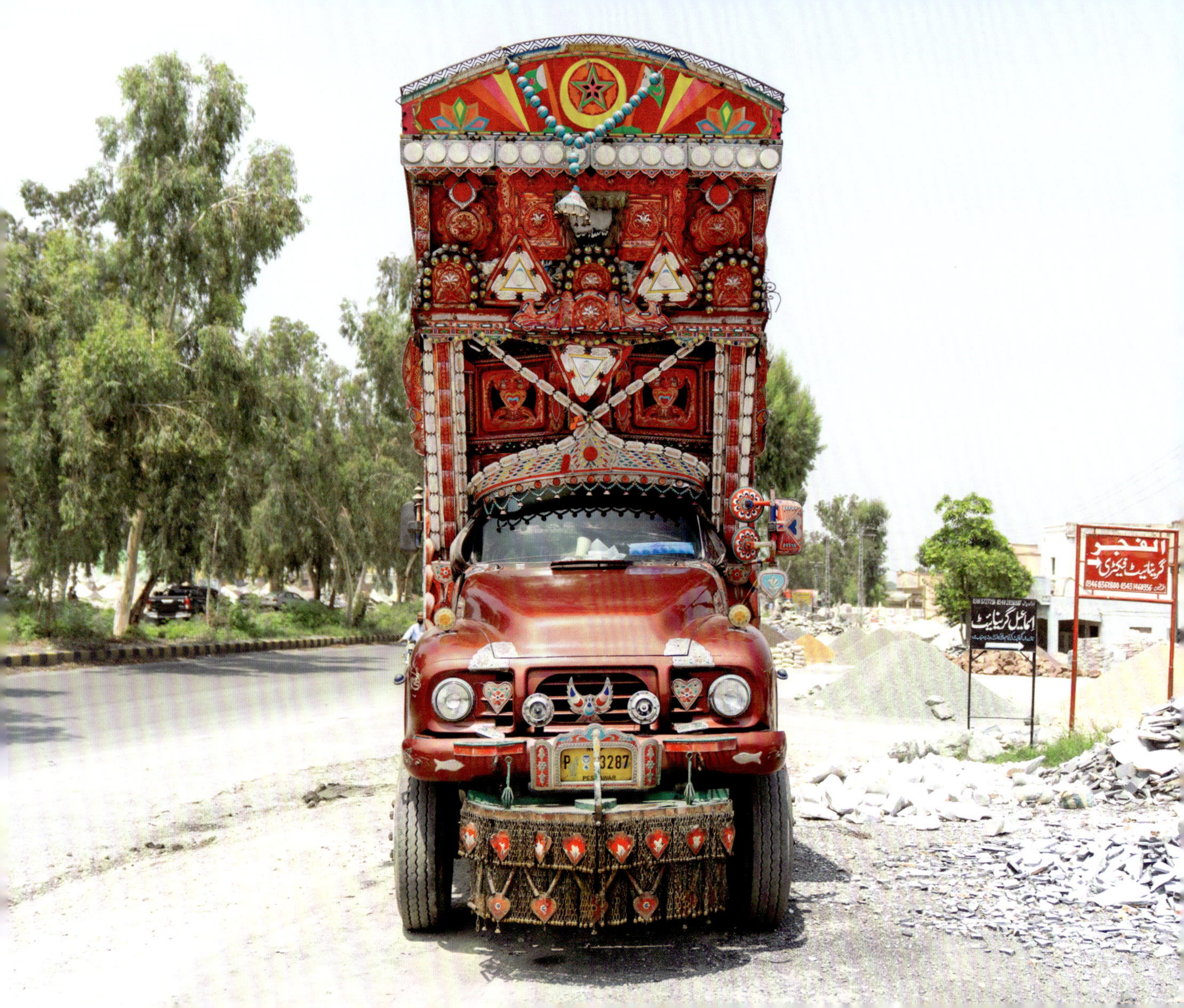
الفجر
گرینائٹ فیکٹری
0346 8361800 0543 1468356
اسماعیل گرینائٹ

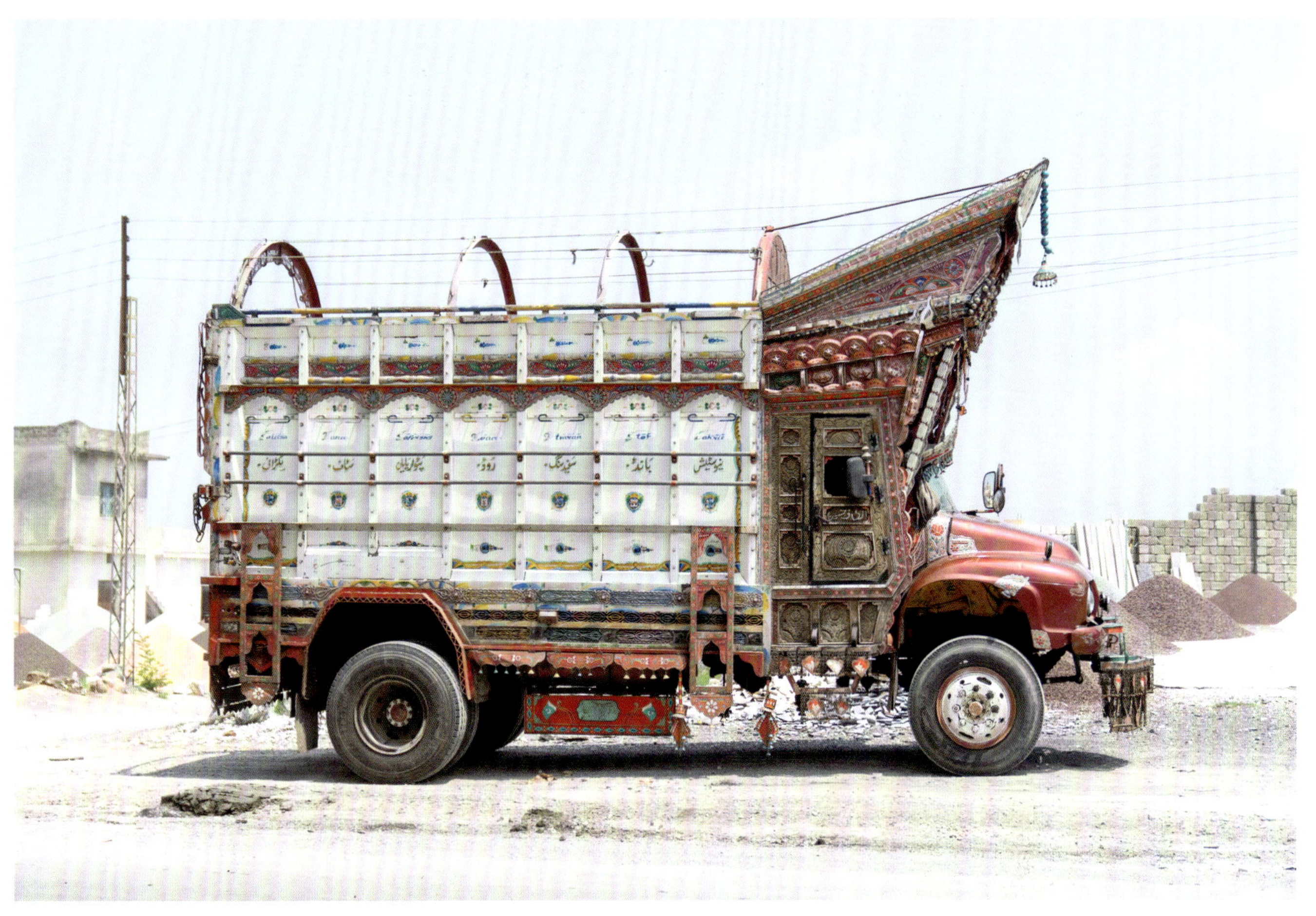

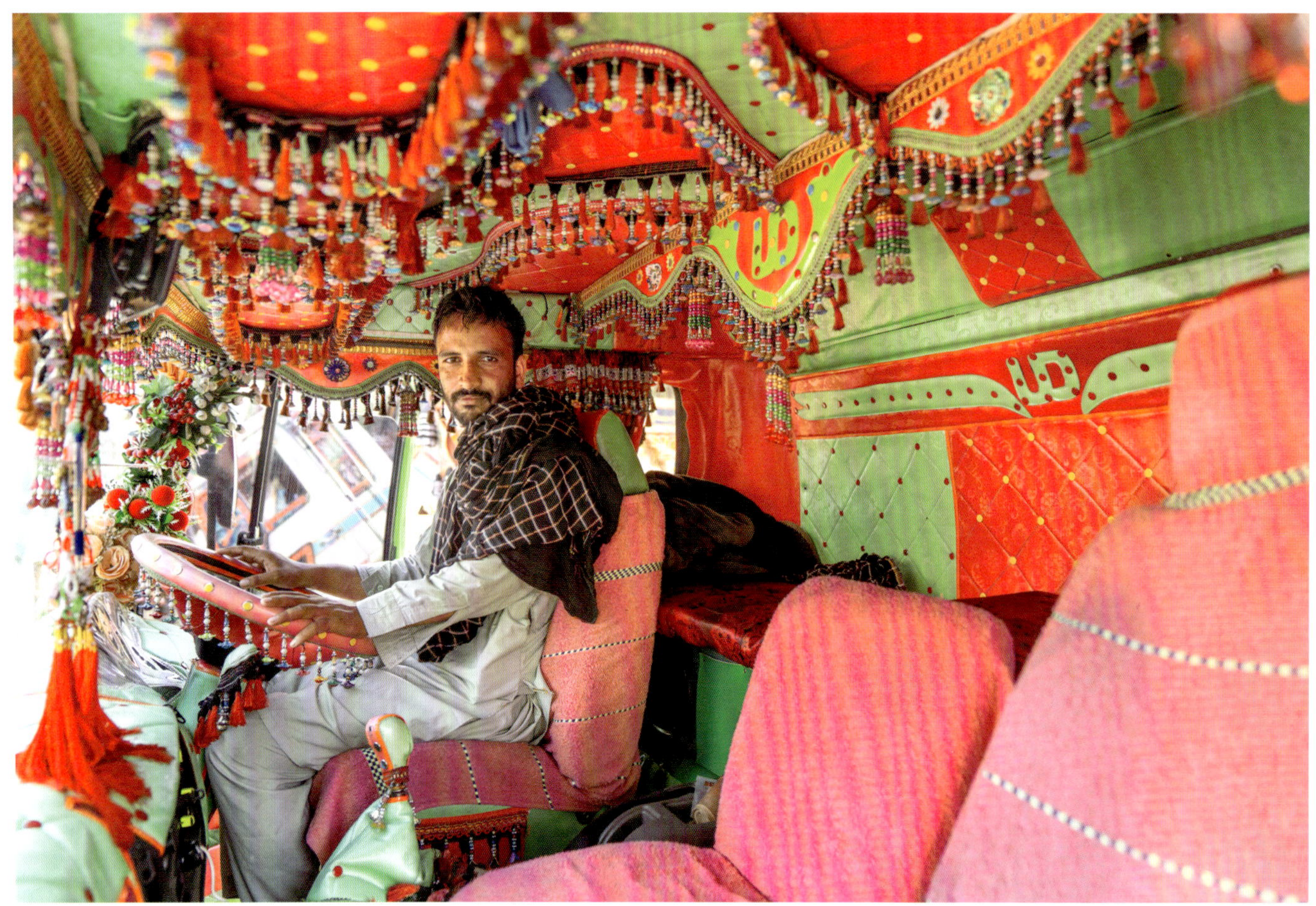

130   Attock, PAKISTAN

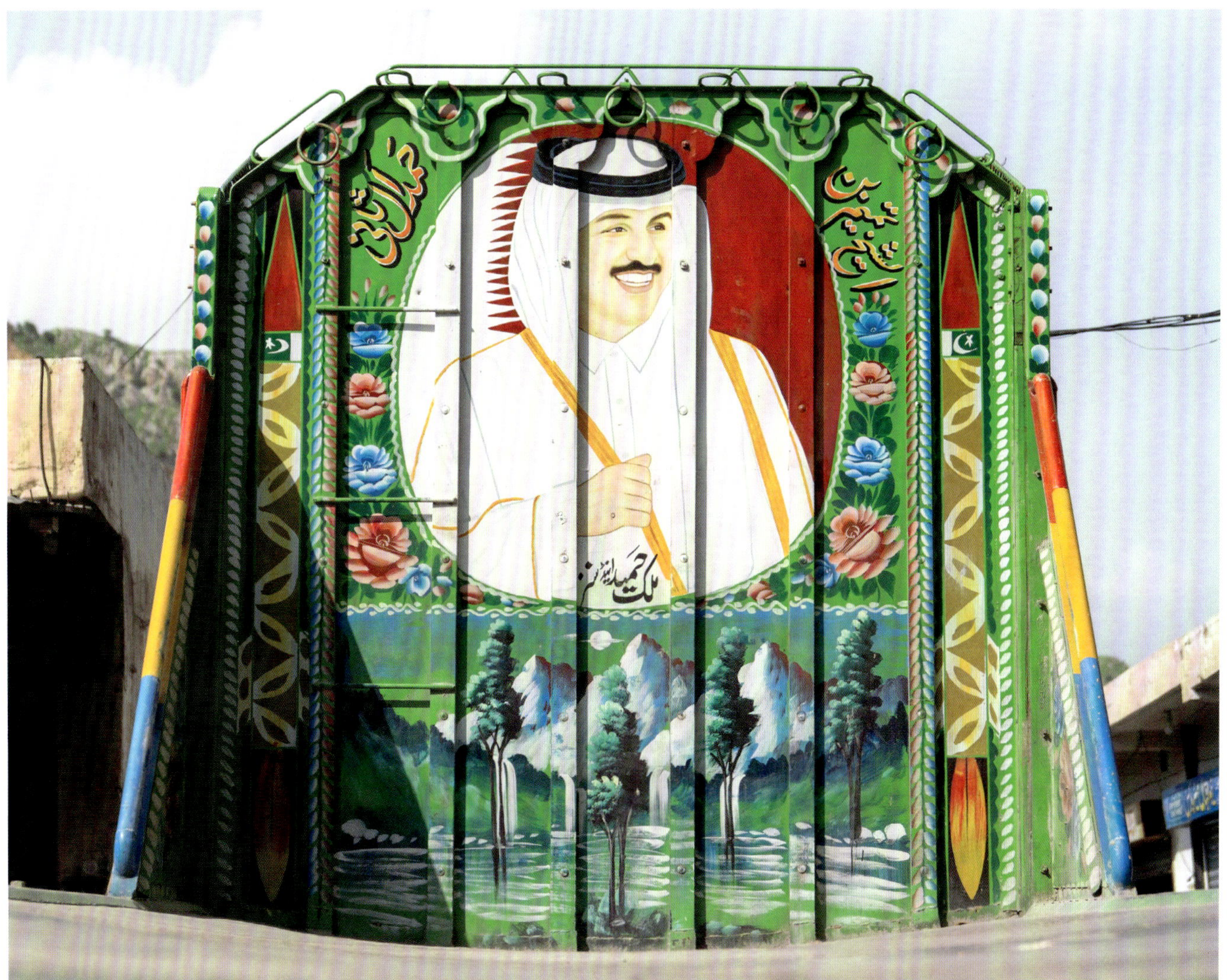

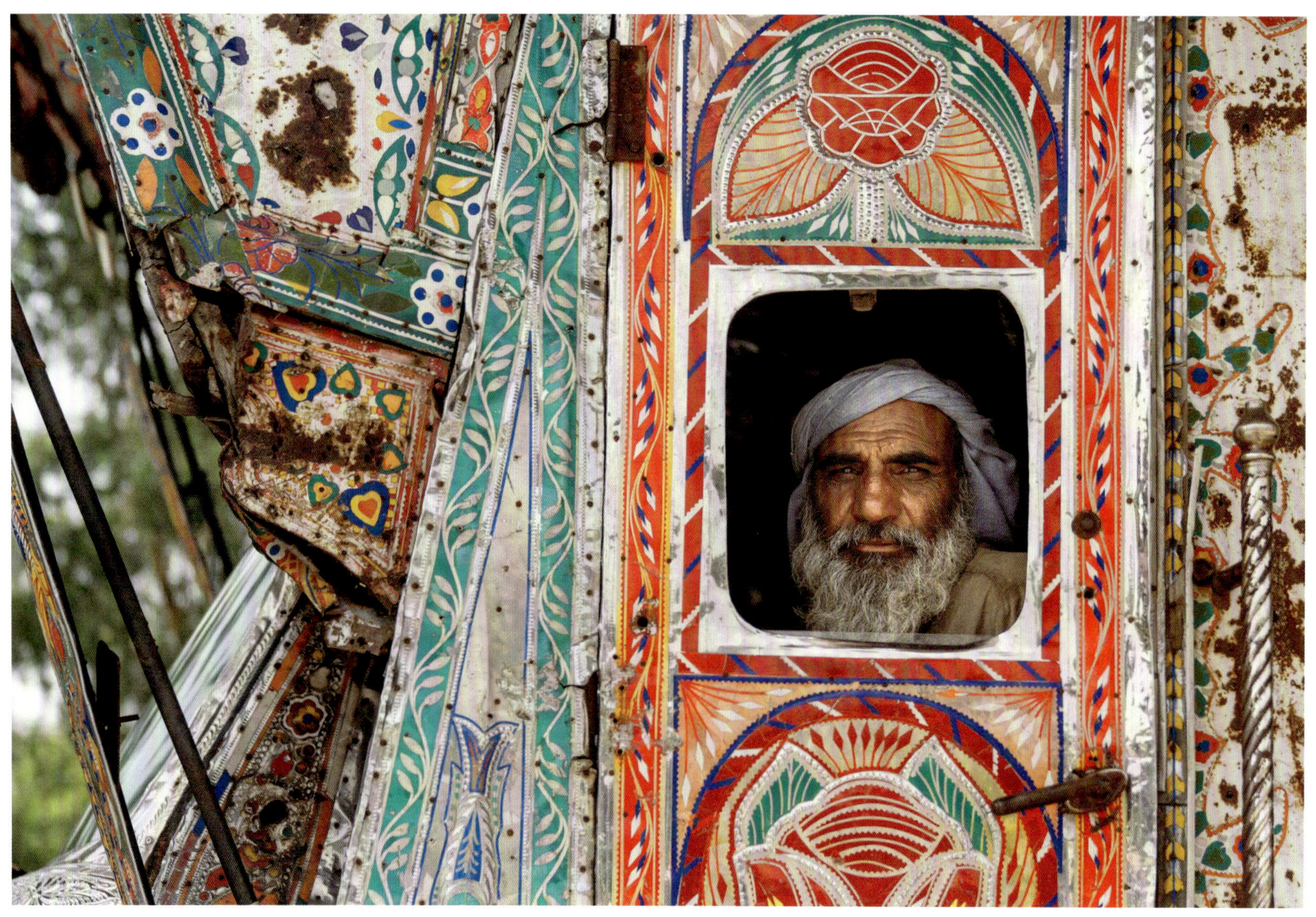

132 Rawalpindi, PAKISTAN

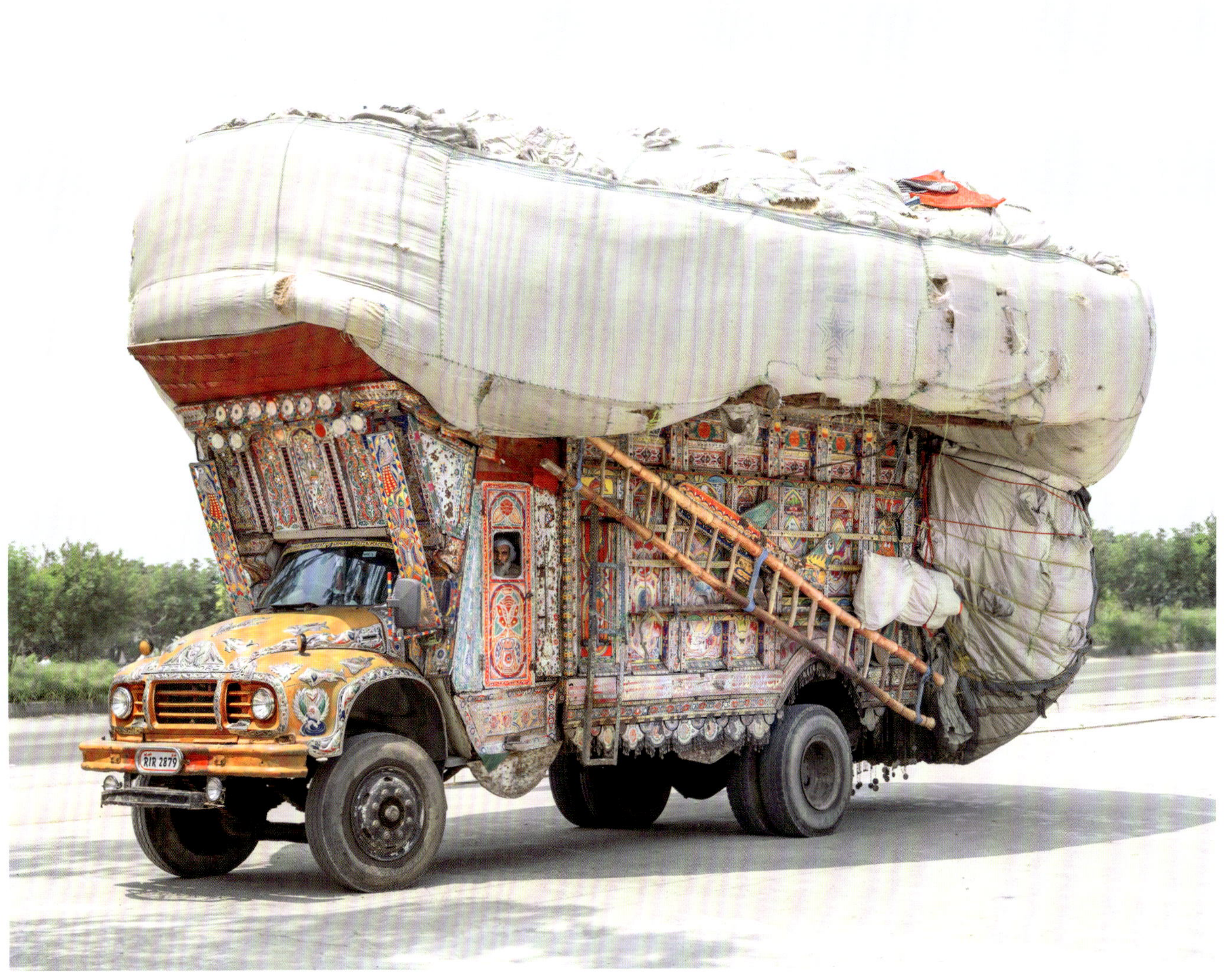

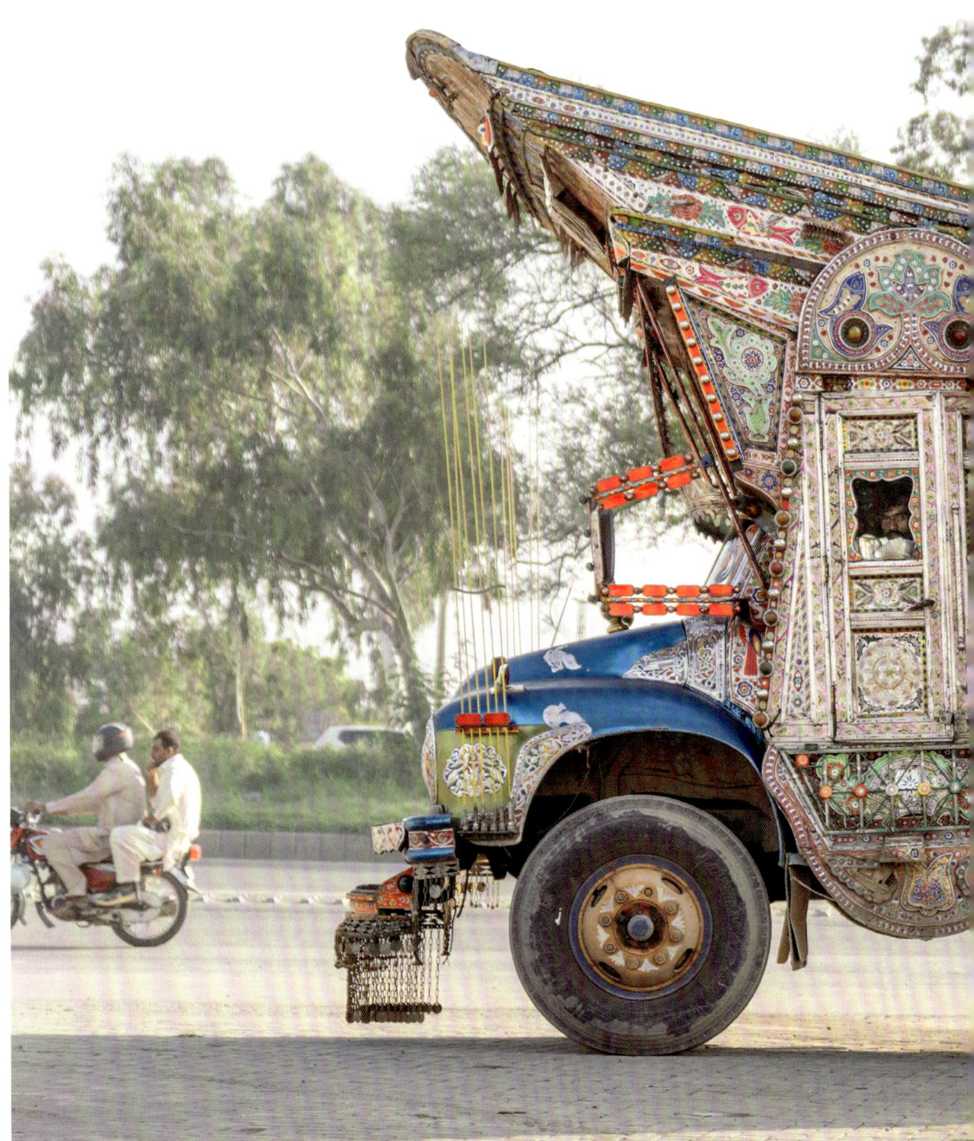

134   Attock, PAKISTAN

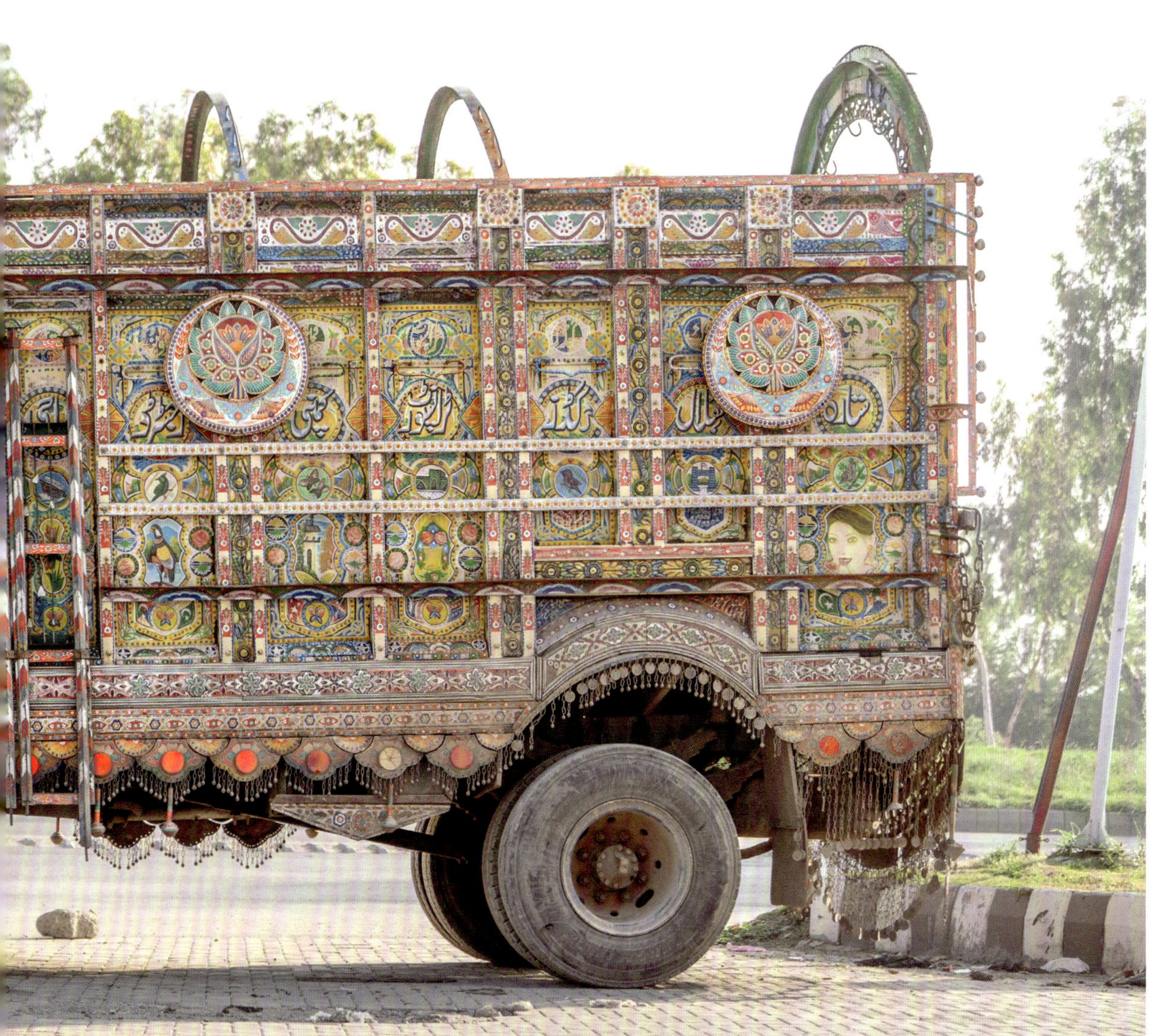

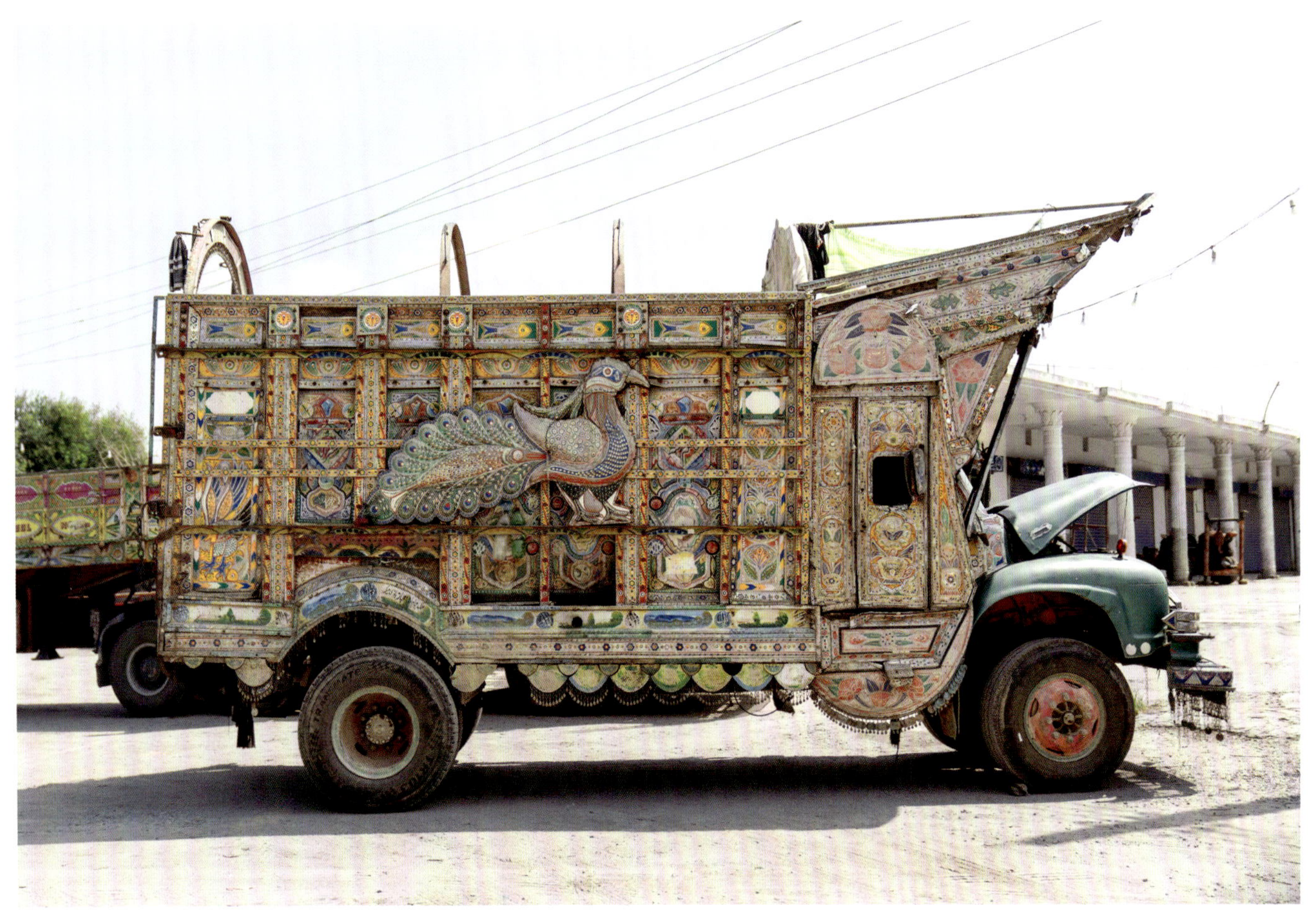

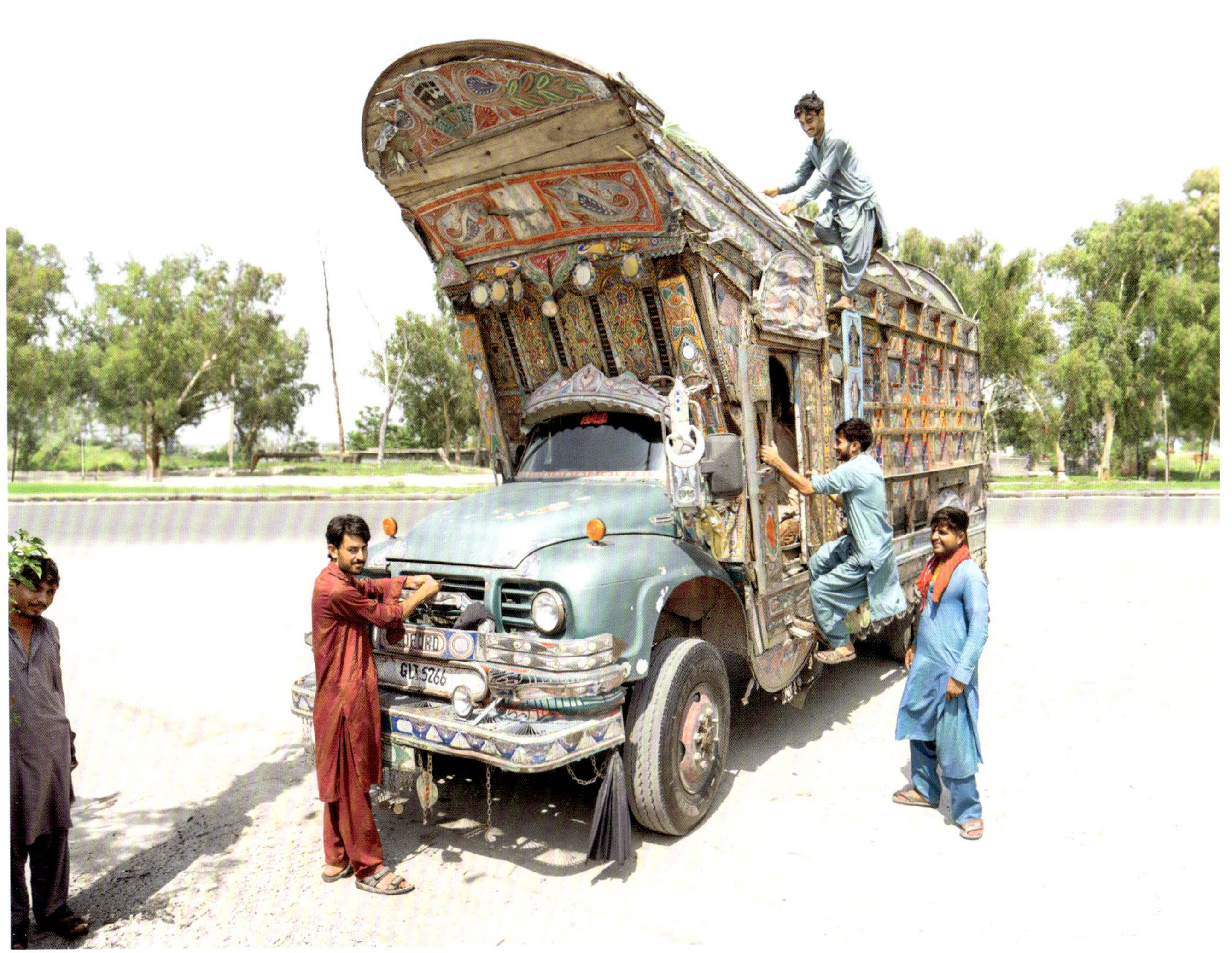

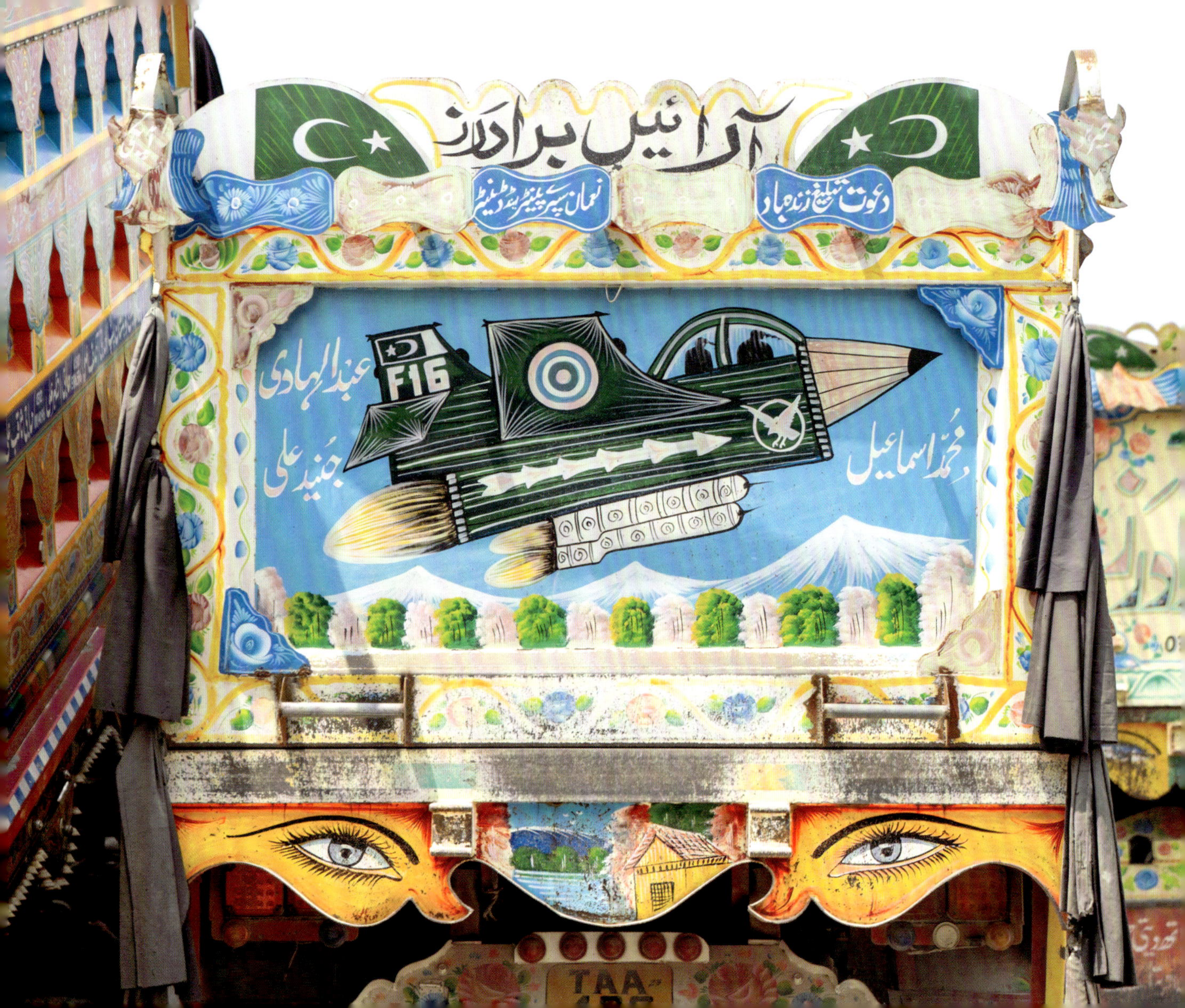

آرائیں برادران
دعوت تبلیغ زندہ باد
عبدالہادی
جنید علی
F16
محمد اسماعیل
TAA

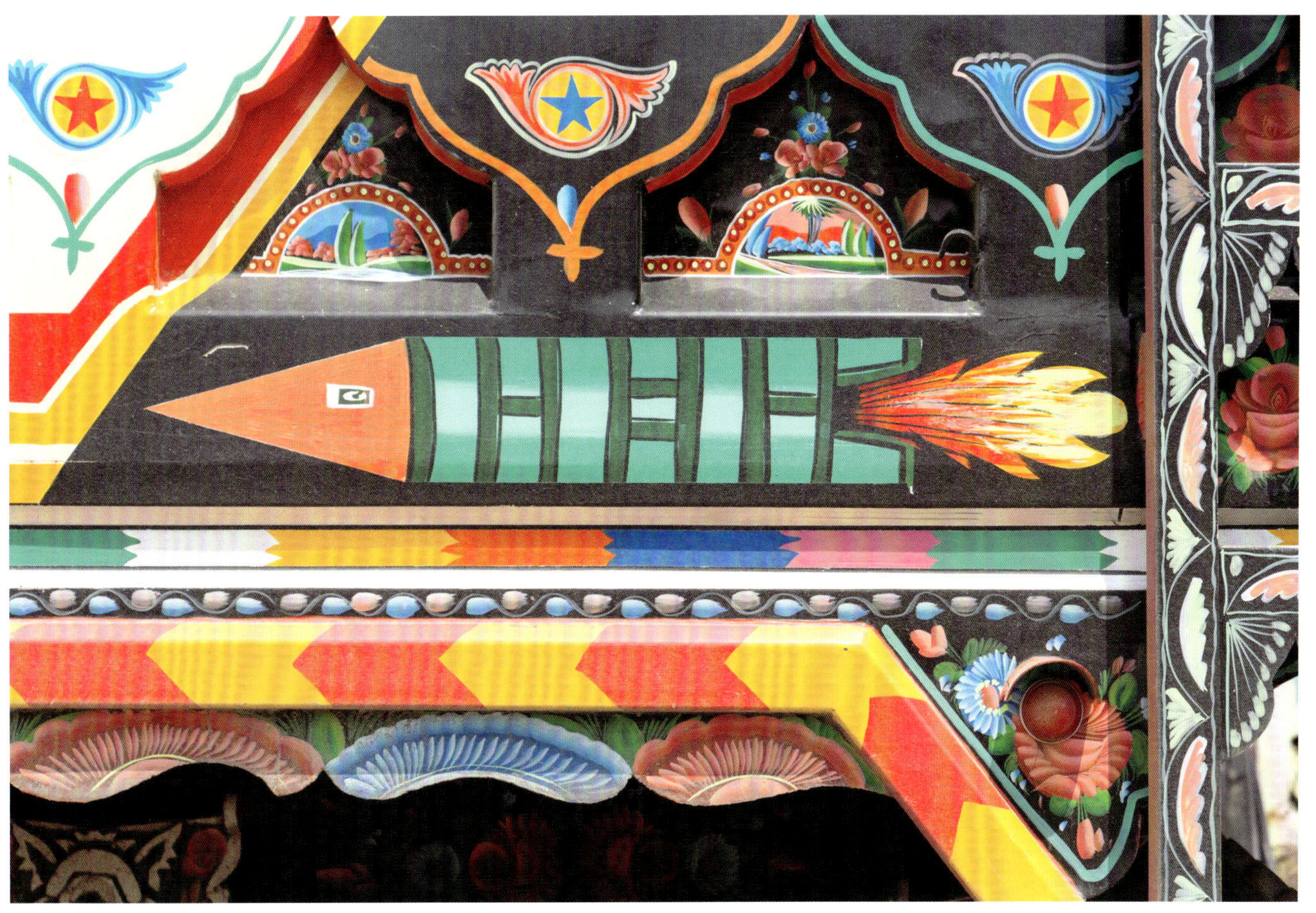

overleaf: Attock, PAKISTAN

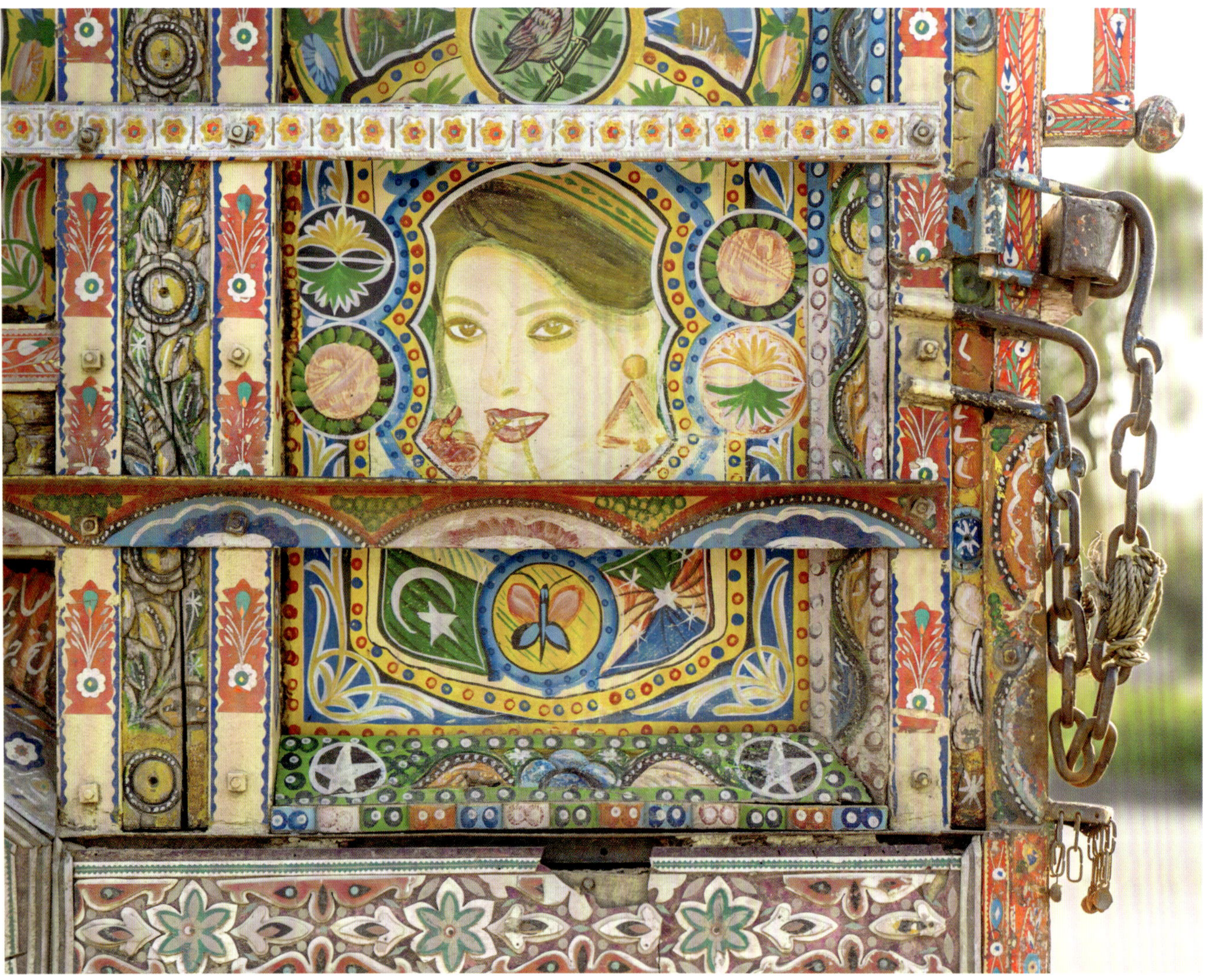

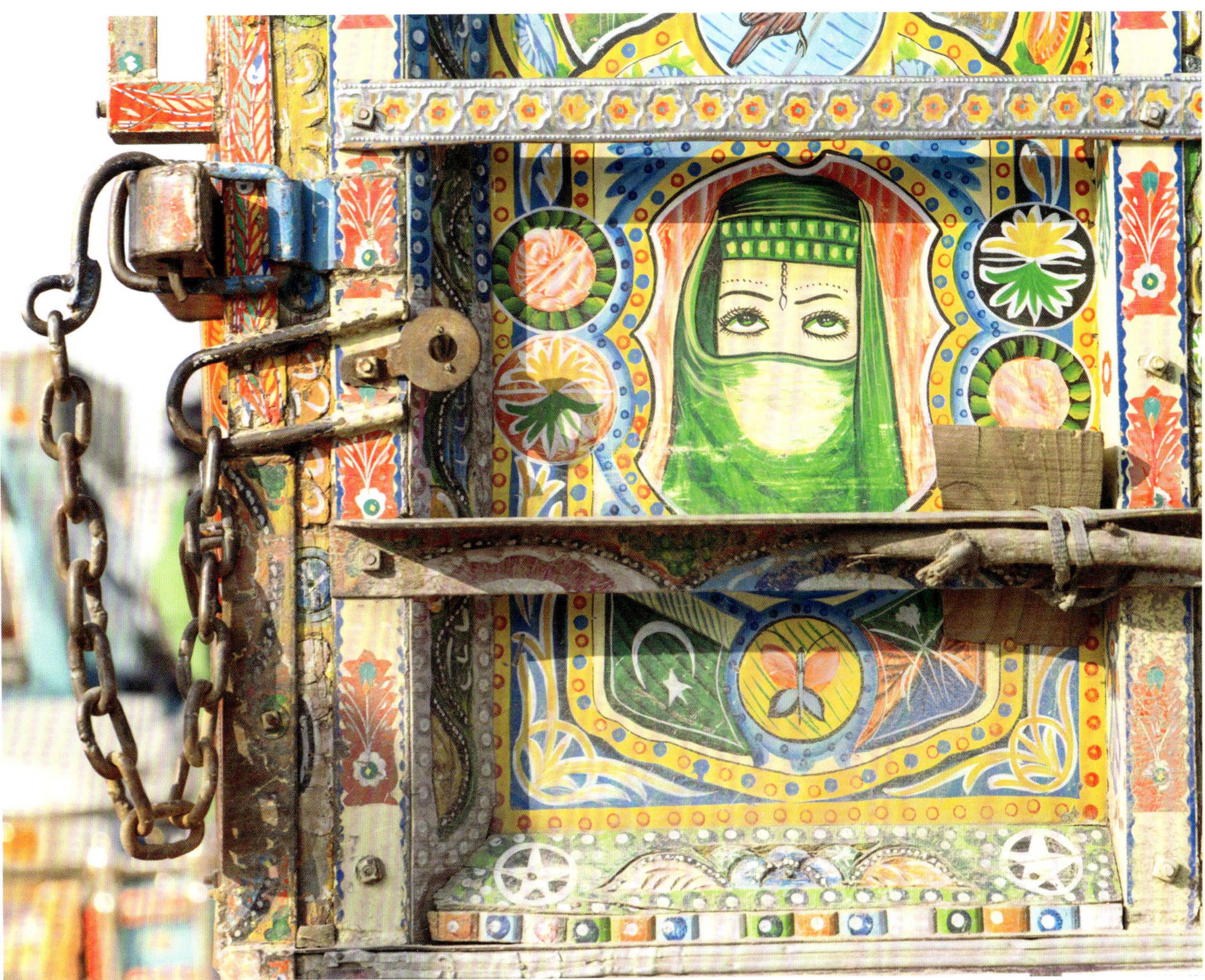

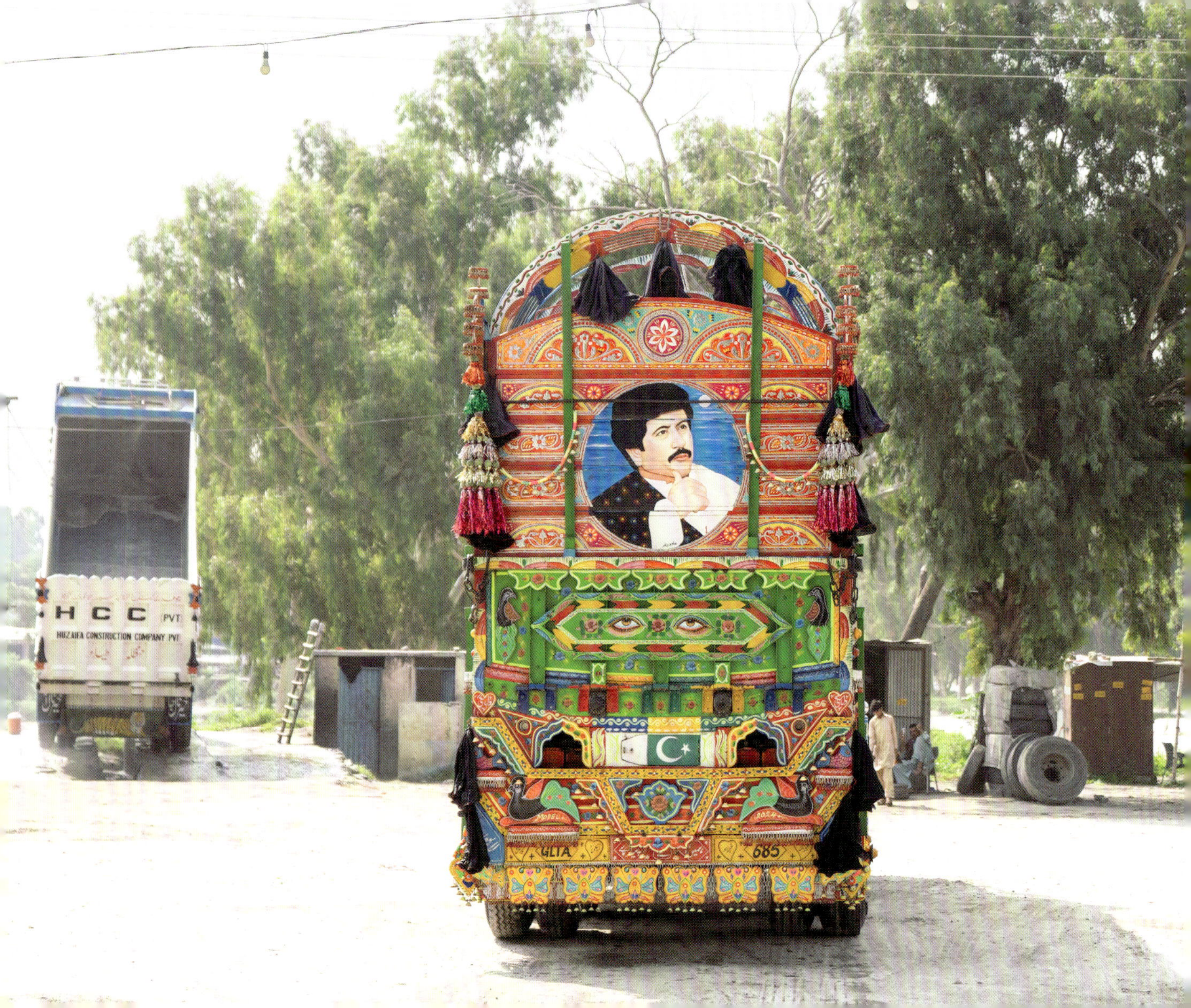

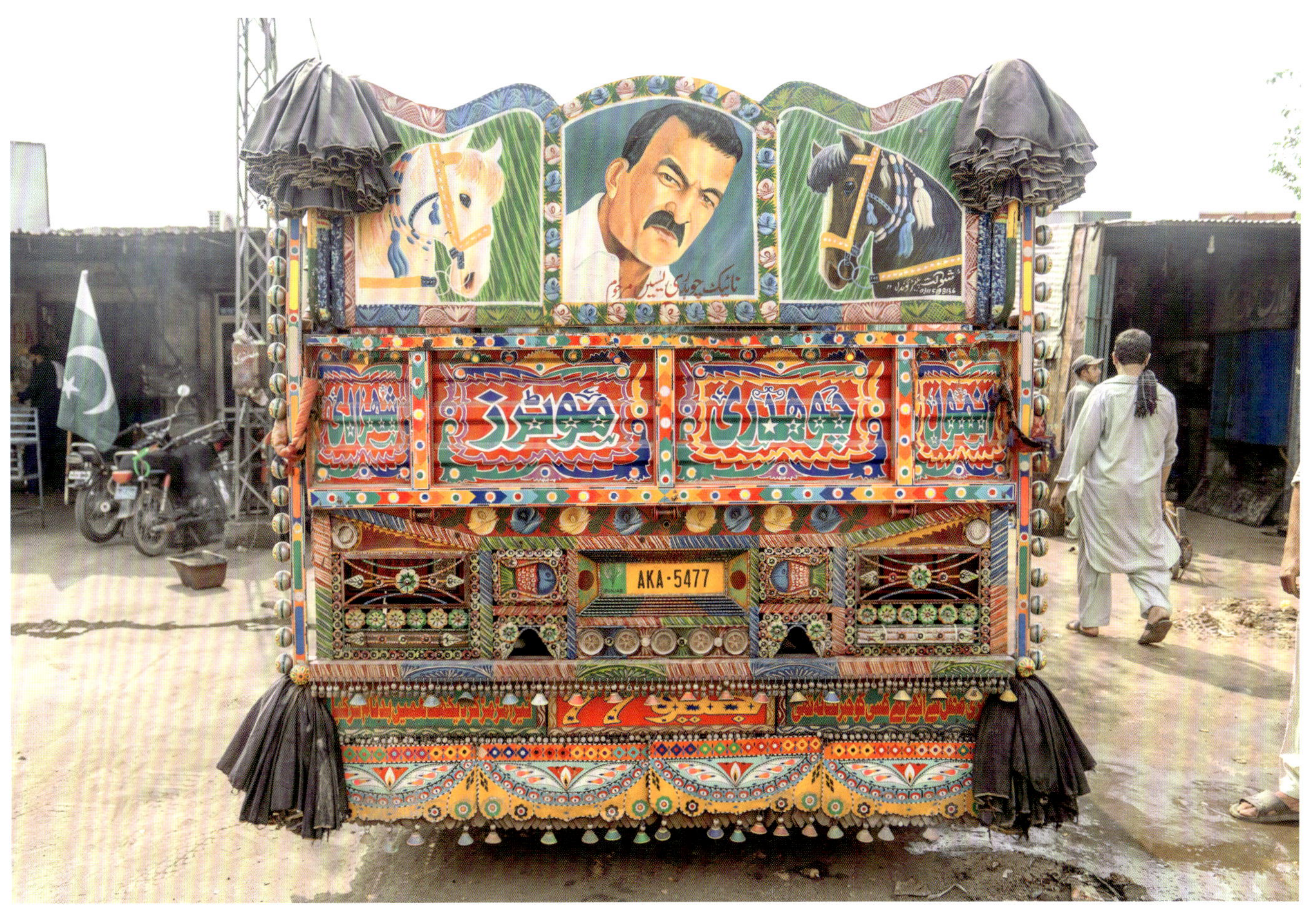

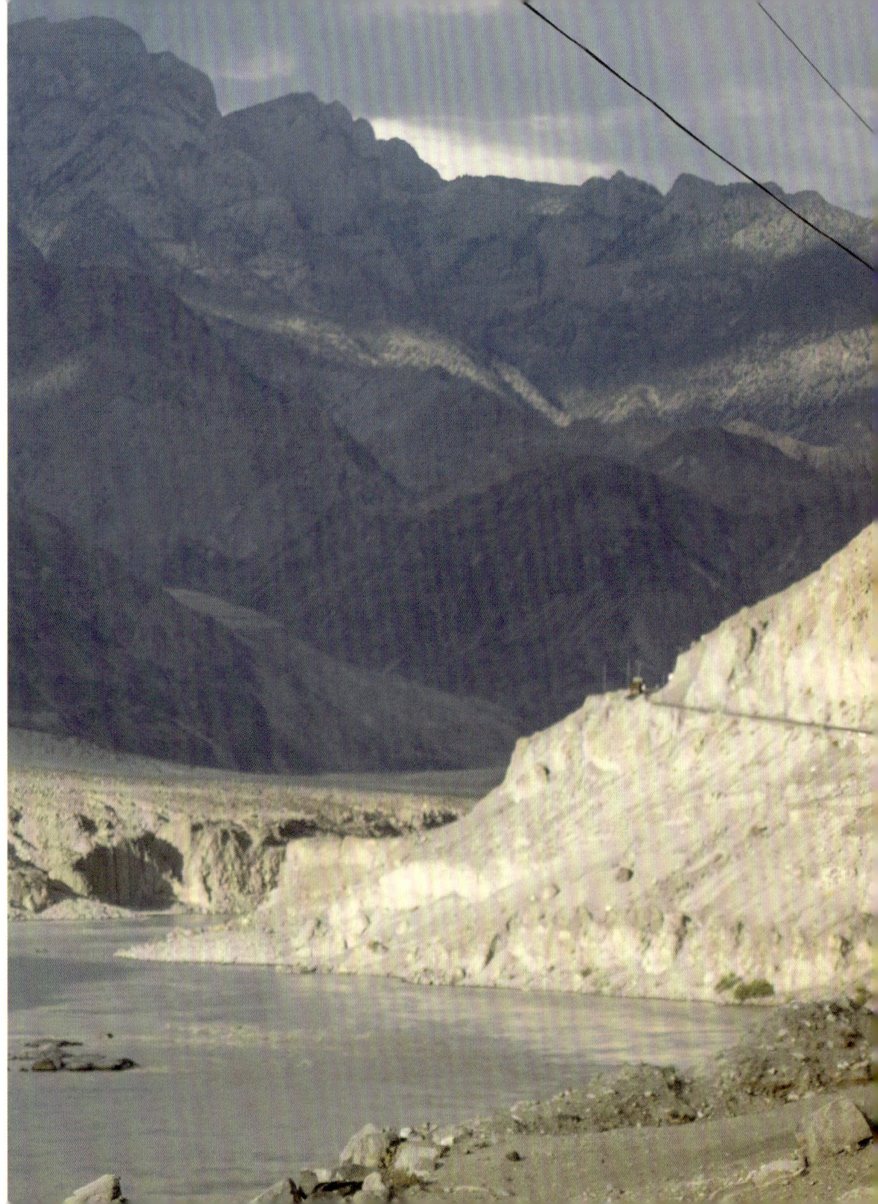

144 Karakoram Highway, PAKISTAN

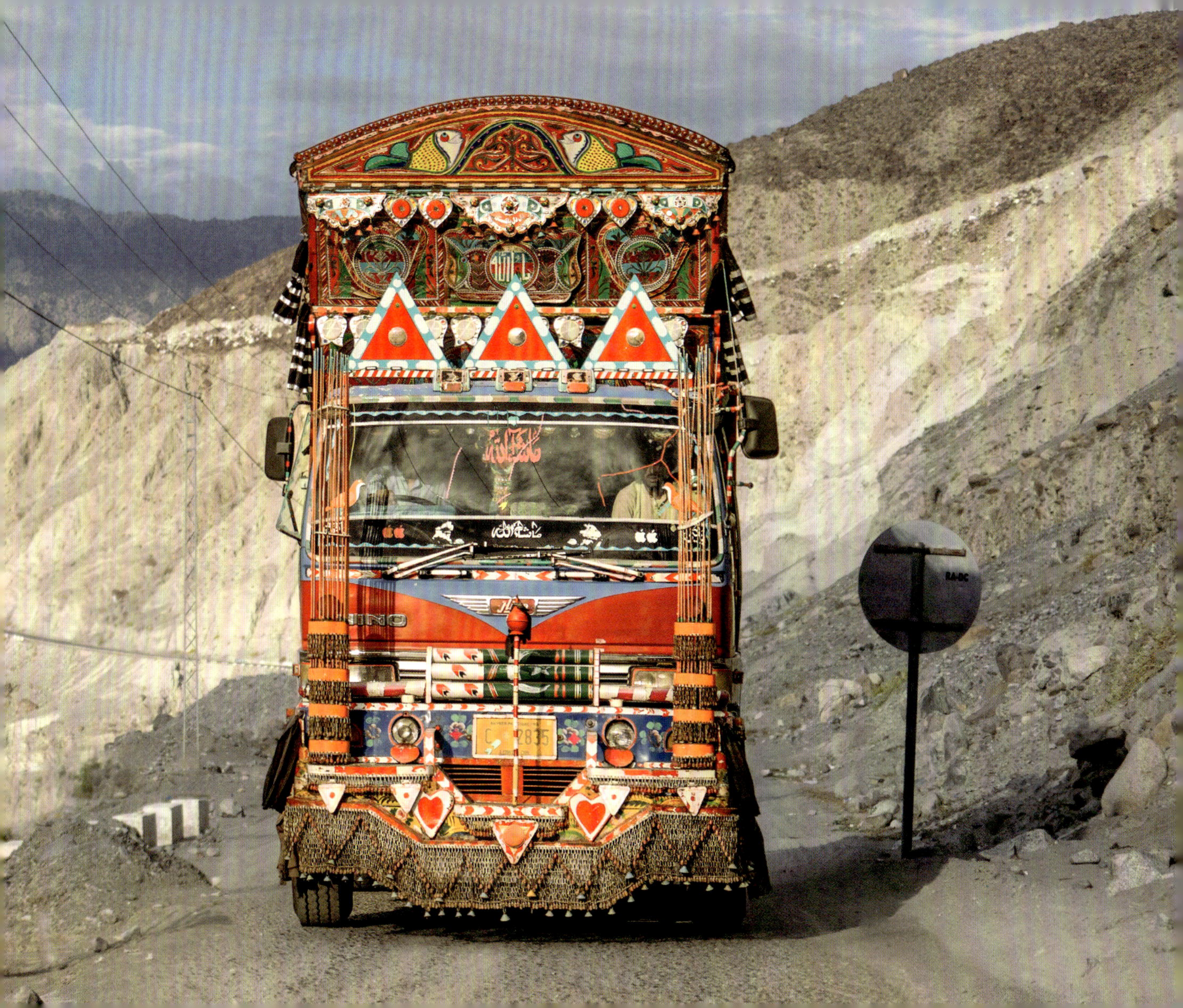

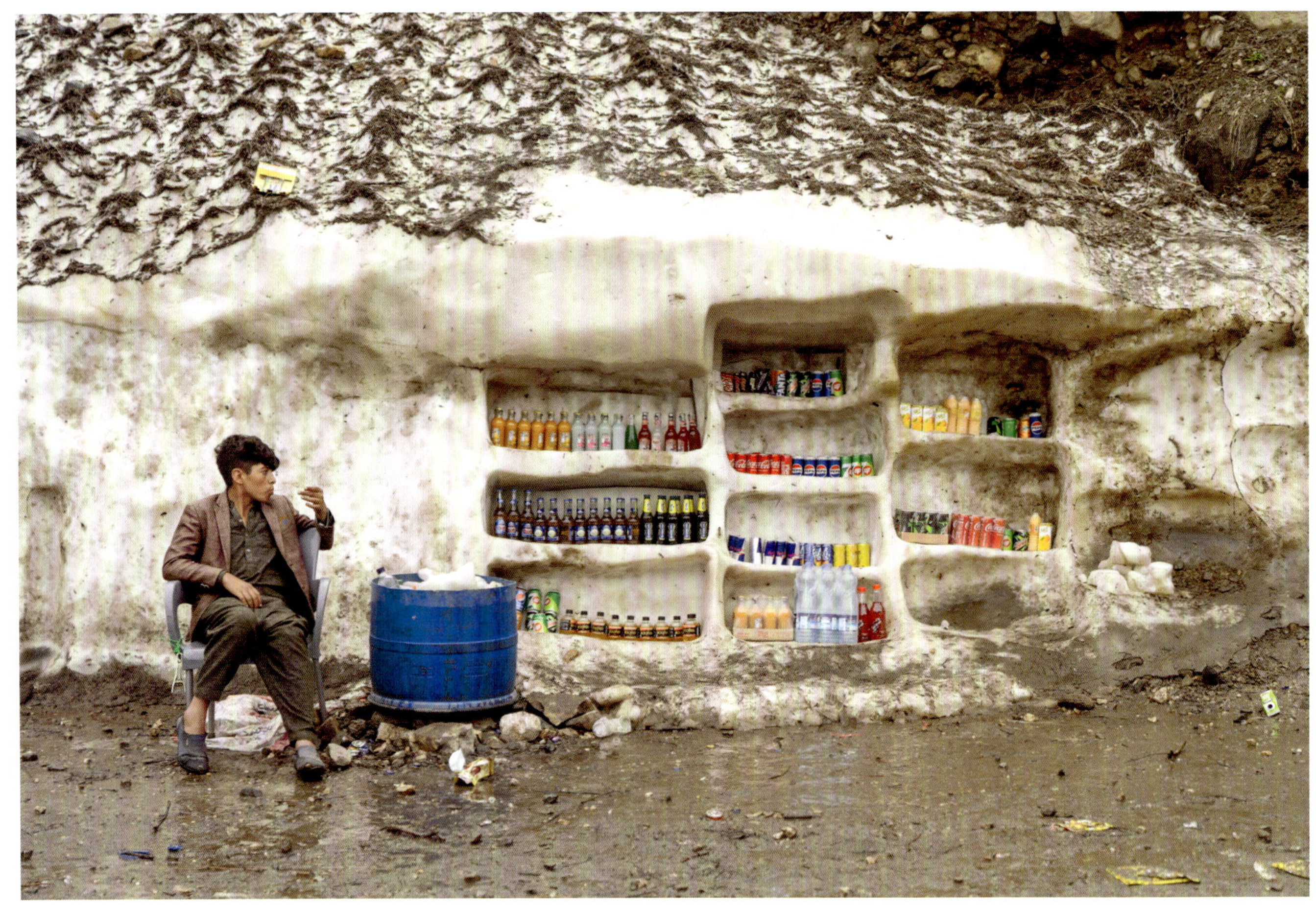

146   Naran, PAKISTAN

Karakoram Highway, PAKISTAN

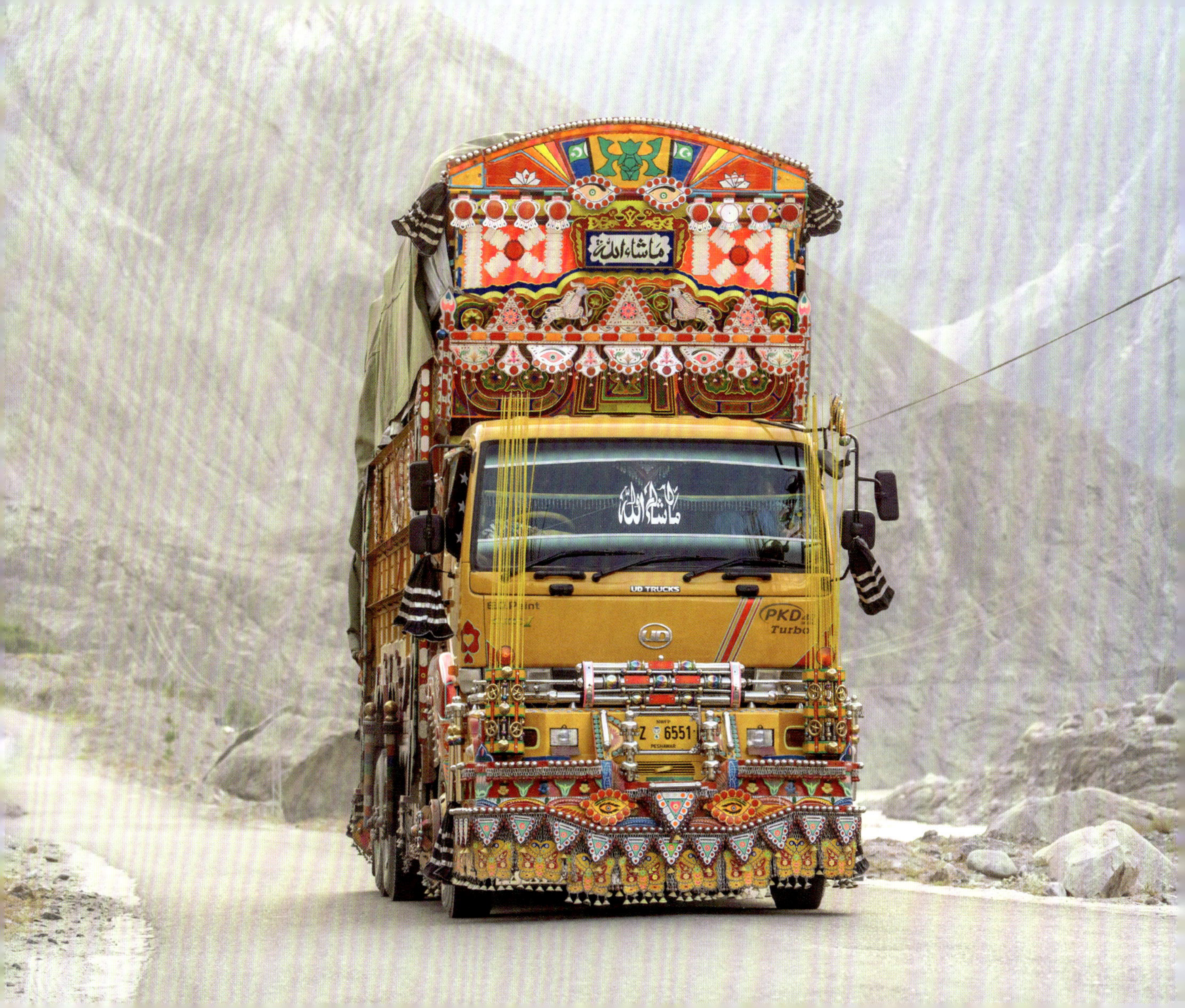
ماشاءاللہ
ماشاءاللہ
UD TRUCKS
PKD
Turbo
NWFP
Z 6551
PESHAWAR

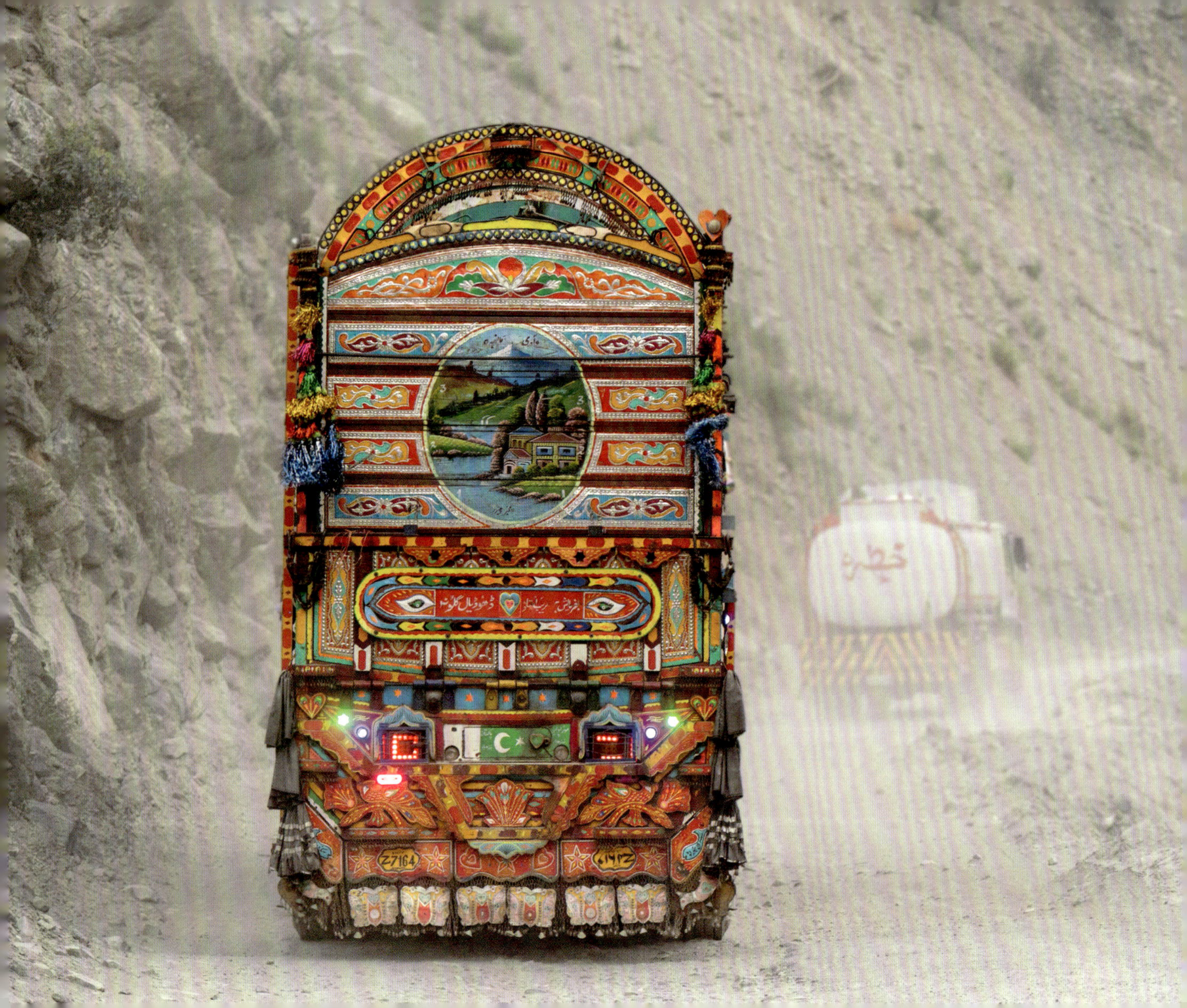

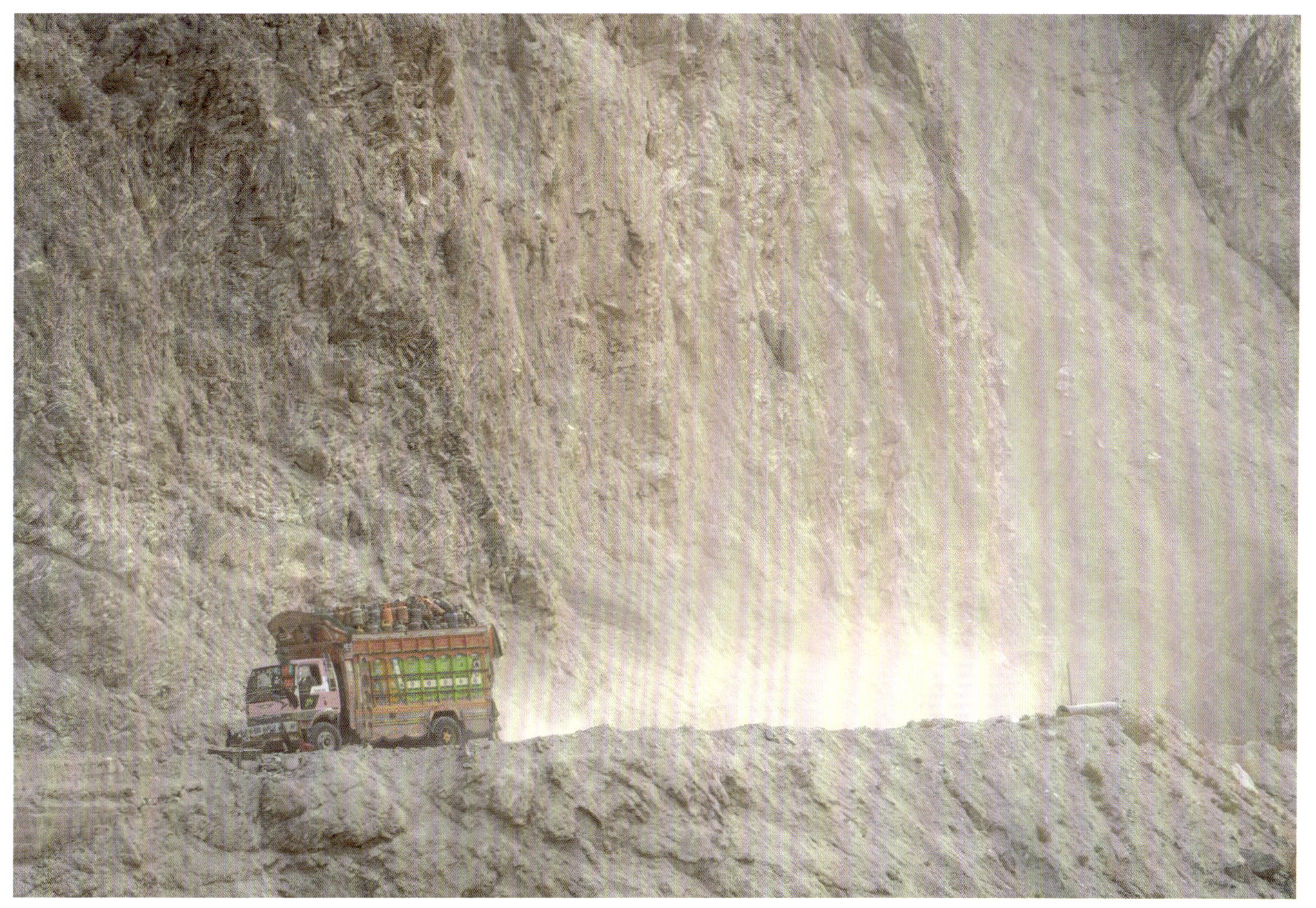

Karakoram Highway, PAKISTAN   149

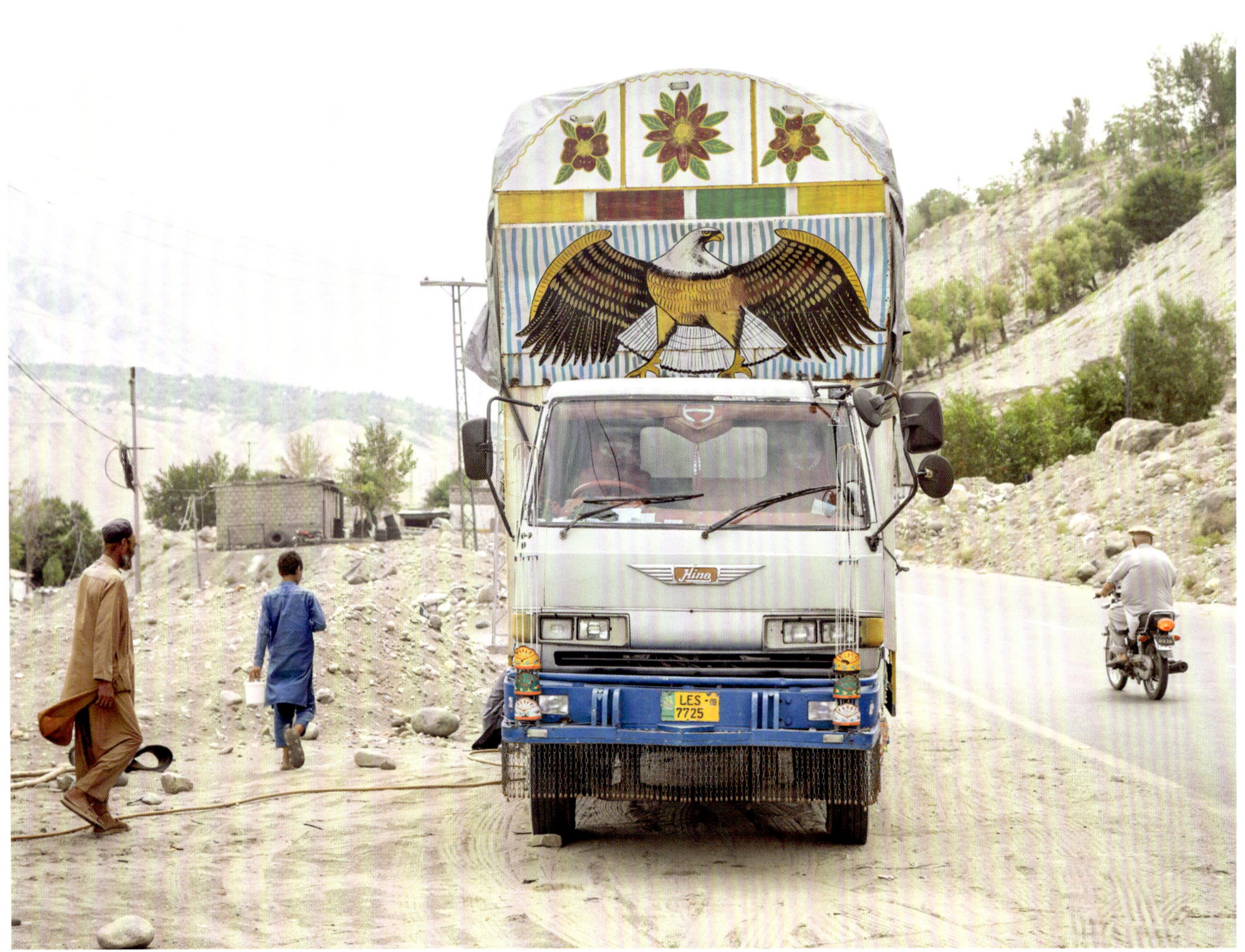

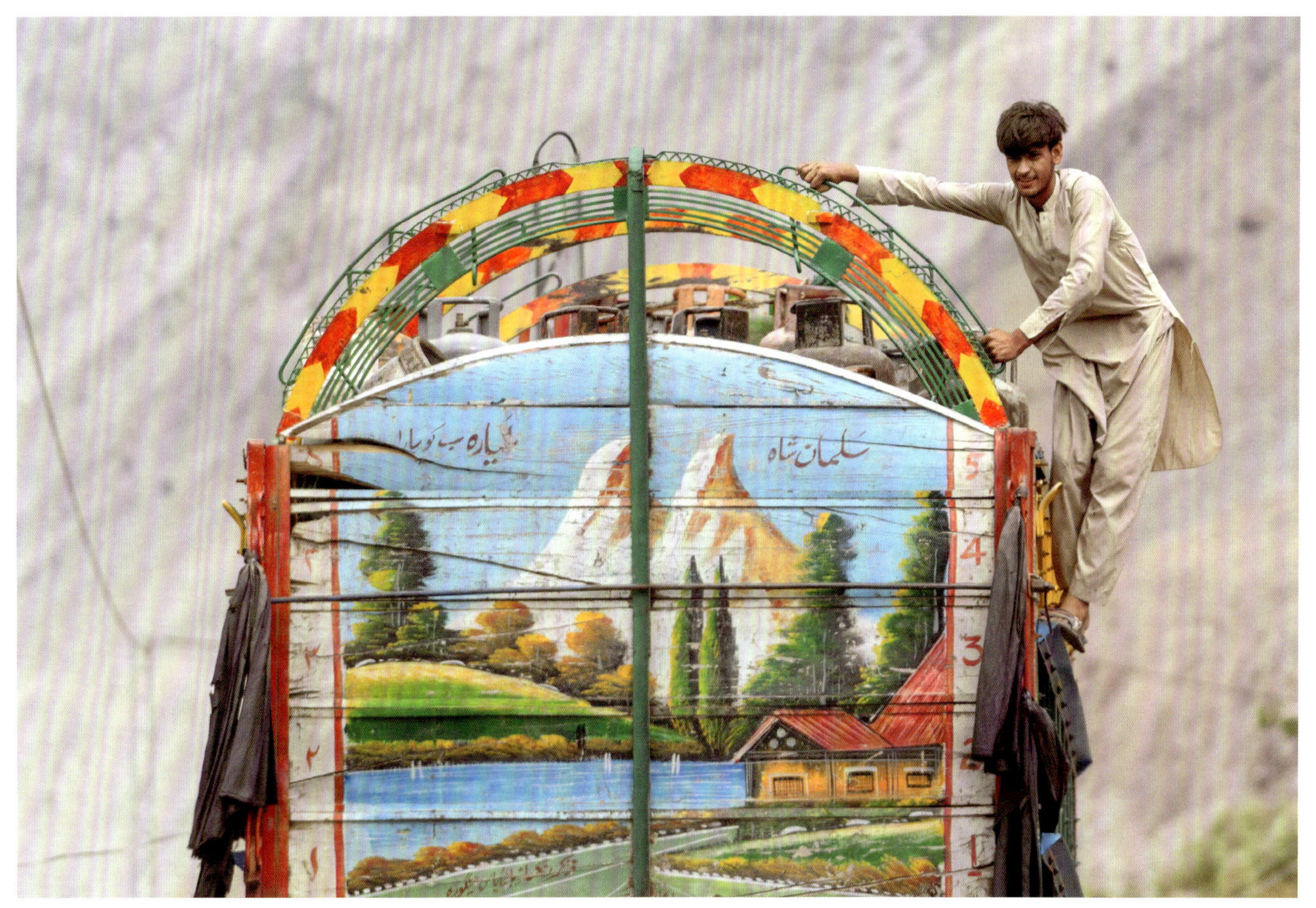

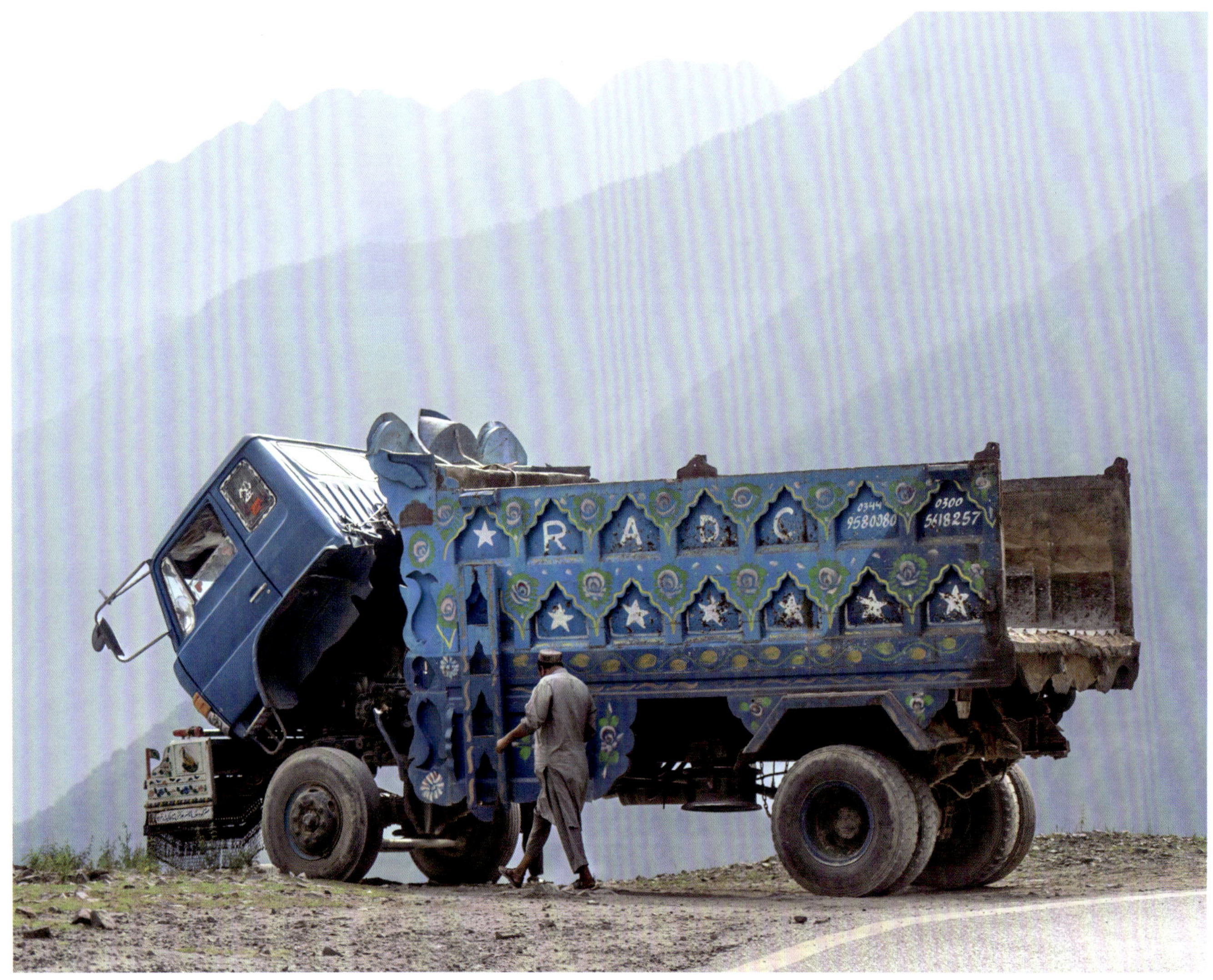

R A D C
0344
9580980
0300
5618257

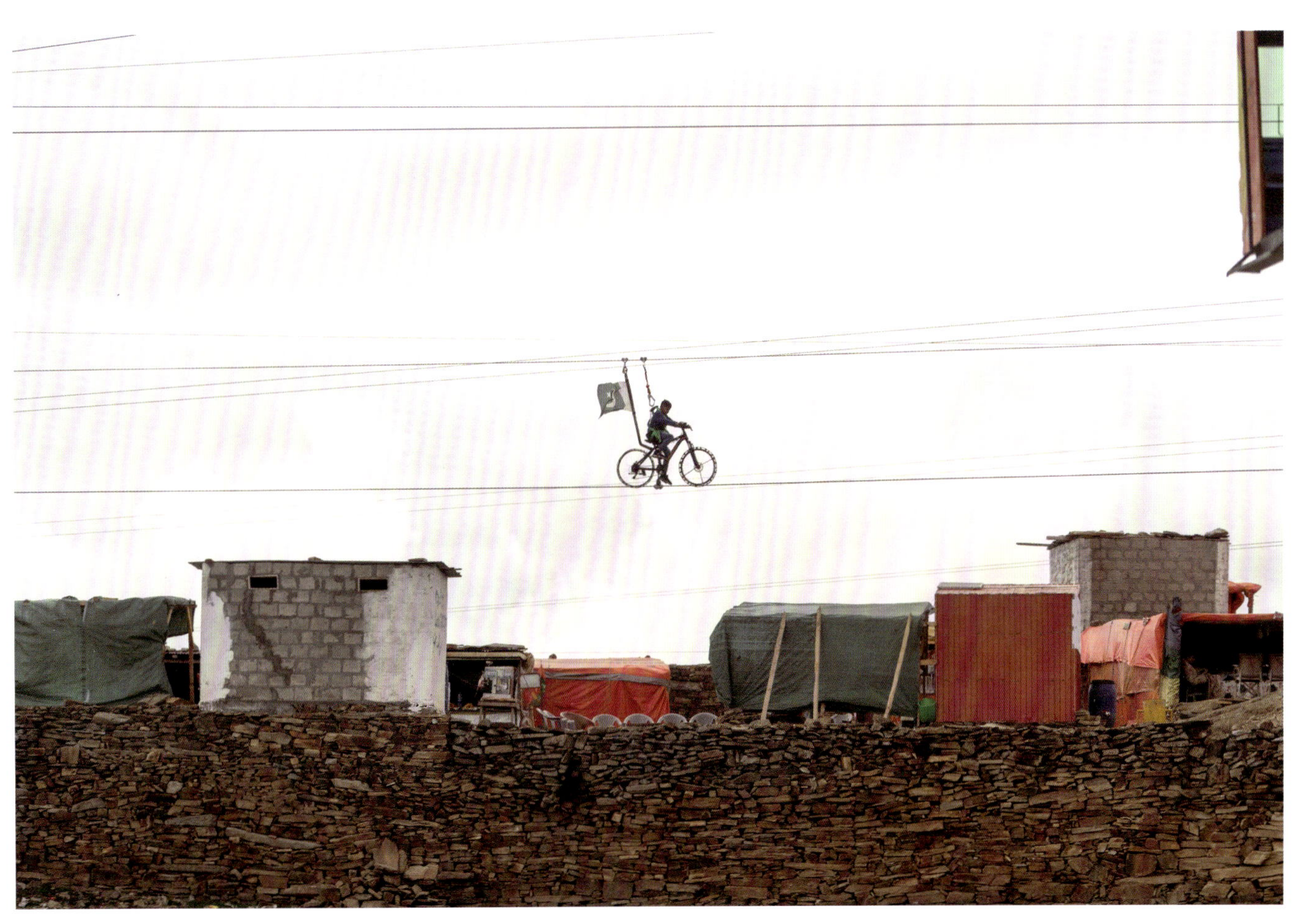

Naran, PAKISTAN

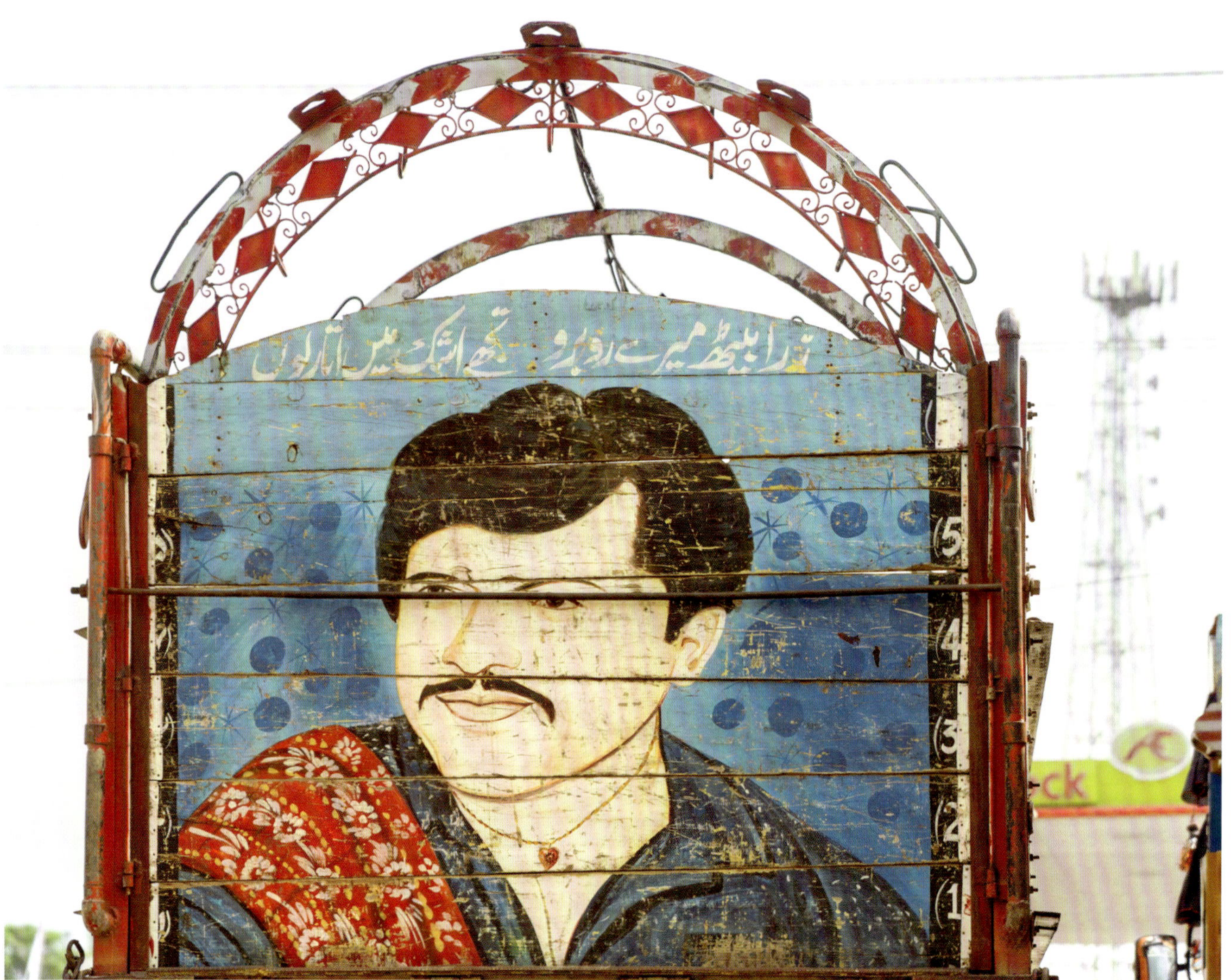

ذرا پلٹ میرے رخ پر و تھے اشک میں اُتر لوں
5
4
3
2
1

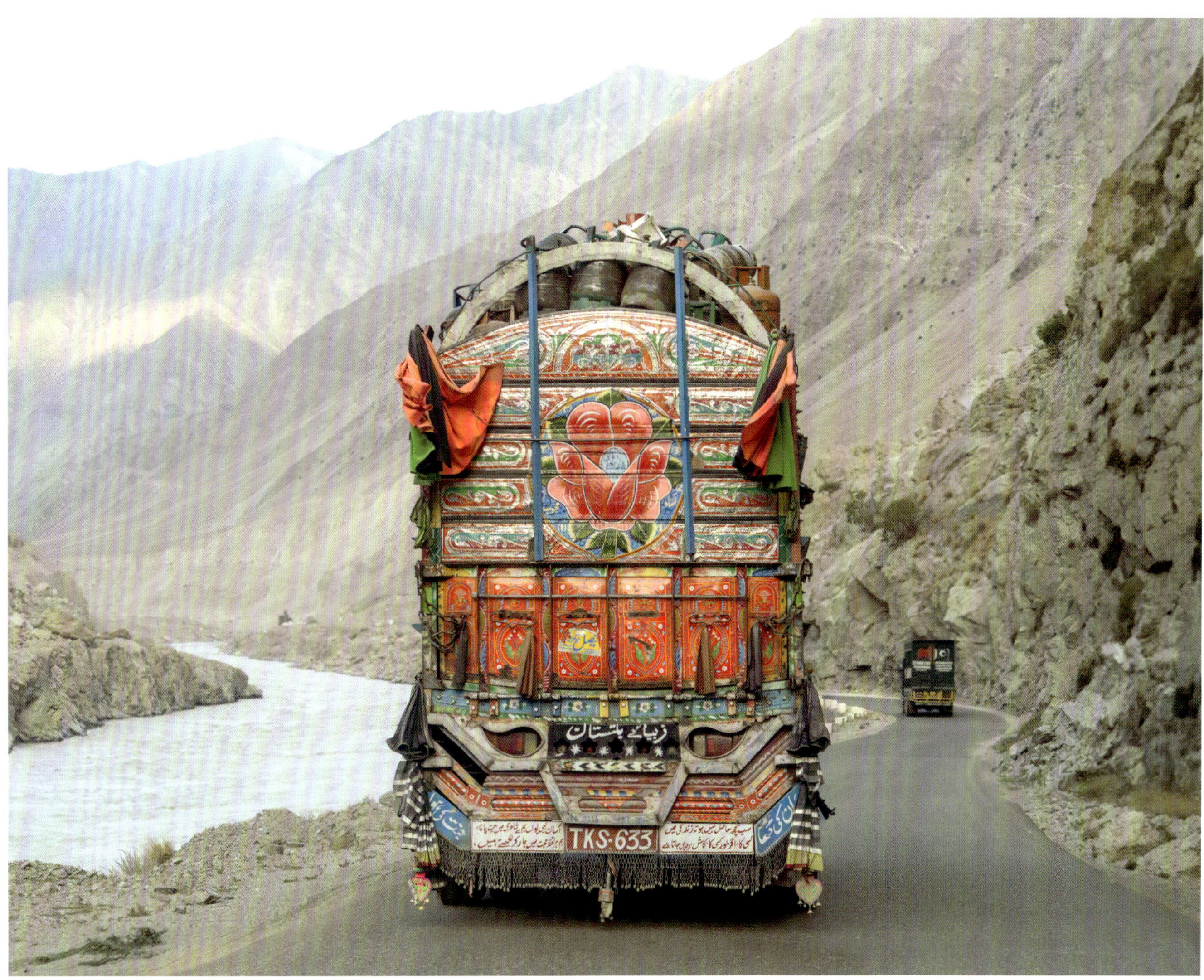

زندہ باد پاکستان
TKS-633

NEPAL

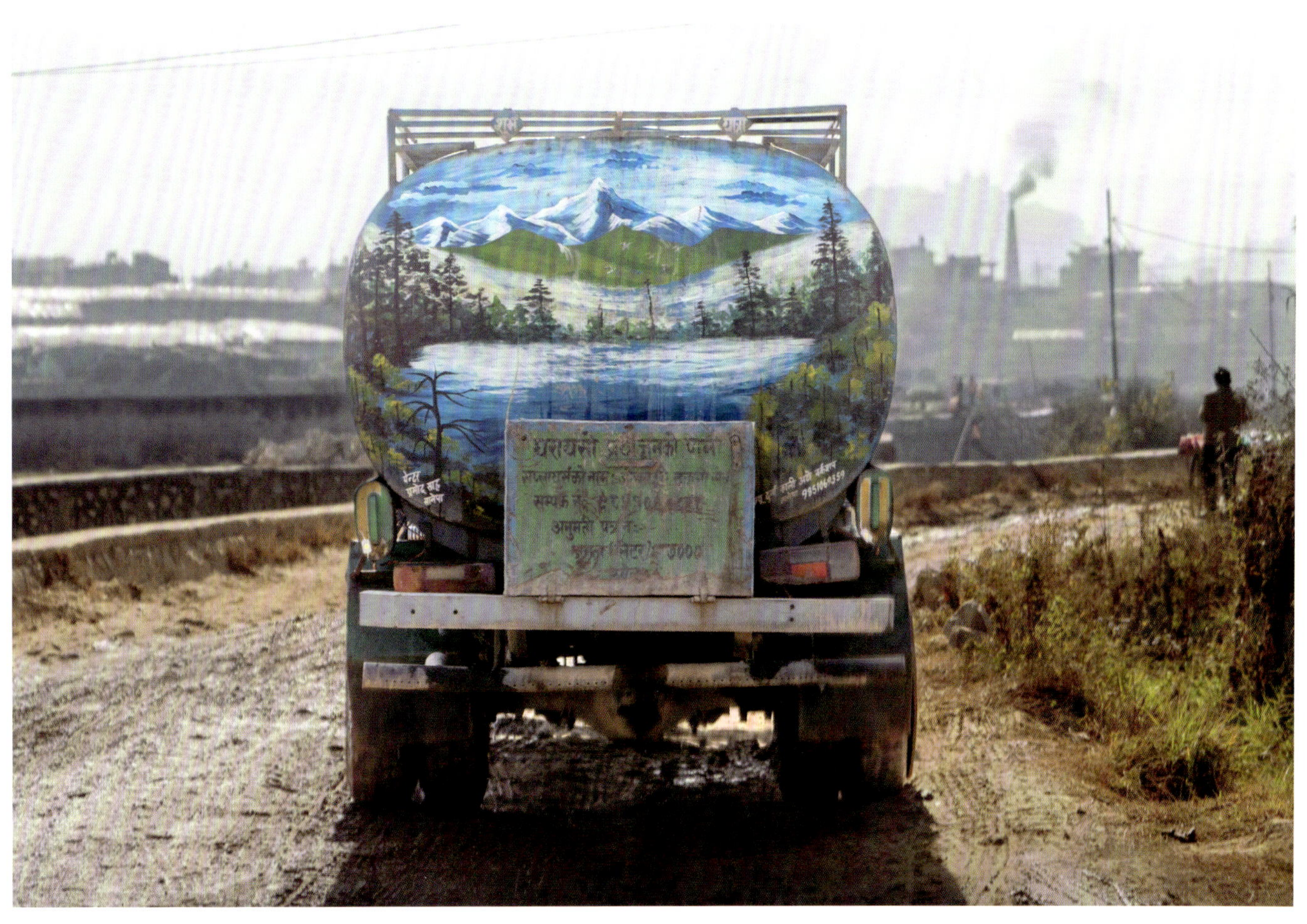

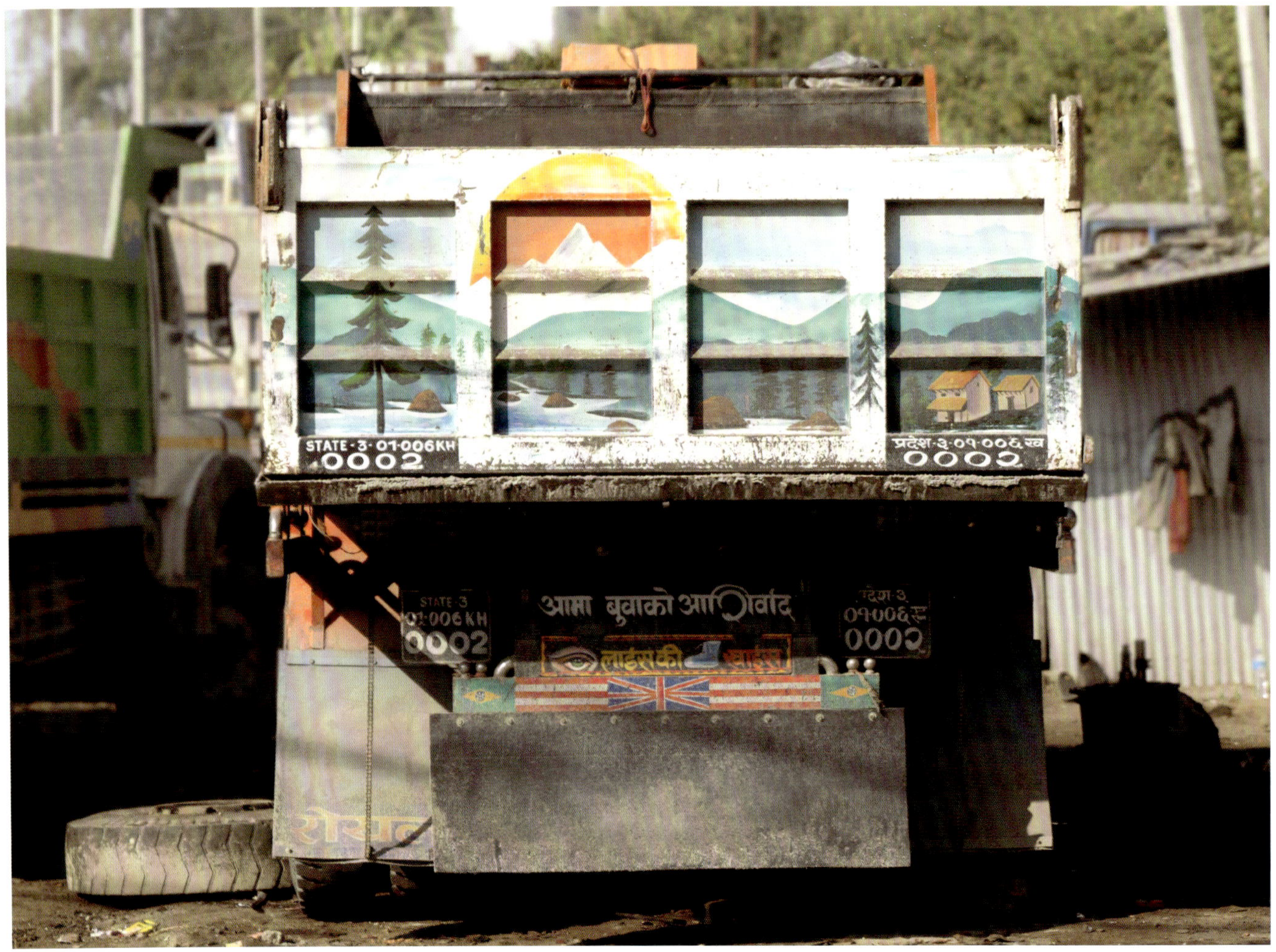

Kathmandu, NEPAL

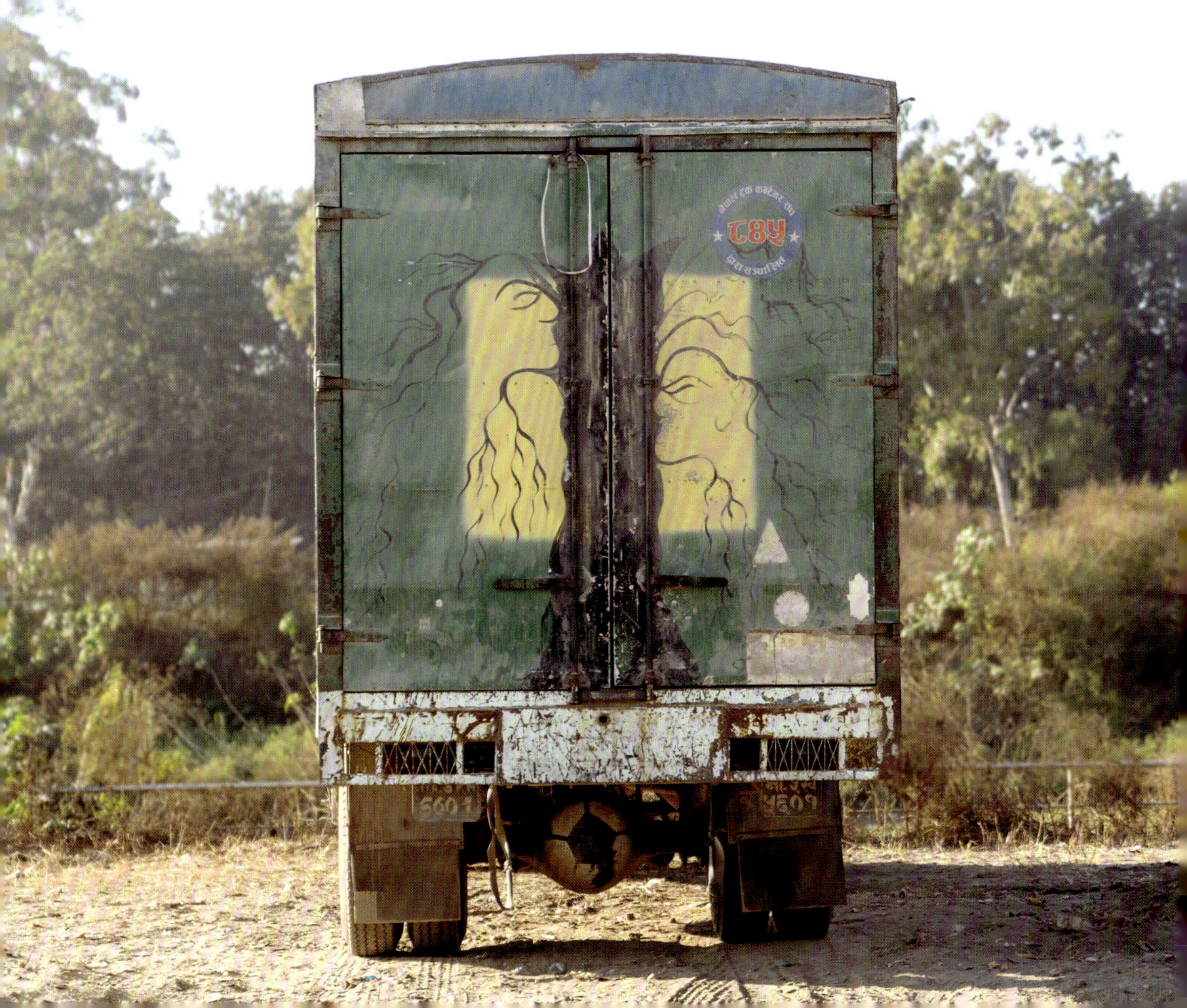

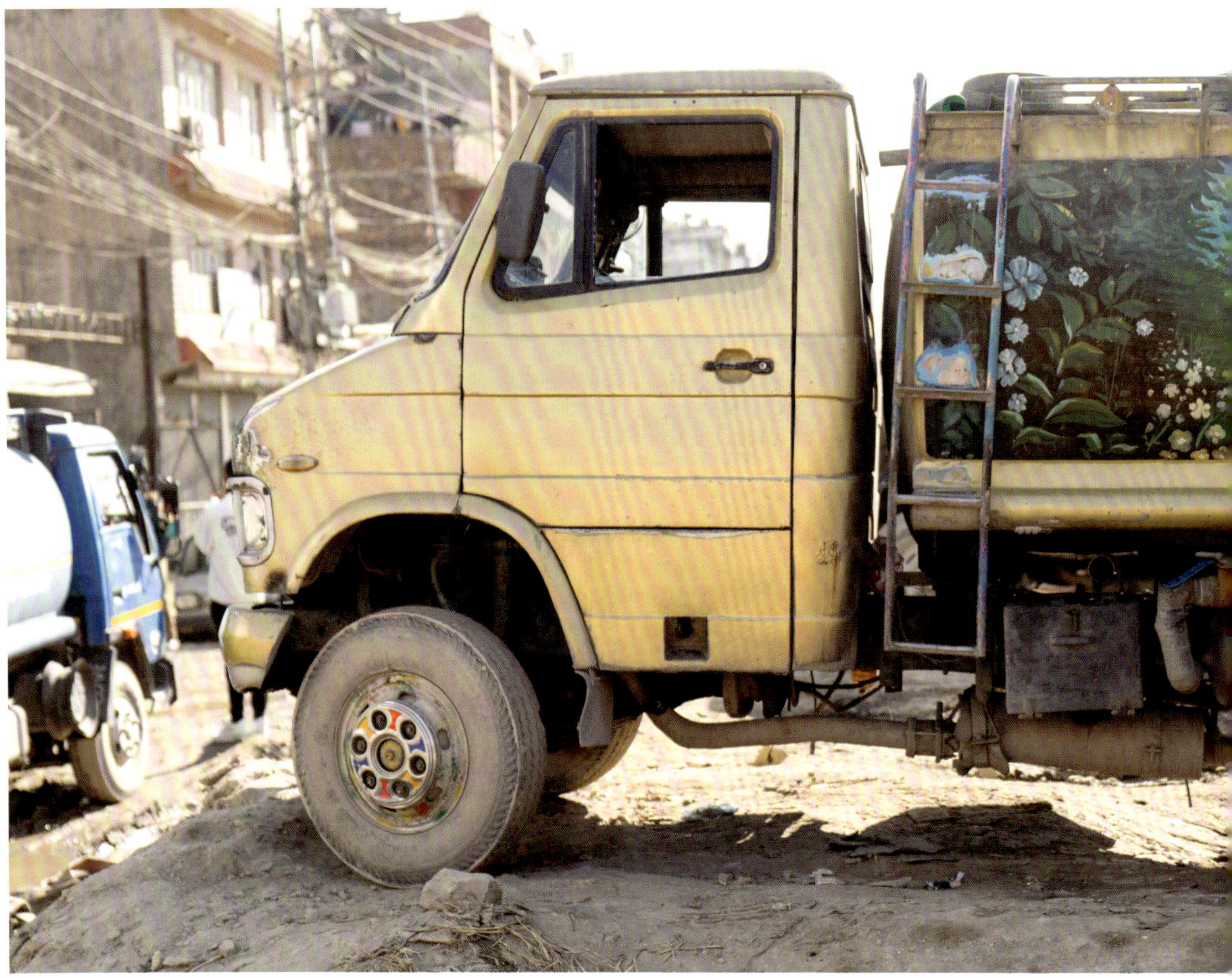

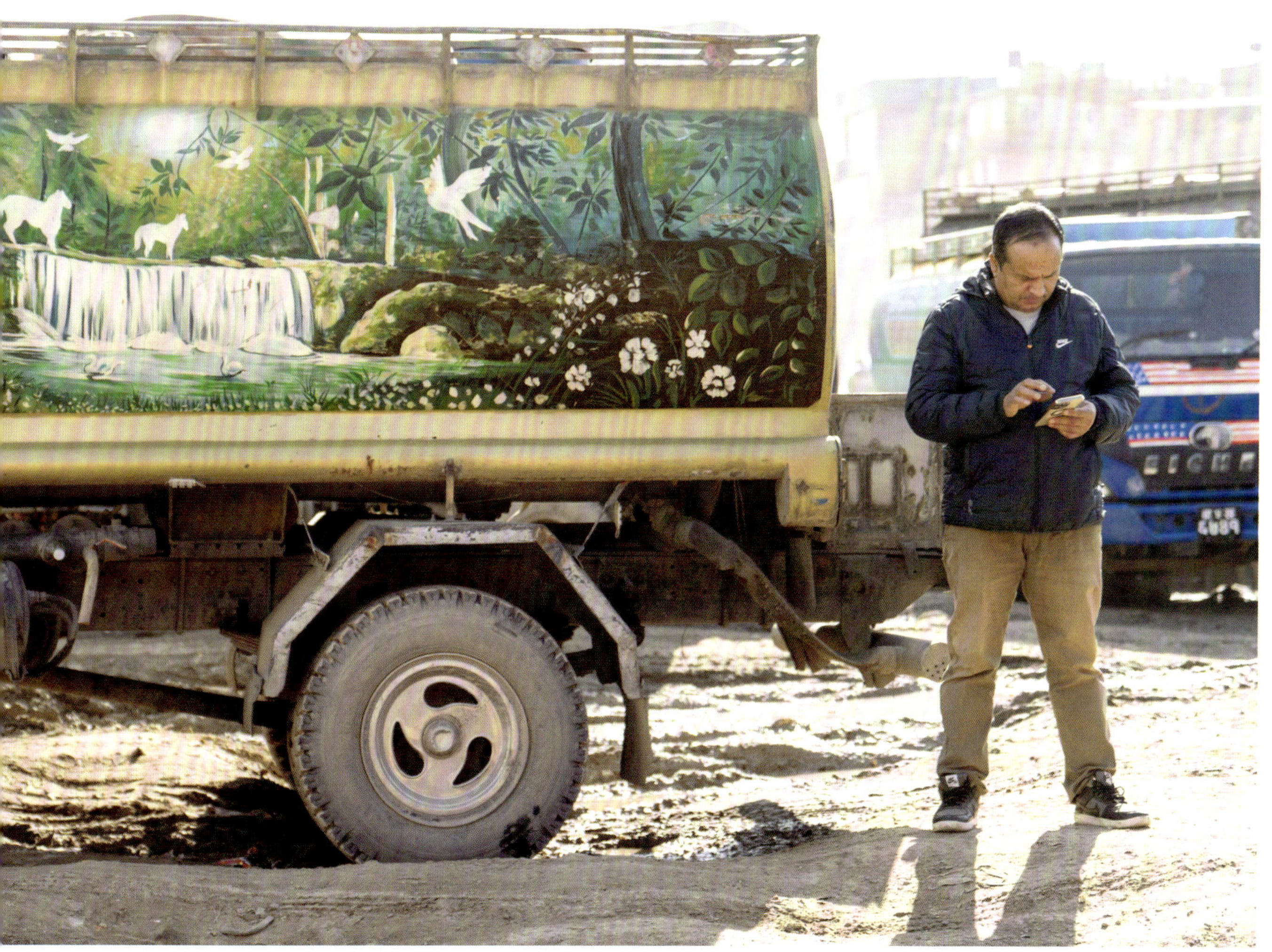

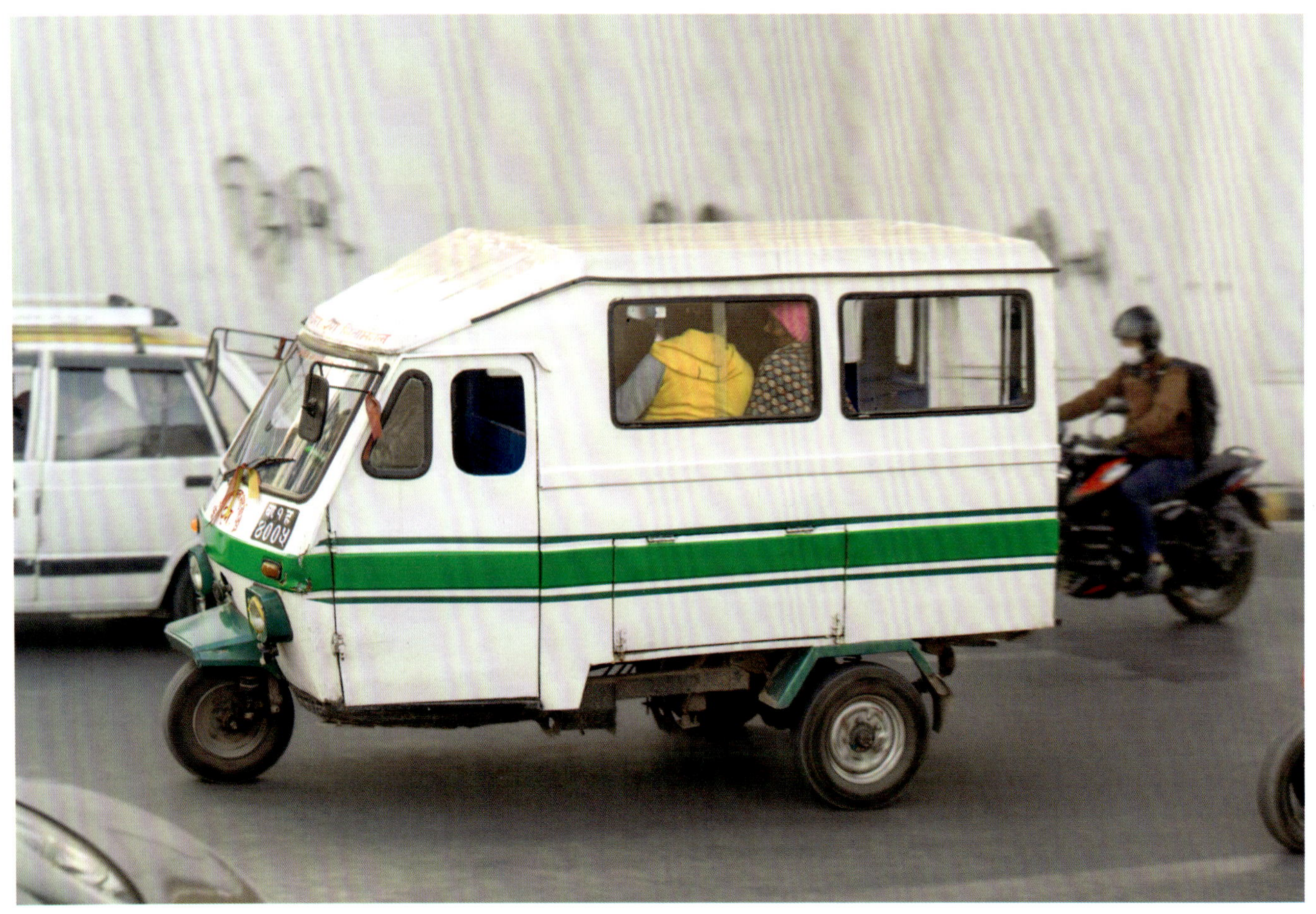

 Kathmandu, NEPAL

previous: Kathmandu, NEPAL

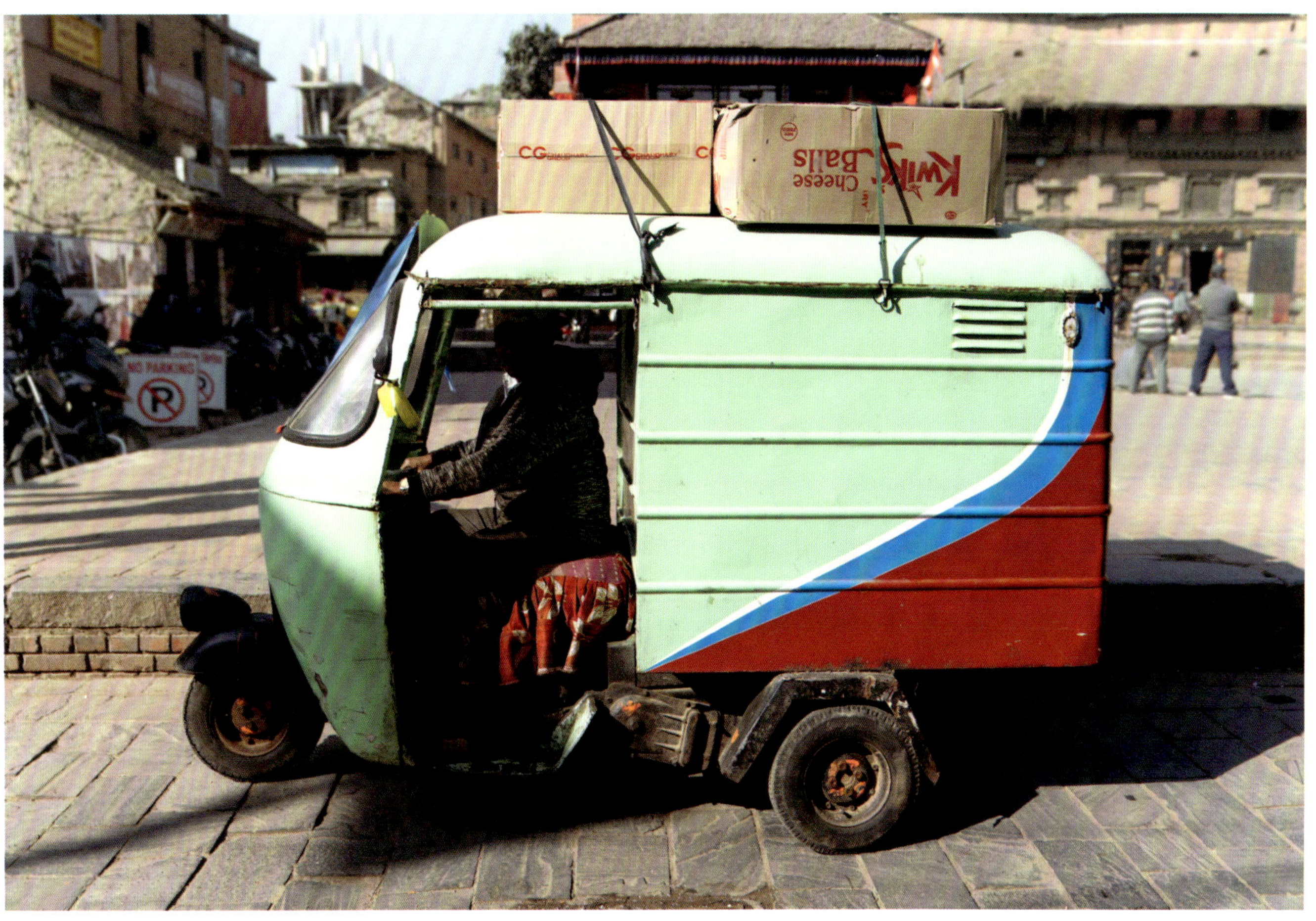

CG
Kwity Cheese Balls
NO PARKING

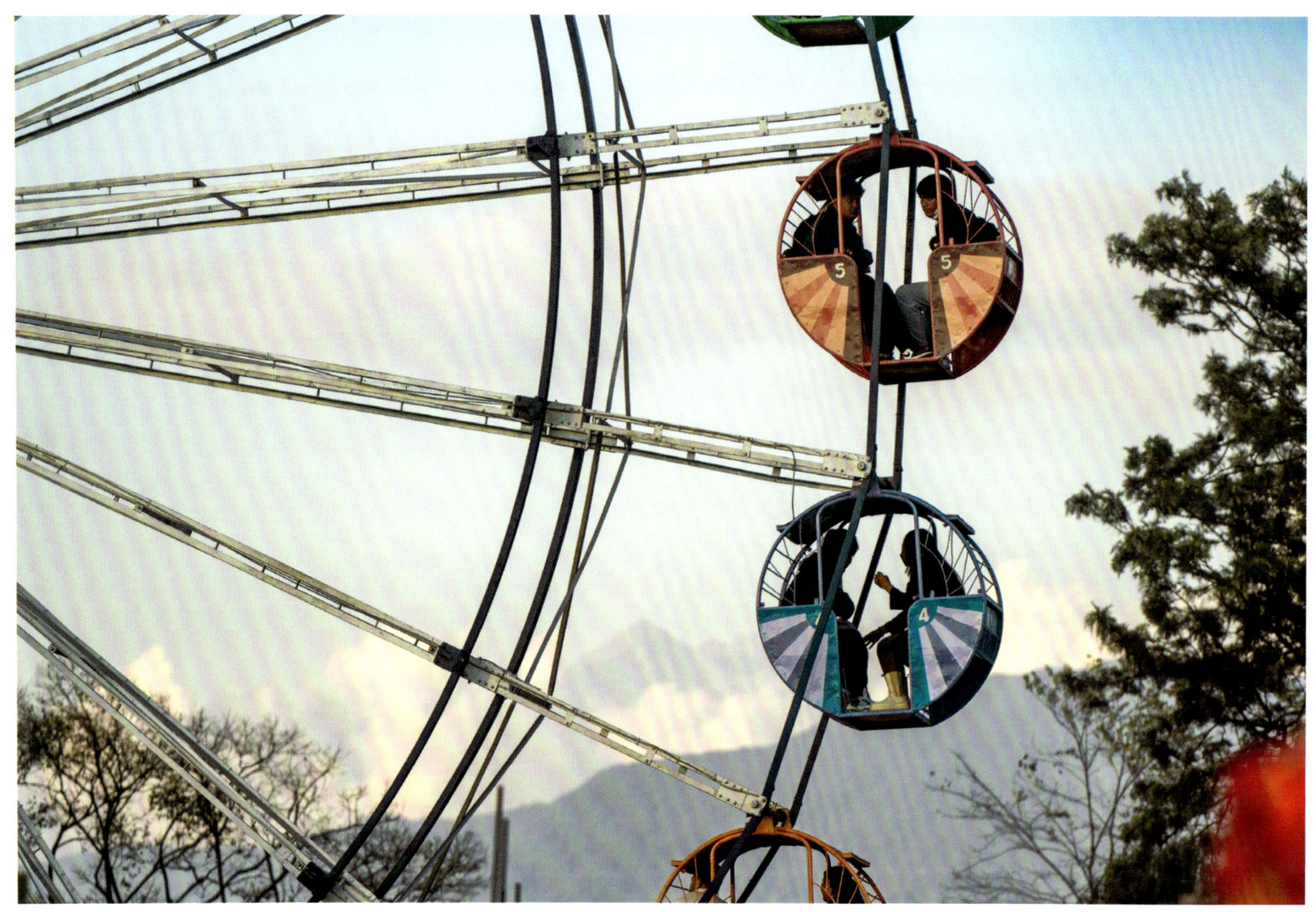

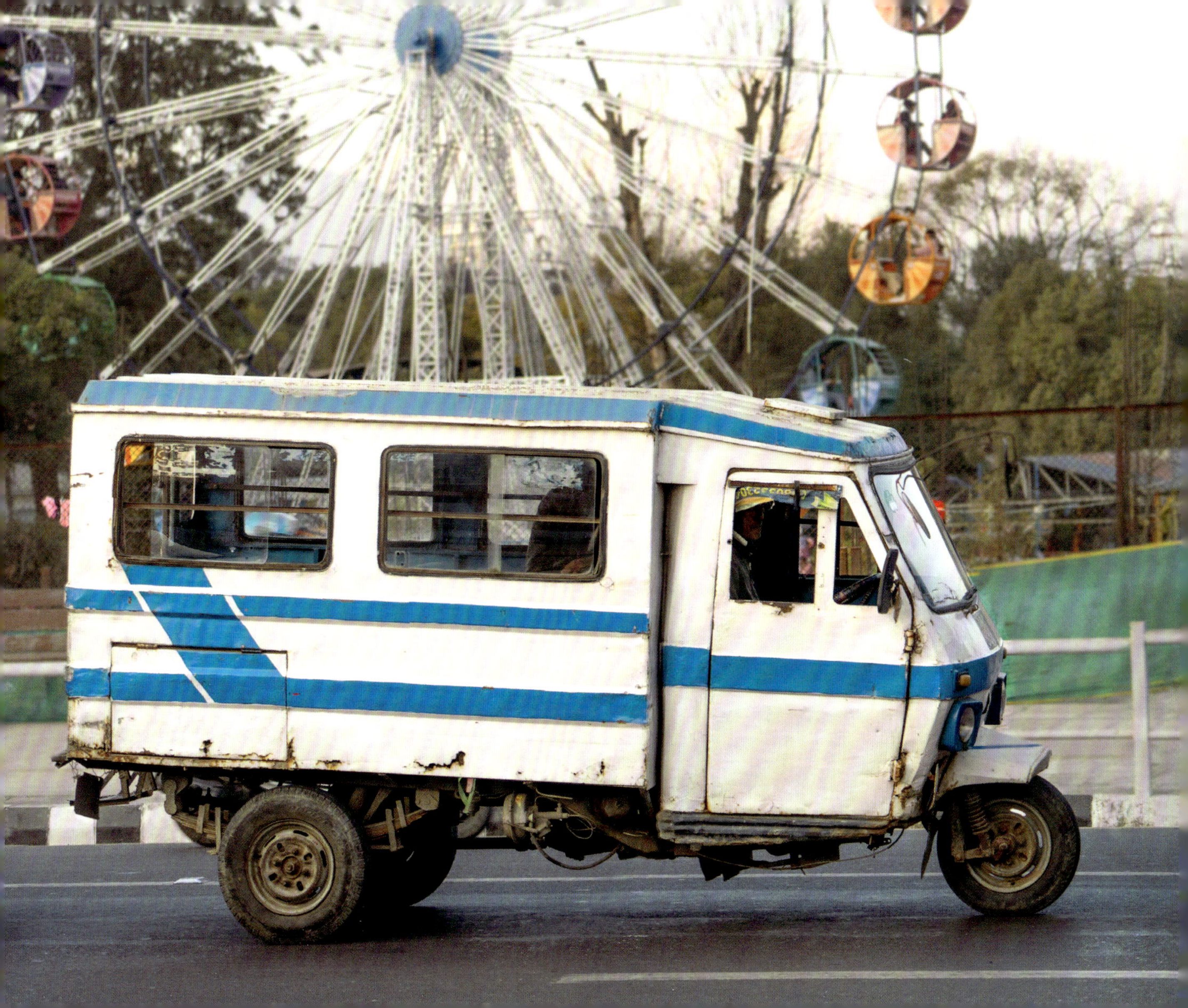

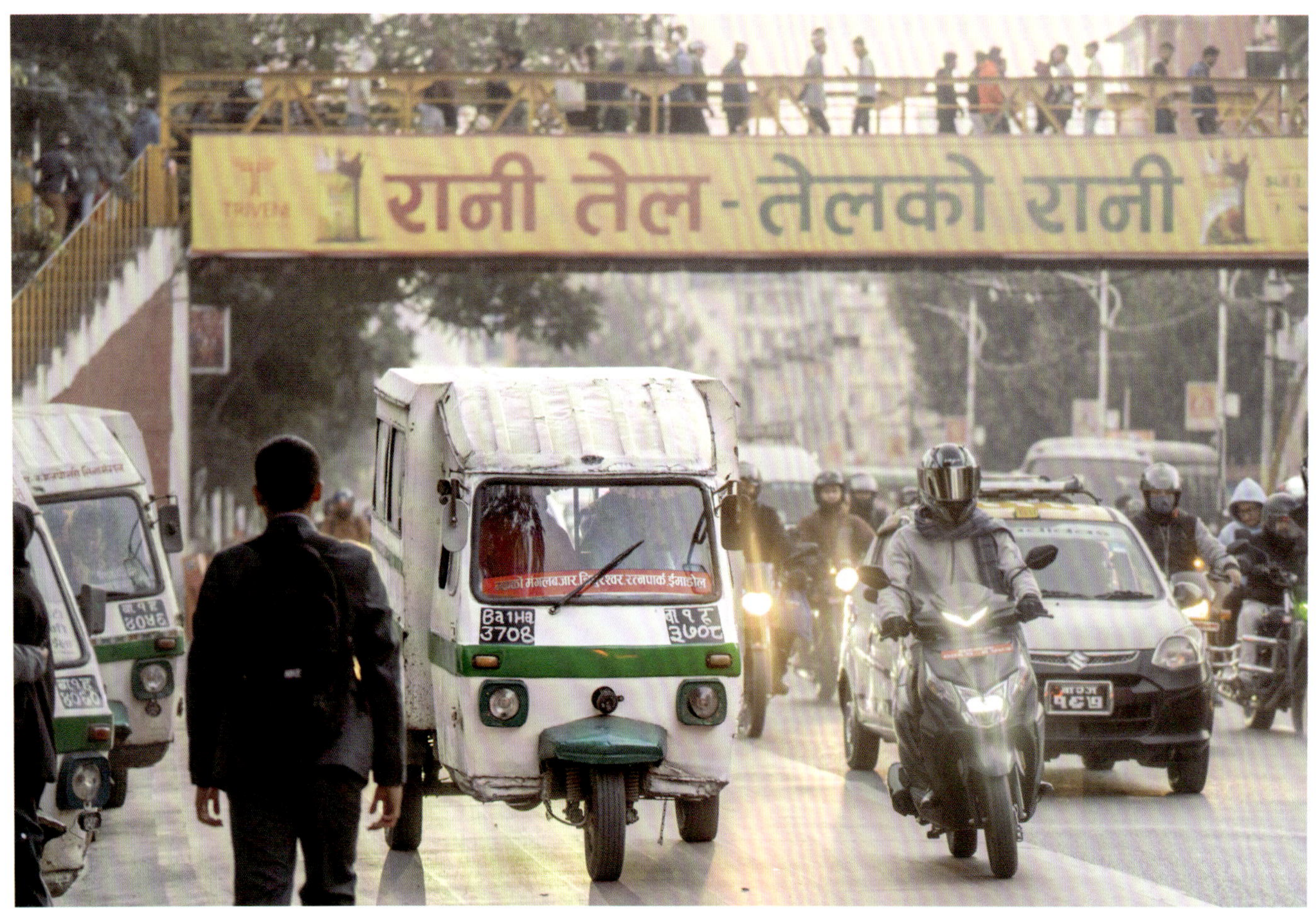

166   Kathmandu, NEPAL

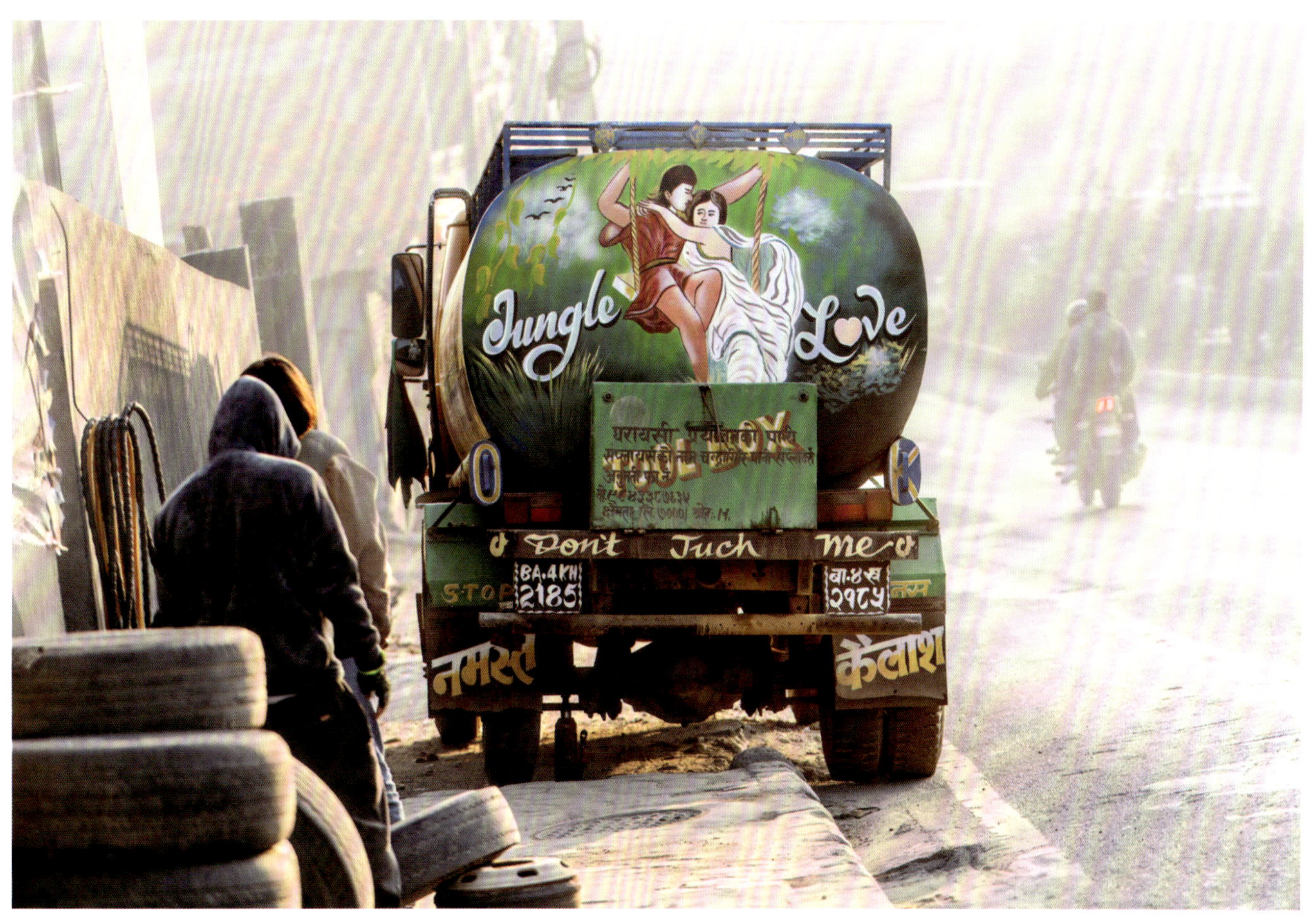Jungle
Love
Don't Juch Me
STOP
BA.4KH
2185
बा.४ख
२१८५
नमस्ते
कैलाश

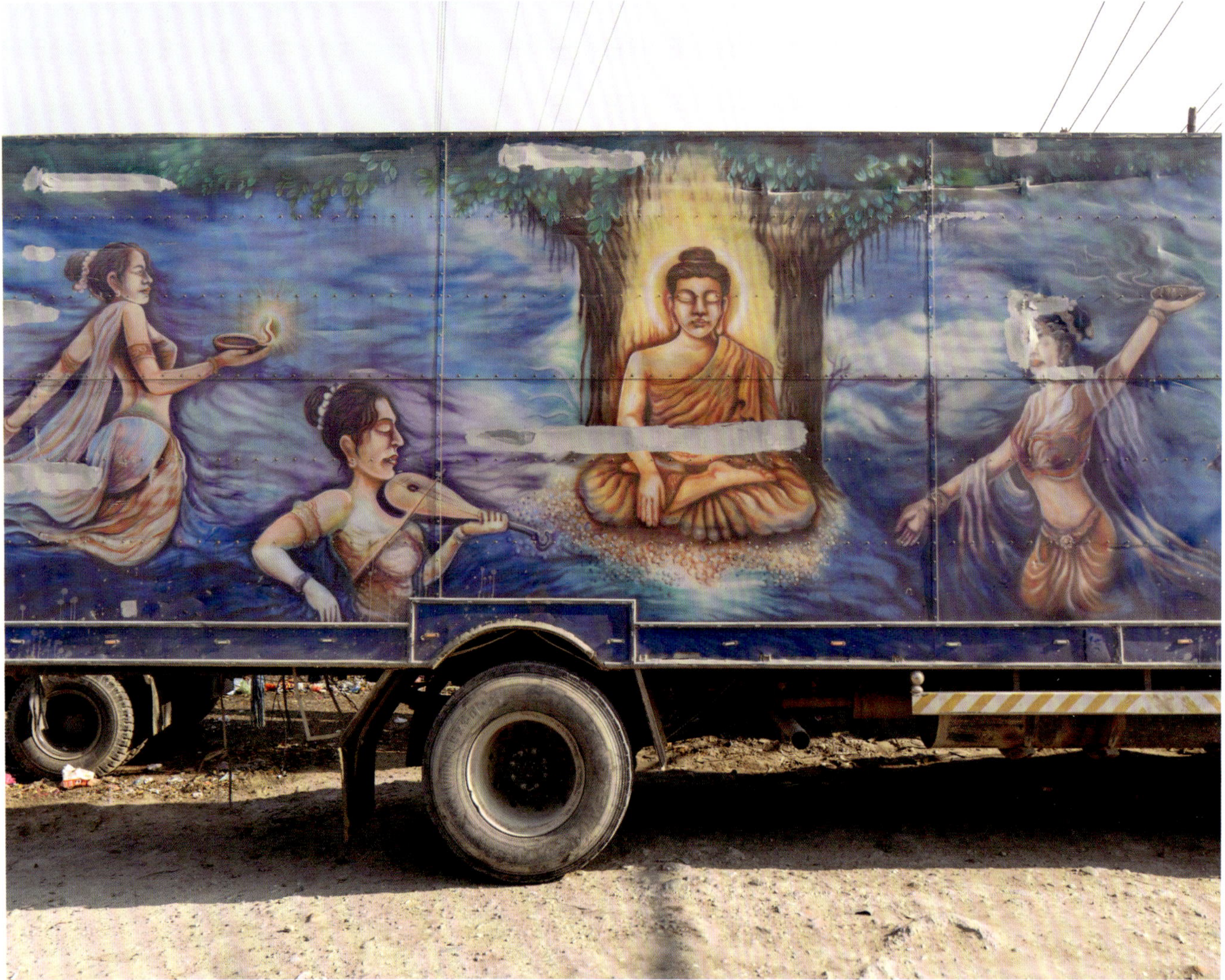

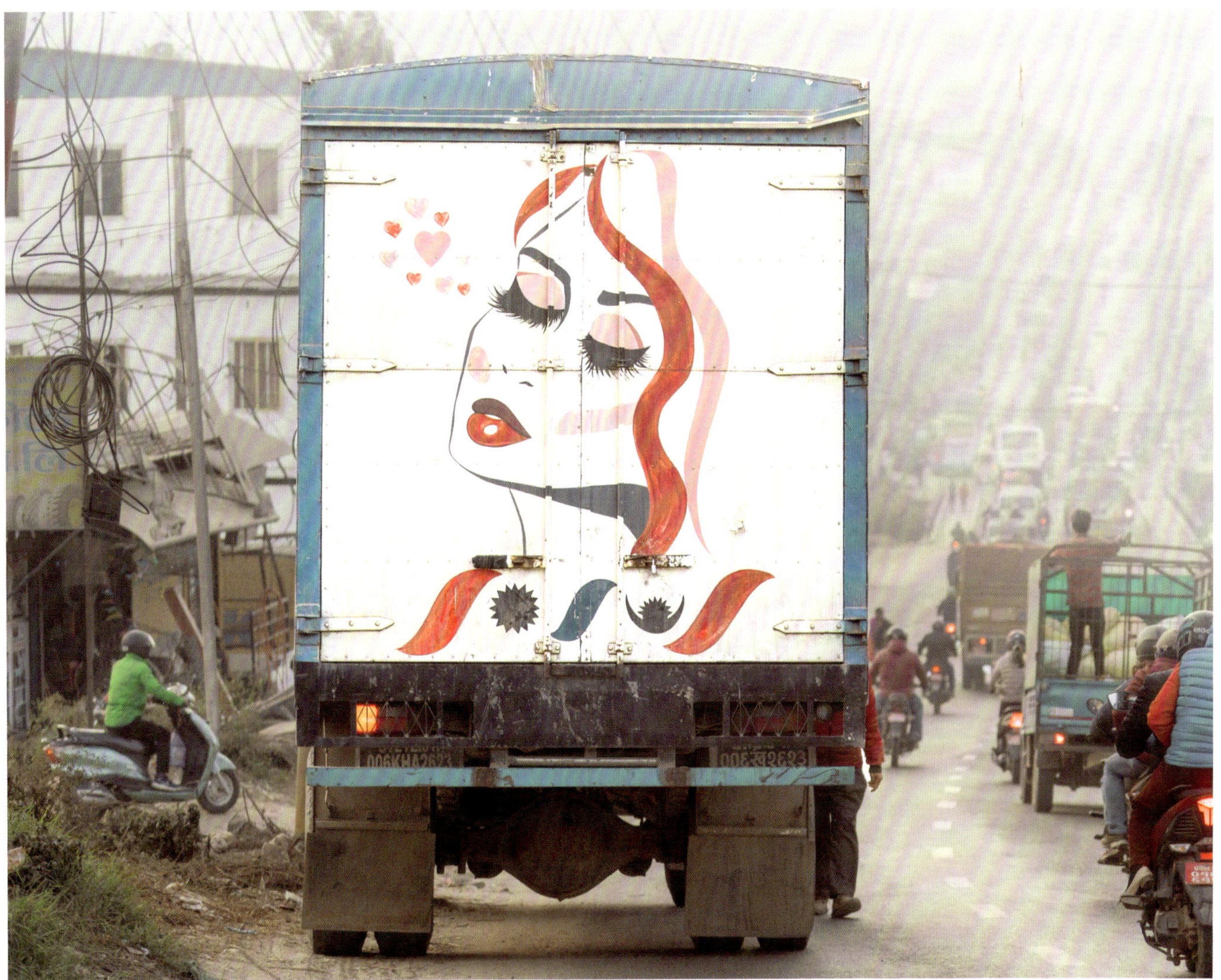

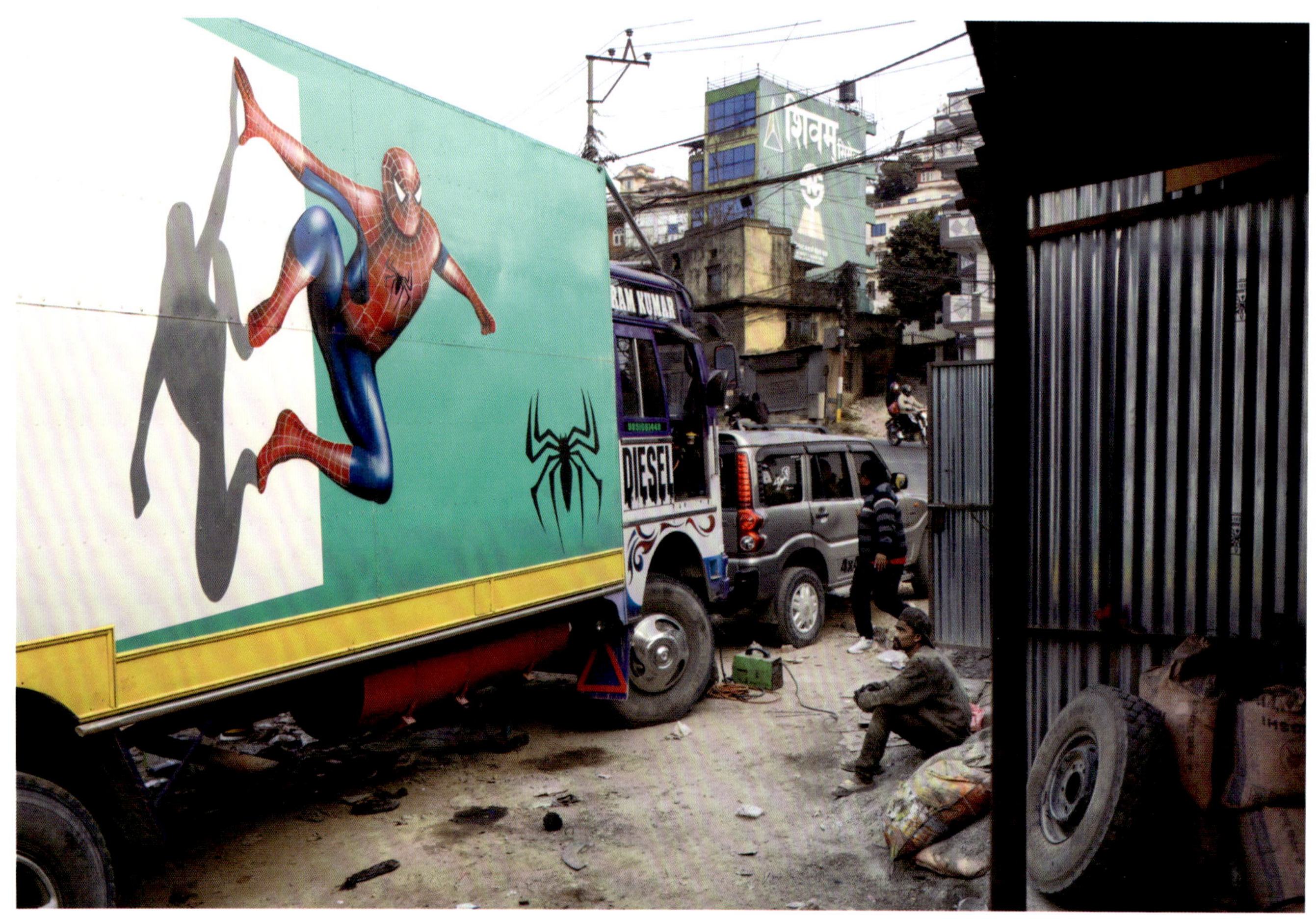

170   Kathmandu, NEPAL

overleaf: Kathmandu, NEPAL

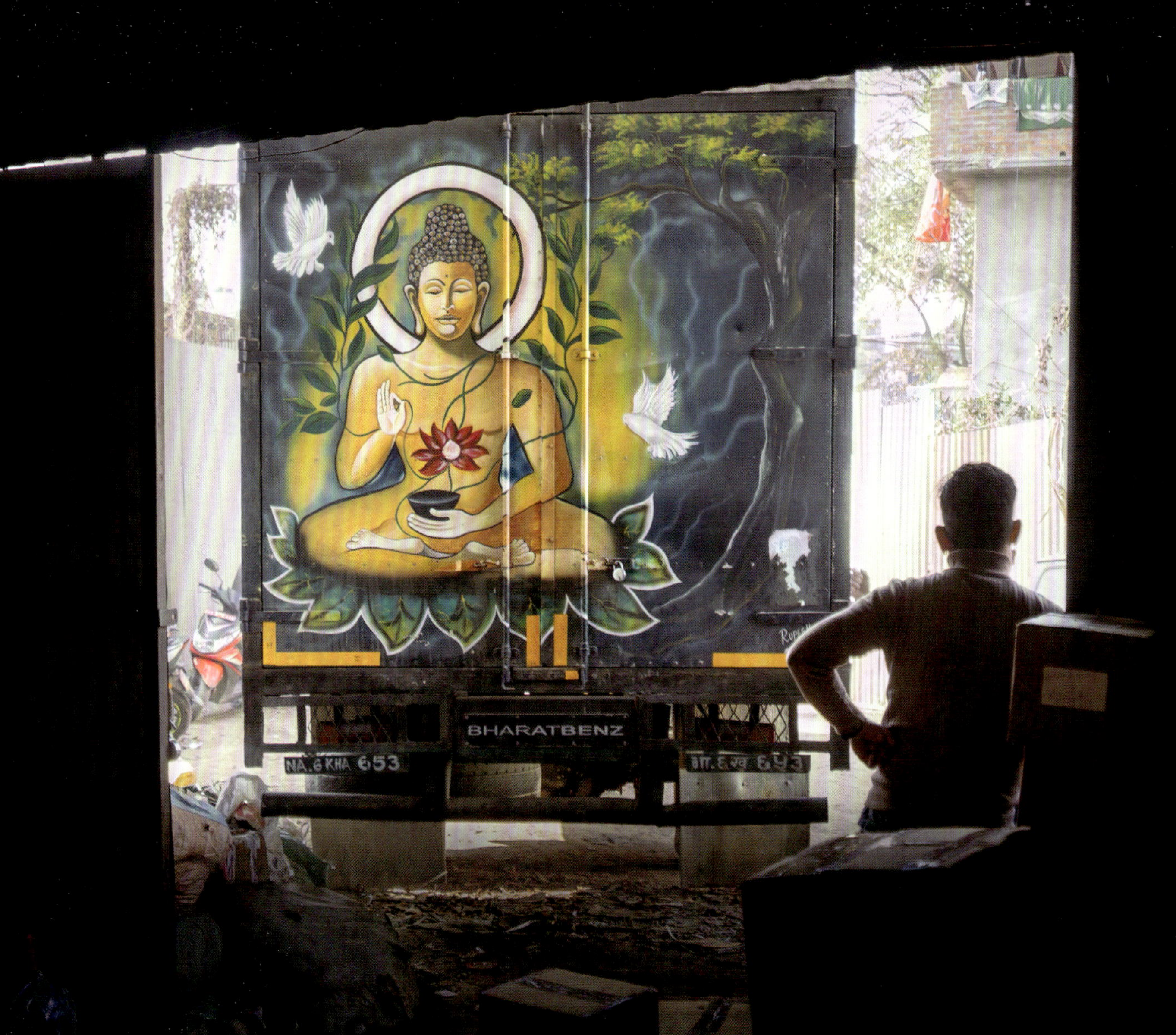

BHARATBENZ
NA.6 KHA 653

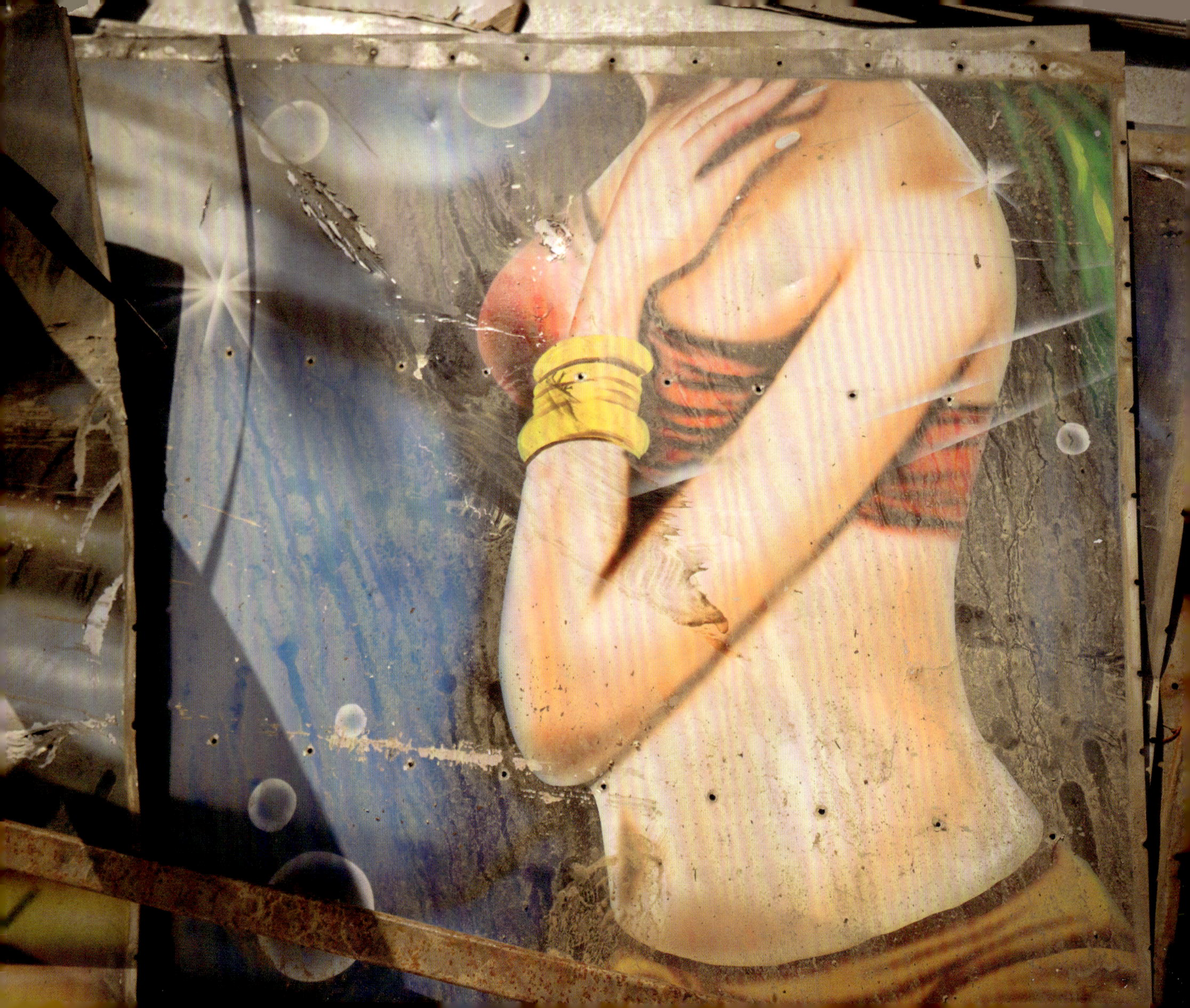

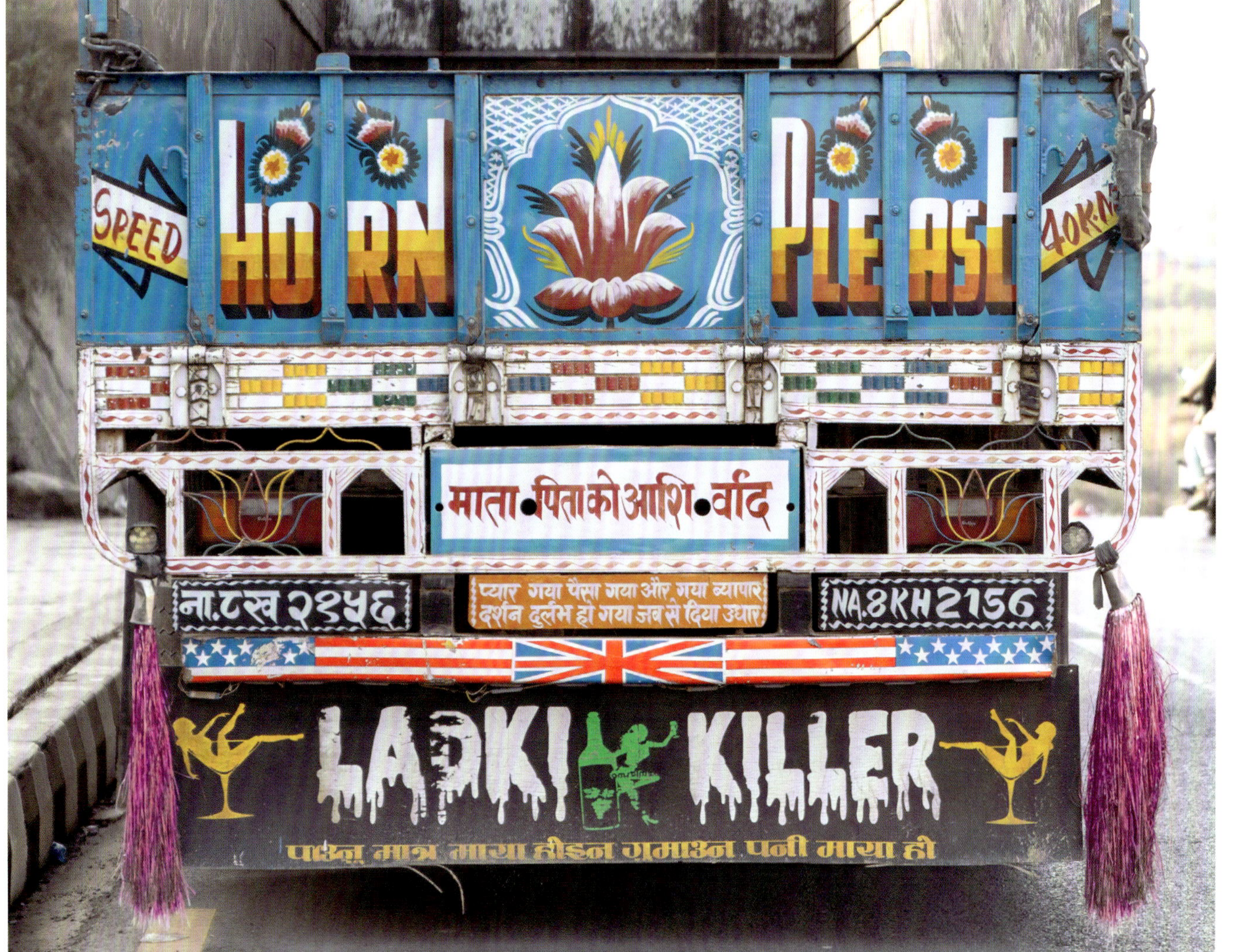

SPEED
HO RN
PLE ASE
4OKM
माता • पिता को आशि • र्वाद
प्यार गया पैसा गया और गया व्यापार
दर्शन दुर्लभ हो गया जब से दिया उधार
ना.ट ख २१५६
NA.8KH 2156
LADKI KILLER
पैसा मात्र माया होइन नमाउन पनी माया हो

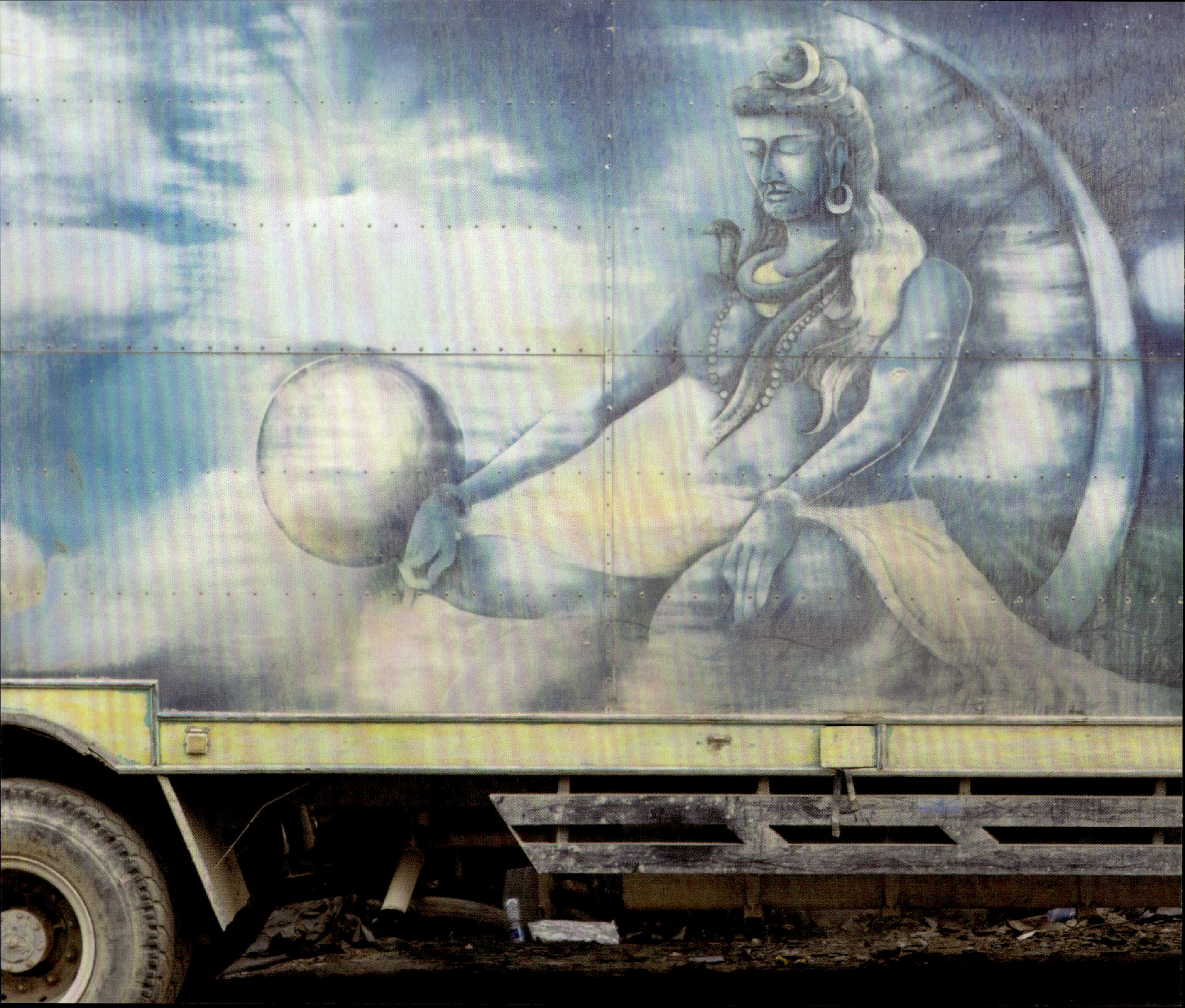

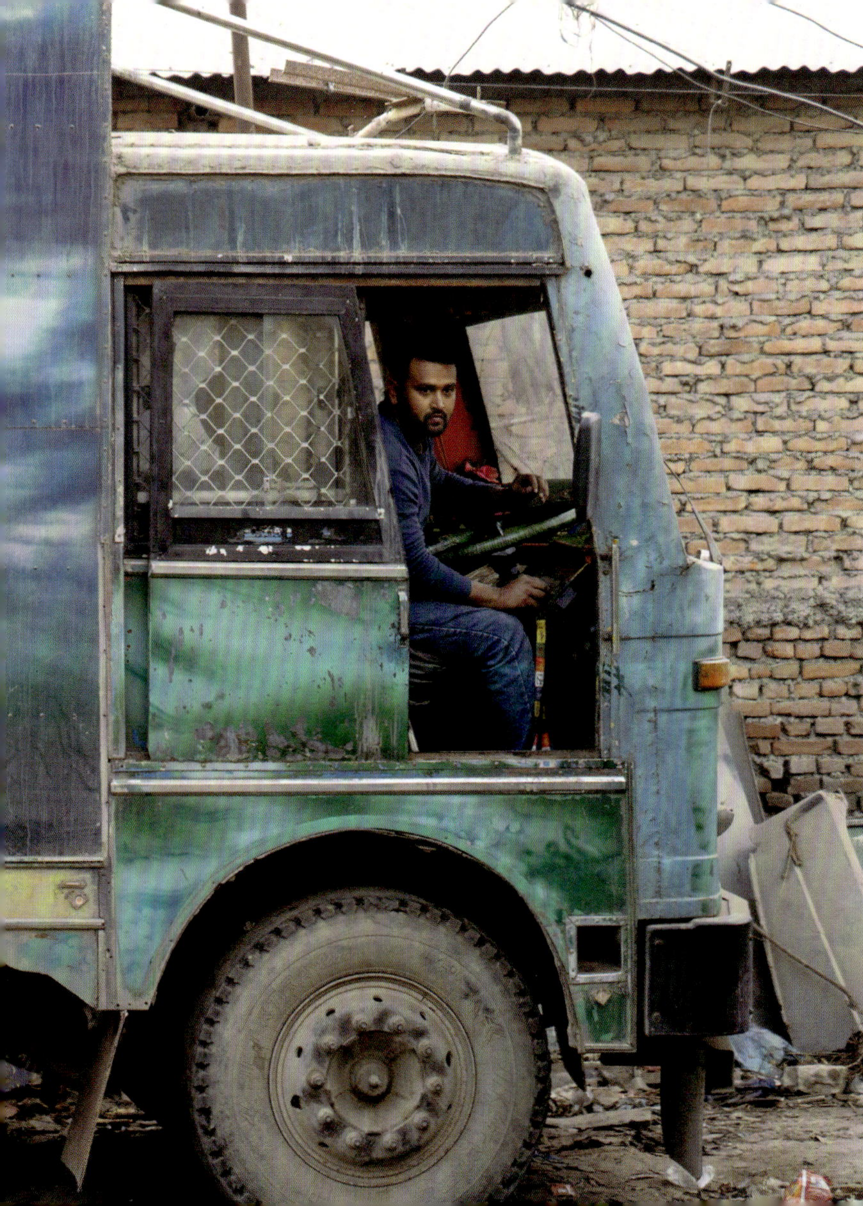

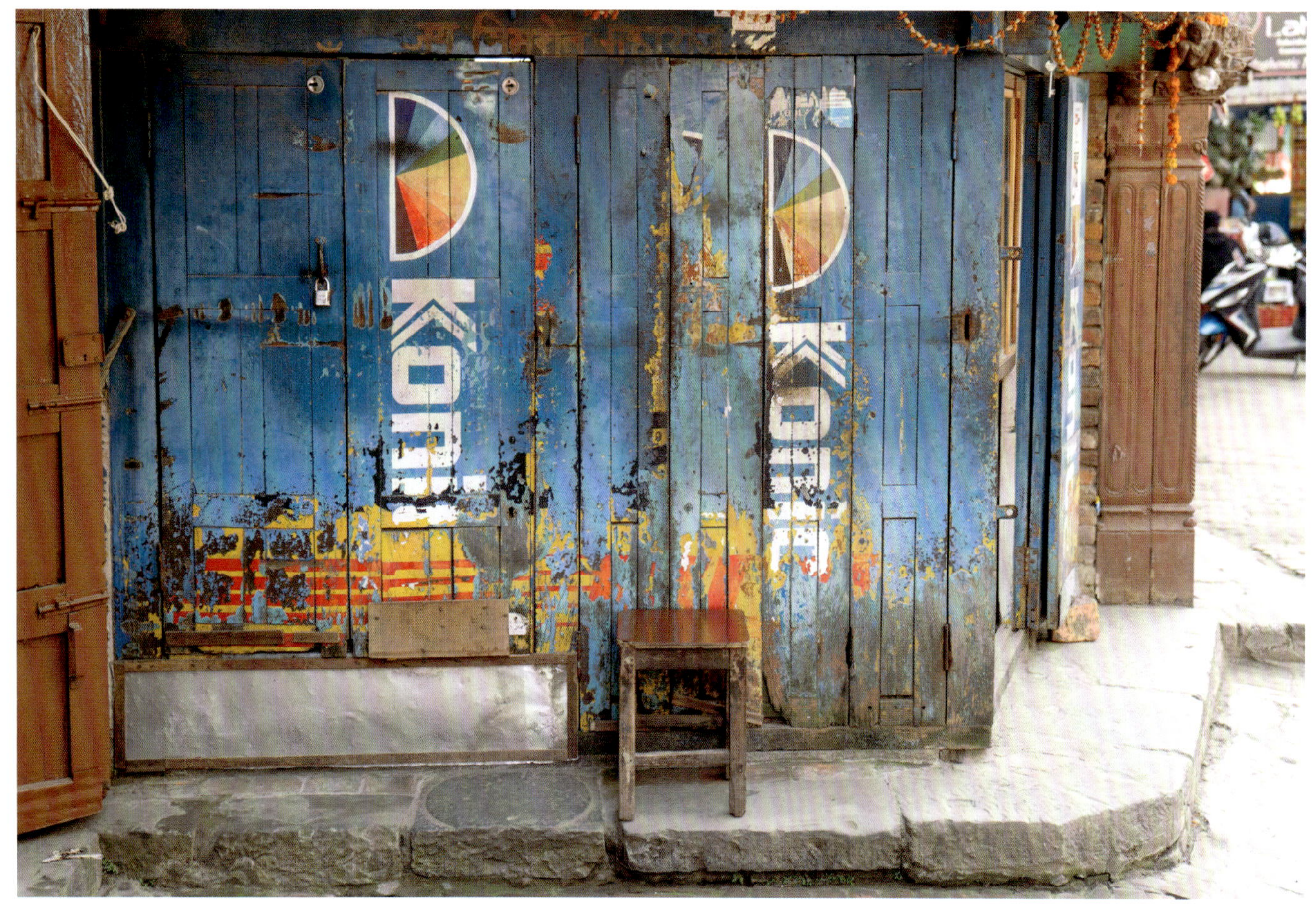

overleaf: Kathmandu, NEPAL

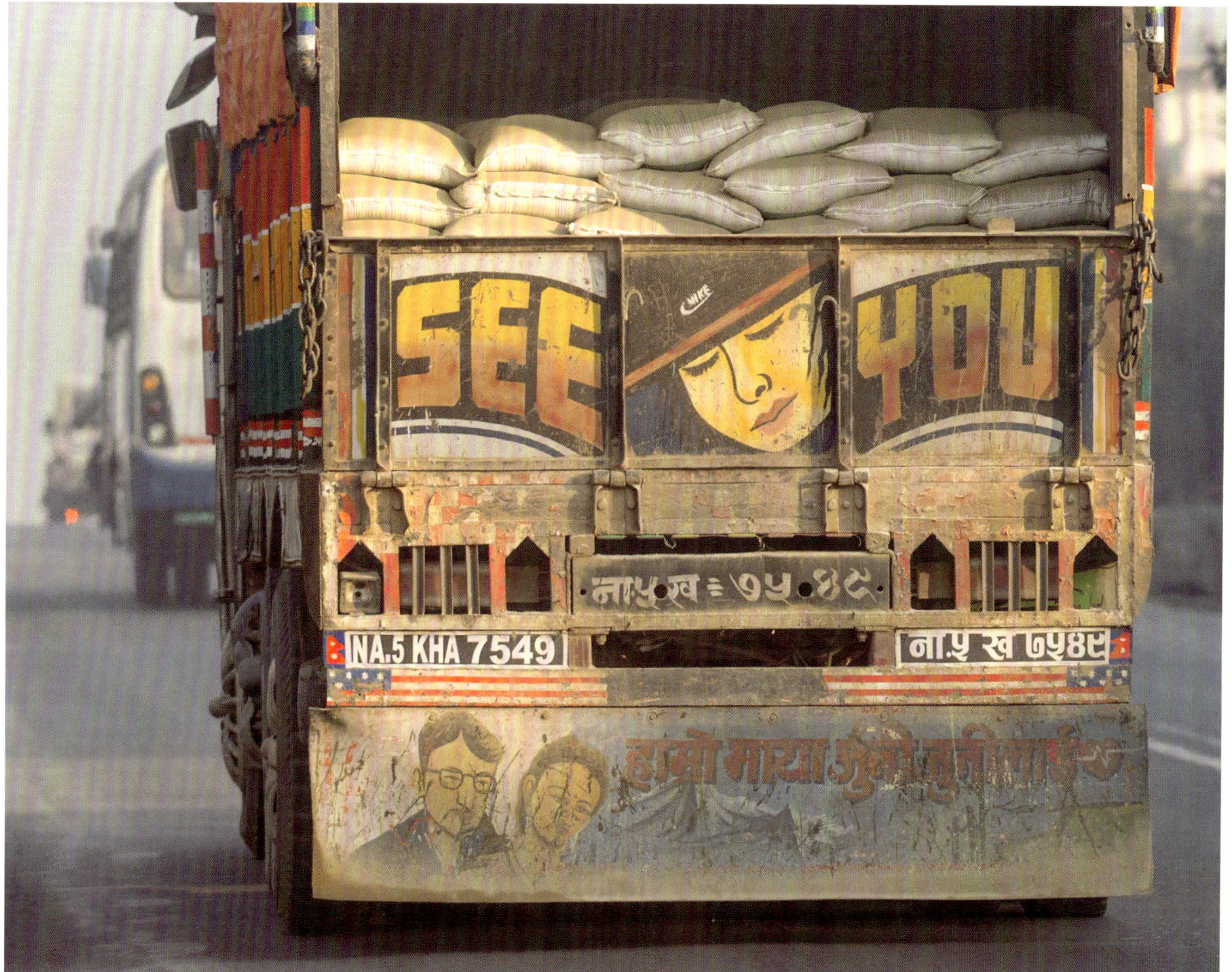

SEE
YOU
NIKE
NA.5 KHA 7549
ना.५ ख ७५४९

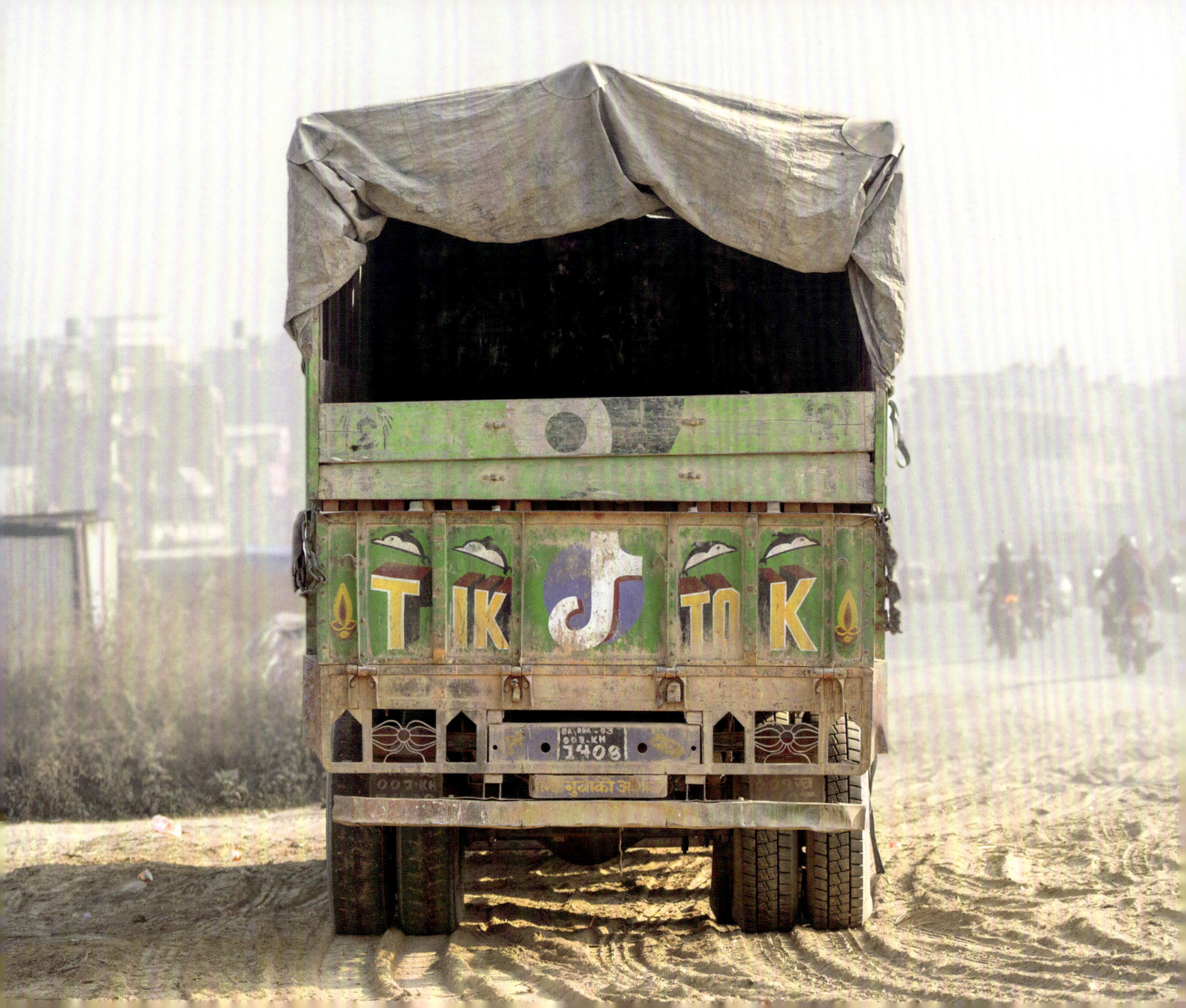

TIK TOK

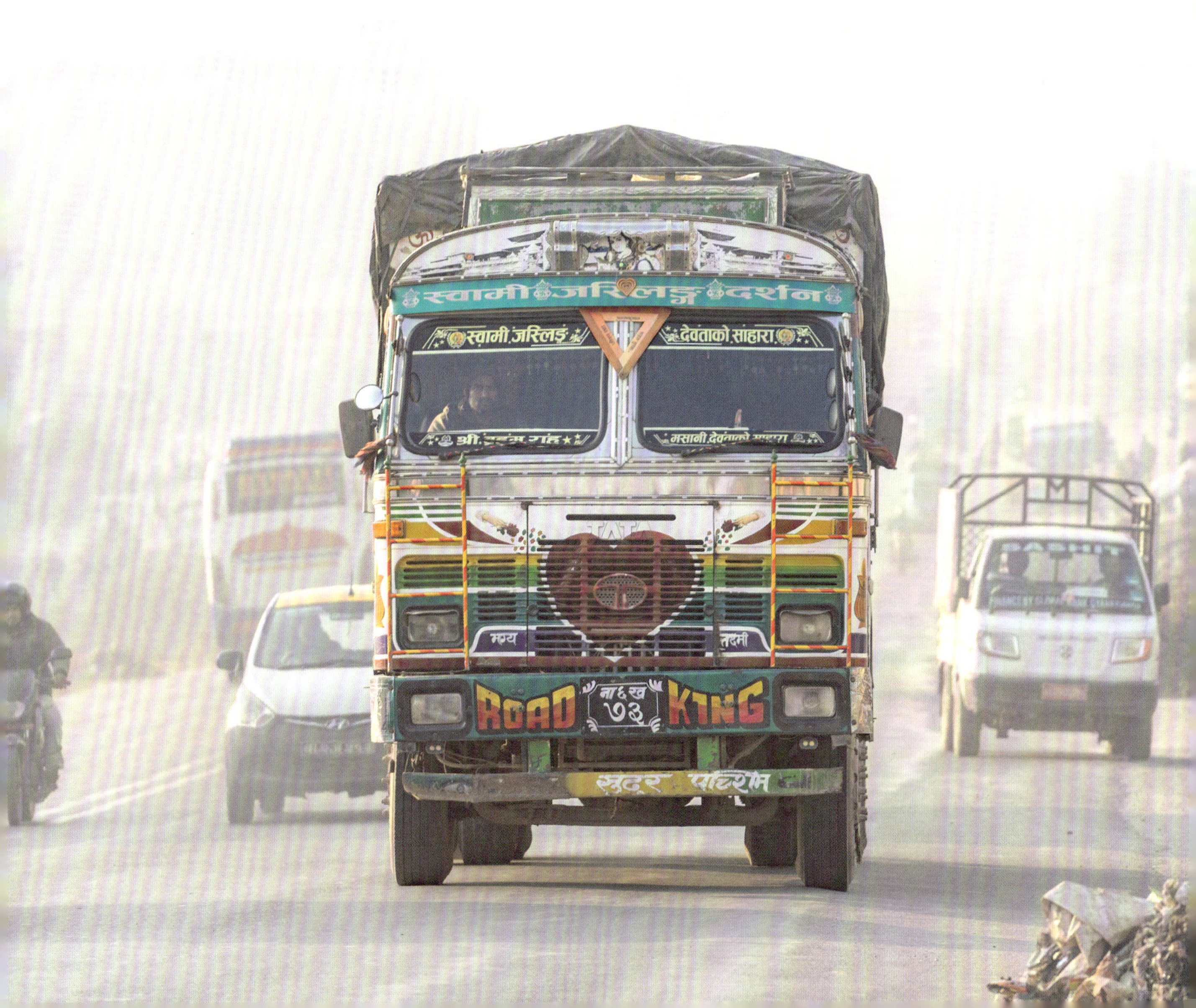
स्वामी जसिलङ्ग दर्शन
स्वामी जसिलइ
देवताको सहारा
श्री रत्न गान्ठ
मसानी देवताको सहारा
TATA
ROAD KING
ना६ख ७३
सुन्दर सतीराम

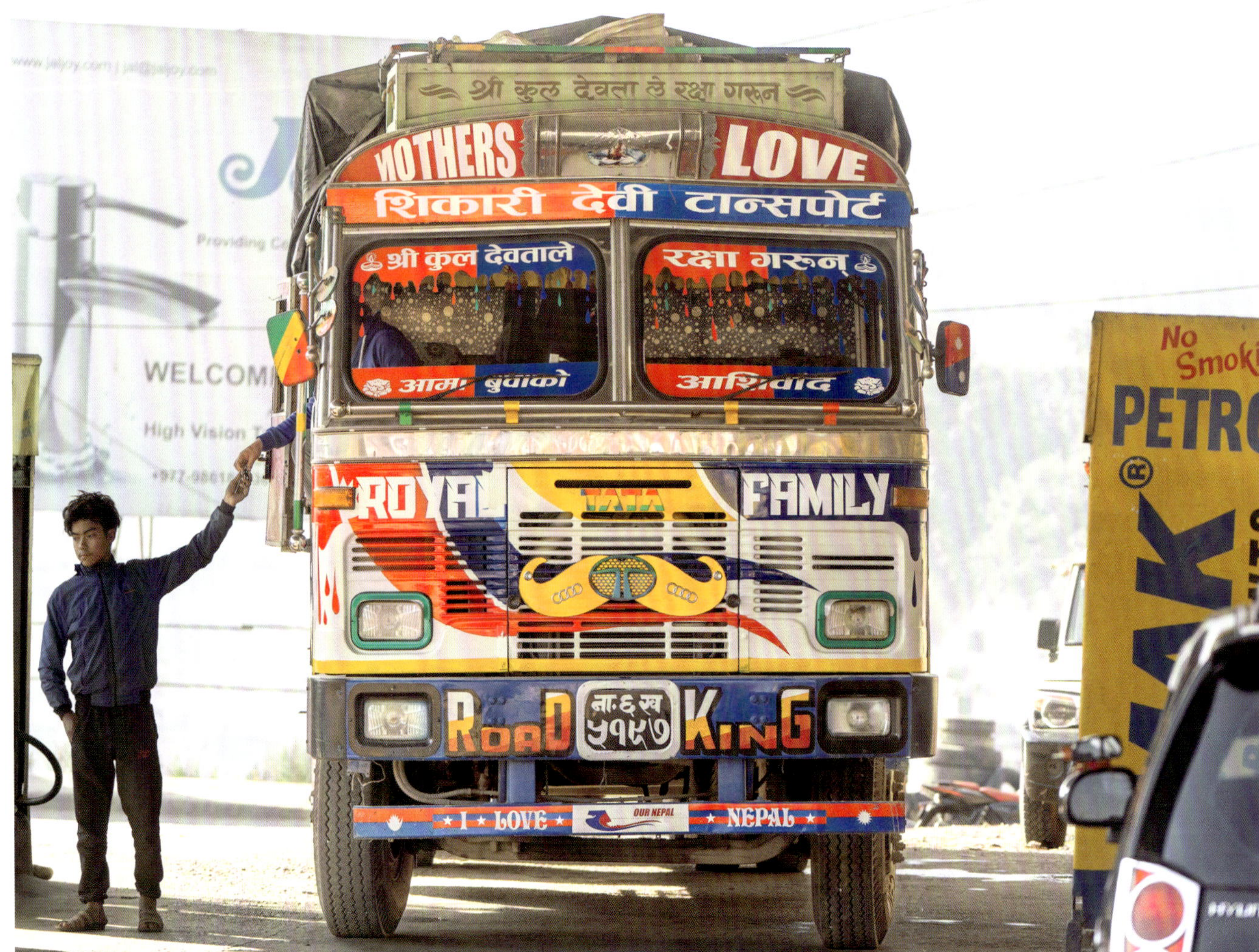
श्री कुल देवता ले रक्षा गरुन्
MOTHERS LOVE
शिकारी देवी टान्सपोर्ट
श्री कुल देवताले
रक्षा गरुन्
आमा बुवाको
आशिर्वाद
ROYAL
TATA
FAMILY
ROAD KING
ना. ६ ख
२१५७
I LOVE NEPAL
OUR NEPAL
WELCOME
High Vision
No Smoki
PETRO
JAK

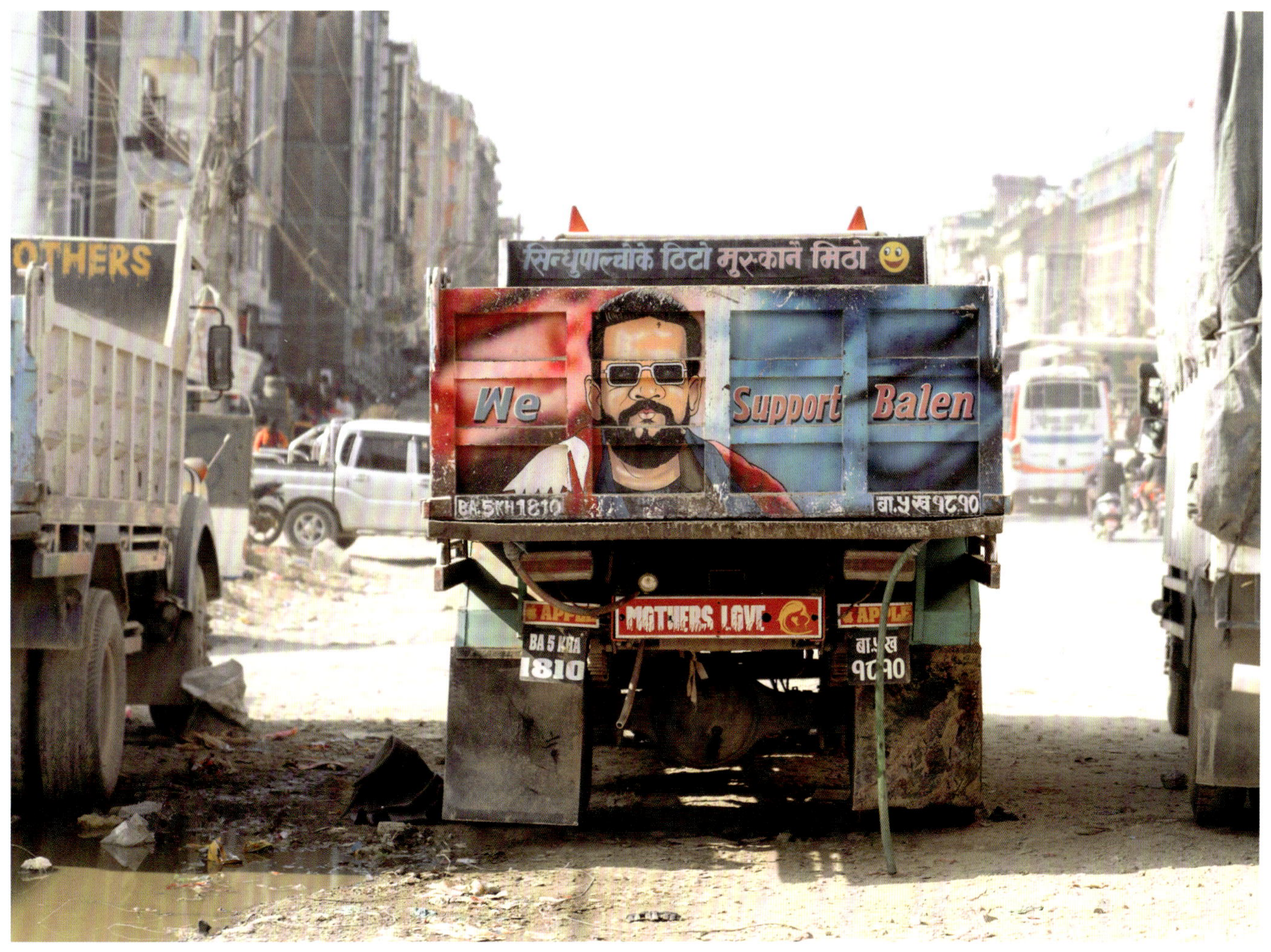
सिन्धुपाल्चोके ठिटो मुस्कानै मिठो
We
Support Balen
BA 5KH 1810
बा.५ख १८१०
MOTHERS LOVE
BA 5 KHA
1810
बा.५ख
१८१०
OTHERS

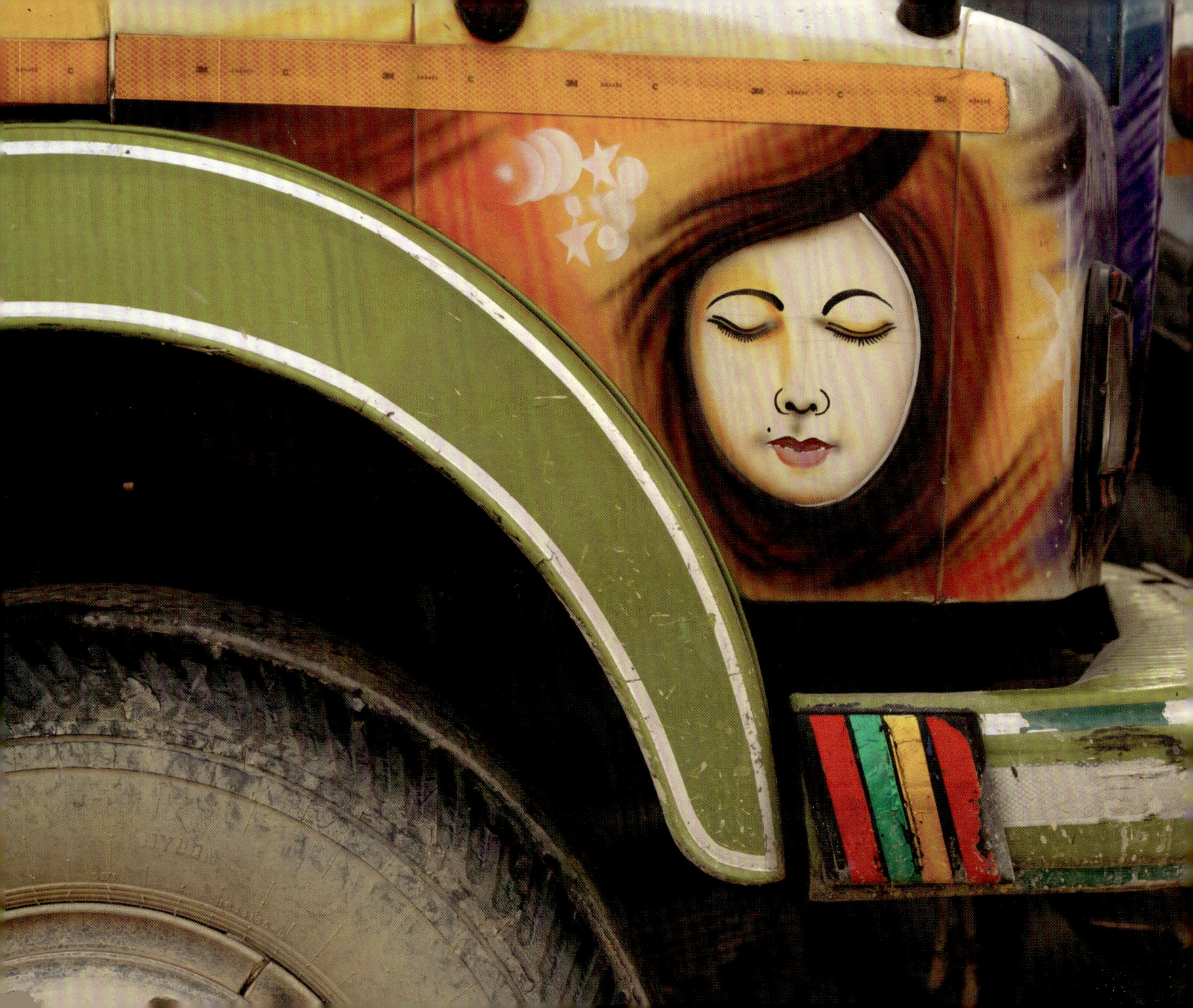

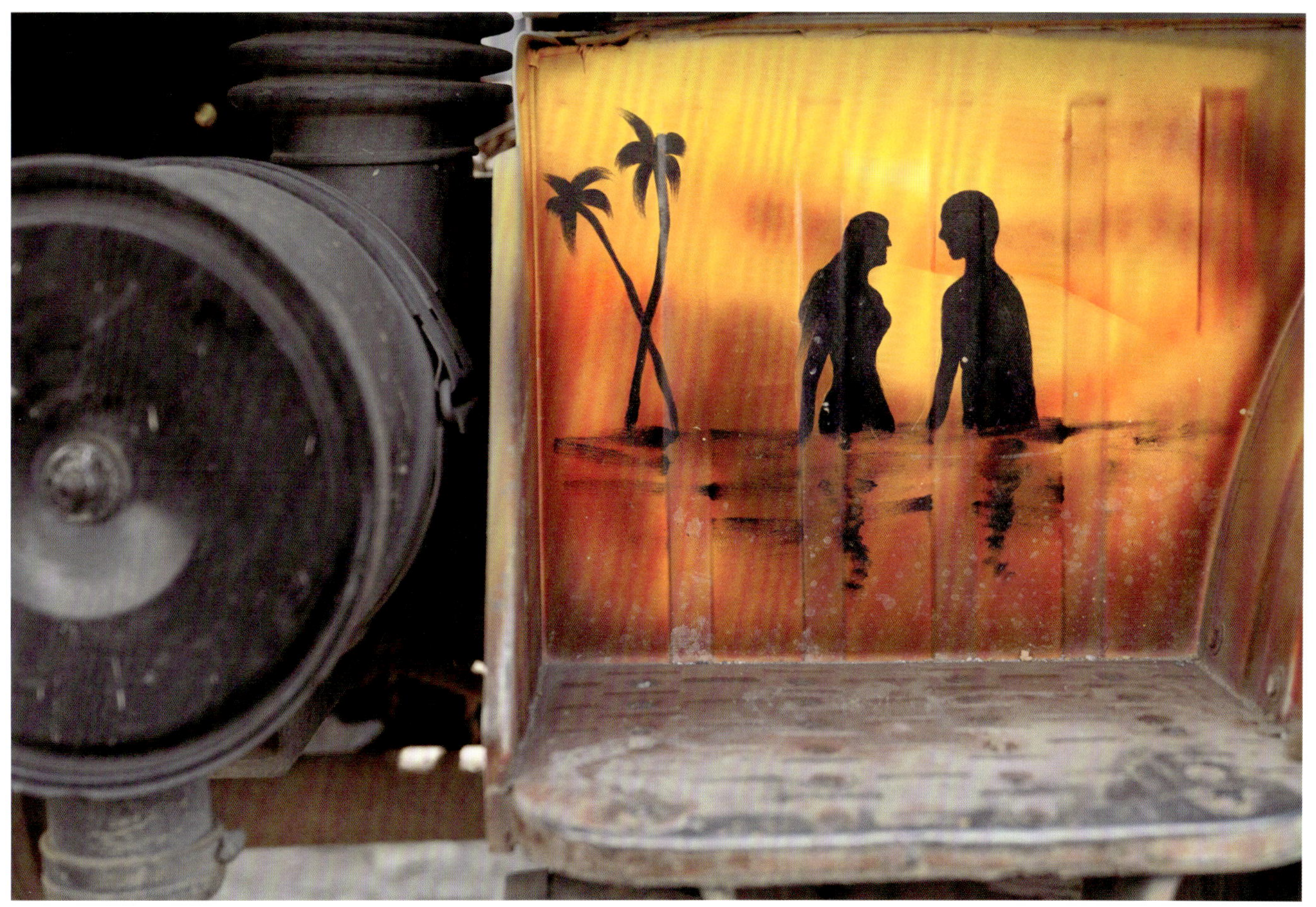

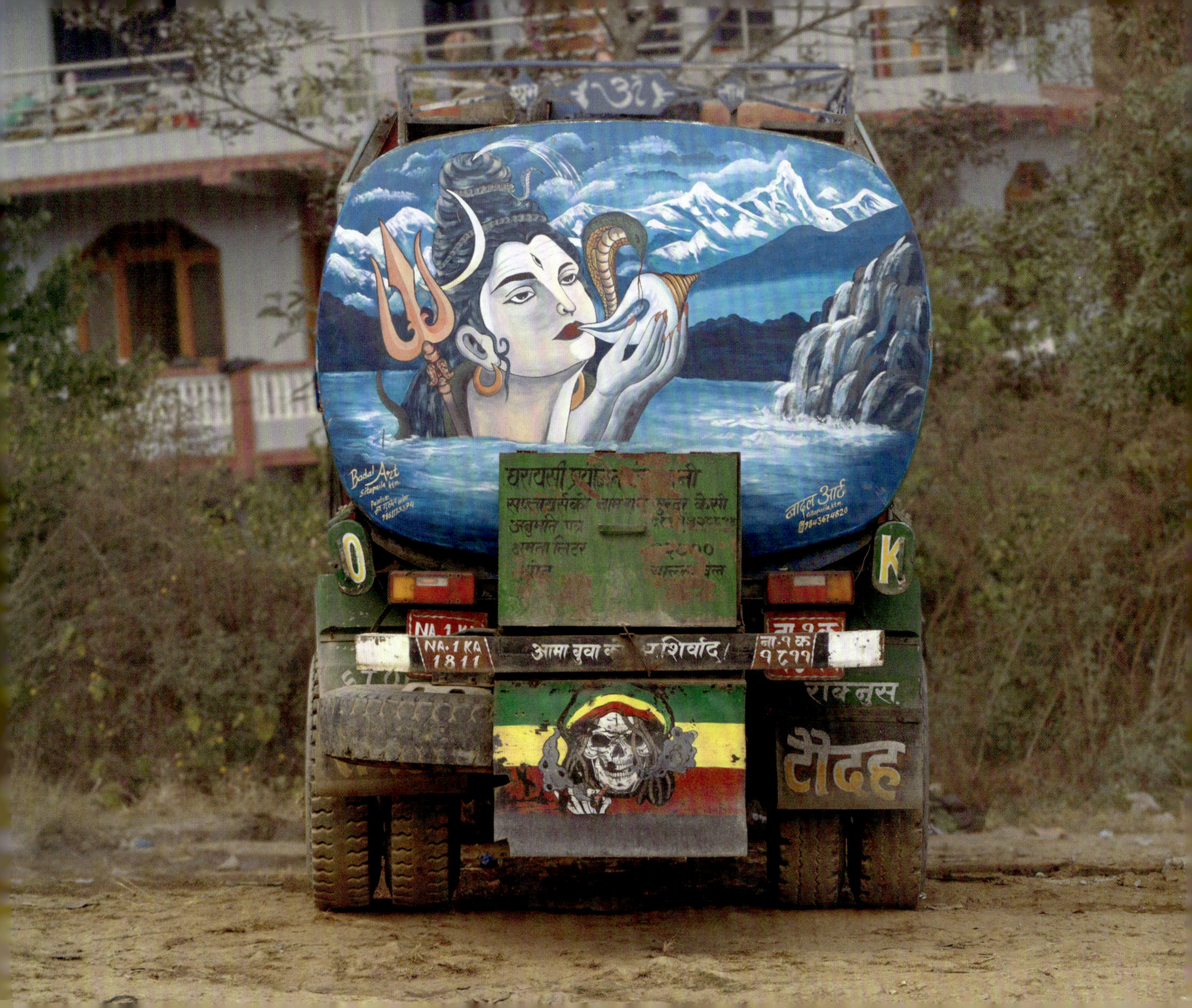

Badal Art
O
K
NA.1 KA
1811
ना.१ क
१८११
आमा बुवा को आशिर्वाद
धौदह

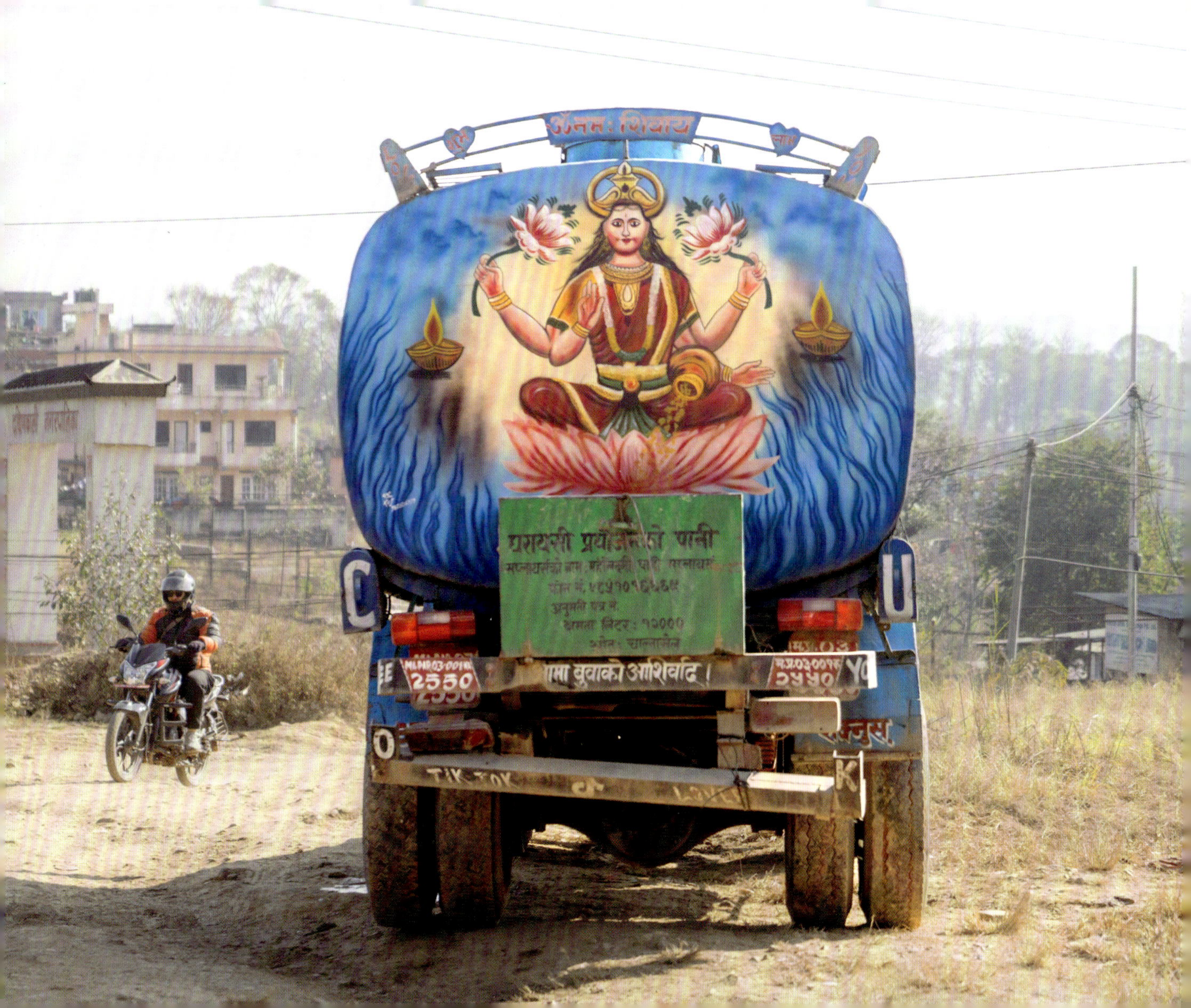
ॐ नमः शिवाय
गायत्री प्रयोजनतो पानी
TIK-TOK
2550
आमा बुवाको आशिर्वाद !

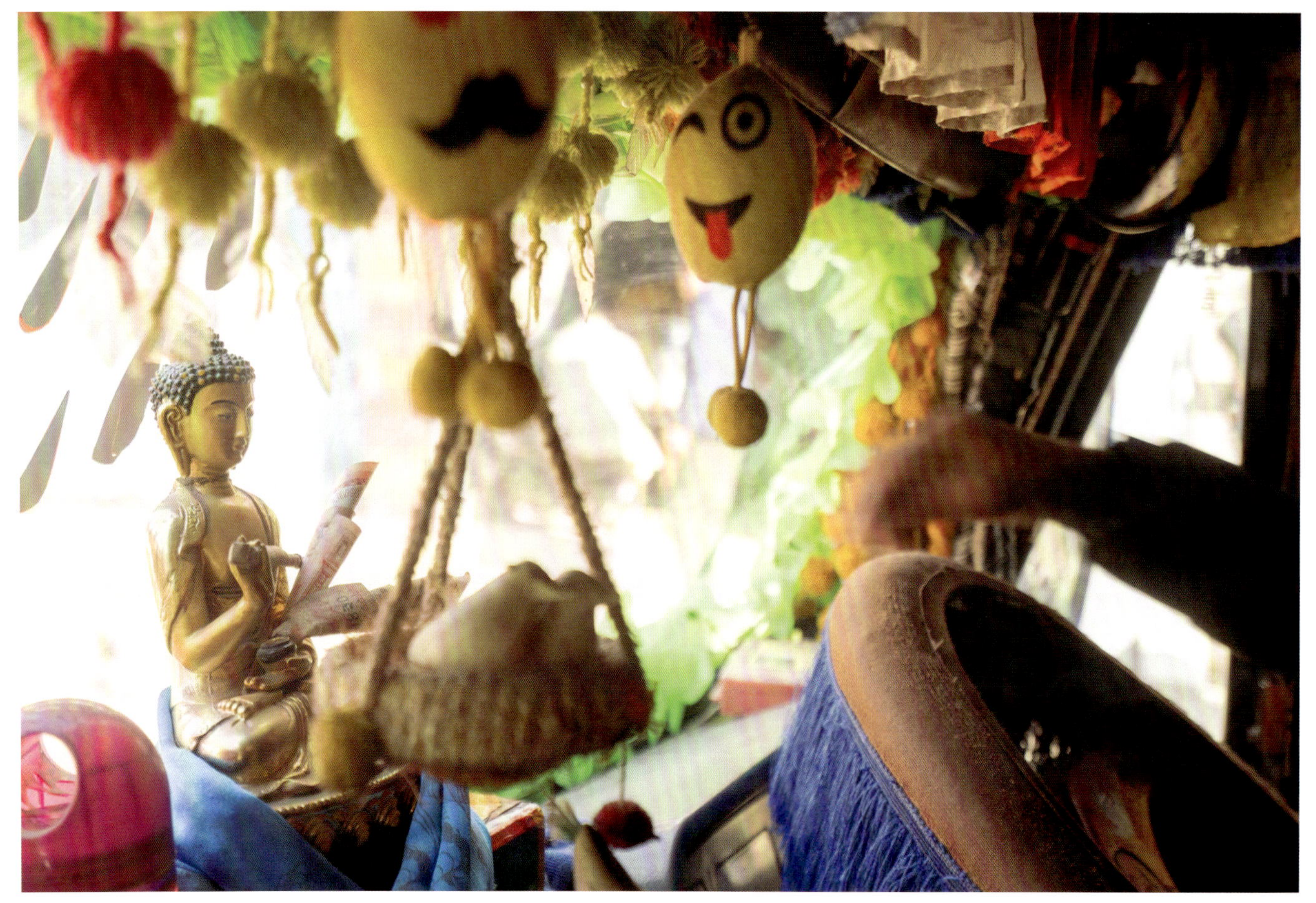

Mahalxmi, NEPAL

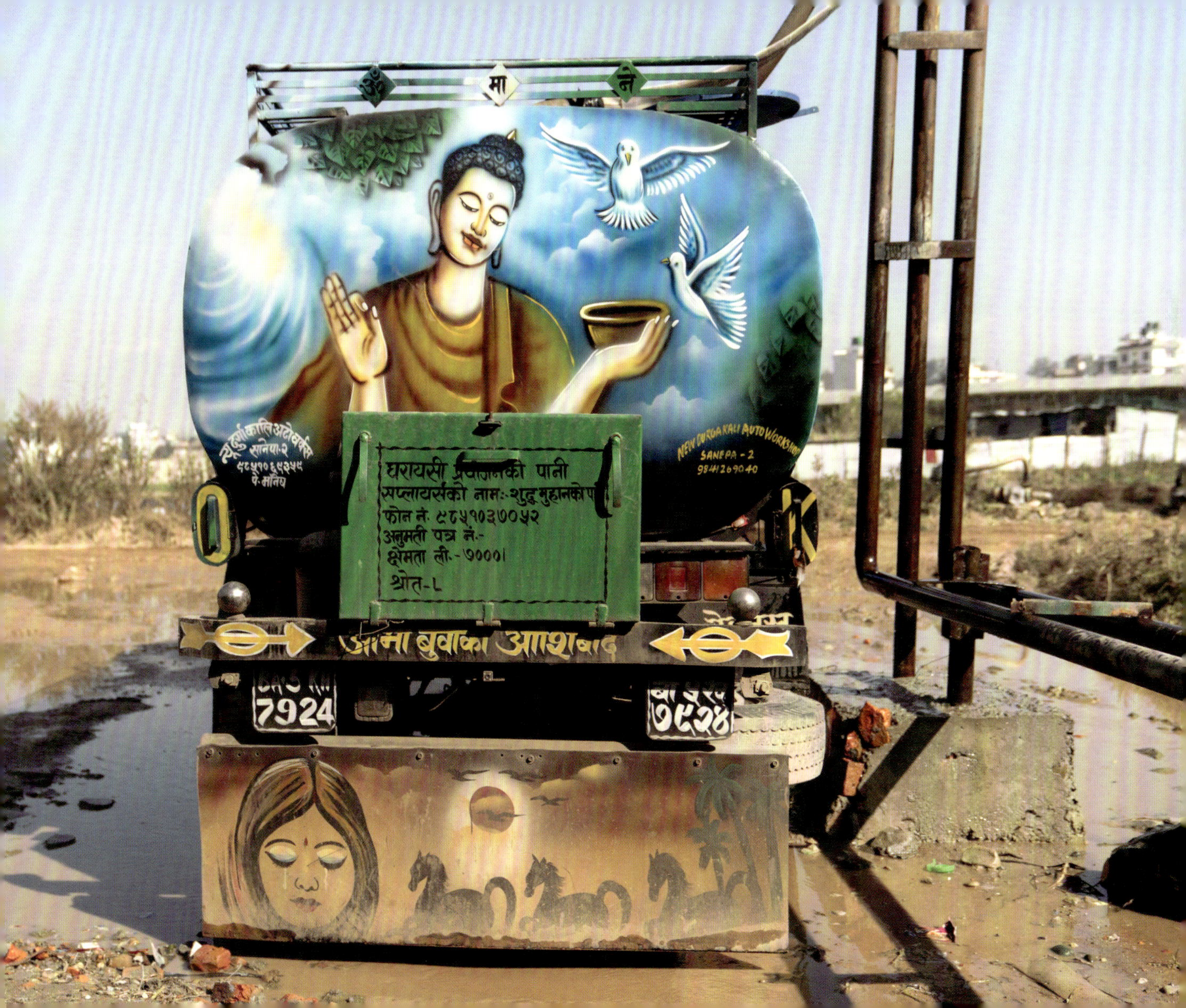
घरायसी प्रयोजनको पानी
सप्लायर्सको नामः- शुद्ध मुहानको प
फोन नं. ८८५१०३७०५२
अनुमती पत्र नं.-
क्षेमता ली.- ७०००।
श्रोत- ८
New Durga Kali Auto Workshop
SANEPA - 2
9841269040
आमा बुवाका आशीवाद
BA 5 KH
7924

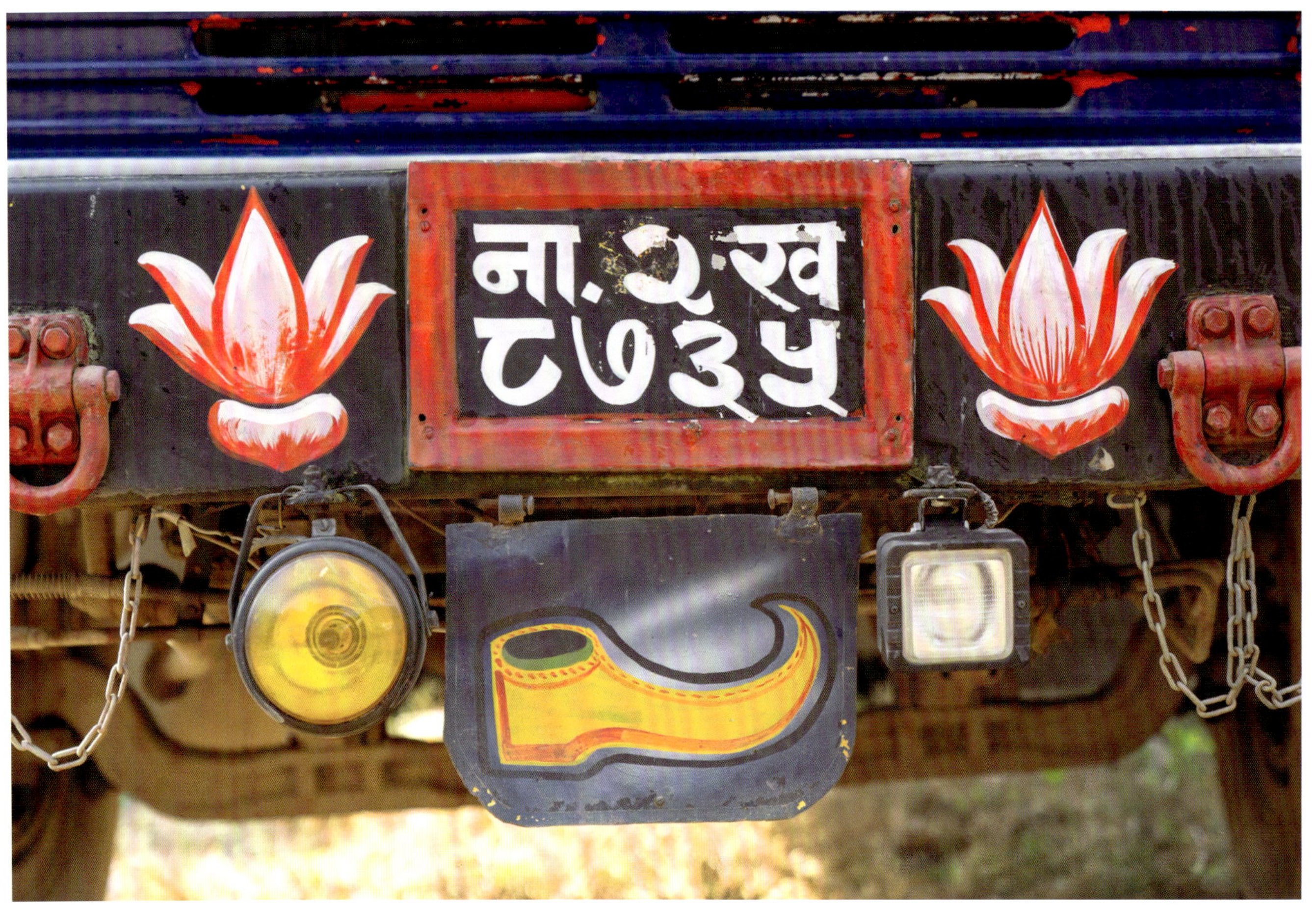

overleaf: Kathmandu, NEPAL

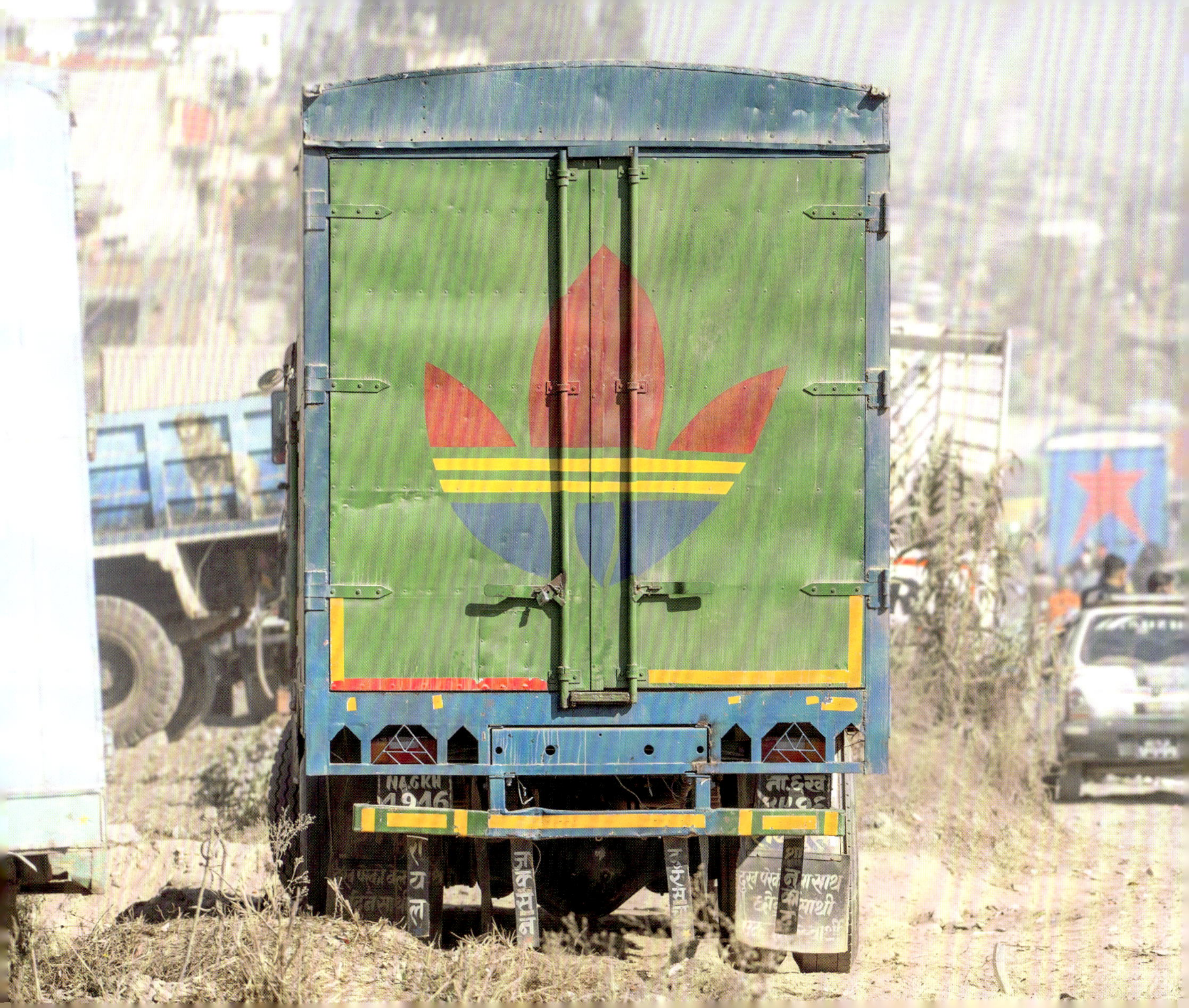

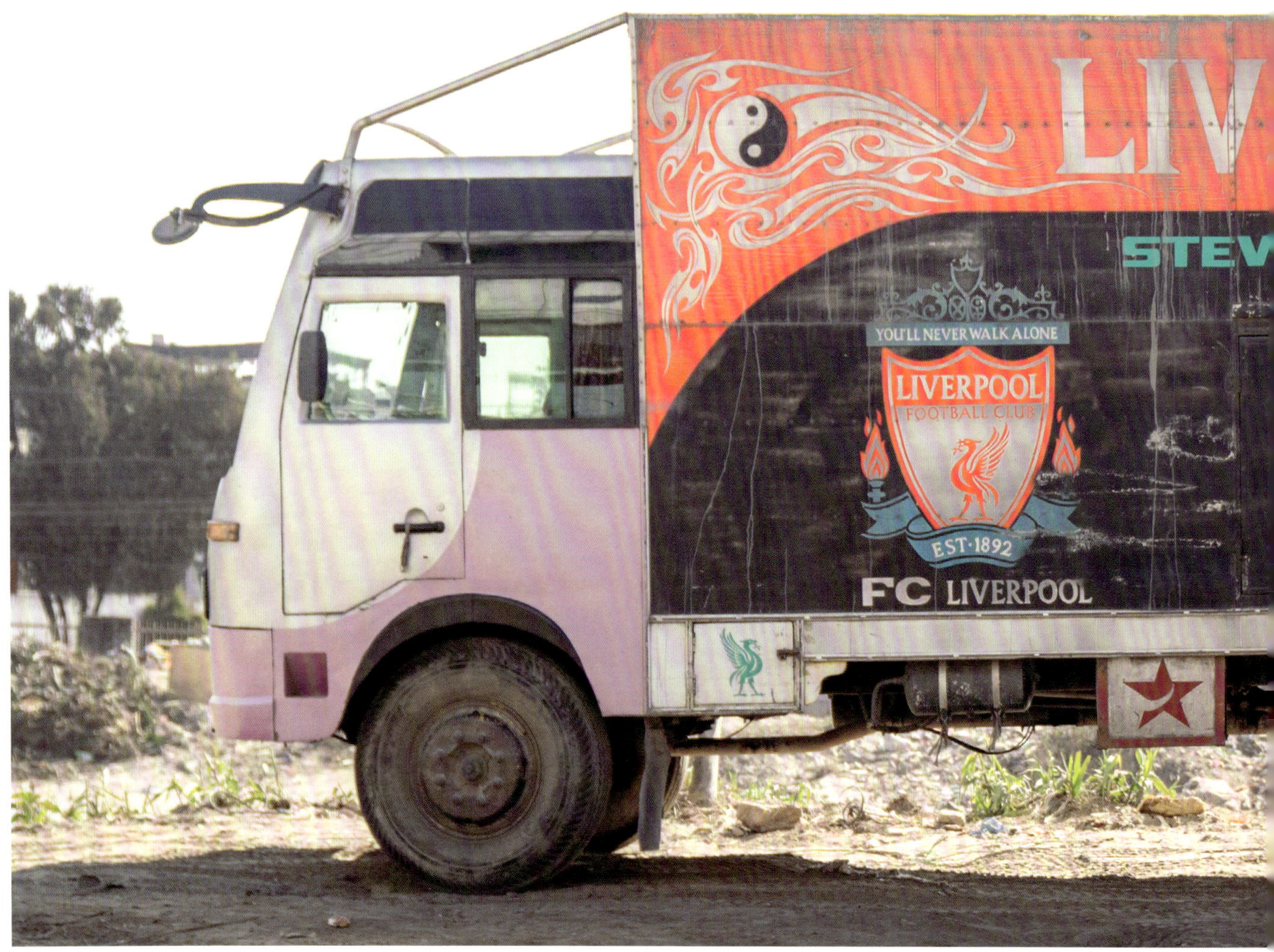

LIV
STEV
YOU'LL NEVER WALK ALONE
LIVERPOOL
FOOTBALL CLUB
EST·1892
FC LIVERPOOL

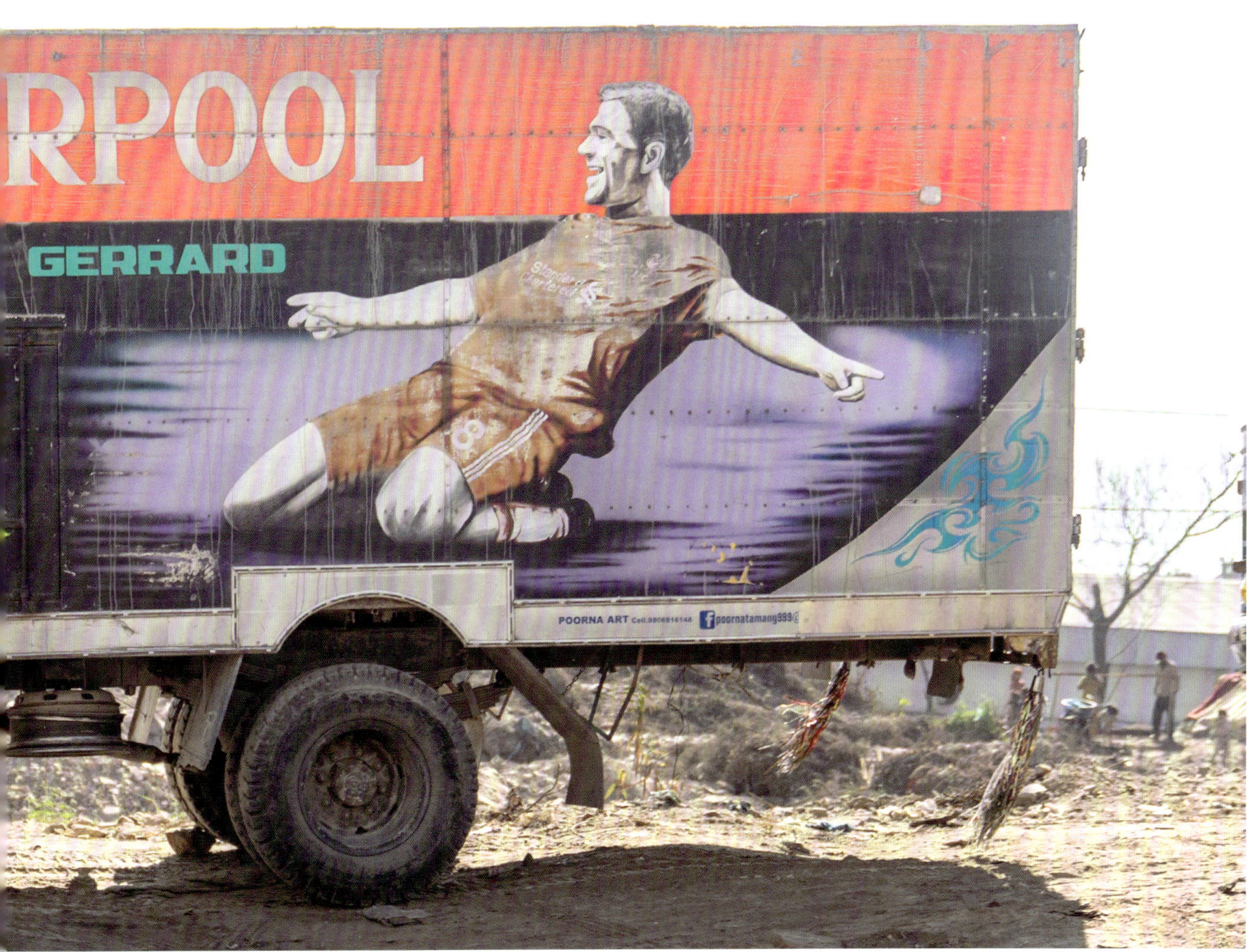
RPOOL
GERRARD
Standard
Chartered
POORNA ART Cell.9806816146 poornatamang999@

BANGLADESH

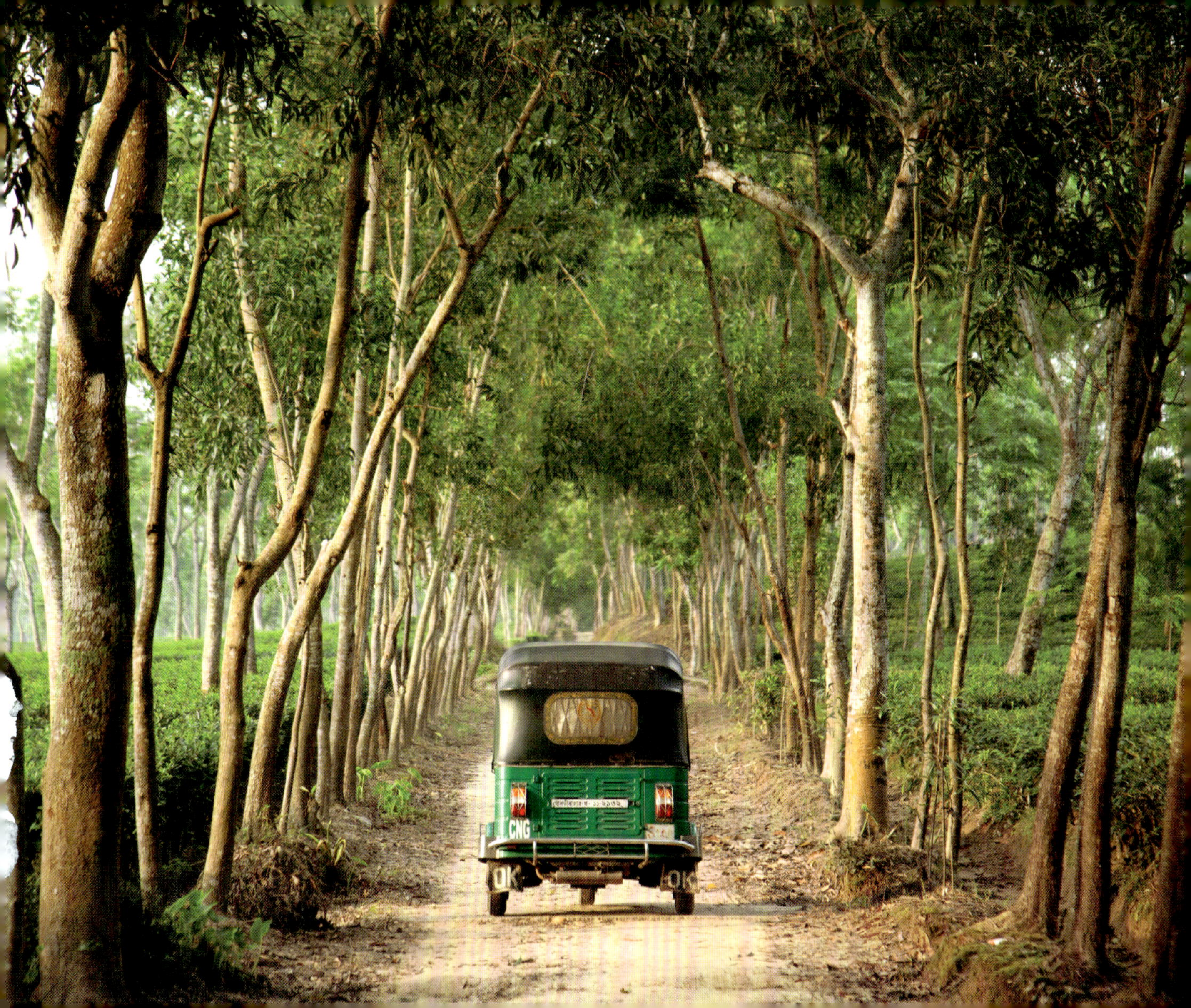

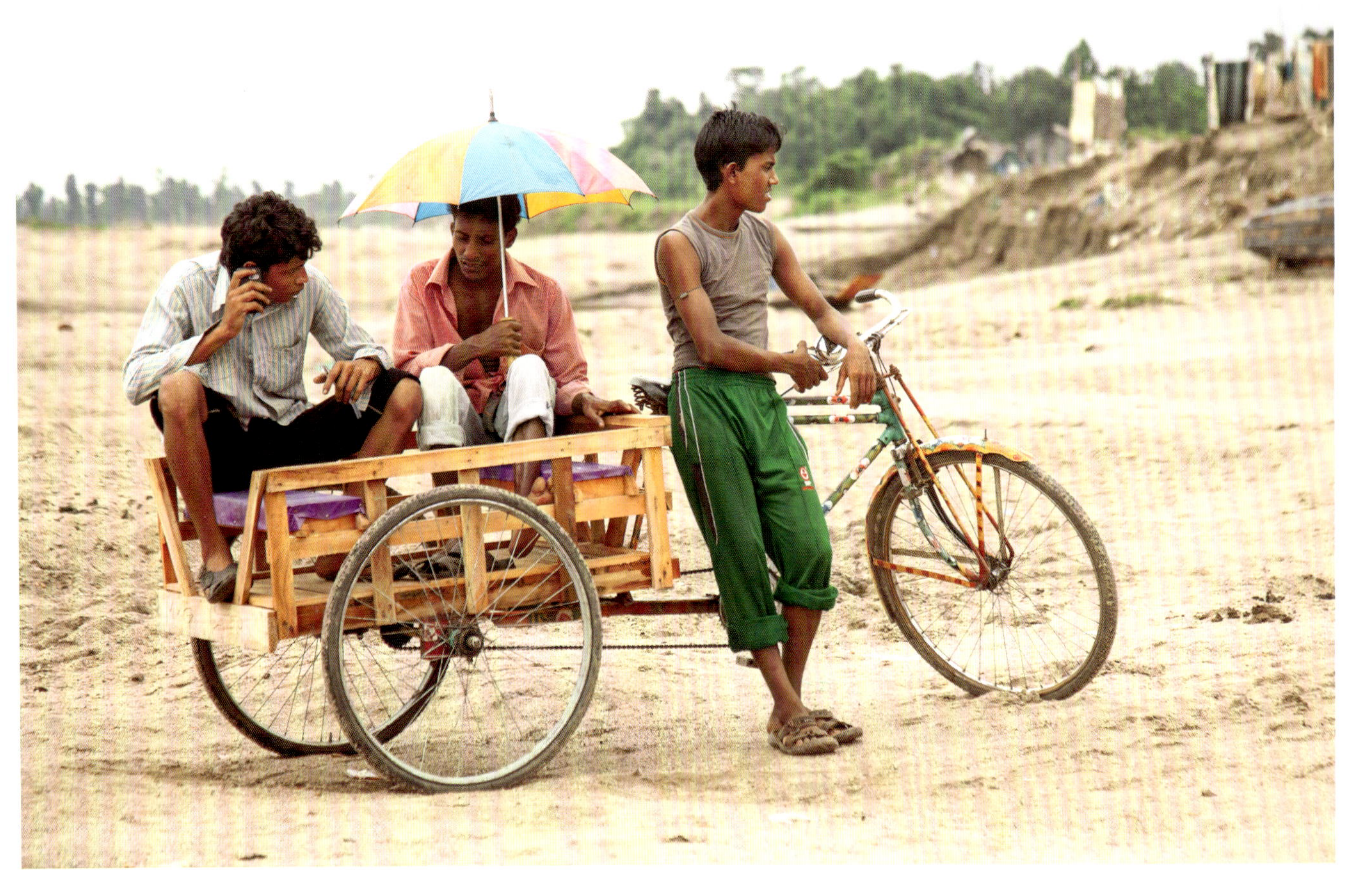

Hatia, BANGLADESH

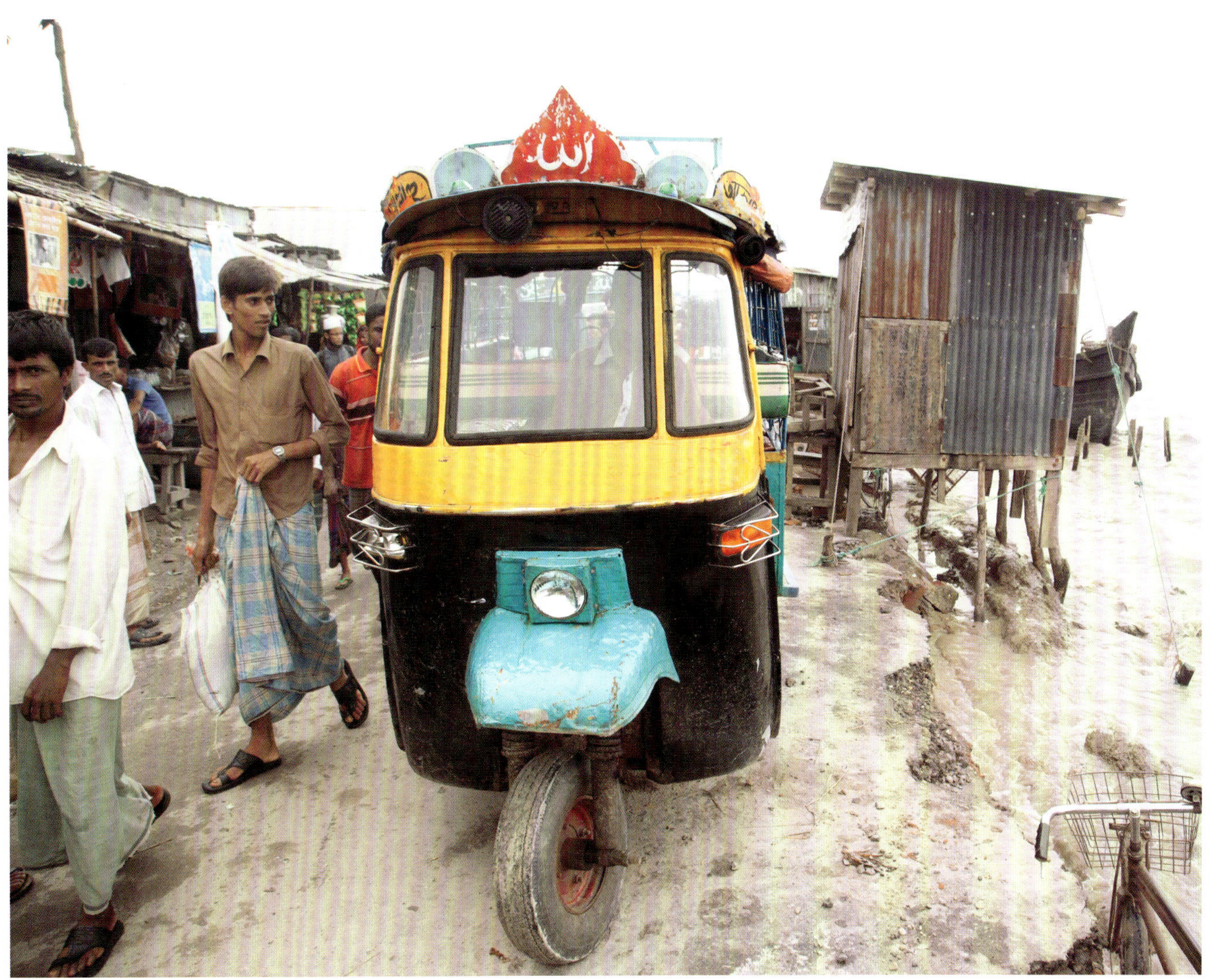

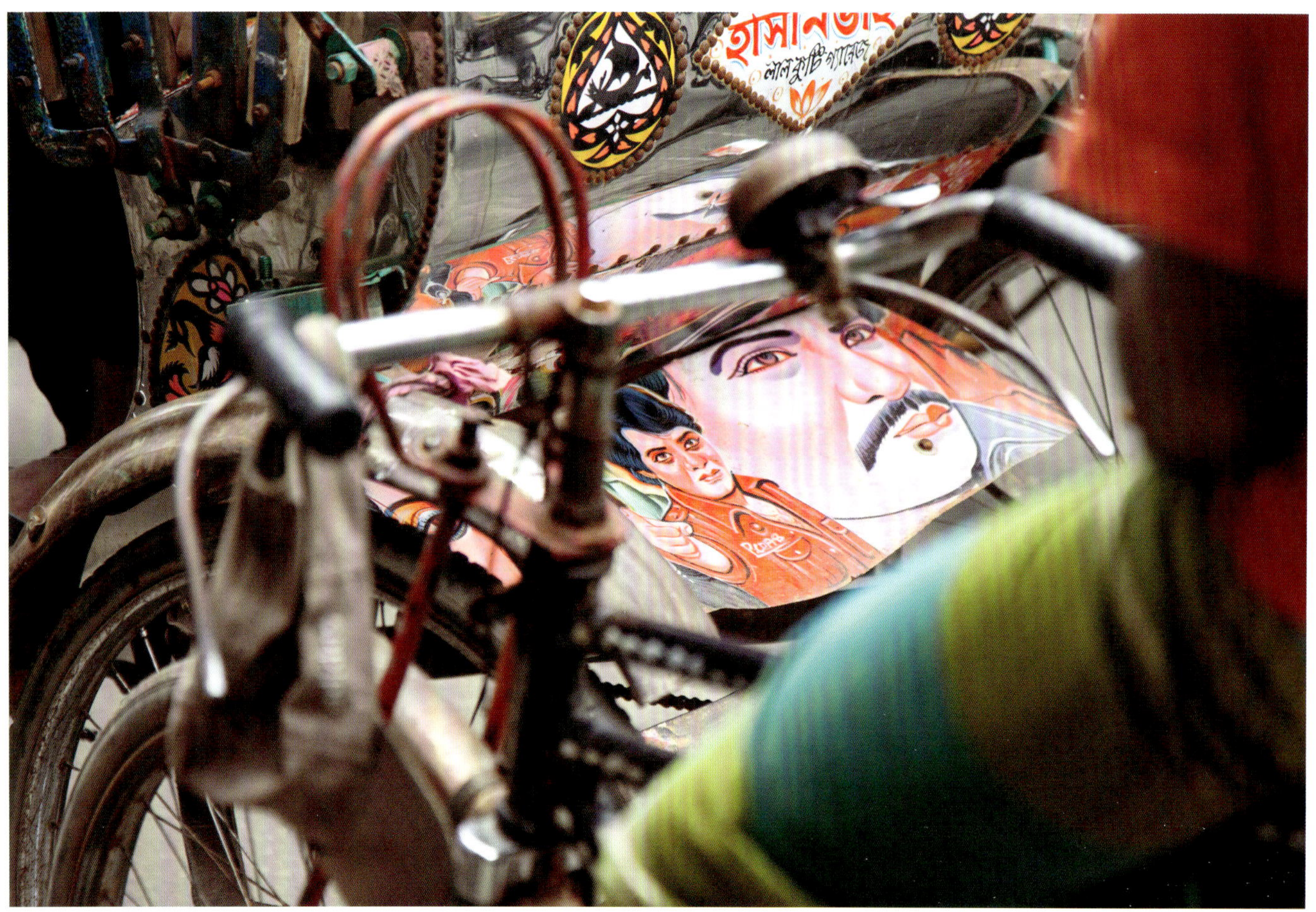

196 Dhaka, BANGLADESH

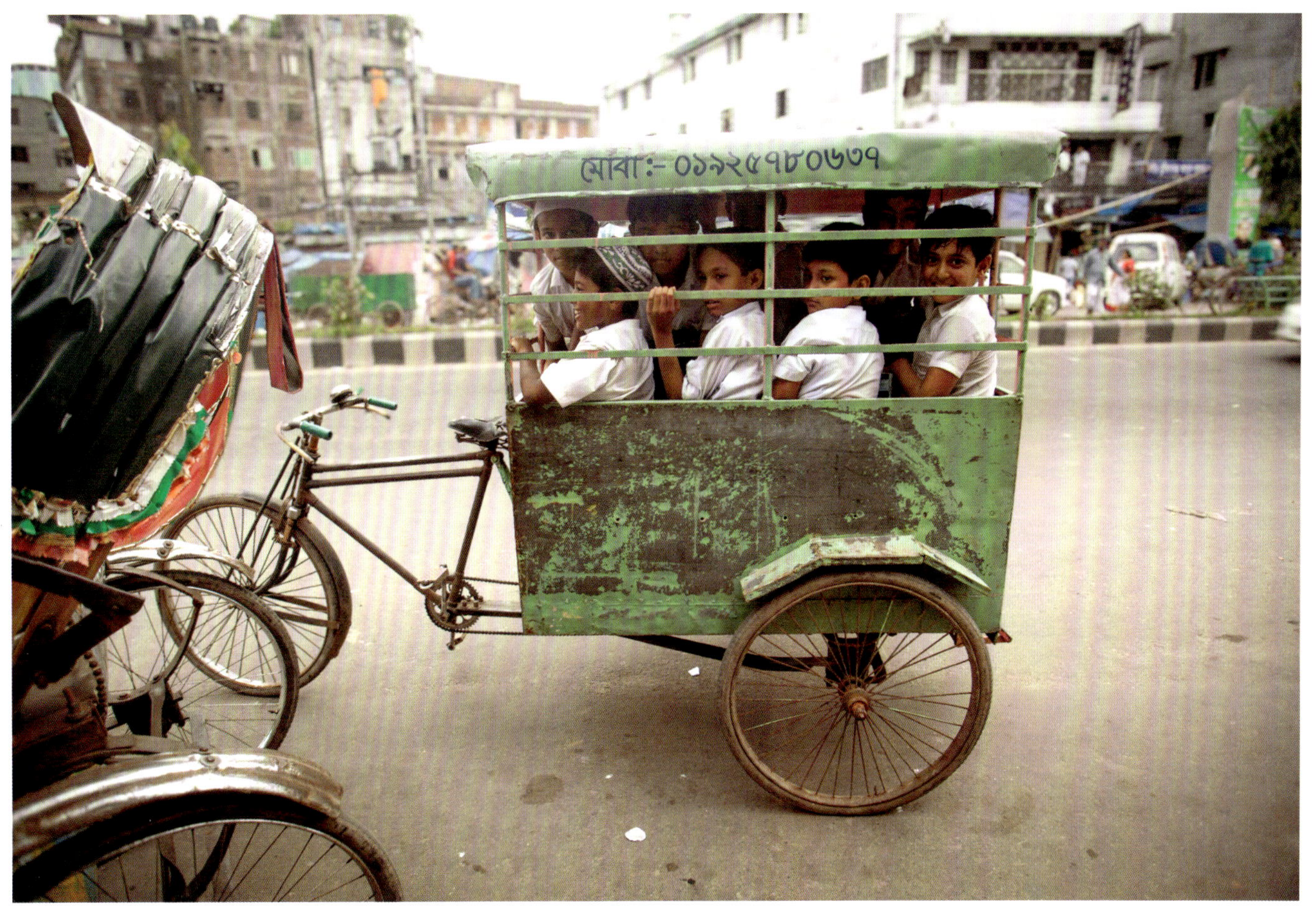#

Dhaka, BANGLADESH   197

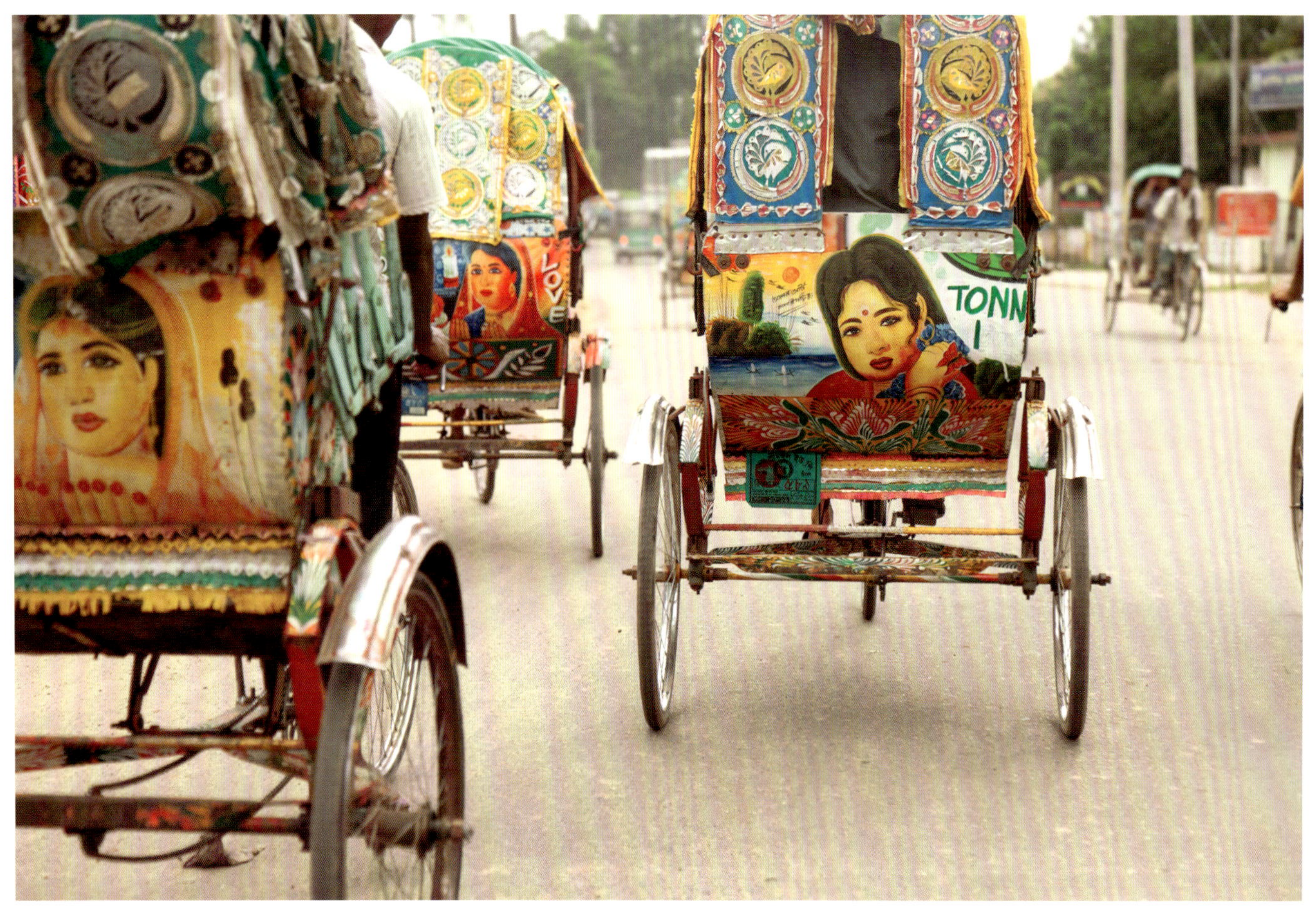

198   Dhaka, BANGLADESH

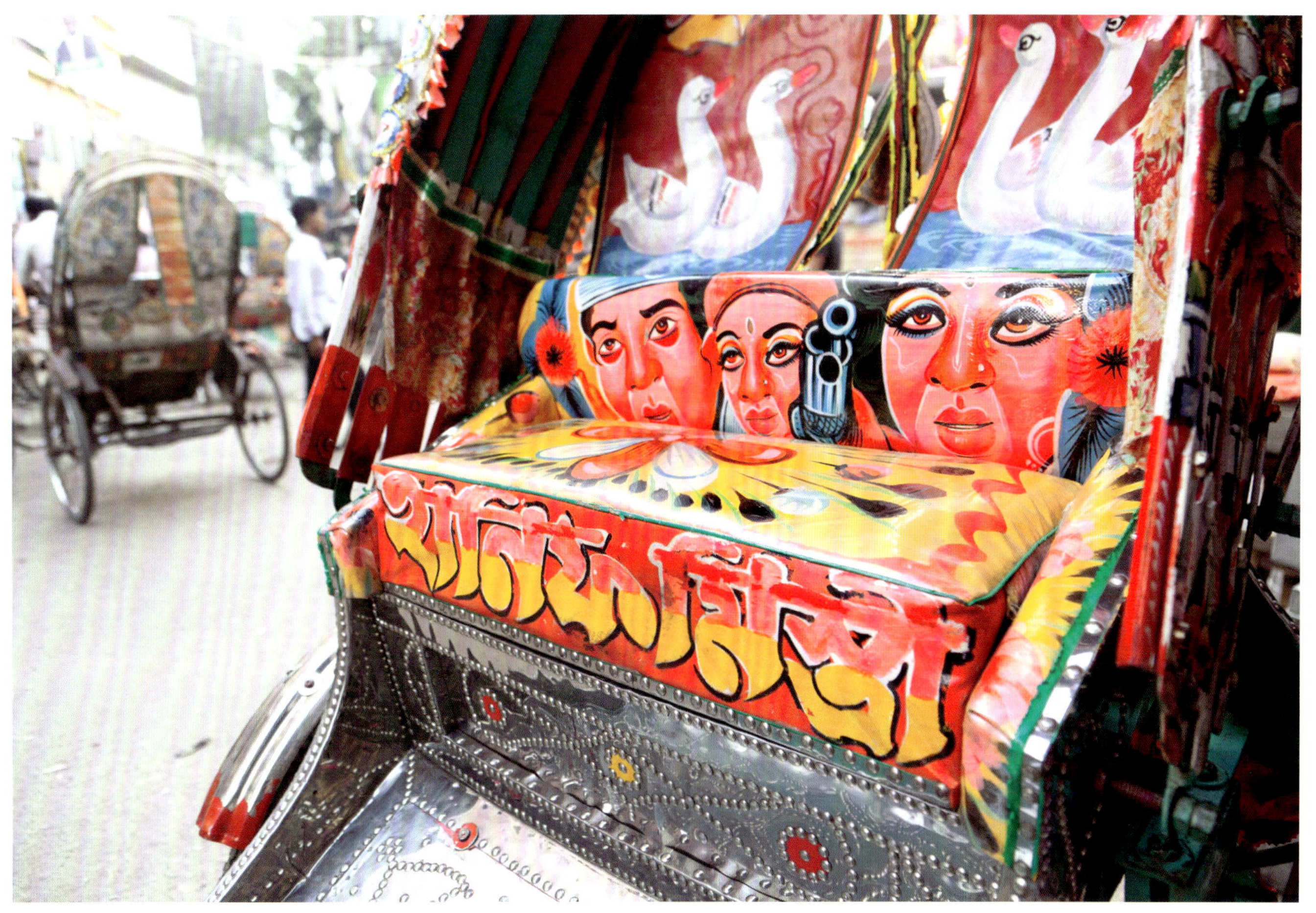

Dhaka, BANGLADESH   199

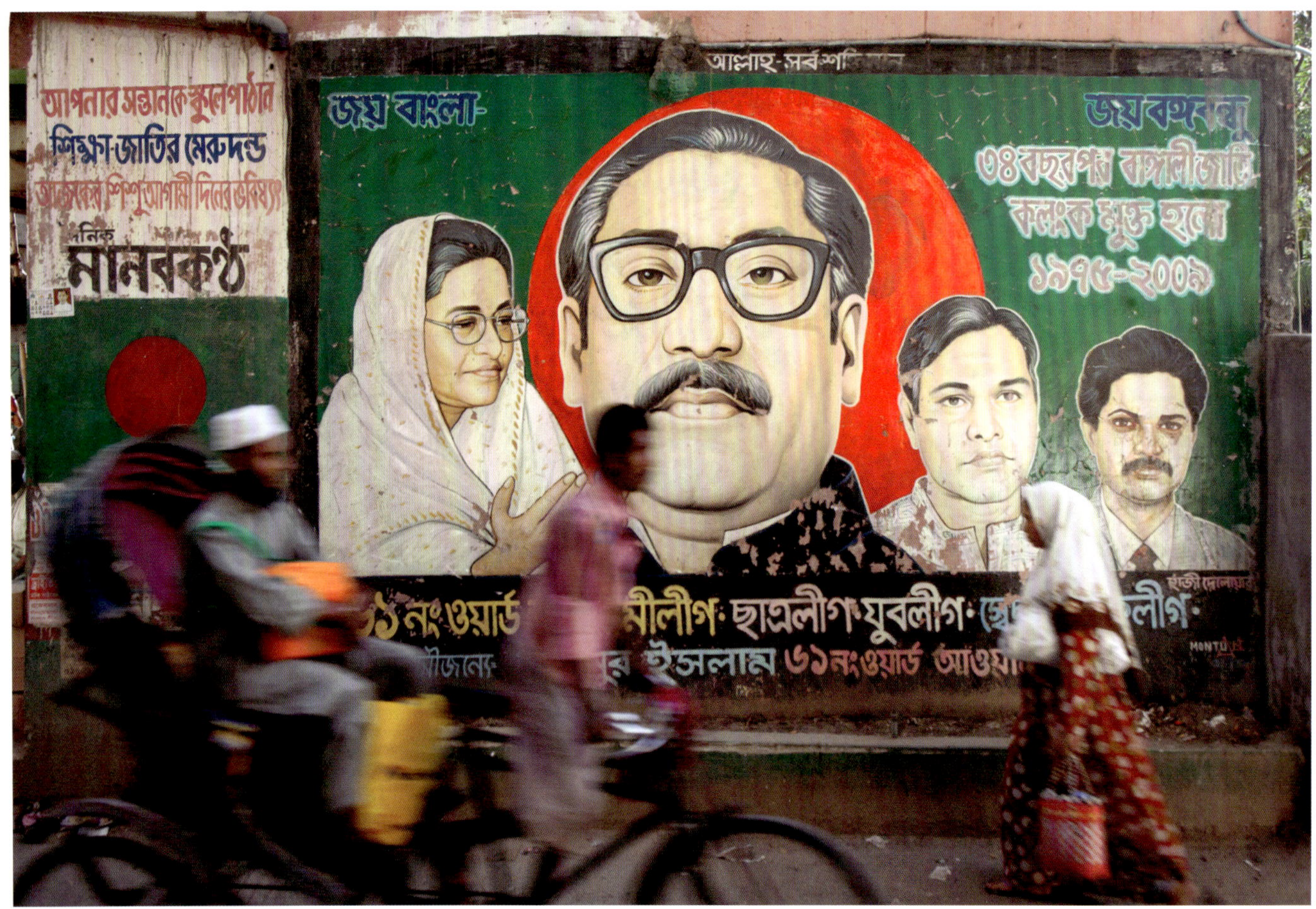

আপনার সন্তানকে স্কুলে পাঠান
শিক্ষা-জাতির মেরুদন্ড
দৈনিক
মানবকণ্ঠ
জয় বাংলা
আল্লাহ-সর্বশক্তিমান
জয় বঙ্গবন্ধু
৩৪ বছর পর বাঙালী জাতি
কলঙ্ক মুক্ত হলো
১৯৭৫-২০০৯
নং ওয়ার্ড
মীলীগ ছাত্রলীগ যুবলীগ
লীগ
ইসলাম ৬১ নংওয়ার্ড আও
MONTU

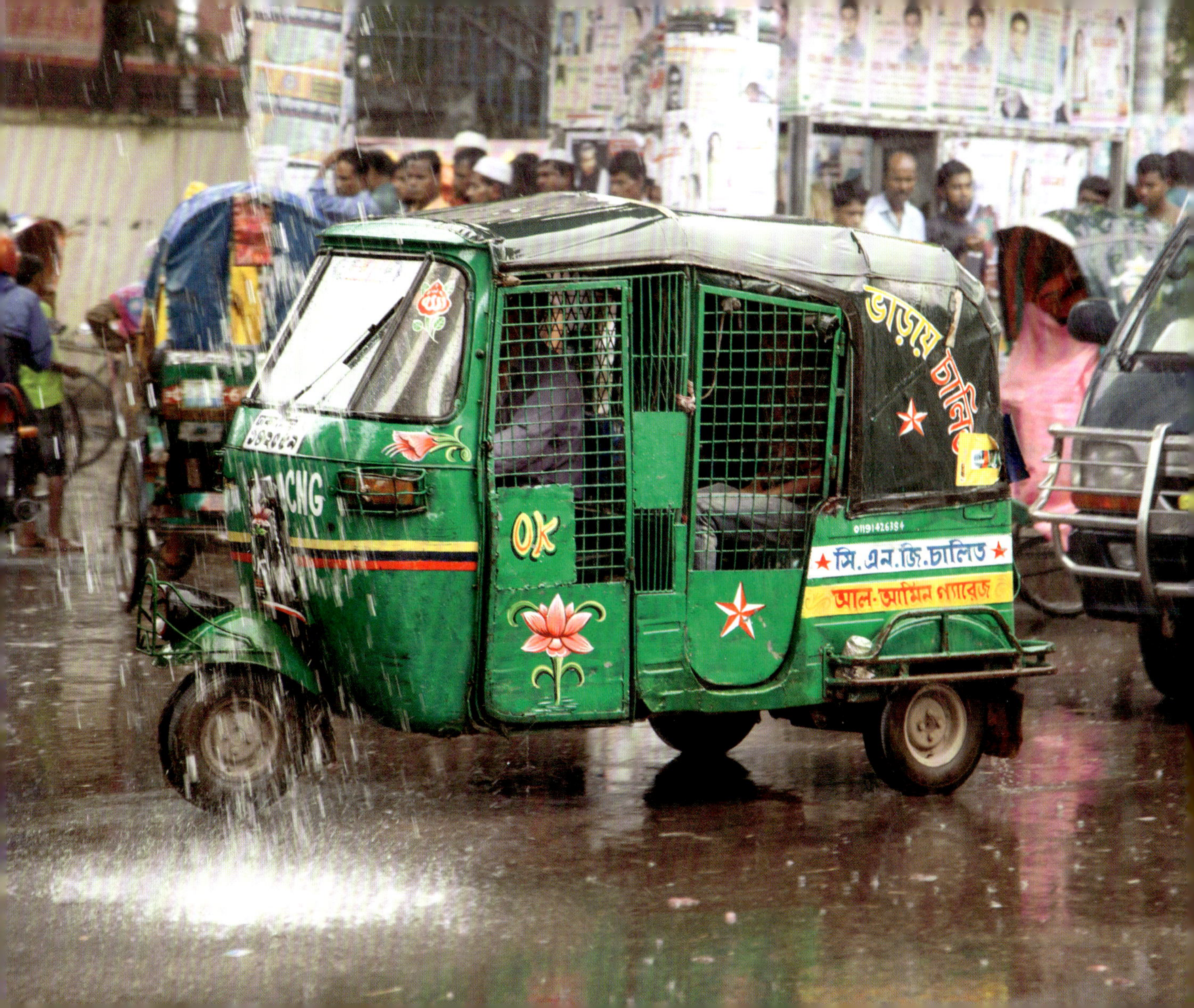
CNG
OK
ভাড়ায় চালি
সি.এন.জি.চালিত
আল-আমিন গ্যারেজ
01191426384

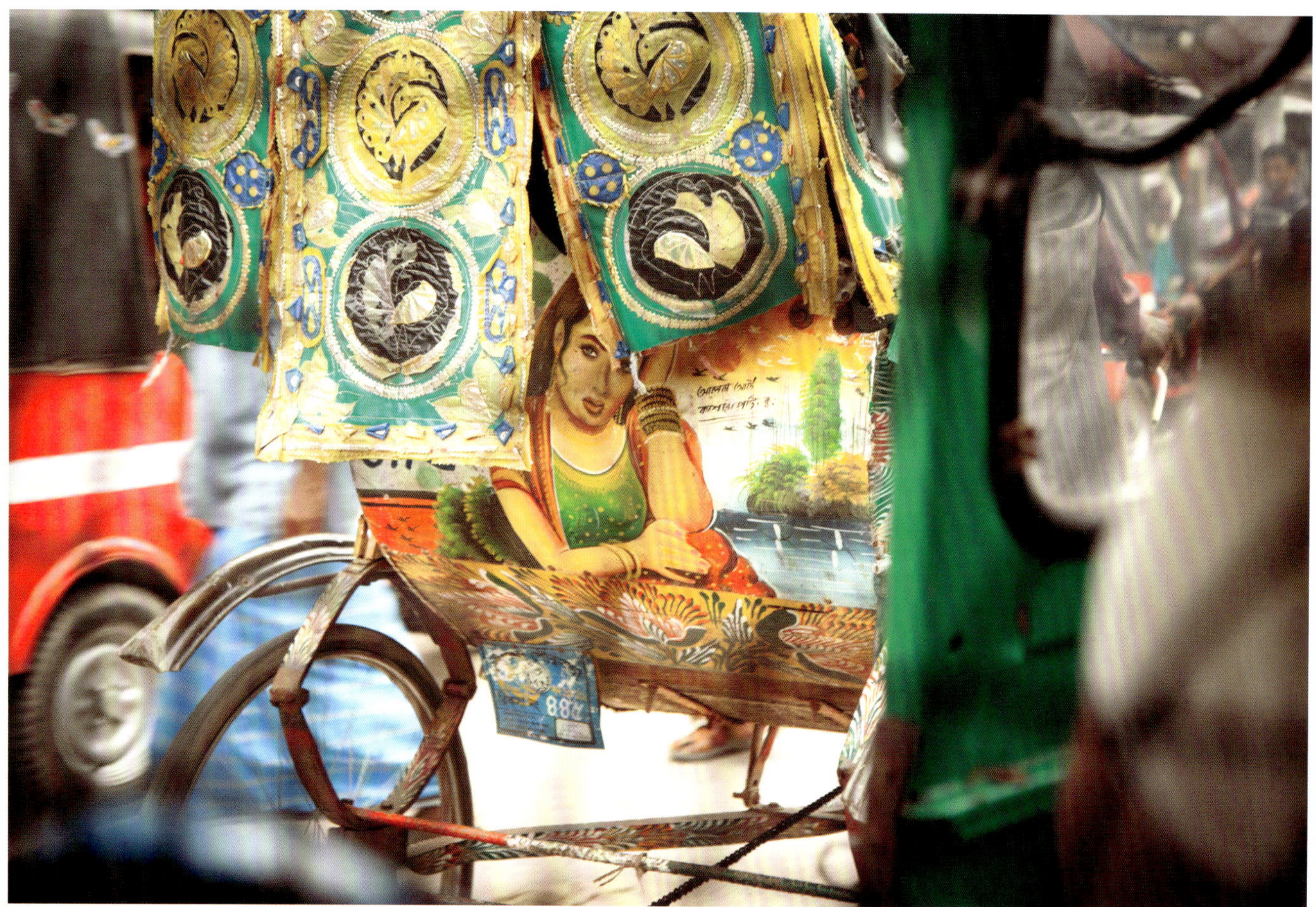

202   Dhaka, BANGLADESH

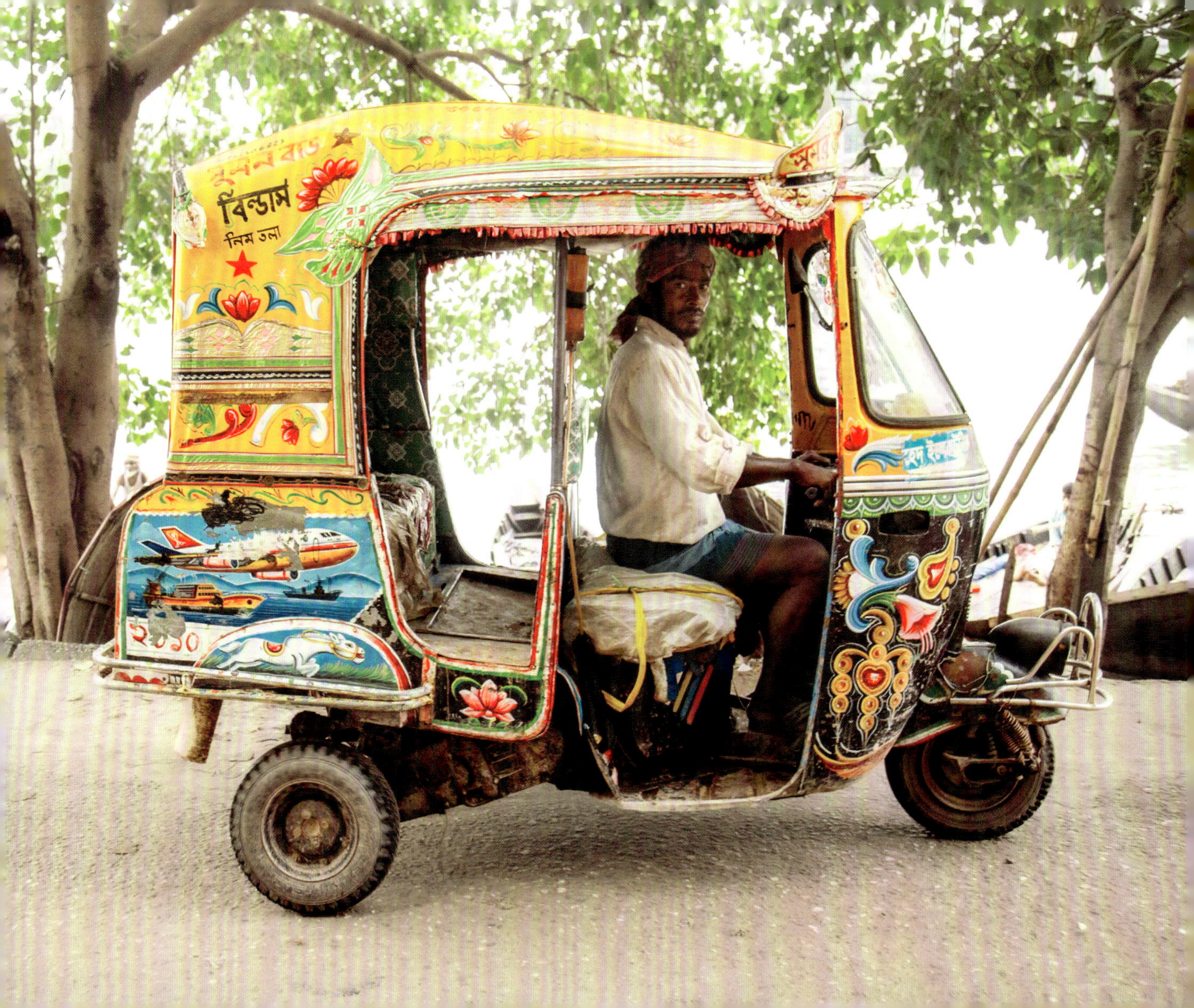

বিন্দাস
নিম তলা
২০১০

Afterword

Christopher Herwig

Like the many bus stops I photographed across the former Soviet Union, this project celebrates individuality, improving one's surroundings with creativity and the value of being able to escape our everyday situation through dreams. While based in Colombo over a period of years, I travelled the region exhaustively: from the towering Hindu Kush Mountains of Pakistan, to the tranquil beaches of Sri Lanka. Unlike the bus stops, the trucks constant movement made them an exciting challenge to hunt down. On a typical day, I might encounter thousands of trucks at numerous locations. Presented with so much amazing material, it was a constant dilemma whether to stop and spend time photographing, or to keep moving, hoping for something even more extraordinary a little further down the road.

The hunt was an opportunity to travel again in the most rewarding way – blind, with eyes wide open. I rarely had a fixed location, my subjects were on the move and could be anywhere, so getting results meant putting in the miles. It was sometimes difficult to explain to taxi drivers that I wanted to drive with no fixed destination. Despite this, a few embraced the challenge, one or two even performing dramatic manoeuvres, chasing down the trucks so I could photograph them.

In Nepal, I found myself literally off the beaten path as a beautifully painted water truck drove past me down a muddy road. I ran after it and slipping, I flipped over, my camera swinging round and smashing me in the face. Bloody and covered in mud, I finally caught up with the truck and photographed it. I now look at the image on page 157 with a greater sense of achievement.

In Pakistan, for my own safety, I spent a day accompanied by several police escorts. Eventually, I found myself at a small-town hotel, where – fearing for my life – the local police insisted I rent an extra room so a heavily armed officer could guard me. Granted, I may have been naive at times, but I can truly say that I only ever encountered generosity, friendship and warm hospitality.

Not all drivers shared my excitement for the hunt. One young man named Amir fell asleep at the wheel twice, drifting off the Grand Trunk Road. Even his favourite rapper – Sidhu Moose Wala – couldn't keep him awake. The project made me reflect on the realities of a life spent behind the wheel. Like many of the truckers, Amir explained that the vehicle he was driving was not his own. He worked long days for the real owner, who paid him just a fraction of the fare, threatening to fire him if he argued. With few employment options, his monthly salary of US$100 was better than nothing.

Walking across a muddy, industrial parking lot, I nervously approached a trucker for the first time. I expected to encounter a hard and aggressive character. Leaning out of his truck, he yelled at me and gestured with his fingers to his mouth. Shamefully, I assumed by his worn clothing and

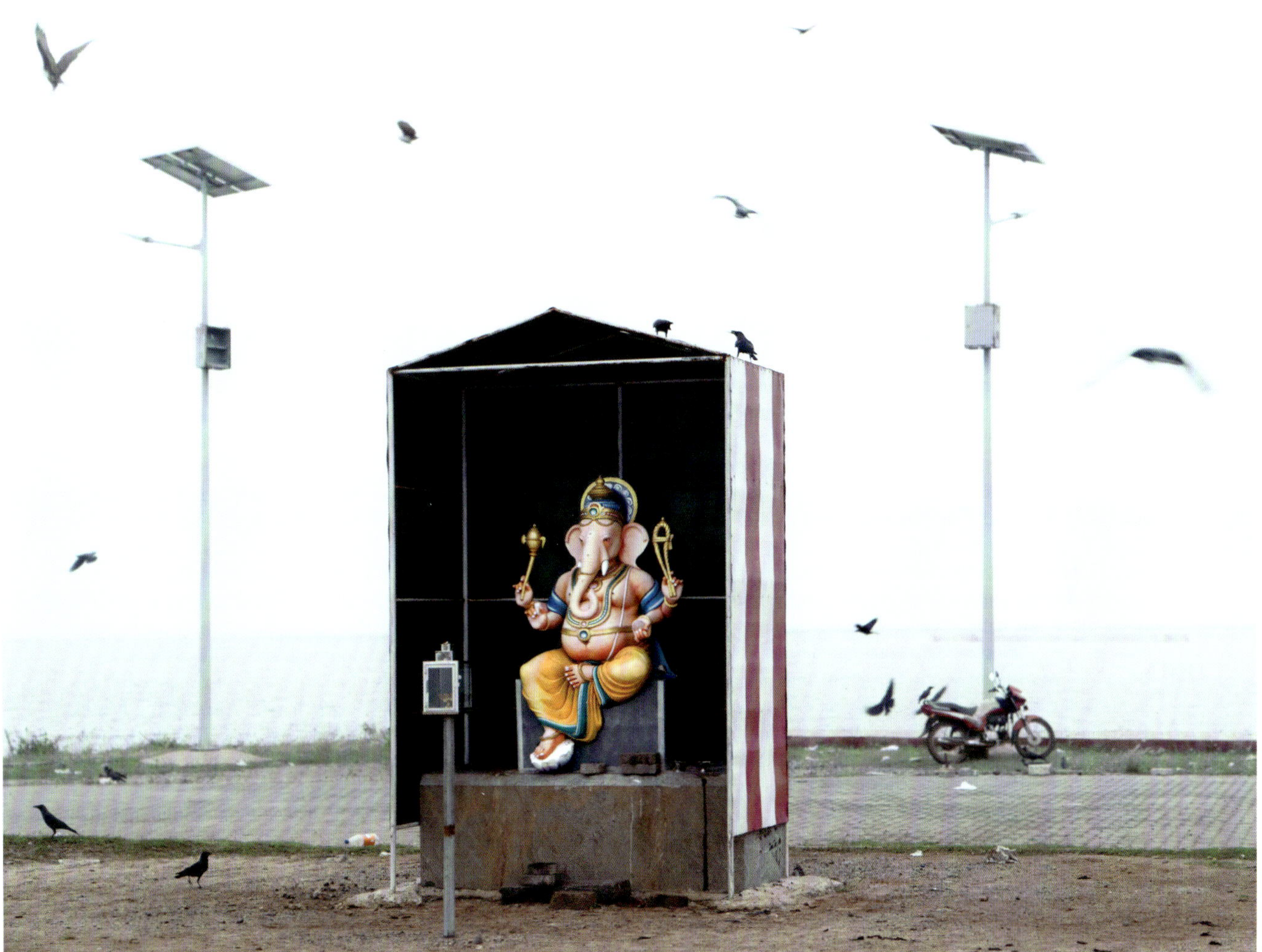

Jaffna, SRI LANKA   205

dishevelled appearance that he was asking me if I had some food to spare. In fact, it was the opposite: he was inviting me to share his dinner.

For truckers like Gopal (opposite), the cab is his entire world. Here he cooks vegetables and rice on a small stove, sleeps, and listens to Bollywood songs. He hopes to one day save enough to buy his own truck and get married.

The Belarusian bus stop designer Armen Saratov described his work as part of 'the Poetry of the Road'. The poetry of the road I found in the trucks and tuks was a complex, individual blend of masculinity and tradition intertwined with expressions of love, tenderness, hope and longing. Invitations for food and tea continued throughout the project; one trucker named Jayachandran even offered a friendly kiss. Alongside the practical elements found in the truckers' cabs, there was often an abundance of visual imagery in marked contrast to their challenging existence. Decorated with elaborate whimsical flare, dangling good luck charms and wallpaper showing idyllic scenes, they revealed a dream life. Traditionally arriving in South Asia as basic components: an engine and a chassis, these vehicles were a completely blank canvas, not only ripe for decoration, but also the customisation of their shape and design.

The truckers do not have it easy. They work long hours, are paid little, and spend long periods of time away from their loved ones. Often, they did not own the vehicles but were simply hired to drive for the lowest possible wage. I met Sekul Khan briefly at a toll booth on a highway south of Jaipur (p64). His story was a universal one: looking tired and stressed, he told me that he was in a rush. If he didn't deliver his cargo of produce by the deadline, he would be fined for every hour he was late. 'It's a constant race against time,' Sekul reflected. 'Carrying perishable items is like running with your own coffin. With the pressure to speed, constant confrontations are unavoidable and the risk of accidents lethal. If I'm late, it's not just a fine – it's a loss that stretches all the way back to the farmers and the people in the markets. Everyone depends on this.' He dreams of owning his own truck one day, planning to have it painted with mountains – a symbol of strength and endurance and a reminder of the last vacation he had with his parents.

As Jagtar (p77) in Indore told us, 'No young person should ever choose this life. With every turn of the wheel, it feels like another part of my dreams dies. But those dreams live on in my children. They'll get an education – I'll make sure of that.' The interior bling of his cab gives him strength – 'they are small decorations, things that may not cost much but mean everything.'

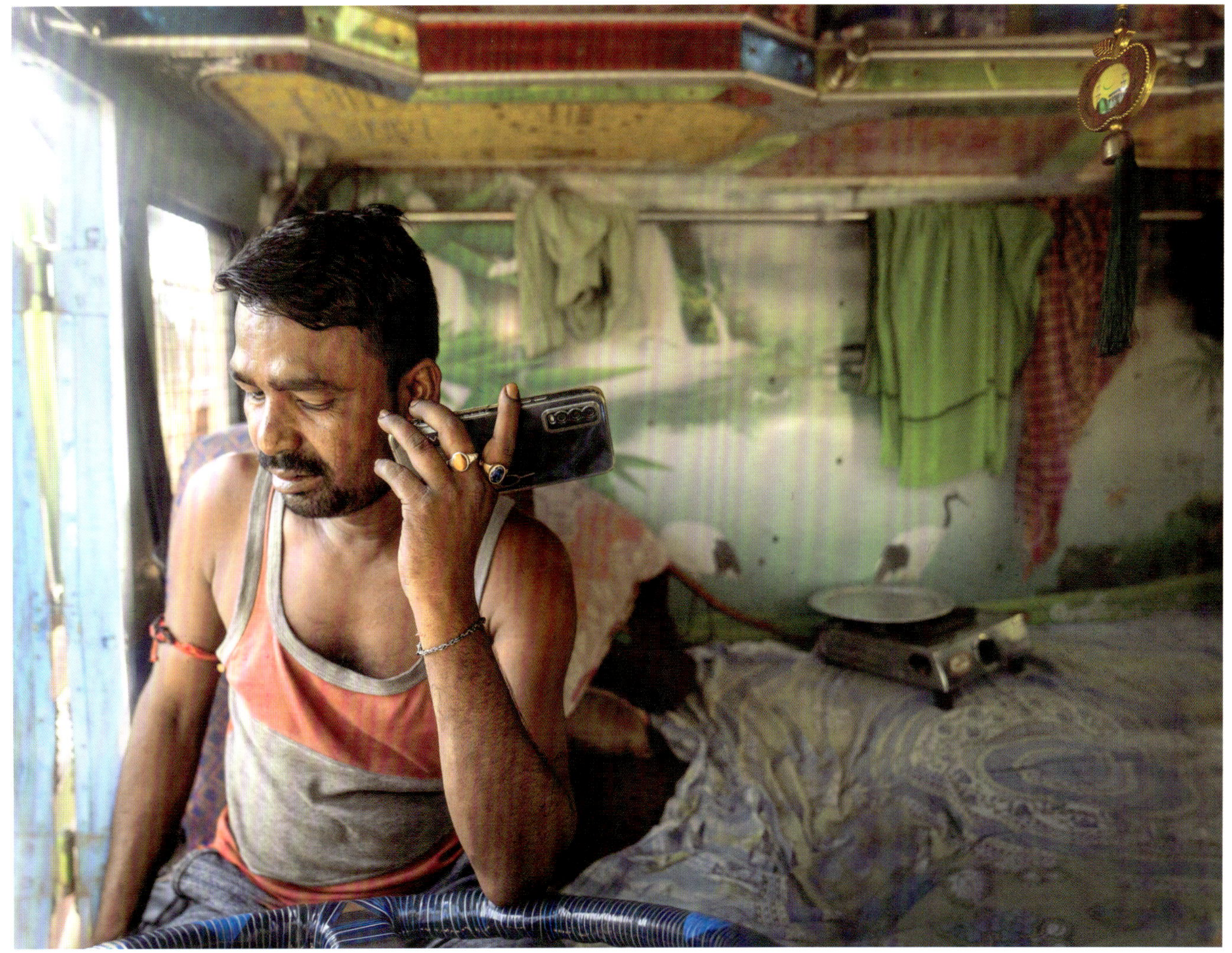

With over twenty-five years of experience in more than ninety countries, Christopher Herwig is a Canadian-born photographer and videographer determined to find beauty and inspiration in all aspects of life. A firm belief that the thrill of exploration is still alive in the world has sent him hitch-hiking from Vancouver to Cape Town, across Iceland by foot and raft, and through Europe on a bike. Currently based in Sri Lanka, his previous homes have included Liberia and Kazakhstan. His photographs of some of the remotest regions of the world – from the Pamir mountains in Tajikistan to the rainforests of West Africa – have been reproduced in publications including *GEO*, *CNN Traveler*, *Geographical* and *Lonely Planet*. He has worked extensively with non-government organisations and UN agencies in some of the most challenging regions, to put a human face to their statistics and bring project proposals to life.

His best-selling books *Soviet Bus Stops*, *Soviet Bus Stops Volume II* and *Soviet Metro Stations* were published by FUEL in 2015, 2017 and 2019. The documentary film *Soviet Bus Stops* was released in 2022.

With a background in art history and criticism, Riya Raagini is a writer and artist whose work explores poetry, gender, ecology, philosophy and South Asian culture.

Thanks to the following people who helped with this project: Ron Ranson, Sudarson Karki, Leyanvi Mirando, Katarina Herneryd, Mohamed Yahya, Nafees Painters, Johnathan Gomesz, Edwina Thomson, Malin, Jasper and Mango Herwig, Pär Borg, Prof. Nuzhat Kazmi, Akhlaq Ahmed, Amit @ Indigo Taxis, Rizwan Khan, Mohammad Wazid, Ejaz Ahmed, Sherjeel Ahmed Bhatt, Sekul Khan, Jagtar Gurjar, Bakeli Gurjar, Arif Khan, Jayachandran, Gopal, Suresh, Ebin, Malayalam, Mahesh Varan, Udara Madhushka, Kuruwitam, EG Premarathna, Shaggy, Malith, Sajith, Pratyush Pushkar, Prabhav Pushkar, Bindu Das, Brajesh Kumar Choudhury, Bharat Tilwani, Neelam Tilwani, Tenzin Sangmo, Shashi Gora, Ven. Tenzin Dekyi, Aliya Ban Hamza, Vishesh, Khem Khowal, Iqbal Abhimanyu, Uddipana Borah, Atul, Amaan Imam Ghazee, Shubham Singhal, Vasudha Vijaysheel, Shayak Alok, Avinash Mishra, Anamika, Makrand Sanon.

Published in 2025

Murray & Sorrell FUEL Ltd
FUEL Design & Publishing
33 Fournier Street
London E1 6QE

fuel-design.com
@fuelpublishing

Design and edit by Murray & Sorrell FUEL

Distribution by Thames & Hudson / Artbook | D.A.P.
ISBN: 978-1-7398878-8-9
Printed in China

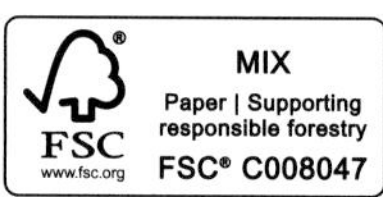

Printed with non mineral ink on FSC (Forest Stewardship Council) certified paper, EUDR (EU Deforestation Regulation) compliant, from responsibly managed forests and recycled materials, ensuring sustainable forestry practices and environmental protection.

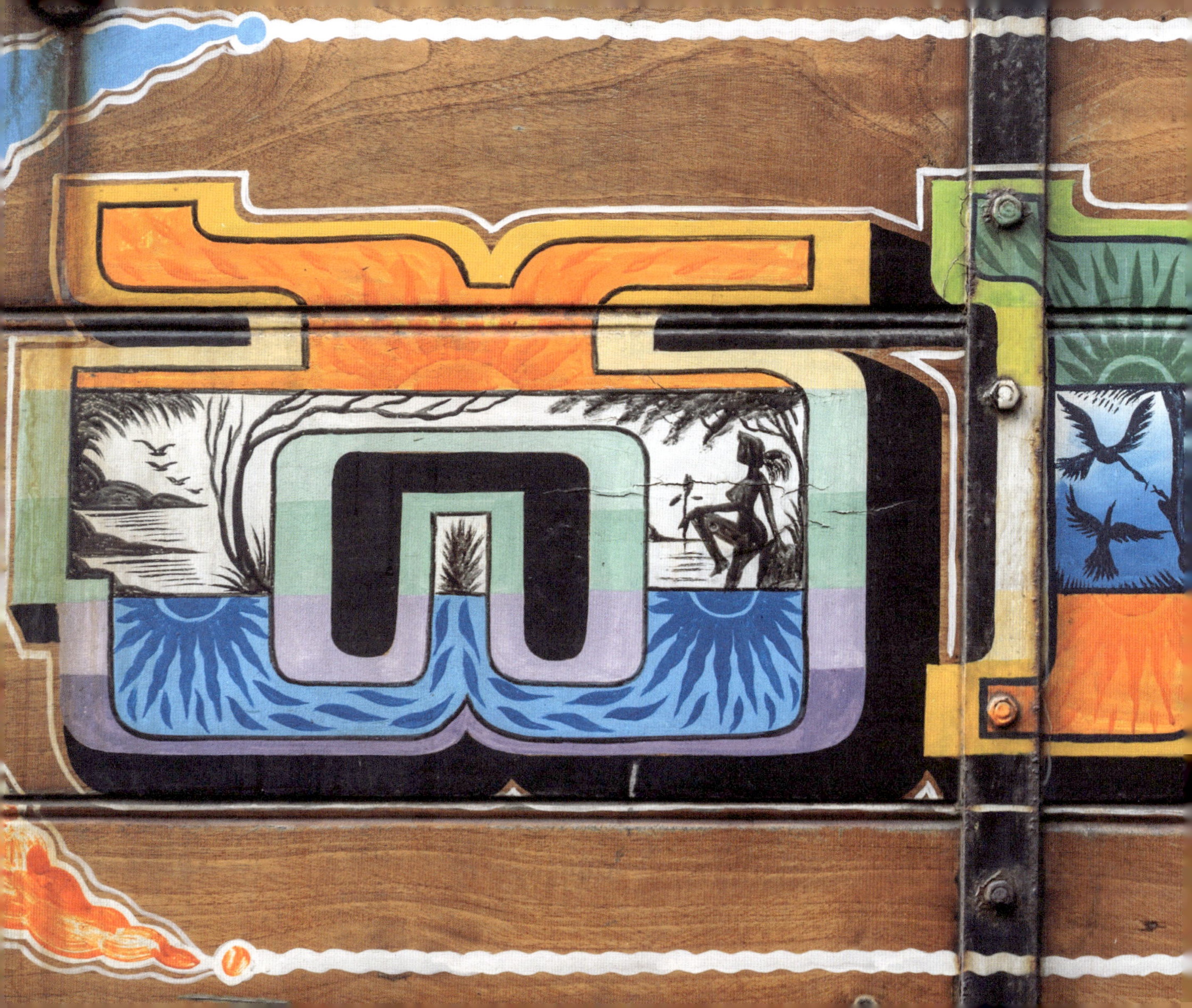

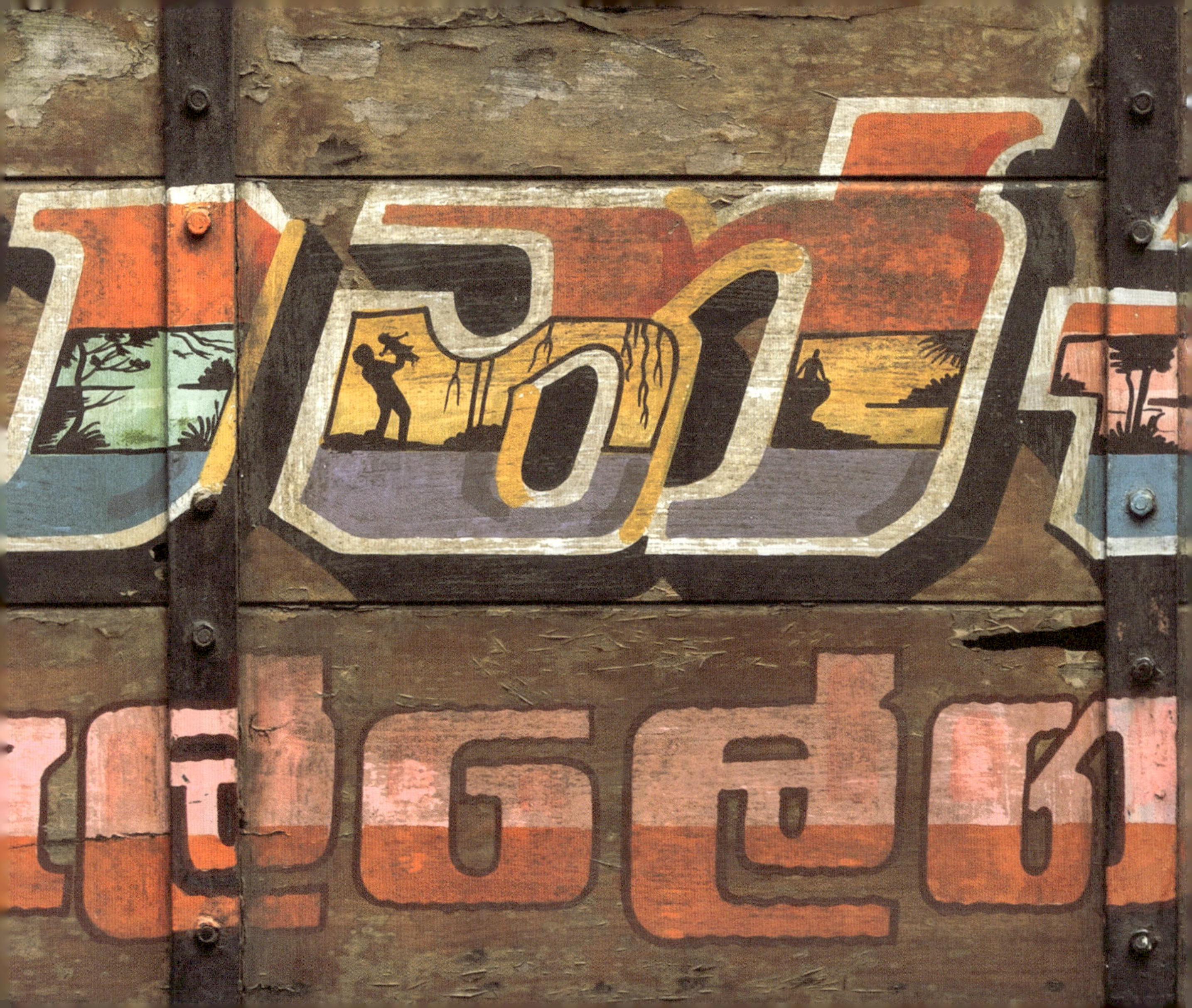